CU00870847

THE TRUE HISTORY

A LITTLE RAGAMUFFIN.

NEW YORK:

HARPER & BROTHERS, PUBLISHERS,

FRANKLIN SQUARE.

1866.

This scarce antiquarian book is included in our special *Legacy Reprint Series*. In the interest of creating a more extensive selection of rare historical book reprints, we have chosen to reproduce this title even though it may possibly have occasional imperfections such as missing and blurred pages, missing text, poor pictures, markings, dark backgrounds and other reproduction issues beyond our control. Because this work is culturally important, we have made it available as a part of our commitment to protecting, preserving and promoting the world's literature.

CONTENTS.

CONTENTS

THE TRUE HISTORY

OF A

LITTLE RAGAMUFFIN.

CHAPTER I.

IN WHICH ARE NARRATED A FEW PARTICULARS OF MY BIRTHPLACE AND PARENTAGE.

I WAS born at Number Nineteen, Fryingpan Alley, Turnmill Street, in the Parish of Clerkenwell.

It is scarcely probable that the reader is acquainted with the locality in question, and even less probable, if he undertook a journey of exploration in search of it, that any great amount of success would attend his labours. This especially, if he addressed himself to the individual best qualified to give him the required information. This would be the Clerkenwell costermonger. He may have resided within ear-shot of Clerkenwell Church bells all his life; nay, he may be a lodger in Turk's Head Alley, which is not more than twenty paces from *my* alley, and still he will shake his head ignorantly in reply to your question. Fryingpan Alley, Turnmill Street! He never heard tell of it. He knows all the courts and alleys thereabout. There's Rose Alley, and Lamb and Flag Court, and Crozier's Alley, and *Fringpun* Alley. The last-mentioned comes closest to what you are inquiring after; but that can't be the one, because it is in *Tummel* Street. Even though he had a suspicion that your "Fryingpan" and his "Fringpun," and his "Tummel" and your "Turnmill" were identical, it is very doubtful if you would gain advantage, your use of the full and proper terms being regarded by him as priggish affectation; and against all such it is the costermonger's creed to set his countenance.

Nevertheless, Fryingpan Alley is a fact; a disgraceful one, probably, but one that is undeniable. Passing Clerkenwell Sessions House from Coppice Row, it is the second alley on the left-hand side of the way; and coming at it down Turnmill Street from the Smithfield end, it is on the right, past the coppersmith's and the great distillery, and next to Turk's Head Alley. Except that the stone step at the mouth of the alley is worn quite through to the bricks beneath, and the name-board above has been renewed, its outward appearance is exactly the same as when, nearly twenty years ago, I used to live there: the same dingy, low-arched entry—so low that the scavenger, with his basket on his shoulder, is obliged to slacken at his knees to enable him to pass under it, and so narrow that a shop-shutter—a coffin-lid, almost—would serve as a gate for it.

As a boy, I was not particularly jovial or light-hearted, and the subject of coffins and funerals used to occupy a considerable share of my attention. There were always plenty of funerals going on in our alley, especially in the summer time; indeed, if it were not so, it would be no great wonder that Fryingpan Alley and coffins should be intimately associated in my mind, since it was a funeral of a very woeful sort that roused me from babyhood to boyhood, as it were, and set me seriously reflecting on the world and its ways. However, it will be time enough to give the particulars of that melancholy business when I have fulfilled the promise made at the beginning of this chapter.

The breadth of coffins and the narrowness of our alley used to occupy my thoughts a great deal, and there were very few of our neighbours whose height and breadth I had not considered, and settled within my mind how hard or how easy it would be to carry his body out.

Two persons in particular caused me tremendous anxiety on this account—the one being the landlord of the "Dog and Stile," out in Turnmill Street; and the other an elderly lady, who lived near the mouth of the alley. The publican, although he did not reside in the alley, was, nevertheless, there a great deal, chiefly in consequence of the many difficulties that stood in the way of his recovery of the pots and cans he lent to his customers; and if Mr. Piggot sometimes lost his temper while in pursuit of his property, it was really not to be wondered at. It was not at all an uncommon thing for him to discover the bright pewter borrowed of him overnight resting on the hob of a fire-place, half filled with the dregs of the coffee that had been boiled in it at breakfast, and so burnt and blackened as to require a vigorous application of Mr. Piggot's broad, fat thumb, wetted and roughened with cinder-ash, before he could convince himself that the vessel bore his name and sign. He had been known to enter a room (he had a way of never knocking at a door) to take an Irish stew or a dinner of cabbage and bacon off the fire, and, tilting it all into the fender, walk off triumphantly with the gallon can it was cooking in. He used to work himself into the most dreadful passions on these and similar occasions, and to stamp and swear till his eyes rolled and the pimples on his nose stood out in a way that was terrible to witness. "You shall never have a pot or can out of my house again—may I drop dead if you do !" was the threat he was constantly using, rolling his glaring eyes up towards the ceiling as he spoke. But he never kept his oath. The very worst defaulter was never refused after a second, or, at the outside, a third application; and it would only have been what he was always asking for if, one fine morning, Death had taken him by the heels and laid him flat along the cobble-stones of our alley.

I often thought about it. What if such a horrible thing should happen ! How ever would they lift him up and carry him round to his public-house ? Even now, when he passed out loaded, though he went shoulder first and sidling, his cans rasped and clanked against the wall. True, he did not appear to be a very solidly-built man, and there were fellows in our alley who, as pushers of loads, would give in to no man; still, if once Mr. Piggot's shoulders got blocked in the doorway, it was very certain that the harder they pushed the rounder he would become, and that they certainly would have a great deal of trouble with him.

But if I felt concern on poor Mr. Piggot's behalf, what were my sensations as I pondered on the chances of Mrs. Winkship's demise, and its inevitable consequences ? Mrs. Winkship was an elderly lady living at the entrance of the alley. If a single pound, she was full five stone heavier than Mr. Piggot, to say nothing of her being considerably shorter and thicker. But it was not entirely on account of her superior size that I felt more interest in Mrs. Winkship's case than in the publican's. As for Mr. Piggot, so long as they succeeded in removing his body, *how* would not have troubled me in the least; indeed, so far from being affected by the fact of his dying, I have no doubt that, had I been informed that that event had taken place on his own premises, I should have greatly rejoiced that now all chances of the occurrence of the calamity that haunted me were at an end; but in Mrs. Winkship's case, respect — not to say downright love and gratitude—entered very considerably into the question. She was a woman of business. I don't know exactly what she called herself, but she followed the business left by her husband, which was that of lending barrows and money to the many fruit-hawkers that lived in our alley. It was Mrs. Winkship's boast that since Mr. W.'s death, which had happened thirteen years ago, she had never journeyed out of Turnmill Street, except on the one occasion of her venturing as far as the Royal Coburg Theatre, at Lambeth, in the pantomime season, when she had slipped down the gallery stairs and sprained her ancle. Her constant station was the threshold of her own house, where, seated on an upturned coke-measure, with a nosebag full of chaff for a cushion, she kept watch the livelong day. The peculiar nature of her business, or, more properly speaking, of her customers, compelled it. Unless she caught the fellows when they returned home after disposing of their stock, and insisted on their "squaring up" before they went indoors, she was sure to be a loser.

The difficulties of her business, however, offered no material hindrance to her enjoying herself in the ways of eating and drinking. In wet weather she sat in the passage; but while it remained fine overhead, neither breakfast, dinner, nor tea would drive her from the nosebag. She had no other lodger but a niece—a lanky, pock-marked young woman, who wore her hair much strained in a backward direction, and there secured in a great bunch. The frightful disease that had so seared her face had also robbed her of an eye, so that altogether she could not be called handsome; but, like her aunt, she was a good-hearted creature, and helped me to a meal many and many a time. She kept the key of the barrow-shed in Dog and Stile Yard, and undertook the house-cleaning for her aunt, and prepared her meals.

They *were* meals ! Since that memorable time it has been my good fortune to partake of many dinners that might fairly be called excellent; but not one of them ever came up to those Mrs. Winkship used to partake of. At breakfast or at tea she was nothing very great; but at dinner she was splendid. The coke-measure, being of the half-bushel size, was of a convenient height for sitting on before a bottom-up apple-sieve. The apple-sieve was the dining-table; and certain as stroke of one o'clock, you might see Mrs. Winkship shift her coke-measure from the doorway to under the parlour-window, and hear her call out, "Ready, Martha, when you are !" and then Martha would raise the parlour-window, and arrange on the window-sill the salt and the vinegar, and the pepper and the mustard; then she would bring out the apple-sieve, already spread with a cloth as white as bran-new calico; and then she would bustle back into the parlour again, and hand the dinner out at the window to Mrs. Winkship.

It was always something with plenty of gravy in it—rich to look at, luscious, and smoking hot; but the most wonderful feature of Mrs. Winkship's dinners was their smell. There are meats by nature delicious-smelling—roast pork, for instance; but—and how Martha managed it I could never, from that day to this, imagine—she seemed to possess the power of conferring an odour of baked crackling on the tamest meats; to conjure out of them a fragrance that seemed to cry aloud with a voice that could be heard from one end of the alley to the other. Certainly, fancy may have had a great deal to do with it; or that smelling being our share, we made the most of it; or it may possibly have happened that Mrs. Winkship's dinner and its odour being altogether without competition, its virtues appeared more forcibly. Whether either of the above conjectures explains the fact, I can't say; I only know that exactly as I have never seen such dinners, so have I never smelt any such. It was a common remark amongst us boys and girls, that it seemed to be always Sunday with Mrs. Winkship. After dinner she drank rum and water—hot, invariably. In the depth of winter, when the snow was on the ground, and she sat on the coke-measure wearing a hairy cap with ear-lappets, and wrapped in a coachman's box-coat, she would drink it; in the summer time, when the cobble-stones of the alley were hot to naked feet, and the gutters too warm for a refreshing dabble in them, she drank it hot and strong as ever.

Did we respect Mrs. Winkship the less on account of this weakness ? Did we despise her, and taunt her, and make fun of her? We did not. How could we, when we saw how jolly it made her, and considered what a profitable weakness it was to us? We used to fetch it for her, three pen'orth at the time. We used to lurk in the shadow of doorways, and peep from window-blinds, keeping a sharp eye on her till the arrival of the moment for action—the moment when she waddled back from the parlour window to the doorway with her seat, and sat herself down thereon, with her fat arms contentedly folded on her lap. We used to take it in turns. The way was to stroll from your lurking-place, and saunter towards her in the most undesigning manner possible, and when you approached close enough to address her innocently, and as though the thought had that moment popped into your head, asking if she happened to want anything fetched. *Her* way, then, was to look up in an astonished manner, and as though she thought you had made a mistake,—taken her for somebody else, possibly.

"Did you speak to me, boy?"

"Yes 'm. I'm going into Tummel Street to fetch some treacle, in a minute, for my mother; I thought perhaps you might want some tea, or something'm."

"No thanky, boy; my tea I've got, and my milk will be here presently. I don't think I stand in need of anything."

When it came to this, the way of the boy was to thank her very civilly, and to look perfectly satisfied, and as though he well knew that since Mrs. Winkship was all right in the matters of tea and milk, she could not by any earthly possibility require anything else. If, on the contrary, the boy acted differently; if he winked, or looked knowing merely, and grinned as much as to say, "Why, what's the use of carrying on with all this jolly nonsense? You know what you always have and what you want, and *I* know what you always have and what you want; give me the halfpence, and say no more about it." I say if he said, or even looked, anything of this sort, he would have been sent about his business in a twinkling, and scratched out of the lady's good books for no end of time; but if he managed the business neatly, and turned away promptly and respectfully when he had got Mrs. Winkship's answer, it was next to a certainty that she would exclaim presently—

"Oh, ah! now you are here, boy, you may as well run round to Mr. Piggot's for me. You know Piggot's?"

"Piggot's! Piggot's! Oh, yes, I know now. Sign of the 'Dog and Stile,' I think it is, mum."

"That's it. Go you there and ask for threepen'orth of best rum, hot, with a bit of lemon; and there's a brown for yourself."

After the ice was thus broken, the business to be transacted during the remainder of the afternoon was comparatively easy, and consisted in keeping a watchful eye on her liquor, and, almost before she had recovered her breath from the finishing gulp, which was invariably a large one, to be seen hovering in her vicinity. I have earned as much as twopence-halfpenny in this way in a single afternoon.

This certainly was more than the average daily earnings of Mrs. Winkship's messengers—more, indeed, than I sometimes took of her in the course of an entire week, because I nearly always had the baby in my arms. But I was al-

ways a bit of a favourite with her; and the good afternoon I speak of was once when I was quite free, in consequence of my stepmother going out to a tea-meeting and taking little Polly with her.

Still I can declare, and with a clear conscience, that it was not on any such mercenary grounds as how much I should be out of pocket that Mrs. Winkship's probable death troubled me. My concern was what would they do with her, supposing she should die? Next to burying her at the water-butt end of the alley, where the rent-collector lived, and which was consequently much the quietest and best-behaved end, the only way out of the difficulty, as it appeared to me, was to fix a tall crane and sling her over the house-tops into Turnmill Street—a notion no doubt put into my head by what I had observed of the crane and its action amongst the wharves and bacon-warehouses in Thames Street, and elsewhere in the neighbourhood of Billingsgate.

I am glad to be able to state, however, that I was spared the spectacle of Mrs. Winkship's removal out of Fryingpan Alley, whatever was its nature. On the memorable morning of my flight from my birthplace, as I ran out of the alley in such a tremendous fright, I passed her enthroned on the coke-measure, humming as was her wont, and looking as hale and hearty as her best friend could wish. As I darted out of the archway, I nearly ran foul of a boy bearing in his hand threepen'orth of hot rum. But she has gone somehow. When, but a few months since, filled with the hope of meeting at least one or two of my very limited number of friends of past times, I went to have a peep at the old place, my first glance up the alley was for the familiar coke-measure; but it was not. My inquiries were vain. Nobody could tell me what had become of the kind old barrow-woman; indeed, as well as I could make out, no one living there at the present day had ever seen or heard of such a person. She was before their time. Nor was this very surprising, after all. Death was never for long a stranger in our alley. His seeds were sown broadcast on that fruitful bit of ground, and the grim reaper often came a-mowing there. Nineteen years is a long time.

In every harvest-field, however, there is always an odd nook or corner, be it never so small a one, that the scythe passes by, leaving a few stalks standing. In one such corner in the neighbourhood of Fryingpan Alley still stood and flourished the shop of the bird-fancying barber who has shaved my father hundreds of times. I, too, had had some dealings with him, though not of a character to invoke the use of the tools of his proper trade. The transactions that had taken place between us were of a purely commercial sort. Once I bought a guinea-pig of him for fivepence; and on another occasion a pigeon, his property, flew in at our window, and was captured by me and returned to the barber on payment of fourpence—the pigeon ransom as fixed by Act of Parliament.

Mr. Slaney, however, had no recollection of me. My brown face, more than half-covered by an Australian-grown beard, passed with him as a perfectly strange face. When I asked him what had become of Mrs. Winkship, he replied that no such a name was known in that locality. I pursued the subject, however, and urged him to rouse his memory, telling him that I was actuated by something more than idle curiosity, (as indeed I was,) and hinted that I should consider the smallest scrap of information cheap at half-a-crown; when it suddenly flashed to Mr. Slaney's mind that he knew Mrs. Winkship and what had become of her. Thirteen years ago that very month, my informant assured me—and old Wagstaff, the basket-maker on the opposite side of the way, could have corroborated his statement if he hadn't died last August—Mrs. W. was arrested for shop-lifting, and the case being very clear against her, she was convicted and transported beyond the seas for the term of fifteen years. I paid the unscrupulous story-teller the half-crown; but neither at the time, nor since, could I bring myself to believe a word that he told me. The bare notion of that great, fat, tender-hearted creature "lifting" or carrying away anything from a shop (unless by sheer weight she had carried away the flooring) was too ridiculous to be seriously thought of for a single moment.

In other respects, however, and as before stated, the alley was in pretty much the same condition as when I had left it. From beside this window hung the rope of onions; from the next, the slabs of dried cod; and from the next, several spits of fresh herrings undergoing the process of conversion to "Yarmouth bloaters." As in the old times, too, it was "washing day" with several of the inhabitants; and likewise, as of old, there were the tattered counterpanes, and scraps of orange-coloured blanketing, and the patched shirts, and the flannel jackets, drying on lines stretched out from the upper window-sills by means of regular clothes-props, or make-shift broomsticks.

As of old, too, there at the upper end of the alley was the great leaky water-butt, and it being nine o'clock in the morning, the water was "on," and the old-fashioned pushing, and driving, and skirmishing for water, was also "on" at full blast. Nineteen years had not improved the water supply in Fryingpan Alley. Three-quarters of an hour was the time during which the precious fluid was kept flowing from the main, and in order to make the most of it, the tap at the bottom of the butt was wholly withdrawn, and the water made to spout out in a tremendous way.

The rush about the butt was the rush of old, or as like it as peas in one pod. There were the big, bony, slatternly women slipshod, and with their hair uproarious, each grasping the handle of her pail as though she would lief use the water vessel as a weapon of war, against anyone who should have the hardihood to insinuate that hers was not the next turn. There was the big hulking Irish boy, with his saucepan to be filled, pushing and elbowing amongst the little girls with their pots and kettles, and treading with his cruel hob-nailed boots on their poor naked toes, to make them get out of the way; and once again, here comes the great bully costermonger, with his oily side locks, and his yellow silk neckerchief big as a bolster, and his short pipe cocked insolently at the corner of his mouth, hauling along a great sack full of oysters. He doesn't hurry himself in the least. He comes along leisurely, making straight for the water-butt; and seeing him coming—hearing the clatter of his clout boots on the stones—the hulking Irish boy, the little drudges with their naked feet, even the

bony pail-grasping shrews fall back, away from the water-spout; or, if the boldest of them ventures on another potful, she leans over for it smirking cringingly at the approaching beast with the oyster-bag. How can they do otherwise? The approaching beast is "Flash Jack." He has the strength of a horse, and the ferocity of a bull-dog. Nothing less than three policemen ever took Jack to the station-house; there is not a man in the alley that Flash Jack cannot lift by the hips, and throw him over his shoulder as easy as he can break a tobacco pipe. If you don't like his "goings on," you are free to take it out of him—any two of you! He has been known to send four moderately able men flying, but then he used his feet, and bit a great deal. Now, who will dispute Flash Jack's right to monopolise the water-spout just so long as it pleases him? Who will peril his pan or pail by leaving it in Jack's way? No one. They are mum as mice. Stay a little while, my friend. If you live long enough you will be growing older by and by, and there are growing up in the alley other Flash Jacks, who one day will then fall on you and give you just such a horrible beating as I suppose you gave the Flash Jack that I used to know, and ever afterwards you will shuffle in and out of the alley, afraid almost to assert that your life is your own. You will be glad to stand aside with your few whelks or winkles in your little basket, and wait until every one is served, even down to the hulking Irish boy. And serve you right, Jack. I'd give sixpence to be there and see it.

Just as it used to be, all this, and among my earliest recollections. Are they the very earliest? Up the alley, and down the alley, I search for something that may suggest earlier, but am unsuccessful, until I begin to scan the houses from top to bottom—until my eyes light on the third-floor windows of Number Nineteen, and it is like returning to the port from which I made sail for my first voyage. The windows are *exactly* the same. There may be a brown paper patch or so the less, or a rag plug or two the more, than in the old days; but brown paper and old rags are the same all the world over, and as I look up, they are so much the self-same windows, that at that moment were the sash to be lifted, and an uproarious red head protruded therefrom, and there was to proceed from it a shrill hoarse voice, screaming—"Jimmy! Jimmy, ye shpalpeen! I'll have the blood of ye if ye don't git off that shtep this minnut, and walk about wid her and shtop her owlin!" I should not be very much astonished. I have been cajoled, and counselled, and abused from those windows many a score of times. In the room to which they belong, my sister Polly was born, when I was little more than five years old. In that room with the paper-patched windows my mother died, shutting her eyes on the world and its troubles within about fifteen minutes after my sister Polly opened hers.

Let me, however, hasten to disabuse the mind of the reader who imagines that the red-haired woman with the shrill voice was my mother. She was my step-mother. Of the kind of woman that my mother was, I retain but a half-and-half sort of remembrance. As I look up at the tattered windows, another face besides the hateful face just alluded to, appears there; dim, however, as though seen through a curtain of gauze. It is the face of a woman, with dark hair and eyes certainly, and a pale face; but whether she is pretty, or ugly as sin, is more than I can say. That is what I mean when I say that I don't recollect what sort of woman she was. As to the sort of mother she was to me, the feeling of love I still cherish toward her, taken in consideration with the short time I knew her, is sufficient to settle *that*. One thing, however, I never could make out. If she was the good and worthy woman I am ready to vouch, how was it that my father was so continually rowing with her, and calling her evil names? Why did he beat her, and make her cry so? One name in particular he took to calling her some months before Polly was born, and that was "Judas." He would shake his great fist in her face and grind his teeth, and call her "Judas! Judas!" as though she were a rat, and he would like to stamp her to death as one. He would curse her eyes and limbs, and throw his boots, and cups and saucers at her, and spank her about the head till her long black hair fell all about her face, and roar out—

"You infernal blood-selling Judas, if it wasn't for the boy's sake I'd strangle you!"

There was a great mystery about this blood-selling business. Ready as was my father to throw it in her teeth, as the saying is, on the slightest provocation, or on no provocation at all, he never went into the details of the case, and, more extraordinary still, she never seemed to expect that he should. She never replied, "It is false," or inquired what he meant by it. That is, to my knowledge. It is very possible that she may have denied it until she grew tired of doing so, finding that it was better to bear the reproach silently.

Again, whatever was my mother's crime, father had his reasons for not making it public. Often enough while quarrelling with her, he would bellow it out loud enough for the whole alley to hear; but if any one—even his most intimate chum—met him next day, and gave a hint that he would like to hear further particulars, my father never would gratify him. I know this as a fact; for at that time I had just come into my first suit of corduroys, and father was very proud, and liked to take me about. He used to take me to the barber's on Sunday mornings, to get his weekly shave, and I used to sit by his side on the form while he was waiting his turn to be lathered.

"Isn't he a star?" one of my father's companions would observe to another, in reference to me. "He all'us looks as though he'd just been fresh 'arthstoned—don't he, Bob?"

"He do so. I never see such a kid; he's a credit to your old woman, Jim, anyhow?"

"Yes, she's a werry good mother, no doubt on it," my father would answer, shortly.

"And a werry good wife, Jim?"

"Strickly as such, there's no denying on it," was Jim's answer.

"P'r'aps you puts it a little too strickly, Jim?"

"Ah! who sees so?".

"No, no; nobody ses so. But you do let her have it awfully hot sometimes, Jim—now don't you?"

"No hotter than she deserves," my father replies, growing fierce, and turning round on his interrogator; "can you, or any man here, stand before me and say as she do get it hotter than she ought?"

"Well, 'course she must deserve it, or else you wouldn't call her"——

"What?" interrupted my father, getting up on his feet.

"Well, names. Of course, nobody can tell why you call 'em her, 'cos nobody knows."

"And nobody ain't going to know," replies father, in the tones a man uses when he wishes it to be understood that there has been enough said on the subject. "It ain't nobody's business to know, nor yet to inquire. *She* knows, and that's enough. When she comes a-grumbling to you, and telling you her grievances, you come and tell me; then we'll see about it."

CHAPTER II.

IN WHICH, BY THE NARRATION OF THE STORY OF MY UNCLE BENJAMIN'S GREAT MISFORTUNE, SOME LIGHT IS THROWN ON THE BLOOD-SELLING MYSTERY.

I BY no means promise that the little light I am able to throw on the blood-selling of which my mother was accused will be entirely satisfactory to the reader. I simply offer it as the best I can give. How it came to my knowledge, whether I was an eye-witness, or heard it from her lips, I shouldn't like to say. Most likely I am indebted pretty equally to both sources.

It was all about my Uncle Benjamin, who was my father's brother. He was a younger man than my father by several years, and slimmer, and more genteel in build. He was better looking, too, and better off; though why he should be, considering that my father worked from morning till night, and Uncle Benjamin never appeared to work at all, was not quite clear. He was a swaggering, joking sort of young man, and smoked cigars. He didn't come much to our house, and I was very glad of it; for although whenever he came he invariably gave me a sixpence, and sent for something to drink for my mother and father, sure as ever he was gone there would be a tremendous row, which was sure to begin out of nothing at all. As, for instance, mother would say, "Don't touch that little drop of gin that's left, Jim; it is for my lunch to-morrow. Ben said so."

"Oh! when did Ben say so? Not in my hearing!"

"He said so when you was down-stairs, Jim."

"Burn you and Ben too; you're always talking, and whispering, and sniggering together when I'm down-stairs, or somewhere else out of sight; butcher me if you ain't. He's a butchering sight too fast; and so are you, you ——!"

In this, or a similar way, the row invariably began and was continued. This, however, was before Uncle Ben got married.

He married a girl named Eliza, who was employed at gaiter-making somewhere in the city. After they got married, Uncle Benjamin came less frequently than ever to our house. Indeed, I think my mother was against the match, as she used to speak in a very cross way about it, and say, "A pretty doll she is to be any man's wife!"

And at this my father would turn on her with

an ugly laugh, and exclaim, "I dessay; very sorry for poor Ben, ain't you, Poll?"

"Sorry? of course I am. So ought you to be; he's your brother!" my mother would answer.

"Ba-a-a! you take me for a poor, soft-headed fool, don't you?" would be my father's next remark. "Don't I know you? Haven't I remarked it, over and over again? Turkey's the place for you, marm!"

There must have been another dreadful mystery couched in this sneer about "Turkey;" for, the first time my father ventured to mention it, my mother flew at him like a tiger, and shook him by the collar of his jacket, at the same time screaming out at him talk of a sort which I did not understand, but he evidently did, and which, combined with the shaking, seemed to completely astonish and take him all aback, making him look quite pale and cowed—so much so, that there was an end to the row, and father took up his cap and went off.

If, however, my poor mother imagined that she had effectually conquered him of his sneering about Turkey, she was grievously mistaken. Without doubt, my father had been turning the subject over in his mind, and upbraiding himself for being such a coward as he had shown himself. The very next evening there was another row, and scarcely was it commenced when father called her something, and told her to "go to Turkey!" Presuming, as I suppose, on his previous success, mother flew at him again; but this time he was cool, and prepared for her. He caught her a hit in the face that sent her staggering to the fender.

"You won't try that again, my beauty," said my father.

And she did not. Whenever he spoke of the eastern country in question as being a proper place for her to reside in, (which was neither more nor less than every time he quarrelled with her,) she would make no reply save a look of contempt, and utter a little laugh that set my father foaming almost.

Uncle Benjamin and Aunt Eliza lived in furnished apartments, in a street somewhere near St. Martin's Lane, Westminster. They ate and drank of the best, and wore such fine clothes as made everybody in Fryingpan Alley stare when, by a rare chance, they came to see us. The business in which Ben Ballisat (my name is James Ballisat, at the reader's service) was engaged was a flourishing one. Each succeeding visit saw him richer than the preceding; till, finally, he came wearing kid gloves and patent-leather boots, while Aunt Eliza was attired in a dress of peach-colored silk, and a bonnet that excited in our alley a universal hum of astonishment and admiration.

Occasionally, my mother went to see Aunt Eliza. She never seemed to care about seeing Uncle Ben, and that was easily avoided if she chose her time; for my uncle invariably went out at about three in the afternoon, and remained out until late. He told Aunt Eliza that he held a situation at a fashionable tavern at the west-end of the town, where there were billiard tables kept.

One Monday afternoon, my mother, who had not seen aunt for nearly a month, made up her mind to go and take a cup of tea with her; and she took me, by way of a treat. It was past three when we arrived; but when Aunt Eliza opened the door (she wore a green silk gown, and had great gold ear-rings in her ears; but she looked very pale and unhappy,) she held up her finger, and pointed back up the stairs she had descended.

"Ben's out, isn't he?" asked my mother.

"Hush! no, he's up-stairs," replied my aunt.

"What! Has he left his place, then; or is he ill?"

"No; he's still in his situation, and he's well enough," said Aunt Eliza; "but he's been getting tipsy again. I'm sure I don't know what is coming to him; he keeps me sitting up night after night, and it is breakfast time before he comes home. It was ten this morning when he came home in a cab, too tipsy to stand. He's lying on the bed asleep, now, just as he came home."

We went up-stairs, and mother went into the bedroom with Aunt Eliza, to take her bonnet off, and I went in after them. There I saw Uncle Benjamin, lying across the white bed, and under the white curtains, with his muddy boots on his feet, and wearing his coat, which looked as though he had had a tumble in the gutter.

"He's been lying like that since he came in," said Aunt Eliza.

"And hasn't he had anything to eat?" said my mother.

"He has been asleep all the time, and I don't like to wake him. It makes him so dreadfully cross to wake him."

"Well, if he was my husband, I should wake him, and give him a strong cup of tea."

"But, my dear, I can't do that," returned my aunt. "The cupboard is empty, Polly. I wish he would rouse; we can't have any tea until he does, for I have not got any money."

"Perhaps he is no richer than you are; how do you know you will be better off for money when he wakes than you are now? It's about ten to one that my Jim has a single penny when he comes home drunk," observed my mother, who, now I come to think of it, seemed rather pleased to have found out that fine gentleman Ben was, after all, no better than her Jim in some respects.

"No fear of that," replied Aunt Eliza, pridefully; "Ben has always got plenty of money, that's one comfort. I know that he has got some loose silver in his waistcoat pocket, for I heard it rattle when he lay down. You can see that he has. Look, Polly, that left-hand pocket is quite bulgy with it."

"Well, of course, we all have our own way of managing," said my mother (we had returned to the front room by this time,) "and you have your way, Liz; but all I know is, that if I had a husband asleep and tipsy, with a pocketful of money, and if I had no money and wanted a cup of tea, you wouldn't catch me sitting like a dummy until it happened to please his lordship to wake up."

This, however, could have been nothing but foolish bragging on my mother's part. She touch a penny of my father's money while he was asleep! She dare not approach him to loosen his neckerchief when he came home helplessly, speechlessly tipsy, and lay sprawling over a chair, with his head all askew, and snorting and gasping at every breath.

I have known my father come home in a state of intoxication, bringing with him a bit of fish for his supper, and when he has thrown it down without a word, and lain down to sleep, my mother has sat, fretting and anxious, *certain* of the thrashing that was in store for her the instant he woke. If she boiled the fish, she would catch it for not frying it, and *vice versa ;* and if she left it uncooked, she would not be a bit better off. "She wouldn't sit there like a dummy," indeed! Why, she would sit so from dark to daylight if he willed it.

"What would you do, then, Polly?" asked Aunt Eliza.

"Do! why, help myself."

"It would serve him right, certainly; and if I thought he would not make a fuss about it "——

"Lor', what nonsense," interrupted my mother. "Where's the harm? What's his is yours, isn't it? But please yourself; don't let me give you advice that may get you into trouble; you know Ben's temper better than I do, of course. He's like all the rest of 'em, I suppose—shows a bit of the devil when he's scratched."

"Oh! I'm not afraid, Polly; don't think that. If he has any of the devil in him, he never shows it to me."

"I'll tell you what we will do for a lark, Liz, if you like," said my mother, presently. "One of us will creep in and take enough money out of that waistcoat pocket to buy something very nice indeed for tea—something that will make him think how kind and good-natured you are; and then, when he has eaten it and we have got him to say how much he liked it, we will laugh at him for standing treat without knowing it. What is there that he likes very much, Liz?"

"Well, there's pickled salmon," replied Aunt Eliza, laughing, and readily agreeing to the joke; "he greatly inclines to that when he wants to sober himself; or there's lobsters, which he likes better still. But lobsters are so dear."

"Never mind," said my mother, "we'll have a lobster; if you are afraid, Liz, I'll take the money out of his pocket, and you shall go and spend it."

So, creeping quietly on tiptoe into the room where Uncle Ben lay still asleep, my mother presently returned with a half-crown and a shilling in her hand.

"Here is the money, Liz," said my mother; "now, you run away and buy a lobster—a big one, mind—and what else you want, while I make the kettle boil."

The lobster was bought, and when the tea was all ready Uncle Ben was awoke. Aunt went in to wake him, and, as we could hear, she told the truth when she said that it made him cross to be awoke out of his sleep. He grumbled and swore at a tremendous rate, until aunt made him understand that we were in the front room, and then he moderated his tones, and presently made his appearance in his shirt-sleeves and his slippers. At first he seemed ashamed that my mother should have found him in such a disgraceful state, and was snappish in his answers to aunt; but he grew better-tempered when he sat down to the lobster, and laughed and told us some funny stories, at which my mother and aunt seemed greatly amused. On the whole, it was as jolly a tea as one could wish to sit down to. When it was at an end, and my uncle had withdrawn from the table, said Aunt Liza, as she was preparing to take away the tea things—

"Well, now you have finished your tea, Ben, perhaps you will tell us how you liked it?"

"I liked it well enough," replied Uncle Benjamin.

"But wasn't it *very* nice, Ben—extra nice?"

"Get out with you," said Uncle Ben, laughing; "you are fishing for what you won't catch, my dear. You want me to praise you up before Polly. I don't mean to do it."

"But wasn't it a lovely lobster, Ben?" asked my mother.

"I don't mind confessing to you that it was a lovely lobster, Polly," replied Uncle Ben; "but I mustn't do as much with Liz. You don't know how artful she is. If I was to say to her that I liked it very much, she would not only want me to give her back the money she gave for it, but something in addition for the trouble of getting it." Then turning to his wife, he continued— "Thank'ee for your lobster, Mrs. Extravagance. I'm glad to see you can afford such luxuries; *I* can't."

So saying, he pulled out a handsome cigar-case, and lit a cigar with the air of a man on perfect good terms with himself. This was capital sport for my mother and Aunt Liza, and they laughed very heartily over it.

"It *is* good to see the clever ones taken in once in a while; isn't it?" said my aunt.

"What do you mean, taken in?" asked Uncle Ben, pausing between the puffs of his cigar. "It *was* a lobster, wasn't it?"

"Yes, and you paid for it, you goose," laughed my mother.

He laughed too, but it was plain that he did not exactly see where the joke was.

"I see," said he; "you mean to say that I shall pay for it in the long run. Not the least doubt of it."

"No: we don't mean anything of the sort," replied my mother, still laughing; "we mean that it is already paid for with ready money—with *your* ready money, Ben."

"*My* ready money!"

"Not half an hour ago," said both women, clapping their hands in great glee, to see how foolish he looked.

"Rubbish!" said Uncle Ben; "I haven't paid for a pen'orth of anything since I've been home, I'll swear. What ready money are you talking about?"

"Some of that you've got in your waistcoat pocket, Benny, dear," answered his wife. "Polly took it out and I spent it."

If he did not see the joke now, he never would see it. Evidently *something* came home to him with appalling suddenness, but it wasn't anything funny. His face went white, as though he were about to faint and fall, and unknown to him, the cigar dropped from between his lips and lay smouldering on the new hearth-rug.

"Out of my pocket—my waistcoat pocket—while I was asleep!" stammered he. "Out of *which* pocket? which? which?"

"The left-hand pocket—yes, *that* one, (he clapped his hand on it.) Not much, dear; only three-and-sixpence, Ben—a shilling and a half crown. I shouldn't have thought of it, only Polly"——

"Hang Polly and you too!" interrupted my uncle, fiercely, bustling about in a tremendous hurry, and putting on his coat and hat. "I want to hear none of your infernal excuses; tell me where you palm—where you passed the half-crown and the shilling?"

"The fishmonger in Castle Street had the half-crown, and the grocer next to the trunk shop had the shilling," replied my Aunt Eliza, beginning to cry. "Don't be angry, Ben; I'll never do it again."

"Then you are a great fool, Liz," spoke my mother, who was much put out to see the savage way in which Uncle Ben was going on. "Never cry about nothing, girl. Why, what harm have you done?"

"What harm!" repeated Uncle Benjamin, furiously.

"Yes, what harm?" replied my mother, coolly. "I'd be ashamed if I were you, Ben; you, with a pocketful of money, making all this fuss about a trumpery three-and-sixpence. Anybody, to hear you, would think that your money was bad, and that you were afraid of its being brought back to you by the people who had taken it."

Without doubt this was a random shot, but it hit the mark most cruelly. Uncle Benjamin was walking the room to and fro in a bewildered manner when she began to speak, but her words brought him suddenly to a dead standstill. He faced round at mother paler than ever, and with his eyes filled with tears, and laying one hand on her shoulder, he shook his fist in her face:—

"You cruel wretch," cried he; "you wicked wretch! you knew it all along! you knew it, and you came here purposely to sell me."

And as though really she had been guilty of so base a thing, and they who had bought him were in a hurry to complete the transaction, there came a single rap at the street door even while he was speaking. Hearing the knock, Uncle Benjamin made a few hurried steps towards the passage, but before he could reach it the street door was opened by the landlady; and in walked a fishmonger, and a grocer, and a policeman.

"Beg pardon, sir, and ladies both," said the policeman, entering the room with the other two men, and putting his back against the door; "hope we don't disturb you. We've merely called to see if you happen to have any more of this sort of article to dispose of. If so, I'll take it off your hands without further trouble."

As he spoke, he held out a bright new shilling and a half-crown in the palm of his hand.

Uncle Ben was evidently not unprepared for something of the sort. "Oh, yes," said he, in a loud devil-may-care voice; "it's all right; you're come to the right shop, my man, for that sort of coin. I can change you a twenty pun' note if you don't object to take gold as well as silver. Look here."

And so saying, he took from his waistcoat pocket, and from a pocket inside the breast of his waistcoat, several little packets of money done up in soft white paper, and all as spick and span new as the shilling and half-crown the policeman held in his hand. As he recklessly flung down the little packets, the papers burst, and the coins went rolling and chinking amongst the cups and saucers in the tea-tray at a tremendous rate.

"That's the lot, my friend," said Uncle Benjamin, addressing the officer, and at the same time clasping his hands together. "And now, if you've got such a thing as a pair of bracelets about you, I'll thank you to slip them on me quick. If you don't you may have to book a worse charge than that of smashing against me."

Luckily, the policeman did not miss the signi-ficant glance with which Uncle Benjamin regarded my mother as he spoke, nor that his eyes, with a dangerous expression in them, shifted from her to a broad bread-knife lying handily. In a twinkling the handcuffs were produced from the officer's pocket, and Uncle Ben's wrists locked securely together.

It was a perfectly clear case against the passer of counterfeit coin, and Uncle Ben was sentenced to transportation beyond the seas for the term of his natural life. There was no help for it but that my mother should be a witness in the case, and the least she could make of what she had to say told strongly against him, and made him grin with hate and grate his teeth as he stood there in the dock listening to her. He had got it into his obstinate head that she had sold him, and nothing could shake his opinion.

"That is my own brother's wife—that is," spoke he, when my mother had given her evidence. "That's my own brother's wife," said he, at the same time showing her to the people in court with his pointed finger. "She comes to my house, and she eats my bread, and sits, and laughs, and talks with us, and all this after she has set the trap. She wheedles me and my innocent wife, who, as true as there is a Lord above us, knew no more of my ways of getting money than her unborn baby. She comes to us, and eats, and drinks, and laughs, and talks, till presently, them as she had sold me to comes and takes me. Bad luck to you, Polly! Beware of her, Jim!" (my father was in court to hear the trial,) "she is a bad one."

CHAPTER III.

IN WHICH THE READER IS MADE ACQUAINTED WITH AN OCCURRENCE WHICH HAPPENED ON A MEMORABLE FRIDAY.

IT is my sincere belief that my mother no more deserved to be stigmatised as Judas, through her connexion with that unlucky business of Uncle Ben's, than the reader's respected self; at the same time, I am bound to admit that my father appears to have thought otherwise, and for my own part I hardly know whether to wish that such was really his impression. If so, it was some excuse for his brutal behaviour towards her. Only some, however; not enough, by a very long way, to justify him in beating, and taunting, and worrying her to death. And that's what it came to.

At the same time, I must do my father the justice to state my opinion, that while he was bullying and beating her he did not have it in his mind that he was killing her. I am willing to give him credit for thinking that she was of the same hardy and enduring kind as the majority of the women living in our alley. I judge so, from many reasons; from the one which I am about to relate more than any other.

It was on a Friday afternoon, in the summer time, that, coming in from play in the alley, I made my way up-stairs to the front room in which we lived, and, to my great astonishment, was peremptorily refused admittance by a person of the name of Jenkins, who with her husband lodged on the floor below ours, but who on this occasion was in our room. As I turned the latch, I could hear her hurrying towards the door; and putting out her head, she very sharply requested me to run and play, as no little boys were wanted there. I recall with regret the fact that I, smarting under a sense of indignity put on me by Mrs. Jenkins, and further exasperated by hearing the lock click as she turned the key, began to bawl my loudest, and to batter and kick the door, demanding of my mother to turn out Mrs. Jenkins instantly, and to cut me a thick slice of bread and treacle. Presently, however, I was calmed. My mother came to the door.

"Don't make mammy's head ache, Jimmy," said she kindly. "Mammy's ill, dear. Don't cry. Buy a cake, Jim."

And hearing a metallic sound at my feet, I looked down and saw that she had pushed a farthing through the chink at the bottom of the door; so I went off and bought a brandy-ball.

It was near my father's time for returning from the market when I went indoors again. Just, however, as I reached the first landing, there came a hasty creaking of boots behind me, and in an instant I was overtaken and passed by a tall gentleman in black clothes, who took the stairs two at a time, as though in a mighty hurry, and arriving at our room-door, as I could plainly hear, rapped at it and went in, closing the door behind him. This, of course, was a settler for me. I sat down in a corner of the stairs to wait until the creaky boots came down again.

But they didn't come down, and I waited and waited until I dozed off to sleep, and so my father (who that evening happened to be later than usual) found me. He had been drinking a little, I think, and began to bluster and talk loud, asking me where the something my mother was, and why the something else she did not take better care of me.

"Mother's up-stairs, father," said I.

"Up-stairs! and leave you laying about on the stairs to be trod on! We'll thundering soon see what _that_ means."

And raging like a bull, he was stamping up the stairs, when I called after him—

"There's somebody up with her, father."

"Somebody! Who?"

"A gentleman with "——

"A _what!_ a gentleman?"

"A gentleman with a white thing round his neck, and creaky boots. Mrs. Jenkins is up there, too, father."

Hearing this explanation, my father turned slowly back, laughing a little, and tossing his head.

"Come on, Jimmy," said he, softly, taking me up in his arms; "we don't want nothing to say to Mr. Gentleman. I know who he is, Jim. Let's come down to old Jenks, and see what he's got to say about it."

So we went down and knocked at old Jenkins's door. At first it seemed that there was nobody within; but when father knocked again, louder, Mr. Jenkins made his appearance, rubbing his eyes as though he had been awoke out of a sleep. He laid hold on my father by the jacket-sleeve and pulled him into the room.

"You haven't been up, Jim, have you?" asked he, eagerly.

"No, I'm just a-goin'," replied my father; "what's up? anything the matter? Anything uncommon, I mean?"

"Beggar the things! to think that you should have gone past the door and me not hear you," replied Mr. Jenkins, evasively.

"Gone past the door! why shouldn't I?" asked my father, beginning to look serious.

"Come in, that's a good fellow, and I'll tell you all about it. You must know, Jim, that I promised my old woman that I would lay wait for you on the landing, just to give you a hint like; but you see, Jim, I get up so jolly early, and you was so late to-night before you came home, that I"——

"A hint of what?" interrupted my father.

"Dozed off, I suppose," continued Mr. Jenkins, nervously. "I wouldn't go up, Jim, if I was you. Fact, that's what I was laying wait to tell you; leastways I ought to have done. My old woman is up there, you know. She said she would when it happened. Bless you, the place was full of women till the doctor came, and then says he, 'Which of you may I regard as this poor creature's nuss?' 'Will you be so good as to regard me as such, sir?' said my old woman. 'I will so,' said the doctor; 'and now all the rest of you hook it, for this is, I am sorry to say, a case that requires the greatest amount of uninterruption.' Them wasn't the exact words, but my old woman can tell you. He turned 'em all out, howsomever."

"Why, course he did," answered my father. "Get out with you, trying to frighten a fellow. Why, aint you old enough to know that they always _do_ turn 'em out when they find a pack of 'em chattering and jawing together?"

"What's the time, Jim?"

"After six—half-past," my father replied, beginning to whistle, as though to show his superiority to Mr. Jenkins's ungrounded croaking.

"Half-past three—half-past four! Ah, he's been up there, barring the time he run home and back again to fetch something—he's been up there four hours—four solid hours, Jim. That's a good while, don't you know?" observed Mr. Jenkins, wagging his head seriously.

"That aint no manner of odds, I tell you," maintained my father, stoutly; "they always _do_ stay a long while. Why, when this young shaver as I've got in my arms was born "——

"Oh! I never met such a fellow for argument as he is," ejaculated Mr. Jenkins, distressfully turning away, and making a pretence of mending the fire. "Talk about breaking it to him gradual! It 'ud puzzle a lawyer to do it." Then turning in desperation, and with the poker in his hand, towards my father, said he—

"Since you _must_ know, Jim Ballisat, there's something wrong up there;" and he jerked his thumb towards the ceiling.

"How wrong?"

"Altogether wrong, Jim. Al—to—gether wrong."

It wasn't Mr. Jenkins's words, so much as the way in which he delivered them, that seemed to impress my father. He had no heart for further argument. He took off his hairy cap, and lowered himself down on to a chair by the window, with me on his knees.

"When was she took?" he presently asked.

"A little afore tea—so I'm told," replied Mr. Jenkins.

"If it had been on a Sunday I should have been at home," observed my father; "p'r'aps it's best as it is, though. She didn't want me, I'll wager it, Jenks."

"That's where it is, Jim," replied Jenkins. "She *does* want you. She's done nothing but ask after you for this three hours. Bless your soul, yes. Every time she hears the street-door swing, she begins—'Hark! there's my Jim! that's his step, I am sure.' She *has* been going on, I can tell you."

"A-askin' and a-wantin' to see *me!*" replied my father, huskily, and after a considerable pause. "Well, that *is* rum! Don't it strike you as being rum, Jenks?"

"Aint I been trying to make you understand how rum it all is?" replied Mr. Jenkins.

"Ah! but that part in pertickler. A-wanting me and asking after me these three hours! Why, she knows that I'm never home until five. What makes her in such a hurry, I wonder? It's about the rummest thing I ever heard tell of."

"You'd say so if you had heard a few of the queer things she has been saying," returned Mr. Jenkins. "Oh! I can't tell you half, even if I had a mind to. P'r'aps she's light-headed."

"Not she," replied my father, emphatically. "What queer things *did* she talk about? You might tell a fellow, Jenks."

"Oh, you never heard! 'I want him to kiss me,' says she. 'I want him to hold my hand in his and kiss me. I want to be good friends with him before I go,'" said Mr. Jenkins.

I believe, now that the ice was broken and the old fellow had gained courage, that he would have favoured my father with a repetition of some other queer things my mother had given utterance to; but hearing as much as he had, my father got up hastily from his chair, and after walking up and down the room two or three times, (so softly that you could scarcely hear the fall of his hob-nailed boots upon the bare floor,) presently halted, with his back to Mr. Jenkins and his face towards a picture of the Burning of the Houses of Parliament that hung against the wall. Several times I thought that he was about to put his cap on, but he never got it higher than his eyes.

"Jenks," said he, presently, but still continuing his close inspection of the Burning of the Parliament Houses, "Jenks, it mightn't be quite the ticket for me to go up; but an old chap like you are, I don't suppose they'd much mind; d'ye think they would, Jenks?"

"They've got no call to mind me; why should they?" answered Mr. Jenkins, manifestly shirking my father's question.

"You wouldn't mind just going up and saying to your old woman that I should like a word with her, if convenient?"

Mr. Jenkins did not answer immediately. "Of course, Jim, I'll go if—if you think it will be any good," he presently remarked, in a hesitating manner.

"Of course it will be good," said my father. "She'll come if you call her, won't she?"

Mr. Jenkins looked very much as though he wasn't quite sure of that. With a delicacy and consideration that did him honour, he did not trouble my father with his private reasons for suspecting that his wife might not respond promptly and cheerfully to his summons; but the fact was, he had already once in the course of that afternoon ventured on exactly the same service as that my father now requested of him. He *had gone up to make inquiries as to when it was*

likely that she would be down to get him his tea, and as I, sitting on the stairs, could hear, was snapped up very short indeed. However, like the kind-hearted old fellow he was, he did not flinch from a second attempt.

All the time Mr. Jenkins was creeping up the stairs, my father continued staring steadfastly at the Burning Houses of Parliament, his chest heaving (as I could tell by the painful pressure of the pearly buttons on his waistcoat against my legs) as though he found it tremendously hard work. We heard the door overhead open, and Mrs. Jenkins say, "I heard him; I was just coming;" and down she came along with her husband.

She had her apron to her eyes as she came down; and as soon as ever she entered the room where we were, she threw up both her hands, and began moaning and shaking her head, as though the scene she had just left was woeful enough, but, borne in mind and taken together with the spectacle which now met her gaze, was too excruciating for human endurance, and cut her up completely. She sank into a chair, and covering her head with her apron, rocked, and choked, and sobbed in a way that frightened me very much.

"Has mother got up yet, ma'am?" I asked her.

But the circumstance of my addressing her seemed to throw her into acuter agony even than before; such, at least, might be fairly assumed from her behaviour.

"Has she got up? No, my poor lamb," she gasped; "no, you poor motherless orphan, you! She'll *never* get up again."

For a moment my father withdrew his gaze from the Houses of Parliament, and looked at Mrs. Jenkins as though he had something to say; but he said nothing. He hastened back with all speed to the conflagration, indenting my calves with his pearly buttons most cruelly.

"She's sinking fast, Jim!" pursued Mrs. Jenkins. "The doctor says that it is only her sufferings that keeps her alive; and that when they are over, which is expected minute by minute, it will be *all* over."

Having thus, with many gasps and chokings, delivered herself of the dreadful intelligence, Mrs. Jenkins renewed her rocking and moaning, while her old husband walked round her and hugged her, to comfort her. As for me, although my mind was too childish to grasp the full meaning of what Mrs. Jenkins told us, I found quite enough in it to frighten me; so, slipping down out of my father's arms, I ran to Mrs. Jenkins and buried my head in her lap.

No movement of mine, however, or of Mrs. Jenkins, or of her distressed husband, could distract my father's attention from the picture against the wall. His interest in it appeared to become more absorbing each moment, so that his forehead presently sank down upon it; and between the fitful pauses in Mrs. Jenkins's lamentations, a strange noise of "Pit! pat! pit!" could be plainly heard. The picture of the Burning of the Houses of Parliament was a cheap and flimsy affair, and, being gummed only at the top, the heat had caused its bottom part to curl up, scrollwise. My father leaning his head against the wall, I think it must have been his tears dropping into this scroll that caused the sound of "Pit! pat!" Suddenly, however, and by a tremendous effort, he seemed to smother his grief; and, taking his pocket-handkerchief from his jacket pocket, he dried his eyes.

"The doctor up there still?" asked he.

"Bless the dear man, yes. Heavens! James Ballisat! you don't suppose that I could be such a heartless wretch as "——

"Anybody else up there besides the doctor?" interrupted my father.

"Nobody but the doctor, Jim. Why?"

"Because *I'm* going up," said my father, resolutely.

"You? Why, you're talking like a madman," replied the aghast Mrs. Jenkins, rising and standing in the path to the door.

"I tell you, I'm going. Poor gal! She to want to hold the hand that has so often hurt her! She to beg *me* to be friends with her! Don't you come up for a minute or so, Mrs. J. Perhaps she might have something—something private like—to tell me, that she don't want anybody but me to hear."

He was so fully determined to go, that Mrs. Jenkins made no attempt at hindrance. He stepped hastily out of the room, but scarcely had he done so when the door of our room was heard to open hastily, and the doctor's voice called out, impatiently—

"Mrs. What's-o'-name? come up here, ma'am. Bother the woman! what did she want to go away just now for?"

At this summons Mrs. Jenkins jumped up, and hastily composing herself, hurried away. My father followed her.

"Well, sir! and what the dickens do you want?" we heard the doctor say.

"Please, sir, I'm her husband."

"You are not wanted here, whoever you are," replied the doctor, snappishly; and then came the sound of a door being closed in a very fierce and decided manner.

Down came my father again, to take me on his knee, lean his elbows on the corner of the table, and rest his face on his hands, without saying a word.

It was about the middle of September, and the evenings were growing short and chilly. So we sat. Old Jenkins was present: but seeing my father's condition, he took no notice, but moved softly about the room (he kept birds) pottering over a breeding cage for canaries. By and by it grew so deep twilight that, when he wanted to bore a hole to put a wire through, he had to come to the window for the sake of the light. All at once, my father, starting up, spoke with a suddenness that nearly caused the old man to bore the gimlet into his thumb.

"Good Lord! I can't stand this, Harry Jenkins; it'll strangle me if I do;" and as he spoke, he untied and loosened his bulky yellow silk neckerchief. "I can't abide by it another minute, Harry; upon my soul, I can't. What can a fellow do?"

"If I was you, Jim, I'd take a turn out in the fresh air; not to be gone long, you know; just ten minutes. Come on; I'll come with you, Jim."

"But the boy?" said my father.

"P'r'aps he'd be better for it, too."

"I'd rather leave him. D'ye think we might?"

"Course," replied Mr. Jenkins. "He won't mind just for a little while; will you, Jimmy? He will sit here, and see the squirrel run round in his treadmill."

I said I didn't mind, though I did mind a very great deal; and away they went, leaving me alone in the room. By this time it was growing darker, and nearly dark. I did not like Mrs. Jenkins overmuch, and had seldom or never been in her room before. It was a perfectly strange room to me; for though I had now been in it more than an hour, there had been so much else to engross my attention, that I had looked about me scarcely at all. There was now, however, nothing left but to look about me. There were several bird-cages, with birds in them, ranged against the wall; but, with the exception of a blackbird, all the birds were asleep, with their heads under their wings—still as balls of feathers. The blackbird was still, too, all but his eyes, which winked and blinked at me whenever I turned my gaze that way. There were, besides, the blackbird and the squirrel, a whale's tooth on the side-board, and a great-bellied jug with a man's head, with the mouth wide open for a spout. The darker it grew, the stranger everything seemed to get, and bigger and bigger the blinking eyes of the blackbird, till I was afraid to look about me at all, and kept my eyes fixed on the squirrel's cage on the table, with the little squirrel within spinning round and round in his wire wheel.

The Dutch clock in the corner had ticked off very many more than a few minutes; but my father and Mr. Jenkins did not return. It was quite dark now; and I could see nothing of the squirrel but the white patch on his breast, ever shifting, and rising and falling behind the bright bars of his prison, as he whirled it swiftly round. When I say that this was all I could see, I mean to say that this was al I tried to see. Had I looked about, no doubt I should have found the blackbird's eyes bigger and fuller of winks than ever; and, possibly, the big-bellied man-jug champing his jaws at me. There was plenty to listen to, however. There was the creaking of the squirrel's wheel, and the clawing of its feet; there was the ticking of the Dutch clock; and plain above the ticking, and the creaking, and the clawing, a dull tramp-tramp overhead, in the room above, where my mother was. Not a bustling hither and thither, but a leisurely tramp on a beat that extended from the wall to the window; the walk of somebody waiting for somebody else, who, though tardy, is sure.

At last I grew so terribly hot and frightened that I could stand it no longer; and slipping down off the chair, and shutting my eyes that I might not see that dreadful blackbird as I passed him, I groped my way out of Jenkins's room, and, creeping up the stairs about half-way, there sat down. Had nobody been with my mother but Mrs. Jenkins, I should certainly have gone all the way up; but every now and then I could make out the creaking boots, which effectually warned me off. How could I dare venture to face a man who was so little afraid of my big, strong father that he told him he wasn't wanted, and shut the door in his face? It wasn't very comfortable sitting on the pitchy-dark, hard stairs; but it was twenty times preferable to staying in that frightful room below. Besides, there was a real bit of comfort to be found on the stairs, that was as welcome as it was unexpected. There came through the keyhole of our door a bright streak of light, long and narrow, and just enough to illuminate a solitary banister-rail. I sat on the stair nighest to this bright rail, and laid hold of it with both my hands. It was long past my bed-time; and still holding on to my rail, and laying my face against it, I presently fell fast asleep.

CHAPTER IV.

IN WHICH WORK IS CUT OUT FOR THE UNDERTAKER, AND MY FATHER REFUSES TO BE COMFORTED.

I AWOKE in a great fright. How long I had been sleeping I don't know. The light had vanished from the banister-rail, so that I was completely in the dark; and there came sounds to my ears that completely bewildered me. What with the unaccountable sounds, and the fact of my being but half-awake — and half-dreaming, probably, of the winking blackbird and the big-bellied-man jug, and the other horrors on view in Jenkins's room—it was not surprising that my leading impression should be that, by some means or another, I was in the wrong house. The longer I thought about it, the plainer it appeared that it must be so. There was a baby in this house; in our house there was no baby. So I scuttled down the stairs as fast as I could, and made for the street-door.

Just as I opened it, in came my father and Mr. Jenkins. My father, indeed, nearly stumbled over me.

"Holloa! What! is it you, Jimmy? Got tired of stopping up there by yourself—eh?"

"Bless his young heart!" said Mr. Jenkins. "Don't you see how it is, Jim? He's been watching for us at the window, and he's just come down to let us in."

"No, I didn't," said I, catching hold on father, and mighty glad of the chance, as may be imagined. "We don't live here. You're come to the wrong house, father."

"Wrong house! You're dreaming, Jimmy; it's all right, cock-o'-wax. Come up-stairs."

"It is the wrong house," I persisted. "There's a baby in this house; I heard it crying."

"Heard a baby crying!" exclaimed my father, eagerly. "Are you sure, Jimmy?"

The mysterious baby answered for itself, at that identical moment, in tones loud enough to be plainly heard.

"D'ye hear that, Jenkins?" said my father. "That's jolly, aint it? I begin to think it is all right, after all, old man."

"If it is, we shall precious soon know," replied old Jenkins. "Come on up-stairs."

We went up; and before a light could be struck, I was convinced that we were in the right house by the whirring and burring noise the squirrel was making.

"I wonder whether that disagreeable beggar has gone yet?" said my father, standing in the doorway of Jenkins's room, and evidently of a mind to go up and satisfy himself on the point.

But at that very moment, the disagreeable beggar, as my father called the doctor, made known (or, rather, his boots did for him) that he had not yet departed. Creak! creak! overhead. Creak! creak! to the room-door, the handle of which was turned. Creak! creak! creak! coming down the stairs, which, when my father heard, caused him to beat a sudden retreat, with

long and stealthy steps, to the farther end of Jenkins's room, where he sat down.

"He's off at last, Jenks," said he, rubbing his hands cheerfully; "show him a light, old boy. I think it looks well—his going. He wouldn't go if she was very bad, you know."

But the disagreeable beggar was not off—at least, not straight off. He had got something to say to my father before he went; and when he reached Jenkins's landing he halted, and coughed, and tapped at the half-open door with his walking-stick.

Mr. Jenkins, on the way to show him a light, was just in time to confront him.

"Your name is Ballisat, I believe," said the doctor; "you are the husband of the "——

"No, sir, thanky; it isn't me. Here, Jim!"

"I'm the one you want, sir," said my father, coming boldly forward, with me in his arms; "I'm her husband, at your service, mister. And how might she find herself by this time, mister?"

The doctor was the parish doctor — a tall, round-shouldered old gentleman, with white hair, and wearing spectacles.

"Oh, you are Mr. Ballisat!" said he, speaking in a very different voice from that which he had used to my father when ordering him about his business. "And is this the little fellow she was speaking of?"

"Werry likely, sir," replied my father; "she has been speaking about a goodish many things, so I've been told. Could we go up and have a word with her now, sir? Not as I want to disturb her—of course not; but if so be as "——

"Well, my little man," interrupted the doctor, taking one of my hands in his long, black-gloved own, "you must be a good boy now poor mother has gone, and then you will one day see her again. You must love your little sister, and be kind to her, for mother's sake. Good-night, my dear. Good-night, Mr. Ballisat. You must try and bear up under your loss as a man should. If you and I, my friend, could only live in the meek and forgiving spirit in which she died, we should be happy men. Good-night. If you send round in the morning, I will give you a certificate of the death."

Beyond nodding his head, my father had betrayed no sign that he had heard a word the doctor was saying. He seemed amazed; and his eyes wandered from the doctor to the stairs down which he had just come, as though he could understand it all as far as that, but no farther. When the doctor bade him good-night, he made him no answer beyond a nod; and it was not until old Jenkins was following the doctor down the stairs with the candle, that his speech and understanding came back to him.

"O Lord! O Christ! gone! gone!" he cried, in a harsh, whimpering whisper; and then, staggering back to Jenkins's room all in the dark, he set me between his knees, and cowering, with his face and arms over me, commenced sobbing and shaking like a man with the ague.

That was how old Jenkins found him when he returned with the candle—how Mrs. Jenkins and the minister, whom I had not seen go up (he must have passed me as I lay asleep holding on to the rail) found him. The minister, who was a very young man of stern aspect, endeavoured to comfort father. He pointed out to him how unbecoming it was to grieve, and how that, on th contrary, he ought to rejoice that his wife was snatched away from a world abounding in iniquity. With his eyes so full of bitter tears, however, my father could not be brought to see the matter in this light; instead of giving him any comfort, it only made him savage; and he flatly told the minister that if that was what he meant, the sooner he took himself off the better—which he did, seeming rather glad to get away.

Mrs. Jenkins, although she tried a course exactly opposite to that of the minister, was little more successful. She reminded my father of the excellence of the wife he had lost, and of the many, many kind messages she had intrusted to her (Mrs. Jenkins) for delivery.

"If you had been the best husband in the world to her, Jim, she could not have gone forgiving you freer," said Mrs. Jenkins. At which my father bowed his head lower still, and shook the more.

"Lor'! don't take on so, Jim," continued she. "Think of the two forlorn and motherless babies she has left behind her. Think of this blessed lamb, as it would have been a heavenly mercy if she had never been born. Here, Jim, look up; you hain't seen the baby."

I never dreamed she had it with her. I saw that she had a bundle of some sort, and that was all.

"Do just hold her a minute, Jim," said Mrs. Jenkins; "it will do you good, Jim—sure it will. She's just the spit of the poor dear that's gone; the same eyes and the same hair, to a shade."

And so she wheedled the baby on to my father's lap.

"The sweet angel!" remarked a woman of the alley, (there were a good many of them in the room by this time;) "the dear innocent! with that pretty purple mark on its cheek."

"Which so the mother has, if you remember, ma'am," chimed in another, "showing still on her poor dead face, white as wax-work."

When the woman said this, my father suddenly raised his head and gave such a start that it was a wonder the baby in its blanket did not roll off his lap and fall to the ground. As though it was of no account at all, he bundled it into Mrs. Jenkins's arms, and turned on the woman, with his swollen eyes flashing—

"Let me get out of this!" said he. What d'ye mean by it? Ain't I tormented enough with what's a-passing in my mind, without all of you pecking and jawing at me? Don't you think that I *knowed* all about the bruise on her cheek, that you must twit me about it? Look here! If I could wash out that mark with the blood out of the hand that made it—with this hand— I'd chop it off now before your eyes. But it's there, and it'll have to stop; and it's *there*, (pointing to the baby,) and there it will have to stop, too, staring me in the face all my life. Ain't that punishment enough, don't you think? If you don't, you should feel it. Lord send you could feel for a minute what I've been feeling all through this blessed night! It would teach you better, I'll wager."

And having said all this, very quick and very loud, my father sank down on his chair again, and hid his face on his arms, which rested on the table, as though he wanted no further talk with anybody. The company did not appear to be in a hurry to take the hint; but after an awkward silence of four or five minutes, my father's meaning became so clear that it was impossible to mistake it; and so, by ones and twos, they gradually dispersed; and as Mrs. Jenkins was engaged up-stairs, we were once more left alone with old Jenkins, who shut the door.

"Now, you take my advice, Jim," said he, addressing my father, "and turn in with the boy. There's my son Joe's bed in the back-room, and Joe, as you know, won't be home till the morning. Turn in, Jim; and if you can't sleep, you will be able to get a good spell of quiet."

CHAPTER V.

IN WHICH MY FATHER ENDEAVOURS TO EXPLAIN TO ME THE MEANING OF THE WORDS "DEATH" AND "NEVER."

YOUNG Joe Jenkins's room, in which, after some persuasion, my father and myself consented to pass the night, was not exactly the sort of chamber an over-nice person would have chosen as a sleeping apartment.

Joe Jenkins was a night hand at a blacklead-factory on the Surrey side of the water, and being a long-headed and ingenious young fellow, and having a great deal of daylight at his disposal, had turned his bedroom into a workshop. His father took a great deal to "the fancy," and so did Joe. I say "the fancy," because they called it so. It meant dealing in birds, and dogs, and rabbits, and rats for the rat-pit, and ferrets. Besides "fancying" these various birds and beasts, Joe fancied birdcage-making and bird-stuffing, and the bringing-up from the nest and by hand of all sorts of singing-birds. Likewise he dealt in dog-physic and birdlime, and "salt-cats" for pigeons. The only cupboard in the room was crammed with these sort of things, as was the fireplace; and at all sides underneath the bedstead strange shapes in wood and wire-work protruded. You could not see pots or brushes about, but that painting was carried on in the room, you could smell beyond a doubt.

My father, however, was not an over-nice person. Had the bedstead been the handsomest mahogany four-poster ever built, instead of one of the commonest scissor-pattern; had the bed been down instead of cotton flock, and the counterpane quilted satin in place of faded patch-work; had the apartment been spacious and lofty, instead of small and of a decidedly "cupboardy" odour, my father could not have rested a bit better than he did, which was not at all.

Old Jenkins's prognostication, that if my father could not sleep he would be benefited by a spell of quiet, did not come true. While the people in the house were still up and about, while footsteps up and down the stairs might be heard, and the street cries out in Turnmill Street continued, he lay quiet enough; and had it not been for his fidgeting and tossing his arms about, and the odd noises he from time to time made with his lips, I should have thought that he was asleep. Not that I wanted him to go to sleep. I lay quiet too, but I was painfully broad awake, and could distinctly make out the creaking of the axletree of the squirrel's cylinder in the front room, and the clawing of its feet against the wires. I was a very long way from comfortable in my mind. I didn't exactly know what, but that something dreadful was the matter I had no doubt.

Gradually the noises in the street and in the alley subsided, and all without was quiet. All within was quiet also, except that in the front room overhead the muffled shuffling of feet and an indistinct humming as of two persons conversing in whispers continued. As the other noises died away these last mentioned grew plainer. Knowing the room as I did, I could as easily as possible follow the footsteps, and knew exactly where the two whisperers halted. In about an hour, however, the whisperers came together to the room-door, shut it, locked it on the outside, and hastened down-stairs. When they reached the door of the room where we were, said one to the other—

"What shall we do with the candle?"

"Blow it out, and stand it just outside the door, here."

"Ah, that's the ticket. He and the boy are sleeping in here, you know. I'll put it down along with the lucifer matches."

"No occasion to leave the matches, as I see."

"You don't know: he might take it into his head to want to go up and have a peep, and I don't suppose he would care about going up in the dark."

"I should rather think not," replied the other woman, with a stifled giggle. "If he's the man *I* take him for, he'll be in no hurry to pay her a visit, daylight or dark. At least I should not like to if I was him."

"Why not?"

There was no answer to this, at least no verbal answer. That the party questioned made some sort of response or sign was plain, however, for the other replied—

"Oh! I don't know. Old Nick, you know, is not so black as he is painted, they say. You can't say what you'd do if you stood in his shoes. There's an old saying and a true one, that there is no cure for a burn like holding it to the fire."

"Well, make haste tying your pattens on; we shan't be able to get a drain at the 'Stile' before they shuts up."

"I'm ready when you are."

"How about the key?"

"Well, it's no use leaving him the candle and the matches without we leave him the key. Lay it down with 'em."

"I know a safer way than that. That's how to do it." And as she spoke she pushed the key under the door into the room, as I could tell by the scrooping noise.

Then, as my sense of smell plainly informed me, they blew the candle out and went downstairs. They did not go down in the dark, however. They struck a light with a lucifer match against the wall against which our heads lay. The match, however, went out before they got half-way down; for one of them exclaimed—

"Drat the thing! it's gone out, and I haven't got another! Never mind; come along."

And then they were heard hurrying along the passage towards the street door, which they banged with a heartiness that showed how glad they were to get out of a house where death was.

My father lay quite still while the whispering *was going on without*, and without doubt heard it all as plainly as did I, understanding it much better. Soon, however, as all was quiet, he rose on his elbow, and leaning over the side of the bed, felt about the floor, evidently for the purpose of finding the key the woman had pushed under the door.

What could he want with it? Was it his intention, as the woman said it probably would be, to go up and "take a peep?" Was he going up "to cure his burns by holding them to the fire," whatever *that* meant? This could hardly be, because if he meant to go up to our room, his most natural course would be to get up and light the candle, which he would want to show him the way, and which would make his search after the key an easy matter. No, he was not going upstairs. After groping about for more than a minute, he fished up the key, and lifting up his pillow placed it underneath.

"That's *summat* of a keepsake, anyhow," he whispered; and then he laid his head down, as though at last he really was going to sleep.

But somehow he couldn't manage it. No position suited him for as long as five minutes. He tossed and tumbled this side and that with his face to the wall—with his face to the window—with his arms folded tight over his breast, and then again pressed across his eyes, as though to keep them closed whether they would or no. But he couldn't be still. One thing, however, I could not help remarking. Whichever way he stirred, he was careful to avoid disturbing me. Every time he made an awkward lurch, he would pat me softly on the shoulder, and whisper "hus—sh!" as though afraid that I might wake.

But he need not have taken any pains on that score. I was awake—broad awake—though still as a mouse. My mind was utterly bewildered by the quick succession of marvellous events that had transpired during the day. What, after all, was the matter with mother? That was the foremost puzzle in my mind. Mrs. Jenkins had said she was "gone," and yet the two women were engaged up-stairs hours afterwards,—engaged in our room, and with my mother beyond a doubt; for had not the women when they talked about the key and the candle said, "Perhaps he would like to go up and have a peep at her?" Again, if she was "gone," why had they locked the door? and still, again, if she was *not* gone, but was simply lying abed, why had they locked the door? Had they left her all alone and in the dark because she was ill? Still, if Mrs. Jenkins's word might be taken for it, mother *had* gone. "Poor dear creature, and was you with her, ma'am, when she went?" a woman asked of her, and she answered, "Yes, I was with her till the last." It was altogether a maze to me, and the further I endeavoured to penetrate it the more I became bewildered.

If my mother was gone, where was she gone to, and how long would it be before she returned? She was *never* coming back. That was another remark Mrs. Jenkins had made use of. "How long will it be before mother comes home again, ma'am?" I asked her; and her reply was, "She will *never* come home again, my poor boy. She has gone away for ever to the place where all good people go, and she will never come back any more."

How long was "never?"

Was it a day, a week, a month? Was it fi

ther off than my birthday, or next Christmas? Were there more sorts of "never" than one? I had often heard the word used between my father and mother; but, according to my observation, its meaning was uncertain. I had heard my father say to my mother, "Curse you, I have done with you. I'll never break bread along with you again; if I do, I hope it may choke me." This he would say at breakfast-time; yet he has returned at night and ate his supper with my mother the same as usual, breaking bread and eating it without being choked. "I'll never forgive you, Jim," said my mother that time when he sneered at her about being only fit to live in Turkey, and struck her down beside the fender; "I'll never, never forgive you, Jim, while I've got breath left in my body;" and yet, according to Mrs. Jenkins, she had freely forgiven him. She had been longing all that afternoon that my father might come home that she might tell him so; that she might take his hand in hers, and kiss him, and tell him that they parted good friends. It was plain that "never" meant all sorts of times. But how long was this "never" of my mother's? Certainly, I would put the question to Mrs. Jenkins the very first thing in the morning. Stay! perhaps my father knew. At least there could be no harm in asking him.

"Father, are you asleep?"

"No, Jimmy, I'm awake. Why?"

"When is 'never' father?"

The question fairly startled him on his elbows. No doubt it did come rather suddenly on him.

"Hus—sh! lay down, Jim. You've been a-dreaming," said he.

"I haven't been to sleep yet, father. I can't go for thinking of it. Can't you tell me when 'never' is? Mother's 'never,' I mean?"

"Mother's 'never!'" repeated he. "Well, that's rather a queer question for a young 'un like you to ask. I don't understand you, Jimmy. What has 'never' got to do with mother?"

"That's what I can't make out, I replied; "I thought you might be able to tell me."

"You go to sleep, that's a good boy," said my father, putting my head down on to the pillow, and tucking me in to make me comfortable; "you go to sleep, Jimmy; don't you trouble your head about 'never;' 'never' is a long day."

"Only a day? only a long day? I'm glad of that. I'm glad it ain't more; ain't you, father?"

"Not particular glad, Jimmy; what's it got to do with me? Long day or short day, it's about the same, I reckon."

"It isn't the same to mother, is it, father?"

"There you are again," replied my father, once more rising on his elbows and looking down on me; "what's it got to do with mother?"

"'Never' is the time when mother is coming back to us. You'll be glad to see her come back, won't you, father?"

He rose up high on his elbows when I said this, and regarded me, as I could see by the dim moonlight that came in at the window, with not a little dismay.

"Who's been putting *that* into his young head?" said he.

"Mrs. Jenkins, father," I promptly replied.

"Mrs. Jenkins is a precious jackass for her pains, then," said my father, savagely. "Don't you mind what she says, Jimmy. It isn't no use of her trying to keep your pluck up by telling you a parcel of lies. Mother's gone, Jimmy. She isn't coming back. She *can't* come back. Bushels and sackfuls of money wouldn't fetch her back. How can she, Jimmy, when she's dead? You knew that mother was dead, didn't you?"

"Dead!"

"Dead!" echoed my father, in a whisper. "You see that bird on the shelf there" (one which young Joe Jenkins had taken in hand, and was preparing for stuffing. By the dim moonlight I could make it out pretty well; and a terribly grim sight it was, without eyes, with its beak wide agape, and with bright iron skewers run through all parts of its body.) "You see that, Jimmy; well, *that's* death. Mother can no more come to life again, and get up and walk, than that bullfinch can hop down off the shelf and begin to pick up crumbs, and sing, and fly about the room."

"And is that 'never,' too, father?" I asked, eyeing the horrible bullfinch. "Does death mean the same as 'never?'"

"Pretty much, I suppose," returned he. "Howsomever, *that's* being dead, my boy, and so you see."

"I thought 'dead' meant 'gone,' father. The finch hasn't gone. Hasn't mother gone? Is she up-stairs with sharp things all stuck in her?"

"No, no! good Lord! what a fancy for a kid to lay hold on! Beggar that mother Jenkins! Look here; you know what keeps you going, don't you?"

"Keeps me going, father?" I didn't know. How should I.

"Keeps you walking and breathing, and that; and makes you—well, blest if I know how to bring it home to him!—makes you know what things are when you look at 'em."

"I know," said I. "My eyes."

"No; more than that. Your eyes ain't no more than your hands to see with, 'cept for the power what's give to 'em. It's your soul what's the power, Jimmy. It's your soul what keeps you going. What goes out of you and brings you to be like that finch, is your soul, my boy—what God'll save, if you be a good boy, like the doctor told you, and say your prayers. And when it has gone out of you, there you are; can't cry out, can't move, nor hear, nor breathe, nor see. You can't feel the least in the world. If you was pinned through and through, like that finch is, it would be all the same to you as leaving you alone. It doesn't matter who it comes to, Jimmy; it's the same thing. Death don't know nothing about Lord Mayors, nor magistrates, nor nobs and swells, as ride about in carriages; they're all the same as crossing-sweepers to him. And your mother's dead; and by and by they will bring a coffin and lay her in it, and carry her out on their shoulders and lay her in the pit-hole. My poor Polly! my poor cherry-lipped gal! and that's what they *will* do," continued my father, carried sheer out of his depth in his earnest (though, I am bound to confess, not completely successful) endeavours to make me understand what death was; "that is what they will do to my poor gal; and me laying here without having kissed you before you went, as you wanted me, or even bidding you good-bye."

At this point he broke down completely, and, burying his face in the pillow, fairly shook the scissor bedstead with the strength of his grief. The sorrow he had manifested in the early part of the evening was as nothing compared with it; and I take it to be a lucky circumstance that, affrighted by the dismal turn affairs had taken, I, too, now began to cry, and howl, and shriek, setting my pipes to the highest pitch. It was lucky for this reason, that lest every lodger in the house should be roused and alarmed by the tremendous row I was creating, my father exerted himself to stanch his grief, that he might be at liberty to abate mine.

But I was not to be easily pacified. The terrible picture of death that my father had drawn filled me with horror. The truth was bad enough before, seen as I had seen it through a haze of uncertainty and ignorance; but now, when, in his rough way, he whipped up the curtain, and exposed to my gaze the hard, grisly reality, it was altogether more than I could bear. It was all in vain that he endeavoured to quiet me. He in turn tried threats, coaxing, and compensation. He volunteered to tell me a story; and at once plunged, to the best of his ability, into one in which a dreadful ogre, with seven heads, had little children boiled regularly every morning for his breakfast. As may be imagined, I derived no sort of comfort from such a narrative. He felt out of bed for his trousers, and taking his canvas bag, gave it me with its contents. He promised me a ride on his barrow to Covent Garden Market in the morning. Knowing how much I liked Yarmouth bloaters, he pledged his word that if I would hold my row, I should have a whole one all to myself for my breakfast in the morning. There was a rocking-horse maker out in Aylesbury Street, and often had I expressed a desire to possess one of the splendid saddled and stirruped steeds exhibited in the shop—a desire that had invariably met with refusal, uncompromising and hopeless: now the handsomest rocking-horse to be bought for money should be mine in the morning, if I would only lie down and be a good boy.

No! no! no! I wanted my mother, and would be satisfied with nothing less. According to my father's own statement, she was lying all alone, speared through and through with spikes, as was Joe Jenkins's bullfinch, (or, if not, she was reduced to that deplorable condition, that whether they run spikes through or no would make no difference to her—which was much the same thing;) and what I insisted on, and would consent to leave off crying on no other terms, was that my father and I should go up-stairs and let mother out. He had the key of the door under his pillow, I reminded him; and begged and implored that he would go up and see what could be done for poor mother.

"No; I won't do it. I can't do it. I wouldn't do it for a hundred good pounds told down," replied he, emphatically; "and since you won't be good for nothing less, why p'r'aps you'd better cry until you are tired, and then you'll leave off."

My father had a way of saying things he really meant in a way there was no misunderstanding. The answer above written was of this sort, and speedily led to our coming to terms. On condition that he got up and lit a candle immediately, and, further, that I should see mother the very first thing in the morning, I consented to kiss him and be a good boy.

I have no doubt but that my father congratulated himself on having achieved a victory on such easy conditions; but there were difficulties in the way of the carrying out of the terms of our treaty he had never dreamed of. He got out of bed, and then he made the discovery that old Jenkins had not left us any candle. Stumbling amongst young Joe's wood and wirework, and feeling on the mantle-shelf and in the cupboard, he made the discovery; and it set him growling at a pretty rate. The handiest candle was the one outside the door, that the woman had brought down from the room where my mother was.

"Here's a pretty go, Jim!" said my father, affecting to treat the matter pleasantly, as a lure, I suppose, for me to do the same. "I'm blessed if that old Jenkins hasn't took the candle away. We'll give him a talking to to-morrow morning, won't we?"

"There's a candle outside, and matches as well," I replied. "I heard the woman who came down-stairs put them there."

"Oh, you don't want no candle, Jimmy!" said my father, coaxingly. "See what a man you are gettin'—going to have a bloater for your breakfast, too — a whole bloater! See here; I'll pull aside the curtain, and let a bit more moon in—shall I? There you are! Why, it's as light as afternoon a'most now—ain't it?"

But instead of answering him, I began to cry again, and to call out loudly for my mother. He saw plainly that there was nothing to be done but keep to the terms of our contract; so, after a bit of a growl, he opened the door very softly, and reached in the matches and the candlestick, and lit the candle, and stood it on a shelf.

I was of course too young to think of such things at the time, but it has occurred to me frequently since,—how did my father feel, and what did he think about, as he lay watching that candle burning? In my eyes it was simply a bit of tallow candle; and my only reflection in reference to it was, that it would have been much better had it been somewhat longer, for there was not more than two inches of it, and it was all aslant and guttery. As he lay with his eyes fixed on it, however, it may have filled him with thoughts that were much more serious. It may have come into his mind that this was the candle that had burned all the night through in my mother's room, and that it was gazing on its flame that her dying sight had failed her. Perhaps she had said, as dying people will, under such circumstances, "Bring back the candle; I cannot see; I am in the dark." He may have been led to ponder on the uncertainty of life, and on what a useless thing a body bereft of its soul is. More useless than a scrap of candle, for the candle flame may be quenched, and the candle saved and rekindled; but the body never may until the day of the Great Rekindling comes.

If he got into a train of thought of this sort, goodness knows what else he may have been led to think about. Perhaps of the considerable share he had taken towards putting my mother's life out, and how he would have to answer for it one day. I shouldn't wonder if he did think of this. Certainly, as he lay regarding the candle-flame so intently thoughts of more than ordinary solemnity were busy within him, and I very sincerely trust that the guess I have made is correct, because never before or since do I recollect seeing him so bowed down and humble.

For my part, the bullfinch gave me enough to think of. By the dull light of the moon I had been able to make out little more than its mere shape. Now, however, it was plainly revealed from its head to its tail. My heart has been set against bullfinches from that time; and, as a gift even, I would not accept the best "piper" in London. I believe that most people would as soon entertain the idea of giving house-room to a human skeleton as I to a bird of this species; nor would it be, comparatively, more preposterous, since the bullfinch is, in my eyes, as perfect an emblem of death as could possibly be suggested. It was death itself, and so I regarded it. My eyes were drawn towards it, and would not be withdrawn. Its black, eyeless, bullet-shaped head; its wide-agape beak; its straddle legs; the crimson blurs and smirches that stained its body; the bright, sharp wires which trussed it in every direction, fascinated my gaze completely. Presently the dwindling candle began to sputter, and its flame to gasp for breath, as it were—rising and falling like a man that is drowning, and seeming to make the spitted bird rise and fall, and to wriggle and writhe to get free from the spikes in it. Then, with a struggle, I turned my face to the wall, and, falling asleep, never awoke until I heard the tinkle of the breakfast things in Jenkins's room.

———

CHAPTER VI.

IN WHICH, FOR THE FIRST TIME IN MY LIFE, I SEE THE INSIDE OF A CHURCH, ALSO A PIT-HOLE IN THE YARD BY THE SIDE OF IT.

I DISCOVERED no particular reason for bewailing my mother's death for some considerable time after it happened. On the contrary, indeed, I was decidedly a gainer by the melancholy event; for no sooner did it become generally known that I was an orphan, than every womanly heart in Fryingpan Alley yearned towards me. During the first two or three days, this universal sympathy and commiseration was rather embarrassing to a boy so utterly unused to it. My appearance at the door was the signal for a doleful chorus of "Here comes poor little Jimmy!" and I could scarcely walk as far as the water-butt without having my head patted half-a-dozen times, and more bread and treacle and bits of pudding thrust into my hands that I could have fairly eaten in a day.

Nor did the good-nature of the neighbours stop at presents of victuals. People whom I scarcely knew by sight even stopped me, and, after many tender inquiries of a sort calculated to make me pipe my eye, soothed and comforted me by gifts of halfpence and farthings. The pocket in my little breeches would scarcely hold my riches; and the value of money so depreciated in my eyes, that I was led into all sorts of extravagances. There was no delicacy in the sweetstuff-shop round the corner, from the top to the bottom shelf, with the flavour of which I did not make myself acquainted. My young acquaintances exerted themselves in my behalf to invent novel and curious means for investing my money. At their suggestion, I once bought a market bunch of young and juicy carrots. On the third day after my mother's decease, I became so ill that they fetched the white-headed doctor to see me. I was going after my mother, everybody said; and quite a new start was given to the now slightly-flagging interest in me.

I was the envy of every boy in the Alley. There was one youth in particular, named Pape, whose father used to go about with a tinker's barrow, mending pots and grinding scissors. He it was that recommended the purchase of the carrots, and altogether, at this period, he displayed a great amount of affection for me. He was older than I was, but hardly a bit bigger; and I well remember a conversation he and I had concerning mothers, dead and alive. He had not got a good mother. According to his account, (and I believe I was completely in his confidence at the time,) she was a woman who could consume a large quantity of spirituous liquor without being overcome by it. According to Jerry Pape, Mrs. Pape was malicious to that degree, that she would lay traps for Jerry and his brothers to fall into mischief, and then keep them without their dinner by way of punishment—spending the money that ought to have provided the mid-day meal in gin at the "Dog and Stile."

"I wish there was no mothers," said Jerry; "what's the good on 'em? They on'y whack yer, and get yer into rows when your father comes home. Anybody as is hard up for a mother can have mine, and jolly welcome. I wish she would die."

"P'r'aps she will soon, Jerry," I replied, by way of comforting the poor fellow.

"She'd better," said Jerry, with threatening brows.

"Why had she better, Jerry?"

"Never mind why. You'll know why, one of these days, and so will all the jolly lot on yer as lives in Fryingpan Alley. You know Guy Fox, don't yer? Him as comes about on the fift of Nowember?"

"Yes, yes, Jerry, I know."

"Werry well, then. Don't you ask any more questions, 'cos it's a secret."

"Do tell us, Jerry! Do tell us, and you shall have another bite; up to here, see!"—and I partitioned off a big bit of the apple with my fingers and thumb for Jerry to bite.

"No, not up to there, nor not if you gives me the lot," replied Jerry, eyeing the little apple contemptuously; "why, it's ever such a secret. It 'ud make you funk so, that you'd be afeared to shut your eyes when you went to bed. I might let you into it, if you stood a baked tatur; and that 'ud be like chucking it away."

Five minutes after, Jerry and I were seated on the threshold of a dark warehouse doorway, (it was evening,) in Red Lion Street; and while he discussed the baked potato, he revealed to me the particulars of his terrible secret.

"I'm a savin' up," whispered he. "I've got as high as fippence. Leastways, when I ses fippence, it's fivepen'orth; so it's all the same."

"Fivepen'orth of what, Jerry?"

"Fireworks," replied Jerry, in the lowest of whispers, and with his lips close to my wondering ear. "I've got a Roman candle, nine crackers, and a squib. Sky-rockets would be the things; but they're so jolly dear."

"Where are they, Jerry? Whereabouts is the Roman candle and the crackers? What are you going to do with 'em, Jerry?"

"They 're stuffed in the bed—in our old woman's bed," replied Jerry, cramming the last piece of hot potato into his mouth, his face assuming a most fiendish expression. "I'm a savin' up till I buys enough fireworks to fill the jolly old tick quite full. Then I'm goin' to buy some gunpowder. Then I'm a-goin' to get up early one morning with my gunpowder, and lay a train under the bedstead, and down the stairs, and out into the street. Then I'm a-goin' on the tramp, dropping my gunpowder, mind yer, all the way as I goes; and when I gets about up to Peckham, I'm a-goin' to set light to my train; and up 'll go the old woman over the houses, blowed into little bits."

Whether Jerry Pape seriously contemplated this diabolical murder, or was merely imposing on me, I cannot, of course, be certain. Most probably the latter. I firmly believed in him at the time, however; and for several nights afterwards lay abed trembling, in the dark, in momentary expectation of a tremendous explosion, and one of the largest "bits" of Mrs. Pape falling down our chimney.

To return, however, to my history.

My mother dying on the Friday, her funeral was fixed to take place on the ensuing Tuesday, that being a slack day at the markets, and therefore suitable to my father's convenience.

From the time of my mother's death until the day of her burial, I was so little at home as to be altogether unaware of the preparations that were going on towards that melancholy event. I did not even sleep at home, Mrs. Winkship having considerately placed at my disposal, at her house, the comfortable little crib which her niece Martha had slept in when she was a child. I should even have missed the sight of mother's coffin being carried in at Number Nineteen, had not the lady who lived opposite, and with whom I was taking tea, luckily caught sight of it, and, hurriedly catching me up in her arms, stood me on a table before the window that I might look. "See, Jimmy! see!" said she; "unkivered, with black nails; quite a pictur of a coffin I call that, now!"

There was not much fuss about the Fryingpan Alley funerals. The people were buried in a business-like manner, at a business price, and there was no sentimental nonsense about the matter. I think I have said that I knew nothing of the preparation; but this is not quite correct. It happened that I was in Jenkins's room when the person living in the parlours called up the stairs that here was Mr. Crowl's man "come to take the measure:" and presently, hearing a strange step, I peeped out at the door to see what Mr. Crowl's man was like. I found him to be a dirty-faced man, with hairy arms, and his shirt sleeves tucked above the elbows; and he had a brown paper cap on. He smoked a dirty pipe as high up the stairs as Jenkins's door; but when Mrs. Jenkins gave him the key of our door, he stuck the end of it into the pipe-bowl, and extinguished the fire, and put the pipe in his waistcoat pocket. He carried a pair of trestles on his shoulder, and observed that he thought he might just as well bring them with him now as to come on purpose

to-morrow. He went up by himself, and presently he came down with a square pencil in his mouth and a tape-measure about his neck, conning the "dimensions," as he called them, and which were figured down on the smooth side of a scrap of dirty sandpaper.

It was an old-established custom in Fryingpan Alley, and all the other courts and alleys thereabout, that when a person died, his female relatives wore the regular sort of mourning attire—black bonnets and shawls, &c.—but his male relations wore nothing of the kind. They followed the body to the grave in their ordinary flannels and fustians, and their only emblem of bereavement was a wisp of black crape round the upper part of the arm, after exactly the same fashion, indeed, as soldiers wear their badges of mourning for any defunct member of the Royal family. Sometimes, in addition to the crape armlet, a bit of the same material would be worn round the cap; but this was considered not at all necessary, and as rather approaching what is known as "toffishness"—as near an approach to it, indeed, as could be by any means tolerated. Had any male dwelling in our alley ventured to turn out in a black coat and trousers, and, to crown all, a tall black hat, he would have been subject to the withering scorn of every inhabitant, and the tall black hat would certainly have been knocked from his head before he had reached Turnmill Street.

And yet it must not be imagined that this prejudice against orthodox mourning attire arises out of brutal-mindedness and contempt of death. It has its origin in "fashion." It may seem odd to associate so dandy a thing as fashion with costermongerism, but it is quite true that they are closely associated. No man is more anxious "to do the thing to rights" in the matter of clothes than the prosperous barrow-man. At the period of which I am writing, Spitalfields set the fashion, and not a costermonger in London but scrupulously followed its dictates—from the seal-skin cap upon his head to the arrangement of the clinkers in the "ankle-jacks" in which his feet were encased. Fashion in Spitalfields was as capricious as the goddess that sways her sceptre in Regent Street. It was the correct thing for the costermonger, whatever branch of industry he might pursue, to wear round his throat—bunchy, loosely tied, and elegantly careless—a very large, highly-coloured silk pocket-handkerchief. This the costermonger calls a "kingsman." This season its pattern would be yellow, with a green "bird's-eye" spot; next season it would be red, with a blue splash; and as the cost of a "kingsman" was about seven-and-sixpence, and as there was nothing to be done with the old-fashioned one but to let the pawnbroker have it for as much as he would lend on it, the annual pecuniary sacrifice in this matter alone was not inconsiderable. As regards waistcoats, if my memory serves me, Spitalfields fashion was not quite so inexorable. So long as it was an ample waistcoat, and profusely and cheerfully "sprigged," that was enough. His jacket was of flannel, or velveteen, or fustian—it didn't matter which, so long as the pattern of the buttons was according to the prevailing mode. It was the buttons that stamped the garment. If "plain pearly shankers" were Fashion's latest edict, to sport glass "blue bells," or brass buttons of the game-keeping school, impressed with a horse and hounds, a fox's head, or some other such emblem of the chase, would be to declare yourself a "slow coach" at the very least. Knee-breeches were just going out of fashion when I was a little boy, and "calf-clingers" (that is, trousers made to fit the leg as tight as a worsted stocking,) were "coming in." Even the hair and whiskers of the costermonger, like that of more civilised folk, used to be governed by fashion. Sometimes "jug-loops," (the hair brought straight on to the temples, and turned *under*,) would be the rage; another season, "terrier-crop" would be the style. There were three fashions for whiskers when I was a child, and they were variously known as "blue-cheek," (the whisker shaved off, and leaving the cheek blue;) "bacca-pipe" (the whisker curled in tiny ringlets;) and "touzle" (the whisker worn bushy.) "Terrier-crop" and "blue-cheek" had, I recollect, a long run.

The barrow-man knew nothing of "Sunday," or best clothes. They were his best he could best work in. In these he courted the young lady of his choice; in these he married her, worked for her, and, when she died, followed her to the grave. It was so with my father. The red and blue-splashed neckerchief, and the mouse-coloured fustian, with big white pearl buttons, were the fashion at the time when my mother died; and in these my father, with a pale and troubled face, arrayed himself, by the aid of young Joe Jenkins's shaving-glass, while the undertaker and his men were busy up-stairs. The only articles my father had bought specially for the occasion were a pair of new ankle-jackets for himself, and a black cloth cap with a peak (of the pattern known as "navy") for me. Having ascertained that I was to follow, Mr. Crowl, the undertaker, took my cap, and pinned a long black streamer round it, which trailed down to my heels; but a little time afterwards, happening to pass me in the passage—in the middle of which I was seated, dividing some hardbake with a few sympathising friends—his sad face bristled up as he saw a boy standing on my trailing "weeper," and, fetching him a savage smack on the side of the head, he wiped the dirt off it, and pinned it up to a decent length.

The followers were to be my father, myself, Mrs. Jenkins, carrying the baby, (which, by the by, I had not set eyes on since the evening when Mrs. Jenkins had saved it from falling off my father's lap,) and four male friends of my father's, who had come early, and were now assembled in Jenkins's front room. Two of these four lived in the alley, but the other two were strangers to me. Judging from the smell, however, they were something in the fish way. They wore bits of crape round the sleeves of their flannel jackets; and though they looked anything but comfortable and at their ease, their behaviour was all that could be desired. They sat in a ring with my father, and smoked their pipes and talked but little, and that in solemn whispers. Their conversation, as I recollect, (for I was a good deal in and out of Jenkins's front room that morning,) was all of a melancholy turn, in compliment, I suppose, to my father. Once, when I went in, they were deep in the subject of miracles; and one of the men whom I did not know was expatiating on Jonah's probable sensations while in the bowels of the whale. Another time I caught them discussing the great Plague of London, dwelling particularly on that part where the men came round in the night with a cart and a bell, crying, "Bring out your dead! bring out your dead!" just like our own dustmen, only without fantails and baskets, and "loading up a precious deal more frequent," one of them explained. They had some beer in a gallon can, but, not to make a display of it, it was stood behind the coal-box in the corner; and as their turns came round, they went and stood with their backs there, and took a swig, and then came back again looking more solemn than before.

I was engaged on a neighbouring door-step with my companions, when a woman who had been sent to find me, suddenly spied me out, and bore me away in a hurried and excited manner.

"Come along, Jimmy," said she; "They're ready to start, and only waiting for you." Going along, she kindly damped the corner of her apron, and wiped my face and hands with it.

It was just as she said; the funeral party were already outside Number Nineteen, and waiting that I might be coupled to my father, and all be made right and proper. The graveyard of the old parish church was not more than three hundred yards distant; but the master undertaker, with his shiny boots and his oily hair and his black kid gloves, looked as though he were going out for the day at the least. He walked first, slowly, and after him crept the covered load. I think I must have been rather a dull boy for my age; but truth compels me to confess that, at starting, it never entered my head what the load was. I saw nothing in it but one of the oddest spectacles it was ever my lot to witness; there was a long black thing, very shiny and handsome, and hung about with fringe, walking on eight legs—eight legs and feet, some thin and some thick, and one with a crack in its boot, showing the stocking through.

"What is it, father?" I whispered him.

"What's what, my dear?"

"That thing with the feet, father."

"Hus—sh! that's mother, Jimmy. This is what I was telling you about, don't you know? They're taking of her to the pit-hole." And, saying this, he made a plunge at his jacket-pocket, and, withdrawing his pocket-handkerchief, flung his hand up to his eyes as though sharp sand had blown into them suddenly, filling them with pain. Presently the wind lifting the splendid black cloth, I peeped up under it, and immediately recognised the end of the plain wooden box the woman opposite had lifted me up to the window to see. From this moment my mind became a maze, out of which the grim truth was presently to appear.

It was a lovely bright and sunny afternoon, and on Clerkenwell Green there was a caravan show of an Indian Chief and a Giantess; and hearing the showman banging at his gong, I saw plenty of boys and girls that I knew running past to see. We turned out of the alley, up Turnmill Street, round the corner by the Sessions House, and through the posts, (it gave me quite a turn, as the saying is, to find myself unthinkingly knocking the ashes out of my pipe atop of one of those posts the other day,) creeping along at a very slow rate. It was very hot and close, with the black load shutting out the way before, and the mourners behind, and the crowd that hemmed us in at the sides. This, however, would not have been so bad, only that the navy cap was much too big for me, (my father had guessed at the fit,) and covered my head so that the rim of the peak was on a level with the bridge of my nose, and prevented my seeing except out of the corners of my eyes, where the peak tapered off, and its depth was least. Once or twice I sought relief by tilting the cap towards the back of my head; but as this caused my weeper to trail on the ground, so that Mrs. Jenkins—who came immediately behind us, carrying the baby—stepped on it, she gave the cap a forward tilt that put me in worse case than ever. After a few moments of deep distress I ventured to push it back again, but she righted it instantly, and with such a cross "God bless the child!" that there was nothing left but to submit. As the reader must ere this have discovered, I was never very partial to Mrs. Jenkins. There she was, talking to the baby as it lay in her arms (with a weeper round its hood, just such as I wore round that abominable navy cap)—talking to it and calling it "poor deserted lamb," just for all the world as though it knew all about the business in hand. I liked Mr. Jenkins much better than her, she was such a fussing sort of woman.

Straight up the street, and past the Giant and Dwarf show (from under the eave of my cap I could just see the showman exhibiting the dwarf's hand out of the window of the tiny house it lived in,) past the shop where one day I went with my mother to buy a second-hand pair of boots, across the road, and there we are at the churchyard gate. The gate is open, and the beadle, with his laced coat and his cane, is waiting just inside. We pass inside, the eight legs creeping slower than ever. There is a whole lot of people coming up behind; but when all with crape upon their arms had passed through, the beadle shut the gate and locked it.

Mr. Crowl, the undertaker, still leads the way. There is a long smooth pathway from the gate to the church door, flanked on either side by tall tombstones, treading over which my father, with the new hobnails in his boots, makes a clatter that sets Mr. Crowl's teeth on edge, judging from the expression of his countenance as he looks round.

Arrived at the church door, which is open, Mr. Crowl pauses and faces round, holding up his forefinger as a sign to the bearers to pause too. Then Mr. Crowl takes off his shiny hat, and lays the brim of it to his bosom, at the same time looking more grief-worn than ever, and as though his heart was now racked to the extreme of its power of endurance, and nothing short of pressing the shiny hat over it would save it from breaking. With his head on one side, that he may get a view of the mourners in the rear of the black load, he signs to them to take off their caps before they enter the sacred edifice.

This, however, brings matters to a momentary standstill. My father's four friends seem taken quite aback at Mr. Crowl's request, and regard each other sheepishly, and as though not quite knowing what to do. Perhaps they think of the short pipes in the pockets of their flannel jackets. Anyhow, they confer with each other in whispers, and after a few moments one of them beckons to Mr. Crowl.

"We ain't got to go into the building, Mister, have we?"

"Of course we have," replies Mr. Crowl, reprovingly.

"What! right in? Right where the pulpit and that is?"

"Come along; don't talk foolish, man. You shouldn't have come at all if you meant to act in this absurd way."

"But are we 'bliged to go in, Mister?"

"You are not obliged," returns Mr. Crowl: "still, having come here, as was supposed, for the purpose, and as friends of the deceased, it seems hardly"——

"Wery well, then; since we ain't obliged, we would take the liberty of being 'scused, if it's all the same to you, guv'nor. It's a thing wot none of us is used to. Not out of any slight to you, Jim, nor yet to her; that you know, old boy. Suppose we walks round a bit, and waits for you over there, alongside the—the place. Whereabouts might it be, Mister?"

"The grave is number eleven-two-nine, over by the clog-maker's wall," replied Mr. Crowl, turning about in disgust, and beckoning the bearers to come on.

We went into the church, and we came out again; and that, as far as applies to this stage of my mother's funeral, is about all that I know; for as soon as we got inside we were placed in a tall-sided pew, from which (although Mrs. Jenkins took my cap off) I could get a view of nothing but the ceiling. True, I could hear somebody talking in a loud voice, and now and then somebody breaking in, in quite another sort of voice, but what the two were talking about I had not the least idea. I was thinking all the time about "eleven-two-nine," and adding up the numbers on my fingers, and wondering what that had got to do with it. I was very glad when the two voices ceased, and the old pew-opener came and unlatched the pew and let us out.

We didn't come out at the door we went in at, but at a little door at the farther end of the church; and never having seen the inside of a church before, the view I got of it on the road amazed me exceedingly. I believe I was chiefly impressed by the immense extent of matting laid over the floor, and with the queer pattern of the candlesticks the beautifully white candles were stuck in. We walked as at first, Mr. Crowl heading the bearers, and the black load next, then father and I, and then Mrs. Jenkins and the baby. Outside the church there was another stone-paved path, narrower than the first, but presently we turned off this and struck across a very hilly road, which must have been extremely trying to the eight legs under the black load. To legs of the length of mine, the hills presented obstacles so formidable that my father had to lift me over the biggest ones, till at last he found it more convenient to take me in his arms and carry me.

From my perch on his shoulder I was the first to spy our four mourners who could not be persuaded to come into the church. They were lurking behind a big stone monument, and close by them was a heap of ragged clay and a long black hole. Close by the black hole there was a man dressed all in white, without his hat, and with a book in his hand.

Presently we arrived at the black hole and the bearers came to a stand. Then, all unexpected, there appeared from among the tall tombstones four men in smock-frocks, with their caps all stained with clay, their boots cloddy, and their hands earthy, as though they had just come from a job of digging. They went straight up to the bearers (taking off their clayey caps and stuffing them into the bosoms of their smock-frocks,) and laying hands on the black load, lifted it off the men's shoulders, and placed it on the grass. In an instant the bearers whisked off the grand velvet cover, and shook it, and folded it up with great care, and walked off with it, straightening their backs as they went. Then the four that had come fresh from digging took the long bare box in their earthy hands, and slung ropes about it, and lowered it into the hole before you might count ten.

Now, indeed, I knew all about it—about death and the grave, and *never*. The lifting of the black cover from the coffin had, as it were, lifted from my eyes the haze which even my father's vivid explanation had not removed entirely, and I could see things, and hear and understand them, exactly as they were. It seemed to me that my mother was but just now dead, and that it was the men with the earthy hands who had killed her. If any one of our party felt worse than I did at that moment, I am sure they were much to be pitied; but I think none did. My father was the only one who might, but he had known all about my mother being dead ever since last Friday, and must have grown a little used to it. He knew, at the time of starting, that we were taking my mother to be buried, and could have been in no way astonished at seeing her put into the ground; but it was different with me: I had been brought, as it were, to witness her death—her sudden shutting out from life and the world in the bright sunshine, and a dozen people looking on!

It was no comfort to me that everybody looked sorry. I had seen at least two of my father's friends looking quite as downcast, and even more dejected, when trade was slack; and as for Mrs. Jenkins, I had seen her cry quite as hard, and wring her hands (which now she could not do, having the baby) when Mr. Jenkins came home drunk. The persons who had most cause to cry were dry-eyed enough. My father did not cry. He looked wretched enough to do it, but he didn't; he only stood with his eyes cast to the ground, nibbling the peak of his cap and listening to the parson just as I have afterwards seen a prisoner in the dock listening to a very light sentence from the lips of a judge. I didn't cry. I wanted to cry very bad, but my eyes only burnt and smarted, and the tears wouldn't come. I seemed too full of thoughts pulling this way and that way, and baulking my tears, just as one might fancy the rain-clouds beat about by contrary winds, with no chance of settling to a down-pour. The baby didn't cry, being fast asleep; but I don't think this was Mrs. Jenkins's fault.

The parson having finished his prayers, shut the book and went away, and the party broke up. Mr. Crowl wasn't half so proud as he seemed to be at first, but walked by my father's side, chatting quite familiarly. He showed us a short cut out of the churchyard, into a by-street in which there was a public house, and waiting about just outside were the four men who carried the coffin.

"Shall we go back to the house, or "——

Mr. Crowl finished the sentence by jerking his thumb in a polite manner towards the public-house.

"In here'll do very well for me if it'll do for you," said my father, at the same time tapping his trousers pocket independently.

So the whole party, with the four bearers, went into the public-house, and I, still holding my father's hand, went in too. As we passed the bar, Mr. Crowl nodded and whispered to the landlady; and before we had been in the parlour two minutes, the waiter brought in some beer, and some gin, and some tobacco.

"How much?" asked my father, taking out his bag.

"I settle for this," observed Mr. Crowl, waving his hand towards the bar—as a hint, I suppose, that the landlady knew all about it.

"Now, when I ask a man to drink "—began my father.

"My good friend, I *always* do it—it's a point with me; honour bright, it is," interrupted the undertaker, staying my father's too ready hand by a touch of the splint with which he was about to light his pipe.

"Very good," said my father, "it's all the same; my turn next."

So everybody took to smoking and drinking, and in a very short time the place grew so full of smoke that I could hardly breathe; so after in vain trying to make my father understand that I wanted to go, (he had got into an argument with one of the bearers as to the proper way to pronounce the word "asparagus,") I unpinned my sash, and leaving it on the table, slipped out of the room and ran home.

———◆———

CHAPTER VII.

WHICH CHIEFLY CONCERNS THE WOMAN WHOM CRUEL FATE DECREED TO BE MY STEPMOTHER.

THE houses in Fryingpan Alley were let out in floors and single rooms. On the same floor with us there lived an Irishwoman of the name of Burke. She was a widow; her husband, a slater's labourer, having, a few months after his marriage, fallen from the outer slant of a roof of the ridge-and-furrow pattern, and so hurt his spine, that he died on the evening of the day on which he was carried to Guy's Hospital. Mrs. Burke was no favourite of mine—not because she was old or ugly; on the contrary, she was a much younger woman than my mother, and so merry as to be continually humming or singing, and so good-looking that no wake or other such jollification ever took place in the neighbourhood without Mrs. Burke receiving an invitation to it. My dislike for her did not arise from the fact of her having carroty hair. I was not over-partial to hair of that colour, and am not to this day; but there were a good many people living in the alley whose hair was quite as red as was Mrs. Burke's, and I got along well enough with them.

My chief objection was to her complexion, which was sandy. Her face and neck, and arms and hands, were dotted so closely that you could scarcely stick a pin between, with pinky-yellow spots, which in my ignorance I firmly believed could have been washed off had Mrs. Burke used sufficient soap and energy. That she did not remove them, but allowed them to remain and accumulate, (I suppose that they did not accumulate, but that they did was decidedly my impression at the time,) was to my mind a convincing proof that she was an unclean person, and one whom it would be better to have as little to do with as possible.

Under such circumstances, it was not to be wondered at that I could by no manner of means relish Mrs. Burke's victuals. Nothing she could offer me—and, like all Irish people, she was mighty generous and free-handed, especially with her cupboard store—could conquer my dislike. I have refused her batter pudding (baked under pork, and steaming from the bake-house) on the plea that I wasn't the least hungry, and two minutes afterwards she has met me deep in the enjoyment of a slice of bread of my mother's cutting. If she gave me an apple, I could not eat it until I had pared off the rind ruinously thick. I have taken her baked potatoes and artfully conveyed them down-stairs, and hid them in the dust-bin.

" Did you like the praties, Jimmy ? "

" Yes, thanky, ma'am ; they were very nice."

And at that very moment up has come Mrs. Burke's cat, with one of the identical potatoes in her jaws, laying it, all ashes as it was, on Mrs. Burke's clean hearth, and munching it up under her nose.

There was no love lost between myself and Mrs. Burke after that time. She never met me but she gave me an evil look, and once she called me " a mite of shtuck-up thrumpery," of which I told my mother, who took an early opportunity of asking her what she meant by it. She laughed—

" See now, Mrs. Ballisat ! see the mischief the little rogues might make between friendly folks wid their funny mistakes ! *Me* call the darlint ' a mite of shtuck-up thrumpery,' indeed ! Mary forbid, ma'am. What I did call him ' a mighty tip-top thrumpeter,' and that bekase of the illigant voice he has, for ever making itself heard about the house. Get out wid you, Master Jim ; divil a compliment you 'll get again out of me for one while."

She was always extremely civil to my parents, which was not very surprising, considering the large quantities of vegetables my father used to give her, because of her being a lone woman.

It was Mrs. Burke whom I found occupying our room when I ran home from the public-house where my father was staying. As it was growing towards dusk, nobody noticed me as I came up the alley, and I crept in and went up-stairs. I didn't hurry up, as might be expected of a little boy who had had nothing to eat since breakfast. I had a vague notion that *now* it was all right in our room, but I was far from certain. I kept close to the wall, and stole noiselessly as high as the first landing of our flight, and peeped round the corner. So far all was right; for the door, which for several days had been kept fast locked, and the key kept down in Jenkins's room, was now ajar. I could see the wall that faced the fireplace through the open chink, and to my very great surprise the light of a fire was reflected on it. Never through all my life can I forget the queer sensations that for a moment beset me. Who could have lit the fire in our room?

Who alone had a right to do so ? My mother and no one else. Dusk was my time of coming home from play ; it was tea-time. Times out of number I had come home exactly at this same time, and found my mother busy at the fireplace, putting sticks on the fire to make the kettle boil, ready for my father, so that he might not be kept waiting a moment. The light against the wall was just such as would be made by the reflection of blazing sticks. Was it, after all, a misapprehension on my part ? Was it all a happy mistake about the black load and the pit-hole ? Should I find my mother in the room, as she was when I last entered it five days ago, and saw her there ? I don't mean to say that all these thoughts passed through my mind with the distinctness with which they are here set down, but they all combined to make the glorious maze that suddenly fell on me. In the maze I found my way right up to the door, and there I met with certain cruel facts that brought me to my senses suddenly, as a dash of cold water in the face of one that faints.

I could see a little bit of the floor of our room through the door-chink—a very little bit, but enough to show me that the place had been very recently scrubbed. There was the sound of rocking a chair in the room, and of a woman singing. The voice was a droning voice, and unmistakably Irish. I knew at once that it could belong to no one else but Mrs. Burke.

I ventured to push the door just a very little, and to take a peep inside.

It *was* Mrs. Burke. She was sitting by the fireside, in a clean cotton gown, and with her Sunday cap on, rocking my little baby sister, and singing to her. The tea-things were neatly laid on the table, and the room was filled with the comfortable smell of toast.

Everybody had been so busy that day over my mother's funeral, that (I think I mentioned this before, by the way) I had missed my dinner, and was very hungry. It was a great temptation, but my squeamishness instantly stepped in with a picture of Mrs. Burke's freckled arms and hands. " If I go in," thought I, " she will be sure to ask me to eat some of the toast she has been making, and I would much rather not. I 'd much sooner go without. I 'll wait outside here until my father comes home."

At that unlucky moment, however, Mrs. Burke's cat came out of the back-room, and smelling out where her mistress was, gave a mew, and, butting the door wide open, walked in. Mrs. Burke paused in her droning, and looking round to see who had opened the door, spied me before I could shrink back.

" Ah, thin ! is it yourself, Jimmy, jewel ? " said she, in a kinder voice than I had ever yet heard her use. " Come in, thin, darlint, and take your place on your little shtool by the fire."

" I don't want. I 'm warm out here."

" Come in now, like a dear, and sit ye down, and take your tay like a little gintleman," urged Mrs. Burke, coaxing me forward with her forefinger.

There was no use in refusing; so in I went, sulky enough.

But, wrong-headed boy that I was ! I had scarcely taken six steps in at the doorway before I was filled with remorse for my ungrateful behaviour. The good Irishwoman had made ou place bright as a new pin. *Anyone* might have taken his tea there like a gentleman. Never in my life had I seen our room looking so beautiful. The stove was as black and almost as shiny as Mr. Crowl's hat, and the hearth—even that part of it on which the ashes dropped—was as white as a cut turnip. Ours was not a very nice set of fire-irons—indeed, we only possessed a bent poker and a cinder shovel; but now resting against the fireplace was a magnificent set, bright as silver. They were Mrs. Burke's fire-irons, as I knew instantly from the crinkly pattern of their stems, and the shape of their knobs. The ornaments on the mantel-shelf were polished up, the floor scrubbed white and finely sanded, and before the fireplace a clean bit of carpet was spread. It was Mrs. Burke's tea-tray on which our crockery stood, and the tea-spoons, genteelly placed in the cups, belonged also to Mrs. Burke. I was accustomed to take my tea out of a tin pot, but now, standing in the old place, by the side of my father's cup and saucer, was a china mug, with gold letters on it—"A present from Tunbridge." There was a spoon in the mug, as in the cups. And this was not all. Being a woman without children, and natty in her ways, Mrs. Burke had fixed up a sideboard in her room, and on it were arranged all sorts of odd bits of china and glass. The centre ornament of the lot, and one that she prized before all the others, (as was evident from its having a fancifully-cut piece of yellow satin to stand on,) was a china butter-boat—very old-fashioned, but of gorgeous design, and coloured green and blue, and scarlet—with the heads of the rivets that fastened on the cracked spout, bright as spangles. Well, there was the china butter-boat on the hob, with baby's pap in it, and very beautiful it looked with the light of the fire glowing on its crimson and green side.

"Where's daddy, Jimmy?" asked Mrs. Burke, taking off my cap, and tidily hanging it on a nail behind the door. "Did you leave him in the churchyard, Jimmy?"

"Close by there, ma'am."

"Where's close by, sonny?"

"At the public-house, ma'am."

"Waitin' to take a shmall dhrop at the bar to put him in life a little, poor man," observed Mrs. Burke, raising a corner of her clean apron to her eye. "Never mind. Don't cry, Jimmy," (I wasn't crying nor thinking about it;) "he'll be here directly, I'll be bound."

"He wasn't at the bar, ma'am; he was inside the room, sitting down with the burying-men."

"Sitting down, was he?" said she, chirping to the baby, and tickling its little fat chin kindly. "Cryin', Jimmy, was he?"

"He was smoking his pipe, and having some gin, ma'am."

"Oh! it's a darlin'!" cried Mrs. Burke, with a sudden gush of affection for my little sister. "Did he sind you off, Jim? What did he say?"

"I heard him tell the man that 'them that growed sparrow grass and sold it, ought to know how to spell it better than them who now and then got a sniff of it passing a cook-shop.' He was a good mind to have a row with the man, I think. I heard him say that he always wanted to pull a man's nose when he called things by flash names."

"Was the man callin' him flash names? Did he keep callin' yer daddy 'sir,' and 'Mr. Ballisat,'

and he didn't like it? Course he wouldn't. That's Jim all over. I know him."

"Oh no, ma'am! he didn't call father names; he only would have it that sparrowgrass was something else,—that was all the talk."

Mrs. Burke made no answer, but began laughing and chirping to the baby in a more cheerful way than ever. By and by she laid the baby down on the bed, and, fetching a broom from her own room, swept up some ashes that had fallen, and rearranged the fire-irons. Then she took the china butter-boat off the hob, gave it a polish with her apron, and stood it back again. After giving several other things a finishing touch, she retired outside the door, and then put in her head as a visitor might, and took a rapid glance round; then she crossed over to the fireplace, and altered the butter-boat slightly, so that a looker-in at the door might obtain at a glance a broadside view of its splendour. Convincing herself by a second glance that her arrangements were perfect, she took the baby up and went to the window with it in her arms, and there remained looking towards Turnmill Street till it grew quite dark; then she neatly closed the curtains, and set up a candle in a brass candlestick, that was so bright that you could see your face in it. I think she must have observed the admiring gaze with which I regarded the bright candlestick, for said she—

"We must give the dirty thing a rub, Jimmy; it isn't so clane as you've been used to see it, my man!"

"It is ten times cleaner, ma'am," returned I, honestly; "it's beautiful."

"Well, maybe it'll pass; but your daddy's so perticlar, you know; he'll be grumblin' about that dirthy ould butther-boat, don't ye think, Jimmy?"

"What dirty butter-boat, ma'am?"

"That on the hob with the baby's pap in it, Jimmy."

"Dirty! it isn't dirty; nothing's dirty, except"——

"Except what? out with it! except what, now?"

Mrs. Burke flushed red as she said this, and spoke very quick and sharp; perhaps it was lucky for me that she did, for in my ignorant eyes the only exception to the prevailing cleanliness was her freckled face and hands, and that was what I was about to tell her. Seeing, however, how she was likely to take it, like the little hypocrite I was, I replied to her impatient demand for an explanation—

"Except me, ma'am. Here's dirty hands!"

My sin carried its sting. Uttering an exclamation as though never in the course of her life she had seen hands so hideously dirty (though, in truth, they were more than usually clean,) she laid the baby down, and taking me into her own room, there gave my face as well as my hands such a scrubbing with yellow soap and the corner of a rough towel as brought the tears to my eyes. Then with her own comb she combed my hair, and with her own oil oiled it; and somehow or another, contrived a curl on either temple. Then she turned my pinafore, and brought the brass buckle of my belt well to the front, and gave it a rub to brighten it.

"Will you have your tea now, Jimmy; or will you wait a little till daddy comes home?" asked she, when she had set me on my stool by the fire.

For a considerable time before this I had been contemplating the pile of toast inside the fender, my increasing hunger doing battle against my deep-seated prejudice against Mrs. Burke's freckles. The latter lost ground rapidly. To be sure, she had taken the bread in her hands to cut; but everything objectionable must have departed from it in the process of toasting. But then, she had to butter it! True again; but the butter on the top round was by this time nearly all frizzled in. Thought I, "If she should ask me to have a piece of toast, I will say yes, and take that top piece." But, unfortunately, just as she asked me, "Would I have my tea now, or wait until my father came home?" she stooped to blow off a "black" that had settled on the side of the butter-boat, and her freckled arm actually touched the crust of that very top round.

"I'll wait a little, thanky, ma'am," said I. "I am not very hungry."

Mrs. Burke worked at making potato-sacks; and when I told her that I would rather not begin my tea at present, she went into her own room, and in a minute returned, bringing with her three ready-made sacks and the materials for a fourth. The ready-made sacks she placed on a chair by her side, and then fastening a big canvas apron decently about her, so that her clean cotton gown might not suffer, she sat down to work.

It takes a good while to make a potato-sack. I don't know how long exactly; but by the time Mrs. Burke had finished the one she had taken in hand, the candle had burned down full two inches. Mrs. Burke, during the last half-hour at least, had grown more and more fidgety. From time to time she got up from her work, and looked out at the window, and listened at the door, grumbling and muttering under her breath. Growing sleepy, I disregarded the pains she had been at to arrange my hair, and scratched it into uproar with both my hands. She rapped out at me in the spitefullest manner for this, and called me a name which, thanks to my mother's diligence and solicitude, I did not deserve. She had one corner of the sack pinned to the table with a sort of bradawl.

"Come here, you (something) little pig," said she: "you may as well hould the candle, as sit shnorin' and rootin' there."

So I went and held the candle until the sack was finished; by which time the fire had burnt hollow, and, falling in, made a terrible litter over the white hearth. The toast was scorched dry; and a little gas coal, lurking in a chink at the back of the hob, suddenly spouted out a flame at the china butter-boat, and sputtered against it until you could scarcely tell the red from the blue for soot.

"Devil take the whole bilin'!" exclaimed Mrs. Burke, glaring round fiercely when she saw all this, and at the same time snatching up the butter-boat at the risk of burning her fingers. "Here am I, and there is he; and prisintly he'll be rollin' in as drunk as Davy's sow! It's cashtin' pearls before shwine, intirely;" and for a moment she scowled about her, and at me in particular, as though I had deliberately, and out of malice, set the gas-coal at her butter-boat. But in the same breath as it were, she recovered, and turning her wrath to music, began humming the fag end of a tune.

"Never mind, Jimmy," said she; "there's worse misfortunes at say." And then she turned to, briskly mending the fire, and sweeping and dusting. She wiped the soot from the butter-boat, and gave it a polish on her canvas apron; she turned the pile of toast topside bottom; and fetching her hair-brush from the back room, smoothed my hair with it. Then she folded up the sack she had just finished, and laid it on the top of the other three. Then she went and fetched stuff for another sack, and sat down to work again quite comfortable.

I was roused from dozing on my stool by the sound of my father's footsteps, blundering and uncertain, on the stairs. He pushed open the door and came in.

CHAPTER VIII.

IN WHICH MRS. BURKE COURTS MY FATHER.

"Come in, Mr. Ballisat," said Mrs. Burke, in a kind and cheerful voice, and as though my father had knocked.

My father came in. He took three or four steps into the room, and then he stood still, staring about him in amazement. That he had been drinking rather heavily was evident from the circumstance of his wearing the peak of his cap over his ear, instead of the front of his head. In one hand he carried a large plaice, and in the other a bundle of firewood.

"You've come home earlier than was expicted, Mr. Ballisat, and caught me at work, sir," said Mrs. Burke, apologetically. "You'll pardon the liberty of me sittin' in your room; I'll run away in a minit."

So saying, she got up from her chair and began to bustle about, lifting back to the wall the chair on which the four made sacks were lying, as well as that which she had been sitting on at her work, and there she stood, looking so bright and kind, with the half-made sack on her arm, and her hand resting on the other four.

It was plain to see that my poor father was completely overcome. Balanced, as it were, between the fish and the firewood, he stood in the middle of the room, gazing in serious astonishment, first at the butter-boat on the hob; then at the baby, tucked up so clean and comfortable in bed. Then, with tears in his eyes, he looked at me, and at the toast and the tea-things, wagging his head in the most solemn manner; and presently he sank into a chair and buried his eyes in the cuffs of his jacket, the wood rolling away unheeded, and the plaice sliding from his grasp down on to the sanded floor.

"Shure you're not well, James Ballisat," said Mrs. Burke, solicitously. "The throubles of this day have been too much for you, poor man!"

"No, no; it isn't not that so much. It's—it's"——

"Askin' your pardon; but that's what it is, and nothin' else," said Mrs. Burke. "But don't mind me, poor fellow; it's been my own exsh-perience, and I know exactly the state of your feelin's, Jim."

"No; it isn't that so much," persisted my father; "it's the pictur—the pictur that come afore me when I come in. I reckons it up comin' along, and what do I make on it? 'It's all over now,' thinks I; 'no more comfortable firesides, and kettles a-bilin' ready waitin' for you. The wittles you want, you must cook for yourself; and if you want a plaice, it's no use you a-buyin' of it unless you takes some wood; likewise a bit of drippin' to fry it in.' Look here, ma'am!"

So saying, my father took from his jacket some dripping in a piece of paper, and, with a sob, laid it gently on the table.

"But, shure, Jim Ballisat, if I may go the length of sayin' as much, and knowin', as I well know, how little throuble you give, and how little you expect, shure it might have crossed your mind that there was a craythur at home as lone and unfortunit as yourself, who wouldn't see two motherless babies "——

"I thinks all this," continued my father, pursuing the thread of his lamentation; "and home I comes, and what do I find? Why, I finds everything as though nothin' had happened—as though *more* than nothin' had happened, I might say."

And then he took to weeping more violently than before.

"Shure and shure," observed Mrs. Burke, turning away her head and raising her apron, "it was the very last of my thoughts to make you take on so, Mr. Ballisat; indade and indade it was."

"No, Kitty, no," sobbed my father; "I don't think for a minnit that you thought to hurt my feelin's; you've got too good a heart for that. I always thought your heart was in the right place: now I'm sure of it."

"Shall you want anything else, Mr. Ballisat?" asked Mrs. Burke, respectfully, and as though she had not heard a word of my father's last observation, and she was his humble servant to command, and nothing else. "Shall I pour you out a cup of tea, and then run away to my own room and cook the fish while you are gettin' on?"

"No, thanky, ma'am," returned my father, now slightly recovered, but still deeply despondent; "my 'art's too full, I couldn't tackle it."

"Not a piece of the back part dipped in butther and browned to a turn?" said Mrs. Burke, persuasively.

"I couldn't, really. Your kindness to me, an unfortnit fellow who didn't oughter expect it, has took away all my wantin' for the plaice. Don't say no more to me, please, or I shan't be able to eat any toast either."

"Well, if there's anything you want, you've only to give a call," said Mrs. Burke, moving off towards her own room.

"Do you want to go particlar, missus?"

"I only go to oblige you, Mr. Ballisat."

"Then just sit down and take a cup with us, that's a good soul. It will be another favour what I shall owe you for, if you will be so good."

With an expressive shake of the head, as though she fully understood the state of my father's feelings, and respected him for them, Mrs. Burke yielded to his persuasion, and drew a chair up to the tea-table. Father also drew up a chair.

"Do you like your tea sweet, Jim? Will this be too much?"

"Don't you trouble about me, missus; you look arter yourself," replied my father, politely.

"Tut! throuble indade!" said Mrs. Burke, as she put in the spoonful of sugar, and then tasted the tea in the spoon; and put in a little more su-

gar, and stirred it. "I think you'll find that to your likin',—just thry it."

My father looked grateful, and, with a sigh, stooped forward and helped himself to toast.

"Whisha!" exclaimed Mrs. Burke, in a tone of alarm, as she made a snatch at the slice; "is it for the likes of me to see you atein' the top piece of all, that's been fryin' before the fire this hour and more? Lave that for my atein', if you plase, and let me help ye to a bit that's soft and butthery."

"We shall be spiled, Jimmy, if we're treated like this," observed my father, turning to me as he took the proffered slice.

"You're welcome to your joke, Jim," said Mrs. Burke, with a pleasant little laugh: "but, as you of coorse know, being so long a married man, that it is just these shmall thrifles that make home happy."

"I wasn't a-joking, don't you think it," replied my father, biting the slice of toast to the backbone, and slowly masticating it as he gazed contemplatively on the fire. "It ain't a joking matter; more t'other; as much more t'other, Kitty—'scuse the word, Mrs. B., but seein' you sittin' so familiar-like on that side, and me on this, comes nat'ral to cut your name short"——

("Tut!" said Mrs. Burke, pulling out the bows of her cap-strings)——"as I was sayin', what you was sayin' is as much more t'other from jokin' as anythink I knows on."

"Put your shtool furder in the corner, Jimmy, and then daddy'll get a bit more of the fire," said Mrs. Burke.

"I'm all right, thanky," returned my father. "Now don't you move; fact is, I'd rather the fire didn't ketch my feet. These new 'jacks' do draw 'em so you wouldn't believe, and the fire'll make 'em wus. I shall be precious glad to get 'em off."

"Then why not get out of 'em at once? Don't you know your juty to yer father, Jimmy? Unlace his boots this moment, and get him his shlippers."

"Get out with you," returned my father, with a laugh. "What's the use of your a-talkin' to me about slippers? Anybody to hear you would think you didn't know me, and mistook me for a gentl'man."

"Got no slippers, Jim!" Mrs. Burke couldn't have looked more amazed had my father suddenly disclosed to her as a fact that he had no feet, and that what she had been accustomed to regard as such were in reality but two wooden stumps.

"Never had a pair in all my life," replied my father. "What does a rough and tumble chap like I am warnt with slippers?"

"What should he want wid'm? Shure you shurprise me by axin' the question, James," said the shocked Mrs. Burke. "As to the roughin' and the tumblin', it may be thrue while you are about gettin' your honest livin', but at home it's different intirely. You know nothin' about a wife's affections, Jim, if you don't think that she regards him as a gintleman as soon as he sits by his fireside, and she thrates him as sich if she's the wife she shud be. Unlace your daddy's boots as I bad ye, Jimmy; and if he'll let us we'll have his poor feet in comfort in a jiffy."

It was not the first time I had unlaced my father's boots, and while I busied myself about them, Mrs. Burke slipped into her room, and after, as could plainly be heard, much rummaging and hunting, returned with a pair of slippers in her hand. They were capital slippers, made of fine leather, and warmly lined, and must, when they were new, have cost a sum that no one but a person of means could afford to give. Probably Mrs. Burke had become possessed of them in the course of her charing, and empty-house cleaning experiences.

"They belonged to my good man that's dead and gone—rest his sowl," said Mrs. Burke; "and it's like my preshumption, as you'll say, to offer ye the likes of sich rubbish; but it pains me to hear you complain of achin' feet, poor fellow; and you'll maybe pardon the liberty on that ground. P'r'aps they're a thrifle damp, so we'll warm 'em."

So she did. She went down on her knees, and held the slippers to the fire until they were as warm as the toast by the side of them, by which time I had managed to haul off the heavy ankle-jacks. Then she turned about, still on her knees, and fitted the warm slippers on to my father's feet, clapping her hands, and looking as delighted as though they were her feet that were being comforted, to find that they fitted so nicely.

"Are your feet aisier now, Jim?" she asked.

"They feels as though they was kivered with welwet," replied my father, holding up a foot, and regarding it approvingly. "They must have cost a goodish bit. D'ye mean to say that you was able to screw the price of 'em out of Tim's earnin's?"

"Bedad, it would have puzzled me," laughed Mrs. Burke. "No, Jim, I saved up to buy 'em for him; saved up out of my own earnin's a pinny or so a day."

"You don't mean to say that!' exclaimed my father, leaning back in his chair, and wonderingly regarding Mrs. Burke with his only half-sober eyes.

"And why not? Wasn't it my juty so to do for the man who was workin' and toilin' for me from daylight till dark? If I couldn't do that and a great deal more for the man of my choice and the mate of my hearth; if I hadn't made up my mind to do it fust and forrard, I'm not the woman that would have crossed the church threshold wid him."

After this my father settled down to his tea, without uttering another word, only from time to time regarding Mrs. Burke intently, and tossing his head as though his mind was still occupied with her astounding views of the duties of a wife.

"We ought to be very grateful, Jimmy," said he, as he helped me to a drink out of his saucer; "even when our luck seems deadest out, Jimmy, we never knows what's a-goin' to turn up. As the puty song ses, 'There's a sweet little chirrup what sits in the loft,' don't you know "——

"'Looks after the life of poor Jack,'" softly sang Mrs. Burke, in her pretty voice.

"Ah! and not on'y Jacks but Jims, and any other poor cove what stands in need of it," said my father, wagging his head impressively. "I hope you will never stand in need of it, Jimmy; and if you bears in mind what the doctor said to you the other night, you won't. So just you be a good boy, and mind what Mrs. Burke tells you."

"He didn't tell me to mind what Mrs. Burke told me, father; he told me to "——

"Never mind what he told you; what I tell you is what you've got to act up to, and let's have none of your argyments about it," interrupted my father, with a frown.

"Bless his little heart, he's obejence itself," said Mrs. Burke, at the same time handing me a slice of toast. "Eat this, my good little fellow."

I was obliged to eat it, for she kept her eye on me all the time.

"You must have had a tightish time of it, I should think, marm," my father presently observed, "what with minding the young 'uns, and making the place so beautiful and clean."

"Indade the hintherence the little craythurs have been isn't worth the talk you've wasted on it; they're rather an amusement than a hintherance," replied Mrs. Burke, lightly.

"Well, you're a queer sort," said my father, pleasantly. "There's no keepin' a place tidy where there's a young 'un; at least that's what I've always been give to understand."

"Tut; it just dipinds on the way of going about it," replied Mrs. Burke. "When one's used to tidying a place, the job comes as easy as play. But, there, Mr. Ballisat, I'll lave you to judge for yourself how much and how little throuble they've been to me, for here's the sacks I've made meanwhiles at fourpence ha'penny each."

"What! done all the clearing and made all them sacks?" exclaimed my father, running his thumb up the work to count it. "Earnt eighteenpence, minded two kids, and cleaned a place in one arternoon! Dashed, you're the sort!"

"And not hurried myself nayther," rejoined Mrs. Burke, laughing; "it isn't a thrifle of work that frightens Kitty Burke, anyhow."

Now, as the reader has already been made aware, this was not the truth by a very long way. She had not made all the sacks since she sat down; she had brought in three ready-made, and all she had completed was one and part of another. Thinking that it was merely a mistake on her part, I was about to correct her, but at the very moment of my opening my mouth her eyes caught mine, and, evidently guessing my intention, she shook her head, and frowned in a way that was not to be mistaken. But I didn't care for her; I owed her a grudge for making me hold the candle, to say nothing about the name she had called me. Besides, my father was there, and she daren't touch me. So, said I, edging closer to my father—

"What a wicked story-teller you are, Mrs. Burke!"

Her rage was tremendous. She glared at me till she squinted.

"What's that?" asked my father, turning shortly round on me.

"So she is," I stoutly replied.

"So she is what? Who are you a callin' 'she,' you unmannered little warmint? She's the cat, don't you know? Now, then, what do you mean by sayin' that Mrs. Burke is a story-teller?"

I watched his hand stealing to his waist-belt, and I was afraid to open my mouth.

"Lor' bless his heart, don't be angry with him, Jim; shure he manes no harm. He was only about to tell you of the purty stories I've been tellin' him to keep him awake till his daddy come home. That's what he meant by callin' me story-teller, Jim."

"Oh, that's it! I thought he was going to in

sinivate that you was tellin' a crammer about the sacks."

"How do you mane, Mr. Ballisat?" asked Mrs. Burke, innocently.

"Well, I thought the young stoopid was going to say that you were wrong in the number; not that it's any business of mine, or his'n either, come to that."

"But the thruth is everybody's business, Jim," replied the virtuous woman. Then turning to me, winking and frowning, said she, "See, Jimmy dear, here is four sacks; tell your daddy how many I have made while you have been sitting and watching me."

What was I to do? Evidently my father was more disposed to believe her than me. I had never tasted the strap myself; but I had seen it laid over my mother's shoulders till she screamed murder.

"Four, ma'am," I answered.

"Of course," said Mrs. Burke, quietly; "that's thrue all the world over." And shortly afterwards she gave me a spoonful of sugar.

I think I may say that that was the first deliberate lie I ever told in my life; and I verily believe it was one of the most mischievous. My father being half tipsy at the time, he might have forgotten all about the circumstance by the morning; but, according to my experience of my father's memory, what transpired in his presence at such times was tolerably accurate. To this day, I believe that when Mrs. Burke demonstrated to him how easily she could earn eighteenpence, it made a strong impression on him—stronger even than the Irishwoman's tea-table solicitude and the loan of the slippers. I further believe that the remarks I made tended to raise in his mind doubts as to the truth of her statement, and that the said doubts were completely dissipated by my corroboration of the said statement. If this view of the case is a correct one, I stand convicted of being an accessory to a very lamentable swindle.

At the time, however, I was incapable of this sort of reasoning, and I was inclined even to look gratefully on Mrs. Burke for helping me out of a threatened danger. I was glad that, just in the nick of time, the baby awoke, and put an end to the conversation concerning the sacks.

Mrs. Burke took the baby up, and, composing it comfortably on her lap, begged my father to be good enough to hand her the butter-boat from off the hob; and then she proceeded to feed the little thing, and kiss it, and talk to it in a way that quite went to one's heart to witness. No doubt it would have gone to my father's heart; but becoming drowsy, and feeling warm and at his ease, he presently dropped to sleep—a fact Mrs. Burke was unaware of until he began to snore, when she looked up, and with a little toss of her head finished feeding my sister in silence. The operation completed, she carried the baby off to her own room, and after that only came in once, to carry away the tea-things, waking my father by the clatter she made with them.

"What time will you be risin' in the mornin', Mr. Ballisat?" asked she, respectfully.

"What time, ma'am? oh, about the usual: why?"

"Bekase of your breakfast. If you'll kindly give us the hour, I'll be up and have the kettle biling."

"Breakfast! Lor' bless yer!" laughed my father, "I gets my breakfast in the market."

"And why, may I ask? Shure the bit of breakfast must be more comfortable at your own fireside than in the cowld market, Jim?"

"So it is, but I'm off at five to-morrow morning, and so you see it can't be managed," replied my father.

"And why not?" asked Mrs. Burke, opening her brown eyes in affected astonishment. "Is it bekase you are left alone that you are to go out in the cowld widout the dhrap of coffee to warm you? Shure, sir, I should be no dacent woman, though it wor three o'clock instead of five when you went out. Good night, Mr. Ballisat; no fear but the kettle will be biling in time for yer."

And she kept her word. I slept with my father, and while it was yet quite dark there came a knock at our door.

"There's the pleseman knocking to say it's a quarter to five, Jimmy," said my father, sleepily; "just hop out and tap at the window, my boy."

But at the same moment Mrs. Burke's cheery voice was heard outside the room door—

"It's half afther four, Mr. Ballisat, and the kettle's biling, and there's a nice bit of the fish all hot and a-waitin' for you," said she; and then she tripped back to her own room, humming as gay as a lark. Presently she was back again—

"May I throuble you to bring out the needle off the mantel-shelf, Mr. Ballisat? I've just bethought me I left it there overnight. My silly head will niver save my fingers, which have been itching to get at the bit of work this half an hour."

"All right, ma'am," called my father, and then, in an under-tone, and to himself, he muttered—

"'Send I may live! I never come across such a woman!"

CHAPTER IX.

MY NEW MOTHER. I DERIVE A VALUABLE HINT FROM A CONVERSATION BETWEEN MY FATHER AND HIS PAL.

THE reader, of course, foresees the ending of such a beginning—Mrs. Burke became my step-mother. I cannot exactly state how long a time elapsed from the time of my father burying his first wife to his marrying the second, but it must have been several months—seven, at the least, I should say, for when it happened, my sister Polly had grown to be quite a big child; indeed, I recollect that it was as much as I could do to carry her from one end of the alley to the other without resting. But however long a time it was, it saw no alteration in my sentiments towards Mrs. Burke. It is not enough to say I liked her as little as ever. When I first made her acquaintance I simply disliked her; now I hated her deeply and thoroughly. She hated me, and made no scruple of letting me know it. The very first morning after the memorable day of my mother's funeral she told me her mind without reserve.

"Come here, my dear," said she, gripping me by the arm and pulling me towards her, as she sat on her chair. "You recollect the divil's prank you had it on your tongue's tip to play me lasht night?" She spoke in allusion to the threatened sack exposure.

I made her no answer, but she could of course see that I well understood what she meant.

"You thought you might dare me becase ov yer father being prisint! You thought bekase of me winkin' and coaxin', and givin' you sugar, that I was afeard you'd open your ugly mouth! Hould up your head, you sarpint, and look at me! Listen here, now. You've got the ould un in yer, and I mane to take it out of yer. I'm goin' to be alwis wid you, to look afther and feed you; you'll get nayther bite nor sup but when it's plisant to me to give it you. So mind your behayvour. Dare so much as make a whisper to yer father of what I say or what I do, and I'll make your shkin too hot to hould you."

And seeing how hopeless it was to show fight against such a creature, I am sure I did mind my behaviour. I did her bidding in every particular, and fetched her little private errands, and kept her secrets faithfully; but she didn't treat me at all well. If she didn't make my skin too hot to hold me, it was not for want of trying. From breakfast time to within a few minutes of my father's coming home, I was kept at it, drudge, drudge, drudge, as hard as any charwoman. Indeed, no charwoman would have engaged to perform the many various jobs that were put on me. The baby was my chief care. I was either lugging her about the alley, or sitting on my stool at the street door, or in the back yard, (Mrs. Burke could not bear to hear the baby cry,) hushing her to sleep; and when, after long and patient exertion, this was accomplished, and she was laid in her cradle, I was set to making waxed ends for Mrs. Burke's sack-making, or fetching up coals, or sifting cinders, or slopping about with a house-flannel and scrubbing-brush. Of one sort and another, there was always employment found for me from the time little Polly went to sleep until she woke up again; and all without so much as a kind word or look even.

She was a wicked woman. She used to buy gin with the housekeeping money, and threaten me with all sorts of dreadful punishments if I did not promise to tell my father, should he ask me, what a beautiful dinner I had had. She was artful to that extent, that she would send me to the broken victual shop at Cowcross for a penny or a three-halfpenny bone, and this she would place in the cupboard, so that my father, when he came home, might see it, and believe that it was what was left from the nice little joint we had partaken of at dinner-time. She was always very particular in telling me to be sure and bring a small bone or bones, such as those of the loin of mutton, or a dainty spare-rib of pork, or a blade-bone of lamb—any bone, indeed, that might belong to a joint of meat of a sort that might be bought as a dinner for two persons. Once I recollect bringing back a single lean rib-bone of beef of at least twenty inches in length, which was, of course, ill-suited to her fraudulent designs, and so exasperated her that she banged me about the head with it, and then packed me off to the rag-shop to sell it for a halfpenny. I was terribly hungry at the time, and what little meat there was on the bone was very crisp, and brown, and tempting, and I begged leave to eat it; but she wouldn't hear of it. She didn't want it herself. She would eat scarcely an ounce of meat from Monday till Saturday, liking gin so much better.

She would even go out of her way to do me an injury in the matter of food. There was always a bit of something hot got ready for my father's supper, and when—as happened at least four days out of seven—I had no more than a crust of bread between breakfast and tea, I would contrive to make myself conspicuous, when he sat down to eat, in hopes of getting a bit. If Mrs. Burke's back was turned, I was pretty sure to come in for a mouthful; but so sure as she caught my father in the act of helping me from his plate, she would instantly interfere.

"For the love of Hivin, man, hould your hand, unless you'd have him stretched on a bed of sickness wid over-ateing. He is a very dacent boy, Jim, but his gluttony at his meals is somethin' awful. 'Twas ony this blissed dinner-time—and there he is, and can't deny it—that he was helped three times to biled mutton, and each time enough for a man and his dog, as the sayin' is."

"And yet you comes a-prowlin' round and a-showin' your teeth at me as though you hadn't tasted a bit for a week, you greedy young willin!" my father would observe, savagely. "You're better fed than taught—that's what you are. Be off to bed, now, before you ketch a larruping."

And to bed I would go, an empty-bellied and wretched little boy, not daring to utter a word in explanation.

One day she served me an especially villainous trick, and one that is among the greenest of a hundred such in my memory. A woman called on Mrs. Burke one morning shortly after breakfast, and they drank gin between them until every farthing of the half-crown my father had left to buy our dinner and his supper was consumed. When the woman was gone, and she recovered from her half-fuddled condition, Mrs. Burke began to feel alarm. The money to buy my father's supper *must* be raised somehow; but how? Her other gown—the flat-irons—the chiua butter-boat, even—were already at the "leaving shop," and there was no one in the neighbourhood that would lend to her, or trust her with their goods without cash down. Presently she went out, and in a little while returned in a condition of sad distress, and took to rocking herself in a chair, and crying and moaning in a way that went to my heart to hear.

"Ow, what'll I do? what'll I do?" cried she. "Your daddy'll be comin' home by and by, Jimmy, dear, and there'll be no supper for him, and he'll be beating me till I'm dead. Ow! what'll a poor lone craytur do widout a frind in the world to help her?"

I never could bear to see any one crying. Had Mrs. Burke intimated to me with tearless eyes and in her usual manner of talking, that there was danger of my father falling on her and beating her to death, whatever answer I might have made, I should undoubtedly have thought in my inmost mind that it was exactly what I wished; and I verily believe that I wouldn't have given a button —certainly not a "livery" one—to have turned him from his purpose. But her moaning and weeping, and calling me Jimmy dear, was altogther more than I could bear; and approaching her, I tried to console her, and told her how willingly I would help her if I knew how.

"So you say, Jimmy; so you say; but you don't mane it," replied Mrs. Burke, wringing her hands in the extremity of her woe. "How can yer mane it, Jimmy, afther me bad tratement of you?—which I sore repint of, me little jewel, and sorra a bit will I ever raise a finger against you agin, Jimmy, while I've a ar-rm hanging to me body."

"You only tell me how I can help you, and you shall see, ma'am," said I, eagerly, and catching hold of her speckled hand, so carried away was I to see her so filled with remorse and penitence; "you only just tell me how, now!"

"Shure, and there is a way of helpin' me, Jimmy, me little fellow, but it goes agin me to ask it of you. Still, you are a good boy for so kindly offerin', and here's three-ha'pence to spend and do just as you like wid."

I suppose she must have borrowed the three-half-pence when she went out, as I know I took her last fourpence for the last quartern o' gin I fetched. Her generosity completely astonished me: never before, since she had been my father's housekeeper, had she given me so much as a single farthing. Now, more than ever, I pressed her to tell me in what way I could help her out of her scrape.

"I was thinkin', Jimmy, that you might tell your daddy that you lost the half-crown," said she, patting my head kindly.

"How could I lose it? You changed it. It was a shilling I took when I went to buy the first quartern of gin."

"Whist about gin, Jimmy dear! Mightn't we say that I sint you for a pen'orth of aniseed for the baby, wid the half-crown to pay for it, and you made a shlip, and dropt it down a gully hole? That 'ud be aisy to say, Jimmy dear."

"Ah! but see the tow'lling I should get."

"Devil a bit of tow'lling, Jimmy, while I was wid you. Be shure, dear, I'll tell him as how that a great hulkin' chap run agin you, and that you couldn't help it a bit. Never fear for the tow'lling, Jimmy; I'll bring you clane out of that, you may freely depind. And you may cut away now, and spind the three-ha'pence as fast as you like."

I went off, though not without some misgivings; and I spent the three-halfpence. It was some time since I had had a ramble, and I thought as she was in such a wonderfully kind humour, I might venture to indulge in one. I went as far as Farringdon Market, and I spent the afternoon there. The market clock striking five reminded me that it was high time I went home.

But I didn't hurry. Thought I, I'll let father get home first, and Mrs. Burke will tell him about the half-crown, and it will be all over when I go in.

I don't know how long he had been home, but when I went up and opened the door, there he was, standing up, and waiting for me, with the waist-belt in his hand. I was for dodging out again, but he caught me by the ear.

"Stop a minnit, young feller," said he, quite pale with passion; "I warnts a whisper with you. What have you done with that there half-crown?"

"I lost it, father," said I, in a terrible fright, and looking appealingly towards Mrs. Burke.

"Oh, you lost it! Where did you lose it?"

"Down a gully-hole, father. Ask Mrs. Burke—she knows."

"I ain't a-talkin' to Mrs. Burke; I'm a-talkin' to you. Now then, out with it, and—mind yer—let us have no lies." And as he spoke he spat in his hand, and wagged the strap in it.

"Well," said I, "I was a-going for a pen'orth of stuff for baby, and a chap ran against me, and—and—knocked the money out of my hand."

"And you 'spect I'm a-going to believe that, do yer?"

I was not much surprised to hear my father say this; but what did surprise me—what completely astounded and appalled me—was to hear Mrs. Burke exclaim, with a derisive laugh—

"Yes; that's how he expicts to come it over us, Jim; that's the purty yarn he pitched to me when he came back wid the empty cup. Ask him where he has been all the afthernoon, Jim, and how them shtains came on the breast ov his pinafore."

There were stains on the breast of my pinafore. I had bought a kidney pie with a penny of my three-halfpence, and in the ardour of enjoyment must have overlooked a leak in the bottom of the pastry, through which the gravy had oozed.

"D—n your young eyes," said my father, shaking me by the shoulder, "you've been and prigged that arf-crown, and you've been a-spending it all the arternoon."

"And so it's my belief, Jim; but it wasn't my place to shpeak first," said the wicked wretch; "and though it goes to the heart of me to recommend it, if you'll take my advice you'll let him have it hot and shtrong, Jim. 'Shpare the rod and spile the child,' as the scriptur ses, bear in mind."

And she stood by while my father laid into me with the thick leather strap till the blood trickled. As well as I could, and as plain as my agony would let me, I cried out the whole story to him while the beating was going on, but he heeded not a word that I said, and flogged away till his arm was tired. I felt brimful of fury against her. When the flogging was over, and I had been kicked into the back-room to wait there in the dark till bed-time, she presently came in to fetch something. Loud enough for my father to hear, said she—

"I hope the dressin' you've had will do you good, me boy. Mind you don't forget when you go to bed to say your prayers for forgiveness."

"Hang you, I hate you!" I raged at her; and then thinking of the worst thing I had ever heard to say to her, I called out as she went sniggering out at the door—

"Judas! Judas! you ought to live in Turkey."

But the words did not seem to affect her in the least! she merely turned, with the same ugly smile on her face, to tell me that she hoped I would keep my hands from picking and stealing, and my tongue from lying for the future.

"What was that he said?" I heard my father ask her, in a voice as though his temper had suddenly cooled.

"He ses he hates me. Never mind him, Jim; he'll know better some day," said Mrs. Burke, soothingly.

"But what did he say about—about Judas?"

"Did he? I didn't hear," replied Mrs. Burke, lightly. "It's my opinion, Jim, he's so full of the ould un he don't know what he's sayin'."

If by the "ould un" she meant the devil, Mrs. Burke was quite right when she said that I was full of him. My wrath against her made my throat swell and my eyes feel hot as fire. For the time I felt nothing of the cruel weals that scored my body. Nobody but the devil could

3

have filled my young head with such terrible wishes against her. I wished she might die. I wished that death—my image of death, the dreadful eyeless bird with the sharp spikes—might creep into her bed in the night, and sting and tear her till she was glad to run and hide in the pit-hole.

But nothing of the sort happened. She made her appearance bright and brisk as ever next morning and for many succeeding mornings, until that one came when my father married her.

The wedding was a very quiet one. Not a single individual in the alley knew anything about it, and even I was in utter ignorance that so important an event was about to take place. One evening, however, they — my father and Mrs. Burke—came home together, (I knew that she had dressed in her smartest and gone out in the morning, but that was not a circumstance of such unfrequent occurrence to excite my curiosity,) and they brought home with them a young man, a friend of my father's, who had, it appeared, obligingly kept an eye on my father's barrow while he and Mrs. Burke stepped into the church. I was about with the baby when they came home, and was called in and sent for a pint of rum.

When the rum was brought the strange young man filled a glass.

"Well," said he, "Lord bless every happy couple, I says. May you live long and die happy, both on yer. I looks to'ords you, ma'am."

Mrs. Burke acknowledged the compliment by looking towards the young man and inclining her head smilingly; whereon the young man inclined *his* head smilingly, and drank off half his rum.

"And I looks to'ords you, Jim," continued he, grasping my father's hand. "If you make her as good a husband as wot you are a pal, she won't have nothink to holler about."

My father nodded in an affable manner, and the young man having emptied the glass, my father took it and filled it.

"Here's the foresaid," said he, (as a rule he was a man very sparing of his words,) and tossed off the rum at a draught; an example that Mrs. Burke dutifully followed.

She had put the baby into my arms again, and finding nothing to interest me in the conversation that ensued on the rum-drinking, I was about to leave the room when my father called me back.

"Come here, Jim; you see who that is a-sitting on that chair?" and he pointed towards the Irishwoman.

"Of course I do," I replied, and laughing that he should ask so simple a question.

"Well, who is it?" said he, looking serious.

"Why, Mrs. Burke."

"Say it agin. Think what you are a-goin' to say, and say it slow."

"Mrs. Burke."

"Werry good. Now hark to me. Let that be the last time you let that name pass your lips, 'cos it's wrong. Her name ain't no more Burke than it is Green or Tomkins."

"Isn't it? What is it then, father?"

"It's *mother*, that's what it is. You've had a good long spell of rest off calling anybody mother, so now you can go at it agin hearty. D' ye understand? You've got to call her mother, and to act by her *as* a mother. If you don't you'll ketch something wot you won't like; so I tell yer."

There was not much to cry about in this last observation of my father's, but somehow I fell directly to crying instead of answering him. It couldn't be that I was grieved to hear the news of his marriage, for what possible difference could it make to me? That it gave Mrs. Burke more authority over me was true from a legal point of view, but unless it likewise conferred on her additional powers of spite and muscle, I couldn't possibly be a loser by the change.

"Well; what do you say?" continued my father, gruffly. "Ain't you got so much as thanky to say? Ain't you glad to get another mother?"

I made him no answer. I don't know whether it was owing to his using the word mother so repeatedly, but I couldn't speak for crying.

"Now what's the little beggar snivelling about?" observed my father, savagely; and turning to Mrs. Burke, "Well, I'm cust! I suppose I am to ask his pinion as to what's good for me, am I?"

"Don't mind him, my dear," said his new wife; "he can be as cross-grained as Ould Nick when he takes it into his head, as well to my sorrow I have been made to know many and many's the time, though I was never the woman to throuble you, Jim, wid my complaints. But there, I needn't tell you nothing wus of him than you know."

. I know that she alluded to the scandalous affair of the half-crown, (she was continually alluding to it as a means of turning my father's wrath against me when it suited her purpose,) and I had it on my tongue to give her a saucy answer. I suppose the strange young man detected my intention, for he winked at me in a good-humoured sort of way to hold my tongue, and beckoned me towards him.

"Lor, don't be too hard on the youngster," said he. "It ain't them as is hurt cries most. P'r'aps he's crying because he's so jolly glad to get another mother. How old is he, Jim?"

"I don' know; how old is he, Kitty?" asked my father of Mrs. Burke.

"Bortherin on siwin."

"Hain't he amost old enough to begin to think about cutting his own grass, Jim?"

"Quite old enough," chimed in my stepmother, promptly, "and quite big enough. He'll have to do it too before he's much older."

"Well, he do go puty nigh to'ords doin' it, don't he?" asked my father, with a bit of a scowl, which must have made known to his wife, if before she was ignorant of it, what an uncertain-tempered man he was.

"I'd be glad to know how," sneered she.

"How? why, luggin' young Poll about mornin', noon, and night, that's how. Pr'aps you don't think that's work?"

"Work, indade! Shquatting about wid a mite of a thing on his lap, and as often jining in play wid he rest as not!"

"What do *you* think, Jack?" asked my father of the stranger.

The stranger emphatically replied that soon than nurse a kid he would prefer "shoring" oj ters from morning till night.

"Of course you would. Werry well I recc lects the time when you had a kid to nuss,' (th perhaps accounted for the stranger's sympatl with me.) "Work, indeed! If there's one jc for payin' out the back more than another, it nursing a baby."

"I knows that I was precious glad to cut it as soon as I saw an opening, though it was to go at nothing better than barking."

As the good-natured stranger made this last observation, he slipped a penny into my hand, and in consequence of my anxiety to get away to spend it, I lost the rest of the conversation.

The words the strange young man had uttered, however, sank deep into my mind—"he was precious glad to cut it and get a place as barker," he had said. Well, and so should I be very glad to cut it and become barker.

But what was "barking?" I thought a great deal about the matter, and could arrive at no more feasible conclusion than that a "barker" was a boy that attended a drover, and helped him to drive his sheep by means of imitating the bark of a dog. Living so close to Smithfield market, droves of sheep were not unfrequently to be met with, and I had repeatedly seen boys engaged at the very trade I imagined the stranger to mean. Indeed, more than once, having got rid of the baby for half-an-hour, I had lent a hand at sheep-driving myself, and liked the job very much. I was, however, not nearly so clever at it as were some boys I knew, and who could not only bark like a dog, but even imitate the yelp of the animal when hit with a stick, and that in a manner calculated to impose on the most sensible sheep ever driven to Smithfield.

I had never known, however, that it was a trade at which to work at regularly for a living, and I could not but reflect that it couldn't be a business at which much money was earned. It was clear that the drover's object in hiring a boy instead of a dog must be a study of economy; and if the boy worked for him for a less sum than would buy a dog his daily meat, to say the least of it, he wasn't likely to grow over-fat.

Still the stranger had asserted, and my father had backed the assertion, that "barking" was preferable to carrying a baby about; and this, as I had a right to assume, under the most ordinary circumstances, with a real mother at home who cared for you, and gave you a whacking no oftener than you deserved it. How much more desirable, then, was it for me who had no real mother, a father who didn't care the price of a pot of beer for me, and no more than half a bellyful of victuals! Carrying the baby about was the bane of my existence, and every day it grew worse and worse to bear; and this not only by reason of Polly growing daily bigger and stronger, as the contents of the next chapter will show.

——◆——

CHAPTER X.

DESCRIPTIVE OF MY NOCTURNAL TROUBLES WITH POLLY. I AM PROVOKED TO ASSAULT MY STEP-MOTHER, AND RUN AWAY FROM HOME.

MY supposition that my father's marriage with Mrs. Burke could not make me more uncomfortable than I previously was proved to be altogether fallacious.

Prior to that interesting event, however much I might be fagging about during the day, rest came with the evening. Mrs. Burke relieved me of the baby, and come bed-time, I could sleep uninterruptedly, and rise in the morning perfect-ly refreshed. Now, however, matters were managed differently, It was my stepmother's opinion, and one in which my father agreed, that little Polly might as well sleep in my bed.

And if she had slept, it would have mattered little to me. The chest-of-drawers bedstead in Mrs. Burke's room was of ample size to accommodate both of us, and, as I loved her very much, I should have been rather glad of her company. But she did not sleep. I daresay it was her teeth, poor little soul! but, really, she was dreadfully tiresome. She was laid in my bed in the early part of the evening; and, by dint of creeping in myself with extreme caution, I generally contrived to get to sleep without waking her, and to secure three or four hours' rest. Between one and two o'clock, however, she invariably awoke, squalling her loudest, and refusing to be pacified without an immediate and abundant supply of victuals and drink. To prepare against this, a little stock of bread and butter, and a pot full of milk and water, was always placed by the bedside, and while it held out against her attacks, all went well enough. The worst of it was, it never did hold out long enough. Her appetite for midnight food was something miraculous. Piece after piece would vanish, crust as well as crumb; and when she found that it was all gone, then she set her pipes up. All the cuddling, and hushing, and coaxing, and singing, you could offer her were rejected with shrieks: nothing would pacify her. "Mammy! mammy! mammy!" You might have heard her on the opposite side of the alley.

The amount of ingenuity expended by me towards keeping that child quiet might, properly applied, have served for the invention of the steam-engine or the electric telegraph. "Would she go out a-walking with her Jimmy?" Sometimes, especially if it were a moonlight night, she would agree. Of course, it was only make-believe going a-walking; but she wasn't to know that. We had to dress, as though I meant it. There used to hang up behind the door an old black crape bonnet of Mrs. Burke's, and this I used to tie on her head, wrapping my jacket round her for a cloak. My walking costume consisted solely in an old hairy cap of my father's, reserved and hidden between the bed and the bedstead for the purpose. It was very bad on cold nights to paddle about the uncarpeted floor in this way; but there was no help for it: to have put my trousers on would have jeopardised the success of the scheme.

When we were dressed and ready to start, an imaginary Mrs. Burke would address me through the door, bidding me take that dear baby for a nice walk, and show her the shop where they sold such beautiful sugar-sticks; and to this I would dutifully reply that I was quite ready, and meant to start immediately. Then we would start; but, for our lives, couldn't find the room door. This piece of strategy was the soul of the performance. We couldn't find the door, try our hardest. We wanted to get out to go and buy that sugar-stick, and we couldn't, because that wicked door was hiding. The big crape bonnet was invaluable in carrying out the cheat, its black sides rising like walls on either side of her face, and serving the purpose of "blinkers," so that her vision was limited to the strictly straightforward, and side-glancing rendered impossible. The ack that attended this manœuvre was of three qualities. Under the influence of the first quality, she would in the course of half-an-hour or so, drop off to sleep in my arms, and remain so while I stealthily slid into bed with her; (it was in hopes of this result that I refrained from putting on my trousers before we set out walking.) If my luck was but middling, she would grow so cold and tired as to ask to be put into bed; or she would be brought to see the feasibility of my suggestion that we had better both lie down and watch the window till the naughty door came back again. The worst of this arrangement was, that she frequently would lie still long enough only for us both to become warm and comfortable, and then to insist on going a-walking again. The worst luck of all was, when she would *not* go a-walking with her Jimmy; when she turned a deaf ear to promises of sugar-sticks to-morrow; when my imitations of cats and dogs, and donkeys and mad bullocks, instead of inducing her silent wonder and admiration, drove her frantic from terror, and she *would* have more "bar." "Bar" was her word for bread and butter, and "Bar! bar! bar!" was her only answer to everything I could say.

At such times my stepmother would hammer at the wall with a stick.

"What are you doin' wid the dear child, you young scoundhrill?"

"She wants more 'bar.'"

"And is it too great a throuble for ye to get up and get her some, lazy-bones?"

"How can I? There ain't none."

"How do ye mane, ain't none?"

"She's ate it all. Can't you hear what she keeps hollerin'?"

"Ate it all, you little liar! What! You've been up to your hoggish tricks 'agin, have you? and shtole it all away from the little craythur. Well, you'd betther make her quiet. You know what you'll get if you bring me in there."

She was right. I *did* know "what I should get," having had it so often; and, with tears in my eyes when it came to this, I would beg of Polly to be quiet. Not she. She had heard mammy's voice, and grew more rampagious than ever. Then, with my heart in my mouth, I would presently hear a half-aloud threat from the next room, and a shuffling of hasty feet, and a scrambling at the lock of the door, and, raging like an angry cat, in would rush my stepmother with nothing on but her bed-gown and frilled night-cap. Without a moment's warning, she would fall on me and pummel my unprotected body without mercy; she would wring my head about and knead her bony fists about my sides, till my breath was used up and I could not cry out. My father never knew the extent of the punishment I suffered on these occasions, for all the while she was paying into me, she was clacking in her loudest voice, not about how she *was* serving me, but how she *would* serve me if I ever ate away the baby's food again.

"Don't talk about it; let him have it, the greedy warmint," my father would cry out, as he lay hearing all the threatening, and none of the spanking. "You lets him off too easy, and that's where he takes advantage of you."

"It's little more timpting I can bear before I'll do it," she would answer; "so take care, my fine fellow." And then, when she returned to her own room, she would say, "It's very well to talk of bating him, Jim; but it's best left alone, you may depind. If we can't rule him by kindness, we can't rule him at all. You may bate and bate; but two divils'll come in at the gate you bate one out of."

Strangely enough, soon as ever I had taken my whacking and Mrs. Burke had betaken herself to her own apartment, Polly would cuddle down and be as good as gold, and compose herself to sleep, as though nothing was the matter. Of course, there was nothing objectionable in this as far as it went; the worst of it was, that it really looked as though I could keep her quiet if I liked. Indeed, when at last I mustered courage enough to complain to my father, he told me so.

"I ain't got no pity for you," said he; "an obstinate little beggar like wot you are deserves all he gets and a good deal more."

"Well," I answered, (this was on a morning following a whacking which made my ribs feel as though the skin was all grazed off them,) "she ain't a-goin' to knock me about much longer."

"Ain't she, though?" was my father's scornful reply. "Why ain't she?"

"When I grow a bit bigger I'll show her," I vengefully replied.

My father st...d at me, and then laughed.

"If I was big enough," continued I, encouraged by the laugh, "I'd punch her nose! I'd kick her legs till she didn't have a bit to stand on. I hate her."

My father laughed again, and appeared to have some little trouble in composing his countenance to a proper expression of sternness.

"Come, don't you jaw me in that way, so I tell you; because it ain't my place to stand and hear it," said he.

"She tells you lies—dozens of lies," I further continued; and it coming into my mind what he had said about the hardships of carrying a child about, I thought I might make capital of it. "I never gets no play," said I. "I'm at work from the time I get up till I go to bed, and yet she won't leave me alone."

"How d'ye mean at work?"

"Why, nursing Polly and "——

"Well, and what if you *do* mind the kid?" interrupted he. "The kid can't mind itself, can she, you hard-hearted young wagabone? Do you want to loll about and live on me and yer mother? Why, I'd be ashamed on it if I was as big as you."

"I wish I could get a job of work to go to," said I, earnestly.

"*You* wish!" sneered he. "Jobs of work don't come a-knocking at people's doors and a-asking to be done. If you wanted a job of work you'd go and look arter it."

"Where, father?" I asked eagerly.

"Where? why, anywhere," replied he, warming with the subject. "Hain't there the markets? Why, when I goes to the 'gate (Billingsgate) or the garden (Covent Garden) as early as four and five o'clock, when you are snoring in bed, I sees boys which, in pint o' size you'd make two of, dodgin' about 'bliged to yearn a penny before they can get a cup of coffee to warm 'em."

"But I haven't got no boots nor stockings," said I, "nor yet no cap."

"Well, no more hain't they—yet no shirts, half on 'em. I spose you expect to be togged up afore you goes out to get a livin'? P'r'aps you'd like a blue coat with basket buttons and a chimbly-pot hat?"

I said something about looking respectable.

"Yah!" exclaimed he, with disgust. "Don't talk to me about 'spectability. Don't you think that 'spectability will ever get you a livin', cos, if you do, you're mistaken. The boys I'm a-speaking of carries fish, and tater sieves, and minds carts and barrows; and don't you know if you wore kid gloves and white chokers at that there sort of work you might get 'em spilte? A pretty feller *you* are to talk about what you will stand and what you won't."

And, with increasing disgust, he threw on his hairy cap, lit his short pipe, and walked off.

At the time I had this conversation with my father, Mrs. Burke had been my stepmother for about six months, and I was about seven years old. When I told him that I did not mean to put up with Mrs. Burke's cruelty much longer, I meant it. Every day it grew more and more intolerable, especially since the night when my father came home and found her helplessly drunk, and lying in the middle of the room, and gave her a slap or so about the head by way of sobering her. Up to this time she had always kept up an appearance of a sort of decency before him; but now this all went by the board, and her treatment of me in his presence was little or nothing better than when he was away. Often, indeed, should I have gone hungry had it not been for the kindness of Mrs. Winkship, the person mentioned in the early part of this history. Mrs. Winkship had known my mother for many years, and invariably spoke of her as "as good a gal as ever wore shoe-leather. She was as much too good for your father, Jimmy," she used to say, "as he is too good for the carneying two-faced Irish vagabond who fished for him and hooked him." Her acquaintance with my stepmother was as of long standing as with my mother. I told Mrs. Winkship about the pair of handsome slippers she had given my father, telling him that they belonged to the dead Mr. Burke. I thought Mrs. Winkship would never have done laughing. "Slippers, indeed!" said she; "why, the poor fellow would even carry his Sunday coat about all the week in his tool basket, knowing that she would pawn it for gin if he left it at home. Jim will find her out one day, and then war-hawks to her."

I used to tell all my troubles to Mrs. Winkship. She used to smuggle me into her back kitchen, and give me a tuck-out of anything which might have been left over from dinnertime. Many and many a time has she held my baby for an hour at a stretch while I went off for a game.

I asked Mrs. Winkship what a "barker" was, and she told me. I was wrong in supposing that it was anything to do with sheep-driving. A barker, I was told, was a boy who went along with a barrowman, wheeling his barrow to market, minding it while his master was buying his goods, pushing up behind the load as it was wheeled home, and afterwards going with his master on his "rounds," helping him to bawl out what he had to sell.

I didn't like to let Mrs. Winkship into the secret that I had thoughts of going into the barking line, still I wanted to get out of her all she knew about it.

"Now, how little was the smallest barker you ever saw, ma'am?" I asked her.

"How little? Why, I've seen 'em so little that their heads would come no higher than your shoulder," replied she; "but bless your innocent heart, what's the size got to do with it? It's the call—the voice, you know—that does the business. You might be as big as Goliar and as old as Methusalem, but if you didn't have a proper sort of voice you'd never fetch your salt."

And being in a chatty humour, as she generally was after dinner, and when about the third "brown" had been earned of her, she began to talk exactly as I wished her to. She told me that she had known many costermongers, good buyers and good sellers, and yet who were always kept in the background through having a hoarse, or a gruff, or a hollow voice.

"Of course," said she, "there are things—common things, such as taters, and onions, and cabbages—which are sure to go in whatever voice they're called, if so be that a man has anything like a reg'lar round, because people knows his time and looks out for him; but with goods which comes promisc'ous, and which are only to be got off by forcin', it's different. Now, there's fish. There may be fish to-morrow, and there mayn't. Even the salesmen in the market can't say for certain. And then, it may be cheap, or it may be dear. Say it's cheap. Say it's soles, and that you buy a lot of 'em. How many do you think you'll sell if you go crawling along with 'em, growling out, 'Here's soles, good soles!' in the same voice as does for turnips or taters? Why, you won't take enough to buy fat to fry your own supper in. You must put your heart into it, and try and make yourself believe how wonderful cheap your soles are, till you get into quite a perspiration about 'em. You drive sudden and sharp round corners of streets, and at the same moment you pipe up, 'Dover soles! lovely soles! splendid soles! Big as plaice, and all alive! all alive! all alive!' and this you keep up, driving along brisk and keeping up the tune. Presently you set your eyes on your soles, and see a pair which is so large, and so lovely, that you really can't help stopping, which you do as sudden as you turned the corner. 'Oh, I say,' says you, dropping the tune and taking to conversation, 'here's a pair of whackers! blowed if they don't get finer the lower we get into the pad! Just look here, ladies—there's a pair of soles for you!—three-pence!'

"That's how to sell soles!" chuckled Mrs. Winkship, bringing her fat hands together with a hearty spank to illustrate the manner in which the "pair" should be joined at the very instant their price was disclosed. "It's the same with fruit. Bless your soul, there's a way of crying your fruit, so as to make everybody's mouth water that hears you—specially stone-fruit. Why, when I was a gal," continued Mrs. Winkship, "I was wonderful good at greengages; as good at anything mind you as here and there one, but at 'gages I topped 'em all. It was only the voice, and knowing how to pick your words; 'juicy greengage!' 'blooming greengage!' 'meller greengage for eating or preserving!' Many a hot summer's afternoon have I made a pretty pocket, with only just a silk handkercher over my shoulders, and half a sieve of 'gages under my arm."

Was mine a musical voice? I didn't ask Mrs. Winkship at the time the above narrated conversation took place, but the subject remained pretty constantly in my mind. My stepmother was considered a pretty singer, and there were several of her tunes which I knew completely, and used to sing to the baby of nights; still because I knew and could follow, at least to my own satisfaction, every turn in "Young Riley" and the "Bould Soger Boy," it was by no means certain that I had a voice for Dover soles or greengage plums.

Had I? Never had the question presented itself so forcibly to me as on the morning on which I had expressed to my father my determination to submit no longer to the pummelling of my stepmother. The worst of it was, my only chance of escape from it, as it appeared to me, was to become a barker, and that, according to Mrs. Winkship, on whom I placed every reliance, could never be unless my voice was suitable. It wasn't easy to test it. I tried several calls under my breath with tolerable success, but was I justified in taking the important step I meditated on such inconclusive grounds? So all-engrossing was the subject as I sat on the doorstep with my sister Polly in my arms, that presently she made an unchecked spring, and went with a crash, and a squall, rolling over the stones.

Mrs. Burke was down on me like a thunderbolt. Without waiting for an explanation, or even to pick up Polly, she seized me by the hair, and bumped my head several times against the door-jamb. She made a claw at my ears to wring them, and missing them through a wriggle on my part, scored my cheek with her nails, and set the blood trickling. She punched me about as though she was one prize-fighter, and I was another.

"I'll wring your ugly shnout off, you dirty shwine," said she, and proceeded to take my nose between the knuckles of her fore and middle fingers. The pain was enough to drive me mad. I must have been mad or very nearly, for I made a scramble at her cruel hand, and getting her thumb in my mouth, I dug my teeth into it. It must have hurt her very much, judging from the way she halloed. She let go my face, and in an instant I ducked under her arms, and bolted up the alley as fast as my legs would carry me.

———◆———

CHAPTER XI.

IN WHICH I SPEND AN AFTERNOON IN SMITHFIELD MARKET, AND HAVE A NARROW ESCAPE FROM FALLING ONCE MORE INTO THE CLUTCHES OF MRS. BURKE.

WHETHER Mrs. Burke (I would much rather speak of her so than by any other name, if the reader has no objection) followed me with a view to giving chase, is more than I can say.

Once out of Fryingpan Alley, I never once turned or looked behind me. I passed good Mrs. Winkship sitting on her coke-measure, and she, judging, as I suppose, from my affrighted appearance, that I was fleeing from danger, called out, "Run, Jimmy, run! good luck to you." Arrived at the mouth of the alley, a boy with threepen'orth of hot rum in his hand was at that moment turning in, and to avoid running against him I turned to the left, taking Mrs. Winkship's parting advice earnestly to heart.

When I was thousands of miles from England, the thought would often come into my head, how would it have been if that boy had not been coming in with the rum and water, and I had turned to the right instead of the left? Had I done so, and kept straight on, I should by and by have found myself in the parks, in the fields, out in the country. Then I might have become a ploughboy, a field labourer,—a young fellow with a smock-frock, and a "billycock" hat and cloddy boots; I might ——. But there, where's the use of indulging in "ifs," and "buts," and "might have been?" To the left it was. Down Turnmill Street, through Cow Cross, and still straight on until Smithfield Market was reached.

If it was not my good luck that inclined me to run in this direction, that it was so, was my very decided impression at the time. Had Mrs. Burke followed me, my legs might not have been of much use as against hers in a running-match over a level course; but in Smithfield Market it was odds in my favour. I was well used to the pens, being in the habit of spending my rare playtimes there in the games of "touch" and "chevy;" and unless Mrs. Burke was as good at vaulting and jumping as she was at punching and pummelling, she would have had no chance against me.

It was not a market-day, and the place was as quiet and as deserted as it always is at such times. Finding myself amongst the pens, my instinct of self-defence led me to hurry to that part of the market where the pigs were sold. I had heard boys of my acquaintance say, "Oh, don't let's play in the pig part, it's so precious slippery." So it was, and especially to people who were not used to it.

I climbed to a top bar in the pig shambles, and looked anxiously about me, and soon convinced myself that although Mrs. Burke might have set out after me, she had either lost sight of me or run herself to a standstill. My perch was a capital one for surveying purposes, and I could see all round about for a considerable distance. Everybody, however, that I could make out was quite strange, and did not even look towards me. It was quite as well that they did not, or perhaps one would have stopped, then another, till a mob had got round, and the policeman had come up to inquire what was the matter.

And when I come to reflect on the deplorable pickle I was in, I wonder that somebody did not take notice of me. To be sure, it was a neighbourhood in which ragged and outcast little boys were not scarce, but my appearance was ten times worse than that of the ordinary ragged outcast. Naturally, I had begun to cry when Mrs. Burke took to punishing me with such diabolical cruelty. I had cried all the way as I ran, and I was crying now. Panting from my long run, sobbing with rage, and pain, and spite, with my tears mingling with the blood that trickled from the wounds Mrs. Burke's nails had inflicted on my cheeks and on my nose; with my hair all uproarious and uncovered by a cap; with my naked feet all muddy, and my jacket all torn and tattered; there I sat on a bar in the pig-shambles on the noon of a Wednesday in the merry month of May. This is the picture I see on looking back on those dismal times. When it happened, however,

I thought nothing about it particularly, I'll be bound. Ever since my mother died, now nearly a year and a quarter ago, I had had but one pair of boots; and the navy cap with the big peak, in which I followed the black load to Clerkenwell church-yard, was the last that covered my head. As for my tears, they had grown to be more familiar with me than smiles, and a scratch or a bruise more or less was, thanks to the Irishwoman's liberality, not worth thinking about.

I had ears, eyes, thoughts but for one thing, and that was Mrs. Burke's coming after me. Knowing the sort of woman she was, I was the more apprehensive. Though she had been sure of me by running me down fairly and openly, I knew that she would very much prefer lying in wait for me in the rear and suddenly pouncing out on me. It was to guard against so terrible a calamity that I had to keep a sharp look-out. It was not until the church clocks chimed four that I began seriously to reflect on what I should do.

Should I go home? How dare I? She would kill me; she would wring my head about again, and punch me with her bony knuckles. More than once she had threatened to cut my liver out. No doubt she was cruel enough, and, worse than all, now she had excuse enough; for, however she might treat me, it would be enough for her to hold up her thumb to compel my father to acknowledge that it served me right. What could I say to my father in justification of my savage act? (for I had come to the conclusion that it *was* a savage act.) I had dropped the baby! With nothing else expected of me than to sit still and hold her tight, I had let her go and hurt her, I didn't know how much. This was a feature of the business which hitherto had altogether escaped me—how much was Polly hurt? She went down a tremendous bump, and she screamed in a very frightful manner. Perhaps some of her bones were broken! Perhaps that was the solution to the otherwise unaccountable circumstance of my mother-in-law not following me. Clearly it was no use to think of going home.

Where, then, should I go? By this time it was dusk and the lamplighter was about, and the pig-market became a very dismal place to stay in. I wound my way through the pens till I got to the front row, which is in a line with the thoroughfare called Long Lane, and there I once more sat for further reflection.

I daresay I sat there—on the second bar, with my legs dangling towards the path, my body within the pen, and my arms resting on the top bar—for half-an-hour or more, trying hard to think of my affairs, leaving the "home" aspect quite out of the question; but it was of no use: the darker it grew the hungrier I grew. I found myself thinking more and more on what would be my probable fate if I *did* go home. I called to my mind the most severe whacking I had ever received, with how much it hurt, and whether, supposing on this occasion I got double, (*that* was the least I could expect,) I could possibly stand it. I really believe that I had almost convinced myself that I could, when suddenly I felt something touch my hand, and looking up, saw a gentleman holding two penny-pieces between his finger and thumb.

"Here, you poor little wretch," said he, "take this and buy bread with it;" and before I could recover from my surprise, he passed on and was lost in the darkness.

I had not even said "thanky" for it, and I didn't know whether to be sorry or glad on that score. It was such a queer sort of twopence. I had not earned it. I had not worked for it. I had not expected it. He had voluntarily given it to me. Other people had given me halfpence many a time, and I had spent them without further thought beyond settling what I should buy. But I did not feel at liberty to spend the strange gentleman's twopence so.

Confound his twopence! If he had twopence to give a boy, why didn't he say, "Here's twopence for you," and have done with it? True, I *was* a poor little wretch, and as far as I remember I did not feel particularly hurt at being so called; it was his ordering me to buy bread with his money that made it seem so much like—well—so much like a beggar's twopence. His words rang in my ears till they tingled as though Mrs. Burke had recently pulled them, and I looked up the street and down the street, and was very much relieved to discover that no one had witnessed the little transaction. Finding that it was so, I soothed my injured dignity by uttering aloud and defiantly towards the way the benevolent man had taken, "You be blowed! who are you ordering? I shan't buy bread neither; I shall buy what I like."

So I did. Feeling that the stranger was mine enemy, and one whom it would give me much satisfaction to disobey, I walked down towards Barbican, resolutely turning my gaze from the bakers' shops, (it was, in my hungry condition, no easy matter to do so,) and with my mind bent on luxuries. There was at that time a little old-fashioned shop in Barbican where jams and preserves were sold. It was a wholesale sort of a shop, and the jams were deposited in great gallon jars, each one of which was ticketed with the price per pound of its contents. One in particular took my fancy; it was labelled "greengage," and the mouth of the jar was deliciously smeared with it. Eighteenpence a pound this jar was marked, and after working a difficult sum in long division on my fingers, I discovered that two ounces of it would come to twopence farthing. This was an insurmountable difficulty. True, I might go in and ask for twopen'orth. Twopence was a goodish bit of money. It wasn't like going in and asking for a ha'porth. "Two pen'orth of greengage jam, please." And, after this brief rehearsal, I stepped firmly to the shop door, but had hardly placed a foot on the threshold than I received a box on the ear that sent me reeling.

"Now be off," exclaimed the old woman belonging to the shop, and who, it seems, had mistaken her customer. "I've been watching you these ten minutes, you little prig," and she slammed the door hard and put the catch on.

Hard as I thought my luck at the time, I have no doubt that the old woman did me a real service. What did I want with greengage jam? It was as much as anything out of wanton malice towards my benefactor that I thought of buying it, and I was very properly checked, and at the same time punished. No such proper reflections were mine at that time, however; indeed, I am ashamed to confess that it was when I had rushed vengefully into the road to find a convenient stone to shy through the jam-shop window, that an odour assailed my nostrils of so enticing a sort, that my anger was instantly appeased.

It proceeded from a neighbouring cook-shop. The peas-pudding as well as the baked faggots were "just up," and their fragrance blended, producing a result potent enough to drive a cold and hungry boy mad. Fancy what would have been my sensations if I had invested my twopence in that miserable mite of jam and afterwards approached the cook-shop !

Without a moment's deliberation I marched in and bought my supper—a faggot—(it cost me a pang to be compelled to forego the liberal spoonful of gravy that accompanied each one, in consequence of having no vessel to hold it,) on a big cabbage leaf, a ha'porth of peas-pudding, and a ha'porth of baked potatoes. I longed to be at it at once, but I had heard of unprincipled scoundrels who waylaid children going errands and robbed them of their goods: so I bundled up my supper in the cabbage-leaf, and, hiding it in the breast of my jacket, made haste back to the pig-market, and, sitting in a secluded corner, devoured it with great relish.

I don't mean to say that I couldn't have eaten more—indeed, I am sure that I could have eaten three times as much—still I felt very much better for my supper. I felt better every way; the goodness of the supper had softened my heart as well as assuaged my hunger. How was little Polly ? I thought of her more than of father, home, anything ; nor was it any great wonder that I should. Without doubt she was a dead weight on my liberty during the daytime, and a serious draw-back of nights, but she was a dear little soul. She couldn't speak to me, but she couldn't bear to see me cry ; and often and often after Mrs. Burke had beaten me, and I felt so bad I didn't know what to be at, poor Polly would put her little arms round my neck, and her lips against my cheek to kiss me. She was all the comfort I had, and I believe I was all the comfort she had, poor child.

These and a hundred other such melancholy reflections passed through my mind as I sat in the pig-shambles, until I could bear them no longer, and determined at all hazards to venture home and make inquiries, or at least to approach our alley, and lurk about till I saw somebody who lived there, and of whom I could make inquiries.

It was quite dark by this time, and the way from Smithfield to our alley was not a much frequented one ; nevertheless I stepped along with extreme caution, darting into doorways if I saw approaching any one looking in the distance the least like my father or Mrs. Burke. I met nobody that I knew, however, and presently reached Turnmill Street in safety. As luck would have it, while I was as yet twenty yards from Frying-pan Alley, whom should I run against but my old friend Jerry Pape ?

I have said whom I ran against, but it would be more correct to say that he ran against me. He ran right at me from across the road, and embraced me with both his arms, as though he was so jolly glad to see me he could scarcely contain himself.

"What, Jim ? what cheer, old boy ? Where was you goin' ? " said Master Pape, his affectionate embrace abating nothing.

"I don't know quite where I am going, Jerry," I replied, shaking hands with the good-natured fellow. "I was thinking of going home just to see"——

"Then you hain't been home ? " asked Jerry, eagerly.

"No."

"You hain't been home since the mornin'—not since you hooked it away ? "

Jerry's voice was tremulous with excitement as he asked the question.

"No," I replied, "I've been away all day. How are they all, Jerry ? Have you seen young Polly out this afternoon ? "

Master Pape made no reply to my question.

"If you hain't been home, you'd better come now," said he, griping the collar of my jacket with something more than friendly ardour, and giving me a jerk in the direction in which he wished me to go. "Come on, you've got to go home, you know."

Jerry's behaviour at once aroused my worst suspicions.

"I hain't going home without I like," said I, and down I sat on the pavement.

The treacherous villain appeared to be suddenly made aware of the faultiness of his tactics.

"You hain't a-going home ? " said he with affected astonishment, and at the same time taking his hand from my collar. "Well, you are a rummy chap. You just said you was."

"I can go without your pulling, Jerry Pape. What do you want to pull me for ? "

"Me pull you ? What should I pull yer for, Jimmy ? How is it worth my while to pull yer ? Next time I does you a good turn you'll know it, young feller."

"How's it a good turn, Jerry ? "

"How ! Why, there they are all a-cryin' arter you up the alley."

"Who's cryin' ? "

"Who ? Why, yer father and yer mother and young Poll, and all the whole bilin'. I couldn't stand it no longer. Ses I to myself, 'Here they are a-breakin' their 'arts arter him, and won't get their suppers without he comes home, though it's a stunnin' meat puddin' with hot taters, and all the while p'r'aps he's hangin' about afeard to wenture home, and expectin' a whackin'. Jim knows me,' I ses to myself ; 'I won't say nothink to nobody, but I'll slip out and let him know as it's all right.' And I does do it, and here you are, chucking of yourself on the stones, and as good as callin' me a liar."

There was a gas-lamp near, and as Jerry spoke it was easy to see that he meant every word he had spoken, and that my suspicions as to his fidelity had wounded his feelings very deeply. I couldn't help believing him, and yet what he told me was altogether astounding. Everybody crying for me, and a meat pudding getting cold on my account ! Remorse filled me to the brim, and, sympathizing with my weeping friends, my eyes filled with tears.

"Are you quite sure, Jerry ? " I asked, getting on my legs, and squeezing his friendly hand in gratitude. "You are quite sure you hain't made no mistake ? 'cos it will go very hard against me, you know, Jerry, if you should. It ain't at all unbeknown to you, Jerry, how she punches me about and pulls my hair."

"Mistake about what?" asked the traitor, evasively.

"About the cryin' and that."

"That's right enough, I tell you. They're all a-cryin' arter you like a house a-fire."

"My father too, Jerry?"

"Harder 'un the whole lot put together," replied Master Pape, emphatically. "Don't take my word on it; come up to the alley and arks anybody. You can hear him a owlin' as high up as Winkship's. He'll do hisself a hinjury, that'll be the end on it."

"And little Polly, is she, too, all right Jerry?"

"Right as ninepence; never seed her look better."

"She didn't break any of her bones when I dropped her down the steps this morning? She didn't make her nose bleed, or get another bump on her head, Jerry?"

"Oh, that's what you're afeard on?" said Jerry, lightly. "Lor', bless yer, when they picked her up she was a-larfin fit to kill herself. When they took her to the doctor's"——

"What! took her to the doctor's? Oh! what for, Jerry? I thought you said she wasn't hurt at all, but laughing?"

"Did I say anythink about the doctor's? I've no recollections of it," replied Jerry Pape, turning his head away to hide his embarrassment.

"You did; you did, Jerry. You said they took her to the doctor's."

"Well, did I tell you what they took her for?" asked Jerry, turning about again with the tarnish of perplexity quite cleared off from his brazen countenance.

"No. Do tell me, please, Jerry."

"Didn't I tell you that when they picked her up she was larfin werry hearty?"

"Yes, so you did, but"——

"Werry well, then; it was wus than that. Since you *must* know, she was a-larfin' so that they thought she'd go into conwulsions. *That's* what they took her to the doctor's for."

Completely reassured and comforted by this plausible explanation, I turned towards Frying-pan Alley at a brisk trot, Jerry keeping well up with me and chatting in the cheerfullest manner. It was not until we had arrived within a stone's-cast of the alley that my eyes were opened to his cruel perfidy.

As we were passing Rose Alley, a boy—an acquaintance of mine, and about as big as Jerry Pape—suddenly pounced out and seized me in much the same manner as Jerry had done in the first instance.

"Got him, Jerry? Halves, don't you know?" exclaimed the boy, eagerly.

"Halves, be jiggered," roared Jerry, seizing my other arm. "What's halves for? Ain't I been a huntin' arter him ever since since his father come home? Wasn't I the first to ketch him?"

"Halves, I tell yer," said the first boy, making surer his grip on my arm, and giving me a jerk. "Hain't I been a-keepin' my eye on yer ever since you first come acrost him? You'd never got him home if it hadn't a been for me. No more jaw, Jerry Pape. Bring him along."

"Shan't. What did Jim Ballisat say? Didn't he say the first as ketches him and brings him home, I'll give a shillin' to? He didn't say nothink about the second that ketches him!"

"No more jaw, I tell you," said the first boy, who was stronger than Jerry Pape. "Come on home," (this to me, with a lug that made my shoulder-joints crack.) "I shouldn't like to go *you* halves, my tulip. I 'spect you 'll be werry nigh killed when yer father *does* get hold on yer."

Once more overcome by terror, I wriggled down between my captors and lay on the pavement, crying aloud that I'd sooner die than go another step. Having no shoes on, I couldn't kick very hard, but as well as I was able I let fly at both of them whenever they approached close enough.

The two boys were in despair. Jerry Pape, the treacherous thief, making so sure of my blood-money, and finding himself in a fair way of being baulked of it, was white with rage. Animated by a sudden spurt of courage, (he was known to be a shameful coward,) he unexpectedly turned on his rival, and struck him a heavy blow in the face with his fist.

"Take that," said Jerry, "if it hadn't been for you poking your nose in it, I should have got him home by this time."

This was a rash move on Jerry's part. The boy *did* take it as desired, but, unluckily for Master Pape, he was one of those mahogany-headed boys on whom a blow is lost, unless it downright dents them. For an instant only the mahogany-headed one comforted his assaulted nose with the cuff of his jacket, glaring at Jerry the while. Then he was at him like a terrier with a rat. With tempestuous force he bore him to the earth, and there he pummelled the villain in a way that did my heart good to see. I enjoyed it so much that I stayed dangerously long to witness it. Swift as light the thought came into my head, "Now is my time to be off!"

And with speed swift almost as the thought that suggested it, I sprang up, and away, leaving the baffled combatants struggling in the mud.

CHAPTER XII.

IN WHICH I ENDEAVOUR TO QUALIFY MYSELF FOR "BARKING," AND PICK UP SOME NEW ACQUAINTANCES.

I RAN back in the direction I had come, and speedily found myself in Smithfield again, and in that very part of it in which I had spent such a considerable part of the day. Nobody followed me, and the market was darker and even stiller than when I had left it half-an-hour since.

My errand had been attended by no little peril, and the results it had yielded were by no means satisfactory. It had effectually settled one point, however: it would be little short of insanity—aiding and abetting my own manslaughter—to return home. How could I doubt, after listening to the conversation that had taken place between the perfidious Jerry Pape and his companion, that my father, to say nothing of Mrs. Burke, was furiously incensed against me? My father, indeed, was not able even to contain his wrath until I happened to come home; he was burning and brimming over with it, and so longed to vent it on me, that he had offered the large sum of a shilling for my apprehension. It *was* a large sum for him to offer. It was as much as he could earn, carrying loads fit for a horse to draw, in a quarter of a day. A shilling would buy him three pots of beer.

Going home, then, being so completely out of the question, what *was* to be done? Where was I to sleep? was a question which at once presented itself, and not unnaturally, since never in my life had I as yet slept out of a more or less comfortable bed. Should I sleep where I was? Why not? I had had a good supper, and the nights were not so *very* cold. It wouldn't hurt me for once—just for once—if I cuddled down in a corner, and made myself comfortable. It was light pretty early in the morning, and then——

Ah! and then? I had been thinking about to-morrow in a vague and mystic sort of way all the evening; but now it brought me up as suddenly as though it had been a brick wall. "To-morrow" was not to be shirked. Wherever I slept it was only shutting my eyes and opening them again, and it would be the new day—the day on which I must go single-handed into the world to get my living out of it. Of course I was already "on my own hands," as the vulgar saying is, and had been since the morning; but it had been a patchy sort of a day at best. I had got up that morning at *home ;* I had breakfasted there; I had run away, and gone back, and run away again. I had obtained a meal independently of home—but how? It would never do to begin and go through a new day—my first clear day—in such a manner. I must make up my mind, before I went to sleep, as to the sort of work I thought would suit me, and as soon as I woke I must go at it.

At what? Why, at "barking," to be sure. It was light pretty early in the morning, and I would be off to one of the markets—Covent Garden or Billingsgate, I didn't care which—and I would look out amongst the barrowmen for one that looked likely, and I would offer him my services. If he asked me how much a day I wanted, I would tell him——

Whew! It was all very well to talk about going to the market to look for a master; but suppose it should happen that, after having found one and made terms with him, I couldn't do the work! Suppose, after all, my voice had no tune in it for barking! To be sure I did not know whether it had or not; but what a silly fellow I had been to let the whole afternoon and evening slip by without testing it! I had had the whole market to myself, as I might say, for ever so many hours, and I had done nothing but lounge idly about, as though I had a hundred a year coming in.

I had better see about it at once. It was not yet late—but little after nine o'clock, indeed—and I could not do better than retire to the centre of the pig-market and practise.

For which market should I prepare myself?

At ordinary times I should have found it difficult to choose; but the cold, slippery cobbled stones on which I stood, and the keen night air, had their influence, and I selected Covent Garden before Billingsgate without argument. This preliminary being settled, it next became a consideration what flowers and vegetables, commonly sold about the street, were then in season. What flowers? Let me see; why, wall-flowers, of course, as the most plentiful and favourite.

Ahem !

"Wall-flower! SWEET and pretty WALL-FLOW-er !"

It rang out pretty well as far as voice was concerned, but it was plain enough to my own ears that I hadn't got the proper accent; it would never do to cut the first "wall-flower" so short as I had cut it. Let us try again—this time with my hand to one side of my mouth, to make the sound go further.

"WALL-flow-ER ! sweet AND pret-TY WALL-flow-ER !"

That was a great deal better. I walked up and down one of the dark avenues, and for a quarter of an hour did a roaring trade in the wall-flower line, calling "Whoa !" to an imaginary donkey, and bawling out to my imaginary master for change for a sixpence and a shilling, just as though it was real.

Having polished off the wall-flowers to my perfect satisfaction, I cast about for a seasonable fruit, and found strawberries. I went at them with a confidence based on my first success, but speedily was driven to the conclusion that to an unpractised barker strawberries were decidedly a tickler. There was such a lot to say, and the words wouldn't rhyme.

"STRAW-ber-REE ! FOUR PENCE a MARKET pottle, O BOYS !"

It wasn't neat. There was a bungling hitch between the "ket" of the market, and the "pot" of the pottle. Perhaps altering the price might make a difference.

"FIP-pence a MAR-KET pottle !"

No.

"Thrup-pence a market pottle !"

Same as fip-pence.

"Sixpence a mar"——

It was clear that the price had nothing to do with it. It was the word "market" that spoilt it; if that could be left out it would run smooth enough. But of course it couldn't be left out, at fourpence, or sixpence, or any other price. Ignorant as I was of business matters generally, I knew that buyers of barrow-fruit would no sooner buy pottles of strawberries which were not vended as "market," than they would purchase damsons, or any other sort of small plums, by any other measure than ale-house, or, as the barrowmen more properly styled it, "alias."

By dint of much perseverance, however, and scores of repetitions, I contrived to bring my strawberry call to something like the proper thing. It was mainly effected by sinking the "ket" in market, and making it "mark't," and allowing it to slide easily into pottle. I was getting along very well, when, as I sat on a bar of one of the pens, I was made suddenly aware of the presence of two boys lurking in my rear. My first terrible thought was that it was Jerry Pape and his antagonist, and that, having fought their battle out, they had made it up, and joined in a partnership against me. I thought so the more, because the moment they saw that they were observed, one of them sprang forward and seized me violently by the hair.

"Whoa, boys ! whoa, boys !" exclaimed he, mocking my strawberry-cry, and at each "whoa" giving my hair a cruel tug. "It's werry nigh time you did 'whoa boys.' What do you mean, you wagabone, to be kicking up such a precious row in this here market, when you ought to be in bed—hey, sir ?"

And he imitated the voice and gestures of a very savage policeman, flourishing his fist as though he held a staff in it.

My first feeling on turning round, despite the pain the hair-pulling had occasioned me, was one of thankfulness. The two boys were *not* Jerry Pape and his companion. They were of about the same size, or perhaps a little bigger, but perfectly strange boys to me.

"Do you hear me, sir?" continued the sham policeman, fiercely, feeling in his pockets for a pair of handcuffs. "Are you a-goin' to move on, or am I to put yer where I'll be able to find yer in the mornin'? You'd better go home quiet. I won't take no bails for you, don't you know, if I once gets you to the station."

"Go home yourself," I retorted, wriggling out of his grasp and jumping down from my perch. "Why don't you go home and leave a feller alone?"

"We're a-goin' home," observed the other boy, who had been laughing at the sham policeman until he was compelled to hold on by the bars. "We've been to the gaff, up in Shoreditch, and this is our way home." And then, addressing his companion, said he—

"Come along, Mouldy! We shan't get to Westminister to-night."

Now, I had been to Covent Garden with my father several times, and I knew that it was in or near Westminster; but I had always ridden on the barrow, starting direct from home. From my present position I was much perplexed as to which was the best way to the market; and hearing the boy mention Westminster as a place with which he was familiar, I thought it was a good opportunity to obtain a little information on the subject.

"What part of Westminster do you live in?" I asked of the boy who had last spoken, and who had hair of the same colour as Mrs. Burke's, as was plainly to be seen through the holes in his cap.

"What part? Why, the 'spectable part. Don't we, Ripston?" replied the youth who had been addressed as Mouldy.

"I should ha' thought that he might have knowed that by our 'pearance, without arstin'," observed Ripston.

"But is it near Covent Garden?" I asked.

"What, Common Garden Theayter?" answered Mouldy, cocking his cap and giving his side locks a twist in imitation of the habits of the aristocracy. "Oh, yes! It's just a short ride in our broom from our house to the theayter; and Ripston and me goes whacks in a private box. Don't we, Ripston?"

"What's the use of tellin' such jolly lies?" laughed Ripston. "Where we live *is* nigh Common Garden—both the market and the theayter. We lodges in the 'Delphi—that's where we lodges. Where do you lodge, young un?"

It didn't much matter where I lodged. No doubt I should be able to find a place near the market—perhaps in the market itself—where I might pass the night quite as comfortably as in Smithfield, to say nothing of the advantages of being shown my way and being on the spot in good time in the morning. Without hesitation, I jumped out of the pen and into the pathway where they were.

"Come on," said I; "it's getting late."

"Where are you goin', then?" asked Mouldy, in surprise.

"With you," I boldly replied.

"But we're a-goin' to the 'Delphi, don't I tell you!" said Mouldy.

"So am I."

Mouldy whistled, and looked in astonishment at Ripston.

"What? ain't your lodgin's no nigher than the arches?" asked the latter.

"The 'Delphi, you said; you didn't say anything about arches," said I.

"Well, the 'Delphi is t h arches, and the arches is the 'Delphi—ain't they?" observed Ripston.

"Are they? Well, I didn't know. How should I, when I never was there?"

"Never was there? Why, you just said that you lodged there."

"Well," said I, "if you must know the full particulars, I haven't got no lodgin's to go to."

"No reglar lodgin's, you mean."

"No lodgin's at all," I replied, "only here,"—and I glanced round the pens.

"Oh, that's all gammon, you know!" spoke Mouldy. "Every cove's got a lodgin'! What have you done with your old lodgin'?"

What had I done with it? That was a question blunt as it was unexpected; and by the manner in which the two boys eyed me and each other, it was plain that they saw the confusion it occasioned me. Mouldy pursued his inquiries.

"If you hain't got no lodgin'," said he, "how do you get your wittles?"

"And where do you go of Sundays?" put in Ripston.

I had made up mind to conceal my affairs entirely from my new friends for the present, at least; and here, all of a sudden, I found myself cornered, without any chance of escape. But, after all, where was the danger? To all appearance, they were boys who got their own living, and took care of themselves, without anybody's control. Perhaps it might be to my advantage to tell them how I was situated, or pretty nearly; they might be able to advise me how to set about getting work.

"If I tell you all about it, will you promise that you won't split?" I asked.

Both the lads solemnly assured me that they would suffer death rather than be guilty of such baseness.

"Then," said I, "I used to lodge at home. I lodged there last night."

"What, along with your father and mother, and that?" asked Ripston.

"Yes."

"And you've run away, and don't mean to go back any more?"

"I'll never go back again," I answered, with great sincerity. "I daren't go back."

"I see," said Mouldy, sagaciously nodding his head. "What was it that you nailed?"

"Nailed?"

"Ay! prigged, don't you know? Did they ketch it on you, or did you get clean off with it?"

"What do you mean? Did they ketch what on me?"

"Well, that's good!" laughed Mouldy. "How should I know what it was you stole? I wasn't there, was I?"

"But I didn't steal anything. It was because I was whacked so, that I ran away."

The boys looked incredulous; and Mouldy laid his forefinger along the side of his nose, and winked impressively.

"So you ran away on'y because you was whacked, eh?" observed Ripston.

"Only! If you ever had any such weltings as I've been used to, you wouldn't say 'only.'"

"But did you get reg'lar wittles, and all that?"

"Pretty fair."

"And a reg'lar bed—reg'lar don't you know, with sheets and blankets, and a bolster?"

"Why, of course," I replied.

"Oh! of course, is it?" sneered Ripston; "and you wants us to believe that you gets all this—your wittles, and your bed with sheets to it—and just because you was whacked you run away and are afeard to go home again? You're a jolly liar, that's what you are."

"Else a jolly fool, which is wuss," spoke Mouldy, decidedly.

"You ain't obliged to believe me; but what I've told you is all true," was all I could say.

"Well, strange things *does* happen and so p'r'aps it is," said Ripston; "but what I ses is this—a chap wot runs away from good wittles and comfor'ble lodgin's just because he gets whacked, oughter to be kept out of 'em till he learns the walue of 'em."

"I wish somebody would grub *me*, and give me a comfor'ble lodgin on them terms," interposed Mouldy.

"They wouldn't get much profit on yer, Mouldy," grinned his companion; "but don't you be afeard; he's done something more'n he peaches to, only he won't say, because he thinks we'll split; and werry natural."

Ripston was younger than Mouldy—two years younger, at least; but it was evident from his manner and speech that his worldly experience was very wide.

All the time this conversation had been going on, we had been scudding along at as brisk a pace as Mouldy's slipslop boots would permit, up the Old Bailey and by Newgate, (where my companions having inquired whether I knew at which door they brought people out to hang 'em, and received from me an intimation that I did not, kindly paused for a moment to enlighten me,) out into Ludgate Street, and across the road into turnings and twistings dingier than any I had yet met with. Had it been daylight, the effect of perambulating such narrow, gloomy courts and alleys would have had anything but an enlivening effect on one's spirits; but, instead of daylight, it was pitchy dark; and when I reflected that every step I took carried me farther away from home—from that home which, miserable and cruel as it had been to me, my companions, who might be regarded as competent judges in such matters, had declared that I was a jolly fool for leaving,—I began to be filled with remorse, and tears forced themselves into my eyes. Had I been compelled to talk, I should undoubtedly have betrayed my emotion; but, as luck—good or bad—would have it, my companions had settled down to silence; indeed, the shuffling trot had begun to tell on them, leaving them no spare breath for conversation. So we sped along, I keeping a little in the rear, till at last we suddenly emerged from the dingy alleys and turned into the wide, gas-lit Strand.

CHAPTER XIII.

THE DARK ARCHES AND THE INHABITANTS THERE. I WITNESS A LARK, AS PERFORMED BY THEM. MY FIRST NIGHT'S LODGING IN A VAN.

LATE as it was—nearly eleven o'clock—there was plenty of noise and bustle, and so many people about, that it was as much as we could do to keep up the trot without danger of being knocked over, or at least of having our toes trod on.

"Come on," said Ripston, looking over his shoulder, "we're nearly there."

This remark cheered me considerably. Since we had turned into the Strand, I had been thinking what a beautiful part of the town Mouldy and the other boy lived in, or at least near, and how much I should like to live there too; but then followed the alarming thought that my companions were going "home"—home to their lodgings. They had told me so. I had not been invited to come with them; I had accompanied them voluntarily, and could expect nothing better than that they would presently turn into the house where they lodged, leaving me to get on as best I could. But Ripston had said, "Come on; we are nearly there." Nearly at his lodgings that meant, of course; and I was invited to come on.

I had lagged behind a good bit, partly because I was so very tired, and partly because a minute or so before somebody had trod on my left heel; but I responded to Ripston's invitation as cheerily as possible, and put my best leg foremost. All of a sudden, however, I missed both of them; they had vanished as completely as though they had melted.

Where were they? Perhaps I had run past them. It seemed hardly likely, careful as I had been to keep my eyes on them; but there was no other solution to the mystery.

I turned back a few paces, calling out their names, but nobody answered. I hurried on twenty yards or so, and called out "Ripston" as loud as I was able. Still no reply, and not a trace of them to be seen.

The depression that had fallen on me so heavily while we were making our way through the courts and alleys, and which the glare and liveliness of the highway had nearly dispelled, now returned with greater force than before. My dismal conviction was, that the boys had designedly given me the slip. They didn't like my company, and finding themselves so near home, they had not scrupled to cut me in this unceremonious manner. Perhaps even they had altogether misled me in telling me that they were going near to Covent Garden Market; for all I knew to the contrary, Covent Garden might be altogether another road—I might be miles farther away from it than when I started!

This last reflection was of so overwhelming a character, that I could no longer control my grief. I stepped off the path, and looked disconsolately this way and that down the long endless-looking road, and then I brought up against a lamp-post and began to give vent to my sorrow to a tune which, no doubt, had it been long persisted in would speedily have brought a mob round me.

Suddenly, however, to my great joy, a well recollected voice saluted my ears.

"Smiffield! where are you?"

Smithfield was not my name, but that was the place where my two friends had encountered me, and no doubt they gave me that name from knowing no other. Besides, it was Mouldy's voice, unmistakably.

"Here I am," I replied. "Where are you?"

"Here; don't you see?"

I did not see. The voice seemed to come out of one of the private doorways by the side of the shops just opposite to which I was standing, but which I could not for my life make out. Besides, that was the last place I should have thought of looking, not dreaming that my friends were respectable enough to occupy such splendid lodgings.

Presently, however, a boy darted out of one of the said doorways, for so it seemed, and seized me by the arm.

"Is that you, Mouldy?" I asked.

"'Course it's me," replied he, impatiently, and giving me a jerk forward. "Come on, if you're a-comin'."

I speedily discovered that it was not a private house into which Mouldy had pulled me, but a low and narrow passage, with a paving of cobblestones, just such as Fryingpan Alley was paved with. The air of the place blew against my face, damp and deadly cold, and it was so pitchy dark that to see even a foot before you was impossible. After permitting myself to be led into the frightful passage for a few yards, my terror brought me to a stand-still.

"Is this—this where you live, Mouldy?" I asked.

"Down here," answered he; "down here a good step yet. Come on; what are you frightened of?"

"It's so dark, Mouldy."

"I dessay—to coves wot always gets reg'lar wittles, and burn wax candles in their private bed-rooms; but we ain't so pertikler in these parts. Come on, or leave go my hand, and let me go."

I had him by the hand as tight as I could hold him. I didn't know what to do. Mouldy must have felt my arm tremble, I think.

"Lor', there's nothink to funk about, young 'un," said he, in almost a kind voice. "If we make haste we shall find a wan or a cart, with a good bit of dry straw to lay on. That hain't to be sneezed at, don't you know, on a cold night."

Thus encouraged, I allowed myself to be led farther into the dark, damp passage, which was so very steep and slippery with wet, that if I had had shoes on, I should have slipped forward a dozen times. What Mouldy meant by his allusion to carts and vans, and dry straw, I could not at all understand. If such things were to be found at the bottom of the dismal alley we were descending, they were not to be despised by a poor boy in want of a lodging; and, without doubt, I did want a lodging. Besides, it was very good on Mouldy's part to offer me, quite unsolicited, a share of his bed, humble though it was, and it would seem very unkind to refuse him. So screwing up my courage as I went, I kept up with Mouldy. Down and down, each moment the wind blowing in our faces colder and fouler. Presently we overtook Ripston, who began to growl at a fine rate at the long time we were in

coming, and to prognosticate that every cart and van would be full.

The pavement under our feet grew colder and muddier, and the wind more and more foul.

"Well, I d'n know," spoke Ripston, in the dark, "but it smells to me werry much like spring tides."

"Get out, you fool!" replied Mouldy; "spring tides is all over for this year. Don't you know the smell of a low tide from a high 'un? You oughter by this time."

"Ah! well, I s'pose it's the mud I smells," said Ripston.

"Where are we going?" I asked. "Where does this lead to?"

"Into the river, if we keep straight on," replied Ripston laughing.

"Into the river!"

"What do you want to funk him for?" interposed Mouldy, kindly. "Yes, Smiffield, it do lead into the river if we keep straight on; but we hain't a-goin' to keep straight on; we're goin' to turn off presently."

I was full of fright, and now only allowed myself to be led on, because had I turned to go back I would never have found my way. Besides, it was so dreadfully dark, and if I went back it would be alone. Mouldy still held my hand, and Ripston came on behind, singing a bit of a comic song he had heard that night in Shoreditch probably, and as unconcerned as though he was treading the most clean and cheerful of paths. By and by we turned out of the passage, and down a flight of steps; and when we had reached the bottom, Mouldy said—

"Here we are. Now, you take his t'other hand, Rip, or else he'll be runnin' agin something, and breakin' his legs."

"Lift your feet up, Smiffield," said Ripston; "if you kicks agin anything werry soft and warm, don't you stoop to pick it up, thinkin' it's a lady's muff or somethink; 'cos if you do, it'll bite yer."

"What will bite me?" I asked, most earnestly, wishing in my heart that I had remained all night in the pig market.

"Why, a rat," replied Ripston, maliciously enjoying my terror. "Bless you, they runs about here big as good-sized cats—don't they, Mouldy?"

"Don't you b'lieve him, Smiffield," said his friend; "'course there is rats, but they're jolly glad to get out of the way if they've got the chance, when they see you comin'."

"Oh, yes! they're good at gettin' out of the way, ain't they? Quite perlite; and stands up and makes bows and curtseys to you when you come their road, I shouldn't wonder!" sneered Ripston. "How about the old woman as they part eat the other night; eh, Mouldy? They wasn't werry perlite to her."

"You hold your jaw and come on, that's quite enough for you to do; or p'raps you might be made," replied Mouldy, threateningly; and Master Ripston, taking the hint, said no more.

It was a horrible place. How large, it was impossible to guess; but that it had reeking brick walls could be plainly made out by the light of the few glimmering tallow candles stuck here and there. These scarce scraps of candle were the only means of light, and each of them evidently was private property, and set up for the convenience of the individuals to whom it belonged, and who were lazily grouped about it.

About twenty yards from the spot at which we entered, there was one of these bits of candle stuck against the wall, supported by an old "corkscrew" knife, the screw being wedged in between the green wet bricks, and the broken blade serving as a candle-holder. The light was about three feet from the ground, and squatted in the reflection of it was a ragged and dirty old man, mending a boot. He had the lid of a fish-basket for a seat, and his tools were an old dinner fork and a bit of twine. The fork was for boring holes in the leather; and when he had made a hole, the old man would straighten the end of the twine between his lips, and hold up the dilapidated boot to the candlelight, the better to see where to make the hitch. He had spectacles on—at least a pair of rims, with one glass in—and certainly it did make a queer picture to see the old fellow puckering up his mouth, and with his head on one side, making the most of the solitary glass; his hand shaking so all the while, that even when he had spied the hole in which the twine was to go, he was quite half a minute before he could make good the stitch. Besides revealing him, the old man's candle shone on the wheel and side of a cart a few yards distant. The body of the cart was hidden in the darkness, but, as might be known by their laughing and scrambling, there were several boys in it, and they were amusing themselves by pelting the old man's candle with mud.

"It's old Daddy Riddle, isn't it?" observed Ripston, as the boys stopped for a moment to see the fun.

"Yes, the old beggar," replied Mouldy. "Serve him right. Ha! ha! See that, Smiffield?" (it was because a dab of mud struck the old man on the forehead that Mouldy laughed.) "Hain't it a lark?"

"Why does it serve him right? What has he done to them?" I asked.

"What's he done? Why, he's a miser," replied Mouldy, with much disgust. "They do say that all his money—hundreds and thousands, and all in gold—is hid under a stone somewheres under these arches. Lor' send we might fall acrost that stone—eh, Rip?"

But Ripston was otherwise engaged, and couldn't answer. A well-aimed lump of mud had knocked the boot out of the miser's hand just as he was succeeding in pushing his twine through a hole he had bored, and now he was on his hands and knees groping in the dark to find his old boot again. Such a roar of laughter arose from the cart where the boys were, as made the vaulted roof ring again, and Ripston laughed as loud as anybody.

"Do let me finish the job, there's good lads," exclaimed the old man, when he had found his property. "If you'll only leave off pelting just as long as I can put half-a-dozen more stitches, you shall have the candle to toss or play cards by, just as you like."

"All right, daddy; sing us another song, and we'll be mum as hysters," called some one from the cart.

"Well, well, what shall I sing you?"

"Jolly Nose," "Hot Codlings," "Tippity Witchit."

Hot codlings, however, were in a majority; and in his high, cracked, shaky voice the old man began the song, at the same time making the most of the truce time to finish his cobbling. When he had got through the first verse, and began the "Right tol tiddy-iddy" chorus, the boys joined in it, and just when the old man least expected it, a dab of mud was thrown, completely plastering over the solitary spectacle glass, and then another, extinguishing the candle against the wall with a hiss, and bringing it to the ground, while the mirth in the cart grew more uproarious than before.

"Come on," exclaimed Mouldy; "it's no use stopping here any longer; our wan's up at the furder end."

Catching tight hold on the tails of Mouldy's coat, I followed in his footsteps in the direction indicated.

Evidently he as well as his friend Ripston was used to the place; for while they stepped along without hesitation, I could scarcely put one foot before the other without slipping along the oozy floor, or running foul of cart-shafts and trace-chains, which the little light shed by the few candles failed to render distinguishable from the thick darkness. Besides, nobody's candle but the one by which the old "miser" (he was a poor old used-up Punch-and-Judy man, as I afterwards ascertained) was mending his boots, had a chance of showing much light about the place, each one being surrounded by a mob of boys and young men, squatting, some on the wet ground, and some on wisps of straw, playing cards or gambling with halfpence. As could be seen, some of the players had a bottle amongst them, and all were smoking short pipes, and swearing and laughing at a fine rate.

Presently we came to a standstill.

"Hold hard, Smiffield; this is our wan," said Mouldy; and the next instant I could hear him, although I could not see him, climbing the spokes of the waggon-wheel.

"How is it?" asked Ripston.

"All right," replied Mouldy, from the van.

"Up you goes, then," observed Ripston to me. "Here, put your foot on the spokes, and I'll give you a bunch up."

He did so. He "bunched" me so hard, that I was bundled hands and knees on to the floor of the vehicle.

As Ripston was climbing in, he was heard to sniff loudly. "I thought as how you said it was all right?" said he, addressing Mouldy, in a disappointed voice. "You hain't got no straw in there, I'll lay a farden."

"Not a mite," replied Mouldy.

"I know'd it," returned Ripston. "I know'd it as soon as my nose came acrost the wheel. 'Hallo!' thinks I, 'it's been coals to-day.' Jigger coals, I say;" and the young fellow floundered sulkily into the van.

"I should give warnin', if I was you Rip," observed Mouldy, playfully. "I should write to the cove as the wan belongs to, and tell him that if he can't keep off coals, and do nothink else 'cept move goods, so that there may alwis be a good whack of straw left in the wan, you cert'ny must change your lodgin's."

"It ain't on'y there bein' no straw," replied Ripston, savagely, "it's the jolly coal dust that gets up your nose when the wind blows underneath and up the cracks. What do you say, Smiffield?"

"Is this where we are goin' to sleep?"

"This is the crib, and you are welcome to share on it," replied Mouldy, hospitably.

"But whereabouts is the bed?" I asked.

"The *what?*" asked Mouldy.

"The bed. There *is* a bed, isn't there?"

"Oh, yes; a stunner; all stuffed choke full of goose's feathers, and a lot of pillars and blankets, and that. They're about here somewheres!" And Mouldy went round the van scraping with his foot. "Where *is* that bed, Rip?" continued he; "jiggered if I can find it."

Ripston, whose appreciation of his friend's fun was of the keenest, only laughed, without answering.

"Oh! ah! I recollect now, Smiffield!" said Mouldy, seriously; "it was seized with the rest of our furniture when we had the brokers in the other day. Get out with you! comin' and cockin' it over us with your talk about beds. Hark here! this is *our* bed"—and he rapped with his boot-heel on the boards—"if it ain't soft enough for you, get underneath; which it's mud up to your ankles."

"Don't you mind him," observed the softer-hearted Ripston, when he had had his laugh out; "it ain't so comfor'ble as in general, Smiffield, 'cos of the want of straw. Why, sometimes we finds as much straw in this wan as would fill—well, a sack I was goin' to say, but werry nigh. That's fine, don't you know! Just you fancy comin' in on a cold night, thinkin' what a precious miserable cove you are, and how you are a-goin' to get them aches agin in all the knobby parts of your bones wot presses agin the planks! You think this, and reg'ler in the blues you climbs up into your wan, and there you finds a whole lot of straw—dry straw mind you—and you've only got to rake it together, and bury your head and shoulders in it! Oh!"

And the bare recollection of the luxury made Ripston draw in his breath, with a noise as though he was sipping hot and delicious soup.

"But isn't it cold when you undress yourself?" I asked.

"Dunno," replied Ripston, shortly; "never tried it."

"Never tried undressing yourself to go to bed?"

"The last time I was undressed,—altogether, don't you know," said Ripston, "was—ah, last August, if I recollects right. It was when the plums was ripe, anyhow. You recollects the time, Mouldy; the werry last time we went into the Serpentine. Lor' bless your silly young eyes, Smiffield; if we was to go undressin' and coddlin' of ourselves up, what time do you think we should get up in the mornin'? We've got our livin' to get, don't you know?"

"We sha'n't be up very early to-morrow mornin' if we don't mind," yawned Mouldy; "it must be close upon twelve now. Come on; let's turn in if we're a-goin to."

"I'm ready," replied Ripston. "Stop a bit, though—who's a-goin' to be piller?"

I didn't know in the least what Ripston meant, so I took no notice of his question.

"There's alwis a shyness about bein' pillar when there ain't no straw," laughed Ripston.

"Will *you* be piller, Smiffield?" asked Mouldy.

I felt so perfectly wretched that I didn't care what I was; I told them so.

"Well, we don't want to be hard on you," observed Mouldy; "but now that there's three on us, we may as well enjoy ourselves. You haven't no call to be piller without you like, you know."

"It's all accordin' to what sort of a taste you've got," said Ripston; "some fellows don't care how cold they lay, so long as they lay soft. Other fellows are all t'other way, and 'ud sooner sleep in a brick-kil than anywheres. How do you like it, Smiffield?"

"I like to sleep warm, and soft as well," was my tearful answer.

"What! and both at once, I s'pose," sneered Mouldy. "I wish you might get it. If you're goin' to be piller, down with you; if you ain't, say so, and let somebody else. We don't want no snivellin' in our wan neither, so I can tell yer, jolly young watery head! I'm sorry as we was fools enough to take up with yer!"

I hastened as well as I was able to explain to Mouldy that I was crying because I couldn't help it, and not to give him offence. I assured him that I was quite willing to do anything to make things comfortable; and that if he would show me how to be pillow, I would go at it at once.

"It don't want no showing," replied Mouldy, somewhat mollified. "Piller's the one that lays down for the others to lay their heads on. There can't be anything plainer than that, can there? He's soft for their heads; and they keeps him warm. That squares it comfor'ble, don't yer see?"

"Here, out of the way," exclaimed Ripston, at the same time huddling down into a corner of the van; "don't let us have any more talk about it; I'm piller; come on."

"Now, you do as I do, Smiffield," exclaimed Mouldy, at the same time laying down. But to do as he did was impossible. In the greediest manner he monopolised the whole of Ripston's body, leaving no "piller" for my head to repose on but such as was afforded by Ripston's legs. But there was no use in grumbling, so down I lay.

"Do you feel like going to sleep right off, Rip?" asked Mouldy, after a silence of a few minutes.

"'Course I does; I was half off then, afore you spoke; don't *you* feel like goin' to sleep, Mouldy?"

"I never do somehow arter them combats. My eyes! fancy three coves a-breakin' into your ship like that, and you only with your shirt and trowsis, and a pair of cutlashes to defend yourself!"

"Yes, they puts things on the stage werry neat at that Shoreditch gaff," replied Ripston, sleepily; "good night."

"Good night."

There was another lull of about a minute's duration, and then Mouldy spoke again.

"Sleep, Rip?"

No answer.

"D'ye hear? Sleep, old Rip?"

"Gallus me if I'll be piller at all if you don't keep quiet," replied Ripston, savagely; "*now,* what's the matter?"

"I never see such a chap as you; you never likes to lay awake and talk about what you've seen," said Mouldy, in a conciliatory tone.

"Do you mean to say as you've woke a fellow up to tell him *that!*" said Ripston, with increased ferocity.

"I was on'y goin' to ask you a question, Rip. Do you think it was a *real* body which the robbers chucked down the well?"

"I'm certain on it; I see'd a hand of it through a hole in the sack," replied Ripston, maliciously.

"And do you think it was a reg'ler well, Rip; a reg'ler out-and-out well, right into the bowels of the earth, like Sir Gasper said it was ?"

"No doubt on it," responded Ripston.

"I didn't hear no splash," urged Mouldy.

"That was 'cos you listened too quick," said Ripston. "Bein' so precious deep, you couldn't 'spect to hear the splash all at once. I heard it about three minutes arterwards."

Mouldy breathed very hard, but made no reply. He continued to breathe hard for a considerable time, as though he had something on his mind. Presently he gently called Ripston again, but Ripston instantly began to snore in a manner that put all chance of waking him, by any means short of actual assault, quite out of the question. After a second attempt he desisted, and inclining his head towards me, whispered my name. But I was in no humour for conversation, and I, too, affected to be asleep, and made him no reply.

But I was not asleep by a very long way. With my cheek all wet with tears, as it lay pressing the calf of Ripston's leg, I remained awake thinking of my past career, the foolish step I had taken, and what were my prospects. How different might everything have been by this time, if I had only found pluck enough to have taken the thrashing that Mrs. Burke gave me, as I had taken thrashings almost if not quite as violent, dozens and scores of times! How much better it would have been, even, if when Jerry Pape seized me I had gone home, and once more faced my father and his terrible waist strap! By this time at least it would have been all over, and I should have been snug in my warm bed, in the back-room—snug in bed, and cuddling little Polly. No doubt I should have as yet not quite have done smarting; but at that moment it would have been difficult to have shown me a smart that I would not cheerfully have accepted and endured, the reward for which was that I should be immediately afterwards translated to Fryingpan Alley, with free admission at Number Nineteen, and all my iniquities forgiven.

Poor little Polly! I could not bear to think about her, and yet she was constantly uppermost in my mind. I am sure that the leg of Ripston's trousers must have been saturated with the tears that I shed, as I called to mind her sweet little ways—how pretty she looked when I dressed her up in the night and pretended that we were going a-walking, and how she would nestle down and kiss me when Mrs. Burke came in to bring her more bread and butter, and to wrongfully punch me about for eating the first lot.

Where was Polly now ? What was she doing ? Was she sound asleep—bless her little heart !— in the front-room, or was she at that very moment lying awake in my bed, in the back-room, and expecting me ?

Was she all right, as Jerry Pape had assured me she was ? How could I trust Jerry ? He had shown himself a treacherous rascal. Suppose that instead of looking as well as ever she had in her life—as Jerry had said—she was lying ill ! Perhaps that fall down the steps had broken her arms or legs, and she had them bound up with rags, and sticks of wood, as I had seen the limbs of the people who went in and out at the hospital gate, as I sat in the early part of the day keeping watch in the pig market !

Perhaps Polly was dead ! If such was the case,

then was my father's rage, and his extravagant offer of a shilling for my apprehension, accounted for. Now I came to think of it, Jerry Pape had shown a great deal of confusion when I asked him concerning my little sister. Perhaps Polly was dead, and Jerry knew it. Perhaps the tumble on the cobbled stones had killed her, and she was lying all alone in the room, quiet, and dead as Joe Jenkins's bullfinch !

This last reflection was of so terrible a nature that it stopped my tears, and set my thoughts in altogether a new channel—a very melancholy channel, as in it appeared my mother, with all the strange and terrible circumstances connected with her burial. So I lay awake in the dark until Mouldy was asleep, and snoring as contentedly as Ripston; and the card players and the lads that were tossing halfpence were interrupted in the midst of their wrangling, and cursing, and swearing, by the approach of heavy footsteps, and sent scuttling and climbing into the vans and carts, crying one to the other, "Dowse the glim ! here come the nippers."

That a nipper was a policeman, I well knew; and dreading that Mrs. Burke had placed her case in the hands of the station-house people, I was suddenly filled with a fright that put all my tender thoughts to the rout, and brought to the fore the whole reserve of my selfish solicitude for my own personal safety. As the regular tramping came nearer and nearer, I was so hard driven by apprehension as to be of a great mind to slip over the back of the van, and hide until the police had passed. How I now wished that I had accepted the proposition of my two friends, and become "pillow," so that they might be lying on and concealing me ! Tramp ! tramp ! not of one nipper, but of three at least, and coming straight up to our van ! Straight up, so that my limbs are all atremble, and my face wet with sweat instead of tears; and now the leading nipper hauls himself by the tail-board chain, and with his flashing bull's-eye lantern lights up the van, as though it were on fire.

But to my inexpressible relief he jumps down again without a word, and on the policemen go, talking about nobody's business but their own, till their tramping grows fainter and fainter still, and then dies away altogether, as does every other sound except the snoring of the sleepers and the squealing of the rats, till presently, and all unexpected, I drop into forgetfulness.

CHAPTER XIV.

IN WHICH I ENTER INTO PARTNERSHIP WITH MESSRS. RIPSTON AND MOULDY, AND AGREE TO DO AS THEY DO.

I WAS still sound asleep when the "pillow" wriggled himself away, and let my heavy head fall, with a tremendous bump, against the waggon floor.

Rubbing my eyes open, I perceived that Mouldy had already risen. In the semi-darkness, I could dimly make him out, sitting on the top ledge of the waggon side, yawning, and stirring his great crop of red hair with his fingers in a savage sort of way. For a few moments I felt altogether bewildered. It seemed to me but five minutes ago when the policeman had flashed his lantern light amongst us. Besides, I felt stiff and tired, and as though, as yet, I had had no sleep at all. Without considering the matter further, I curled up into the corner again, with my folded arms for a pillow.

"Now, Smiffield!" exclaimed Ripston, who was no doubt cramped, and excusably cross; "pull yourself together, without you means to stay here all day."

"But it isn't day yet," I grumbled. "How can it be day, when it's quite dark?"

"Oh! don't get a-askin' me none of your riddles. Get up and see if it isn't daylight. Why, it's sunshine. Get up here and have a look."

As he was speaking, Ripston had climbed up to where Mouldy was perched, and, with a little trouble, I, too, climbed up.

"Now, where's the sunshine?"

"Where? Why, on the river down there; see,"

All round about us was dark and dismal indeed; but looking in the direction in which Ripston was pointing, there could be made out what at first seemed like a ball of bright silver. As you looked, however, you found that it was nothing but a round hole, in at which the sun was pouring. It was a wonderful sight—better than any peepshow it had been my lot to see. Looking out at the bright hole, you could see the water of the river all trembling, and, as it were, a-light, and a little bit of blue sky, and a barge laden with hay leisurely floating by.

"Come on," said I, putting a leg over the side of the van.

"Come on where?" asked Mouldy.

"Down there where the sun is; it is better than stopping here in the dark."

"It is all werry well for them as likes it," replied Mouldy, in a surly tone. "If you likes it, you had better go to it."

"But ain't you goin' too—you and Ripston?"

"We are a-goin' to where we always goes," observed Ripston.

"Where's that?"

"Why, to Common Garden, to be sure. Where's the use of going down to the river?"

"Unless you've got a callin' that way, which p'r'aps you have," put in Mouldy.

"P'r'aps he's goin' a-tottin'," (picking up bones,) said Ripston.

"Much good might it do him!—a farden a pound when he gets 'em, and pelted by the barge coves, who puts it down that everybody as goes for a walk on the shore is arter priggin' coals. Are you goin' a-tottin', Smiffield?"

"No," I replied; "I don't know how."

"Then what caper *are* you up to?"

"Well, I ain't pertickler. All I want is, something to do to get me a livin'. Barkin' was what I was thinking of. It ain't such a bad way of gettin' a livin', is it?"

Mouldy looked at Ripston, and both boys laughed.

"You was thinkin' of barkin', oh!" said Mouldy. "What put barkin' into your head, Smiffield?"

"My father."

"Father a coster, then?"

"No; my father is a——isn't a coster."

"Did you ever bark for anybody?"

"Oh, no! Father's pal put me up to it. Never barked for anybody yet. I want to."

"How do you know you *can* bark?" asked Ripston.

"Because I've tried it."

"Well, cert'ny, you *are* a jolly liar! Why, you just said that you never had barked for nobody."

"More I haven't. I've tried it, though. I was trying it last night, in the market, when you come behind me."

"'Course he was," observed Mouldy. "Don't you 'member, Rip? Oh, yes! you've got a werry tidy voice for barkin', Smiffield; no mistake about that."

I was very glad to hear him say this.

"You think, then, that I should do at it, Mouldy?"

"How do yer mean—'do at it'?"

"Please the man what I worked for—earn my livin'."

"Well, you might please the man what you worked for, but as for earning your livin'"—and Mouldy finished his remark by jerking his thumb over his shoulder with a manner that was not to be misunderstood.

"It might suit some coves, don't yer know," he continued; "but it didn't suit *me*. Likewise it didn't suit Ripston."

"Then you've tried it?" I asked, with sinking spirits.

"'Course we have. There's very little we hain't tried—eh, Ripston? Yes, we've tried it, and so has a whole lot of chaps we knows; and what they say is just what we say, and that is, that you won't ketch 'em at it again. There! I'd sooner be a doctor's cove, and go about in a skillington suit with roly buttons. Wouldn't you, Rip?"

"A'most," replied Ripston. "It *is* a life! You're up in the mornin' afore you can see, and fust thing it's drivin' the barrow to market while the man what you works for walks on the path; then it's mindin' the barrow while he goes and buys and loads up; then it's home agin with it, and, if it's vegetables, washin' it and settin' of it out; then it's paddlin' about all day long a-hollerin' of it out."

"And that hain't all," said Mouldy. "S'pose it has been a bad day, and the stock's of a handy sort, what'll go in a basket—such as inguns for picklin', or turmut reddishes—out you go agin by yourself in the evenin', a-hawkin' and a-hollerin' of it, till there ain't no lights in the houses 'cept in the top winders, and it's too late to try any longer. And arter all, what'll you get? Why, your wittles. That's right—ain't it, Ripston?"

"'Cept about the wittles; them you don't always get."

This was not a little alarming. From the very first I had made up mind to become a barker; it was that resolution, indeed, and the fancy that it could be brought about so easily—provided I had any music in my voice—which had all along backed up my yearning to leave home. It was the conviction that I *had* got a musical voice, as was proved by my trials of it in the pig market at Smithfield, which had induced me to go along with Mouldy and the other boy as soon as I was given to understand that they were going near to Covent Garden. Nobody, however, had told me that a barker's life was a jolly one. The young man who had assisted at my father's marriage with Mrs. Burke had merely mentioned that he had taken to barking to escape from a job which

THE TRUE HISTORY OF A LITTLE RAGAMUFFIN.

to his mind, was worse than shoring oysters; and Mrs. Winkship had, after all, said very little in its praise. True, she had drawn a very nice picture of herself, with her silk handkerchief over her shoulders, and without a bonnet, and with half a sieve of ripe greengages under her arm, and making a pretty pocket by strolling round the squares with them on a summer's afternoon, and she had related the little incident to me while describing the particulars of the barking business; but really it had no more to do with barking than with bricklaying. Now here were two boys who had tried the trade of barking, and both of them had abandoned it in disgust. They had found something better to do. What was it?

"What do you chaps do for a livin'?" I asked.

"What do we do? Oh, anythink!" replied Mouldy, vaguely.

By this time we all three had got out of the van, and were making our way towards the passage through which we had come the night before.

"What do you mean by anythink?"

"Well, we picks it up," Ripston explained. "We keeps our eyes open, and when we sees a chance we grabs at it."

"Then you don't go at anything reg'ler?"

"Oh yes, we goes at *everythink* reg'ler," replied Mouldy, laughing. "It's no use bein' pertickler, don't you know; you're 'bliged to do it to pick a crust up. It's all chance work. Sometimes it'll run as high as roast pork—sittin' down to it, mind yer? not eatin' it goin' along—and another time it hain't a lump of bread from the time you turns out in the mornin' till you turns in again at night. It's all luck."

"Ah! but the best on it is, you never knows when the luck is goin' to change," interposed Ripston. "It's that wot keeps the pluck in you. You thinks that your luck is dead out, and that it is no use expectin' it ever to come back again; you turns round a corner, and steps into it slap up to your neck. Why, look on'y at yesterday arternoon! All day long not a mag;—no drop of coffee the fust thing; no breakfus', no dinner—no nothink, 'cept wegetables and that sweepin's! Mouldy he gets down on his luck—which you do, Mouldy, sooner than you ought sometimes—and ses he, 'Wot's the use of us a-prowlin' and a-shiverin' out here any longer, Rip? I thinks we'd better make our ways back to the 'Delphi; it's warmer there than out here.' 'Let's try a bit longer,' ses I; 'let's go round the market three times, and then if nothing don't turn up, we'll go home.' When, scarcely was the words out of my mouth, when somebody hollers, 'Hi!' and there was a gen'lman under the columade as wanted a cab fetched. Mouldy fetched it, which was sixpence for hisself, and a penny the cabman, made sevenpence. So there we was, you see! 'Stead of goin' miser'ble back to the arches, and having to wait p'r'aps three or four hours till your wan came in, there was fippence for grub, and tuppence for the gaff which you see us a-comin' from last night. We often goes to the gaff—don't we, Mouldy?"

"We goes to a benefit to-morrow night, if it can be made to run to it," Mouldy replied.

"Stunnin' piece out too, it is," said Ripston; "'The Wampire Captain; or, the Pirate of the Desert.' Leastways, it *oughter* to be a stunnin' *piece, from the name it's got.*"

"Names is nothink," observed Mouldy. "Look at 'Bleareye, the Bloodsucker,' wot we went to see—wot we went without a bit of wittles all day long to see; and wot did it turn out? Why, Bleareye wasn't a bloodsucker at all; he was on'y a common sort of a cove as lent money a-purpose to ruin young lords, and bring 'em to the work'us. Jigger such pieces as that!"

"Did you ever see a play, Smiffield?" asked Ripston.

"Only in a show," I replied.

"What? a carrywan what a horse draws, I s'pose! It's werry little you knows about plays then, Smiffield," said Ripston, laughing contemptuously. "The place where we go is a *reg'ler* theatre, don't yer know—reg'ler stage, and fightin' with real swords, and characters dressed up real—all welvet, and gold, and diamonds—and blue fire, and that! You ought to go, Smiffield, if you've never been."

By this time we had got out into the Strand, which was very quiet, as well it might be, for just then the churches chimed out five o'clock. Then Mouldy brought us to a stand-still.

"Look here," said he to me; "afore we goes any furder, how are we goin' on? Are you goin' down to the river, or to Common Garden along with me and Ripston?"

"I should like to go with you, if you'll let me."

"Let you! there ain't no lettin's in it. Common Garden is as free to you as to us. The thing is, how are you goin' to work?"

"I don't know anything about the work, let alone how I am goin' to do it," I replied; "that's what I want to go with you for, so that you might put me in the way of it."

"What Mouldy means," observed Ripston, "is this—are you goin' to work on your own hook, or are you goin' pardeners with us?"

Such an offer, under the circumstances, was of course extremely welcome.

"I should like to go pardeners," I replied; "and you are good sorts of fellows to ask it of me."

"Reg'ler pardeners, don't you know," said Ripston, in a whisper; "you works with us, and you grubs with us, and you lodges with us!"

"I understand."

"Fact, you are willin' to go with us, and do 'zactly what we do?" said Mouldy impressively.

"Yes."

"Whack all you finds, or gets, or haves give you," said Ripston, with the utmost gravity; "never sneak off and spend nothink unbeknown!"

"Never. 'Tisn't likely."

"Whenever the beadle catches you, you agree to take your gruel, and never split on your pals; even though splitting would get you off. You agrees to all that?"

"All of it," I replied; although, to tell the truth, I was not quite clear as to some of the terms proposed by Mouldy.

"You'll stick fast to us, and never funk nor flinch?"

"Never."

"Then shake hands," said Mouldy. "Now shake hands with Ripston: now we're pardeners. Come along, and let's get to business at once."

CHAPTER XV.

IN WHICH THE TRUE NATURE OF THE BUSINESS OF OUR FIRM IS MADE APPARENT, AND I BECOME A THIEF FOR THE SAKE OF A PEN'ORTH OF HOT PUDDING.

THERE was no use in hanging back. To think of returning home after being absent a day and a night was altogether more than I dare attempt.

I was in for it, and must make the best of it. According to their own showing, the life led by Mouldy and Ripston was not a particularly hard one,—no harder, at least, and in respect of victuals, than I was well used and seasoned to. Not so hard. The "lump of bread" that my partners seemed to think such hard fare was the best I had got during the past three months; and the roast pork, never. They roamed about as they liked, and where they liked; they had nobody to whack 'em; they had all that they earned to spend and do as they pleased with; and they went to the play. All things considered, it appeared very lucky that I had fallen in with a pair of such jolly fellows; and luckier still, that they had taken to me so kindly. The lodging was the worst part of it. True, I had at present only tried it without straw; and even as it was, after one night's trial, I felt merely a little stiffish, but all right in the main, and should by and by grow quite used to it.

These and kindred reflections occupied my mind until we reached Covent Garden. Here we found business brisk enough, though Mouldy declared that we were at least an hour later than we ought to have been. We didn't enter the covered part of the market, but sauntered about the outskirts of it, where the carts and barrows were being laden. We wandered about in this way for so long a time, that I began to wonder when we were going to begin a job. I was about to ask the question, when Ripston darted away from us, and towards a man who stood holding up his finger by a pile of lettuces.

"Where's Ripston gone?" I asked.

"Gone to work. Didn't you see that cove with his finger held up? That means a job for a boy; if he had held up two fingers, he would have meant that it was a man wot he wanted. Don't you never go when you see two fingers held up, Smiffield, else you might get a knot chucked at you, or something. One finger is what you've got to look out for. The job what Rip's got will get us the coffee; now, if we can find summat else while he's a-doin' of it, that'll be the tommy; which I hopes we shall, 'cos coffee wirout tommy don't make much of a breakfus'. So keep your eyes open, Smiffield."

So I did; but nobody held up his finger—at least, as far as I could make out; and Mouldy was not a bit luckier. In about twenty minutes we made our way towards Bow Street, to a coffee-stall which stood at market end of it; and, after a few minutes' waiting, Ripston made his appearance.

"What luck, Rip?" asked Mouldy.

"Threeha'pence. How have you been doin'?"

Mouldy replied by shrugging his shoulders dismally.

"And Smiffield the same?"

"Jes the same."

"Come on, then. Shall we have our coffee now, or wait till we takes a brown or two, and have somethin' to eat with it?"

"Have it now, I say," replied Mouldy, "I feel reg'ler perished for wants of it. What do you say, Smiffield?"

I was quite inclined to agree with Mouldy's proposition. What with going so short of victuals, and getting up so early in the morning, I began to experience a strange sort of sensation, which I suppose was of the same sort with Mouldy's. I think I never felt so starved and chilly before. So we went to the coffee-stall, and Ripston ordered three ha'p'orths of coffee, which we had in three separate cups, and which was deliciously hot and sweet, though not over strong. When we had drank it, feeling very much refreshed, we turned to again to look for a job.

But our luck didn't seem to better. Hour after hour we tried, but nothing turned up. We scoured the vegetable market through and through and worked in and out of the fruit market in every direction. I should have been ashamed, only that Mouldy did not get on any better than I did; neither did Ripston, except for that first threehalfpence. Another thing that kept me from taking my failure so very much to heart was, that both my companions appeared to be by no means low-spirited; they went cheerily about, cracking their jokes and larking amongst the stalls, as though their bread was already buttered, and only awaited their eating when they were tired of strolling about. About ten o'clock in the morning we quitted the market, and made our way through several back streets and alleys to Drury Lane.

"Well, Smiffield," said Mouldy, "how do you like bein' a pardener? Do you think you shall like to keep on with it?"

"I shall like to keep on with it if we have a little better luck," I replied; "we haven't done much this morning, Mouldy."

"We might ha' done wuss," observed Ripston, "considerin' how jolly late it was afore we begun."

"I believe yer," said Mouldy. "I haven't done so bad; you ought to have done werry well, too, Smiffield."

This I naturally took to be a little joke of Mouldy's, so I laughed as I answered him—

"Oh, yes, I've done splendid; just about as well as you have, Mouldy."

At this my partners winked and laughed too, and we trotted up Drury Lane, merry as crickets. Presently we came to the entrance to a dingy alley somewhere near Little Wild Street, and there we stopped.

"Come on," whispered Mouldy, first looking up and down to see that we were not observed; "tip up, Smiffield."

"Tip up!" I repeated, in amazement, seeing that he as well as Ripston were looking perfectly serious.

"Fork out," said the boy last mentioned, nudging me impatiently; "not all at once; just a few at a time. Here you are; I'll stand before yer."

"I 'spect it's chiefly in new taters," observed Mouldy; "I twigg'd you rubbin' puty close to the sieves—closer than I'd ha' liked to rub. Come on, out with 'em; they're scarce as yet, and will fetch somethink, though nuts pays better, when you come across 'em."

"I don't know what you are talking about," I answered. "I haven't got no new taters."

"Well, let us have it, whatever it is," said Ripston; "the old man wot we deals with lives up here."

I couldn't in the least make out what my partners meant; especially as they pointed to the pockets of my jacket and trousers as they spoke; and presently Mouldy commenced to stroke me down on every side. The result didn't appear to afford him a great amount of satisfaction, judging from the increasing anger of his countenance, and the air of disgust with which he turned to Ripston.

"Ho! ho!" he laughed savagely; "here's a pardener! here's a stunnin' pardener for yer!"

"Wot's the matter with him?" asked Ripston, evidently suspecting what was the true state of the case, but loath to give credit to so preposterous a thing.

"The matter? Why, he hain't got a blessed thing! Not so much even as a goosgog! That's what's the matter."

And for several seconds both my partners stood regarding me in reproachful silence.

"And you calls that stickin' to us!—doin' as we do!" remarked Ripston; "well, you *are* a sort."

"Well, so I did stick to you," I replied; "I'm sure I looked out all I could. If nobody wanted nothink carryin', how could I help it?"

"Yah!" sneered Mouldy, with the utterest contempt.

"I didn't have any money to buy goosgogs," I continued, in explanation; "nor yet to buy new taters, nor anythink. You know'd that I didn't have any money, didn't you?"

"We didn't know you was a jolly fool."

"Besides, if I had got a penny, I shouldn't have bought some goosgogs with it, I can tell you," said I; "I should have bought some bread at breakfus' time."

I never in my life saw a more ferocious face than that of Mouldy's as, on hearing my explanation, he turned towards me. His wrath was altogether too great for speech; so after glaring at me for a moment, he growled deeply, and turning away, looked up the street.

Ripston laughed.

"Don't get out of temper, Mouldy," said he; "Smiffield's green, that's wot it is. See here, Smiffield."

So saying, he took from his jacket pocket, one after the other, seven lovely apples; and then he invited me to peep into his trousers' pockets. I did so. One of them was full of almond nuts, and the other of Spanish nuts.

"My eyes, Smiffield!" said Ripston; "wot a lot of money they must have cost me, mustn't they?"

"But why did you buy nuts and apples?" I asked, in bewilderment.

"Well, I bought 'em to sell agin' don't yer see,' replied Ripston, his whole face, excepting his eyes, perfectly serious; "I deals in 'em."

"When did you buy 'em? I didn't see you."

"Nor did the cove as belonged to 'em. He was servin' somebody else at the time, and I thought he wouldn't like to be disturbed; so I served myself, and didn't wait to have 'em put in a bag. *Now*, do you twig?"

I began to fear that I did. I say, fear; for though I had known Mrs. Burke to be guilty of shameless swindling as regards my father's money, I don't think she would have given her countenance to downright stealing. Neither would my father; as witness the terrible thrashing he gave me when he was led to believe that I had purloined that half-crown. Still, however, I did not like to confess that I did "twig," as Ripston put it, for fear I might be mistaken.

"Yah! you might as well tickle a milestone, and 'spect it to larf, as to try and 'int anythink to him," sneered Mouldy. "Look here, young Smiffield, you see them apples and nuts wot Ripston's got? Well, he nailed 'em! prigged 'em! stole 'em!—is that plain enough for yer! Look here, again," (he opened the mouth of a sort of roundabout pocket in his jacket,) "here's some wot *I* nailed, and I'm jolly sorry that I didn't find the chance to nail some more. Now we're going up this alley to sell our stock, and to buy some wittles with the money."

I don't pretend that I was a particularly sensitive or squeamish sort of boy, even at that time; but really there was something about Mouldy's blunt and brutal assertion that he was a thief that shocked me very much.

"Good Lor'! what a lot to snivel about!" exclaimed Mouldy, mockingly. "You didn't take us for Sunday-school kids, wot minds wot their katekisims and their colicks tells 'm? You was werry much mistaken if you did."

"P'r'aps you, wot's got a home," put in Ripston, with polite sarcasm—"p'r'aps you, wot's got a home as you ran away from, and can run back to when you finds it convenient, can afford to be a little more pertickler. There's one good thing for yer to think on, Smiffield—you ain't in the least 'bliged to have any of the puddin' what we're a-goin' to buy presently. You are a werry good little boy, and are free to hook it as soon as ever you like."

"Which the sooner it is, the better, p'r'aps," observed Mouldy, with an ugly scowl.

And disdaining further conversation with me, they turned about and went up the alley, leaving me standing in the road.

And, indeed, there I was, as Ripton had vulgarly but forcibly expressed it, "free to hook it." If my object was simply to amuse the reader, I should perhaps have refrained from making mention of this important circumstance; but as it is my true history, I have no choice but to relate it. There I was, free to run away. I had tasted a vagabond life; I had unwittingly fallen in with thieves; had eaten, and drank, and slept with them; but, my lucky star prevailing, I had found them out in time, and while I was still an honest boy. It was my chance. I am fully aware of it; and if any one is disposed to accuse me of walking into sin with my eyes open, I have nothing to say in my defence. I humbly confess that my proper course would have been to have screwed up courage and run home. I didn't know the way, it is true; but I could easily have inquired, braving everything. But, ladies and gentlemen, pray bear in mind the peculiarity of my position, and let it weigh with you in your judgment. I was as miserable as the most severe amongst you could have desired, I do assure you. When I thought on how I had met Mouldy and Ripston; how they had invited me home to share their van; how I had slept with them, and talked with them, and shared their coffee,—when I reviewed these hard facts, and, setting them on one side, faced them with the horrid confession the boys had just made to me, the result was that my very ears tingled with shame. I had at least the consolation of knowing that when I took their ha'p'orth of coffee I thought them honest lads, and, further, of being in a position to prove, if necessary, that the money with which it was bought had been honestly earned of the lettuce dealer.

Did I run? I did not. Neither did I, having weighed the facts of the case deliberately, resolve to wait until Mouldy and Ripston re-appeared, and then make up to them again. It would be more correct to say that the balance of my mind was brought to a dead level, and I was inclined neither one way nor the other; and so I stood still. It was terrible to think that the two boys were thieves—indeed, that was the great weight in the scale of good resolution; but, alas! there was another great weight that at least counterbalanced it—my hunger. I was shivering and empty, and Ripston had distinctly said that he was presently going to buy some pudding, a share of which I was not obliged to take unless I liked, clearly enough implying that if I *did* like I might take it. Like a share of pudding! Once more, ladies and gentlemen, I venture to bespeak your merciful consideration to this part of my great temptation. In your ignorance of ragamuffinish ways, you probably underrate the inducement to my stopping. You, of course, know much more about pudding than I did—then at least; you, probably, are aware of twenty sorts or more, some so delicious and of such expensive make that every mouthful costs a shilling; but amongst them all you don't know of one single serving of which would be worth a moment's thought under the circumstances. In answer to this, I make bold to say, that in the first place, you are incapable of understanding the said "circumstances" even. You may have felt shivery, and, perhaps, hungry; but as regards shivering, there is a certain sensation common amongst supperless, out-of-door sleepers, who go breakfastless, and see no prospect of dinner—a peculiar and indescribable numbness of the extremities, and a perpetual ague *within*, compared with which *your* shivering is as nothing at all. Then as to the pudding, you may know of fifty sorts, and yet not of that one which I knew Ripston alluded to; indeed, he could have meant no other, as this one sort is all that is known at the pudding shops of ragamuffin districts. The nearest approach to it within your knowledge is plain suet pudding, inasmuch as it quite plain, and there is suet in it. What else beside suet—and flour—I am not in a position to state; but it is something mysteriously filling; something that holds the heat in such a wonderful way, that the lump you buy continues to warm your hands as you walk along in the cold, until you put the very last piece in your mouth; something that swells a pudding out, so that the piece you get for a penny is as big as any four ordinary dinner-table "servings" of a same-named article—a lump as big as the fourth part of a brick. Just imagine it! Just imagine the picture of a lump of pudding as big as the fourth part of a brick—hot, bear in mind, and of a flavour and quality well known and appreciated—floating before the mind's eye of a weak-minded little hungry vaga-

bond such as I was! Presently I spied Ripston and Mouldy coming back up the court.

There was a great flour-waggon standing at a baker's door close at hand, and behind this I dodged without being seen by them. They seemed very jolly. Ripston had his hands plunged deep into the pockets that had lately held the nuts, and Mouldy was throwing up and catching four or five penny pieces. When they arrived at the top of the alley, they looked about from left to right, and Ripston gave a whistle. No doubt they were looking for me, and that the whistle was meant to attract my attention should I happen to be in the neighbourhood. I kept close behind the wheel, however, and they saw nothing of me, and went down the street laughing.

I crossed over the way, and watched them.

They went along, talking and laughing, until they got nearly to Long Acre, where there was a pudding shop; and while Mouldy went in, Ripston stood outside looking through the window. Presently Mouldy came out with such a pile of pudding of the sort just described, smoking on a cabbage-leaf, as made me draw in my breath to see. It seemed a very cold breath that I drew, and it made me feel more shivery and empty than ever.

I made my way over to their side of the road, and walked a goodish way behind them; not so far, however, but that I could see Ripston take one of the big slices, and raising it to his mouth, bite out of it a bit—ah! ever so large. He kept on raising it and biting it; (you may judge from this, and considering what sort of bites they were, how large were the pen'orths), and I got closer to them. I was dreadfully hungry.

I at last got so close behind them, that I could actually *hear* them eating. I could hear Ripston drawing his breath to and fro to cool the mouthful, and as he now and then turned his head aside I could see the contentment in his eyes.

When they commenced, there were but five lumps on the cabbage-leaf, and they were each well advanced with their second lump. If I *meant* to speak, there was no time to lose.

"What I likes Blinkins's puddin' for is, 'cos of the whackin' lot of suet wot's in it," observed Ripston.

"I b'lieve yer," replied Mouldy, licking his lips; "it's a'most like meat puddin'."

"I feels as though I'd had a'most enough; it's so jolly fillin'," said Ripston.

"Oh, well! don't you go a over-eatin' yourself," laughed Mouldy; "I can eat this other bit."

I could stand it no longer.

"Mouldy!" I exclaimed, laying a hand on his shoulder; "Mouldy, give us a bit!"

Mouldy gave a very violent start as I so quietly touched him, and wriggled downward; he, however, speedily recovered from his fright.

"Oh, it's you, is it!" said he. "Where a' you been? Been home to see if they'll take yer back, and they won't?"

"P'r'aps he's been back to the market to split on us. Have you, Smiffield?"

"I haven't been anywheres; I've been followin' you two," I humbly replied.

"Werry kind on yer; but we don't want anybody a-follerin' us—'specially sneaks," said Mouldy.

"I ain't a sneak, Mouldy," I replied; "do give

us a bit, that's a good fellow; if you know'd how gallus hungry I am, you would, I know."

"I'd be werry sorry to," said the merciless rascal, tantalisingly whipping the last bit of his second lump into his mouth; "don't yer know what the little 'im ses about keeping yer hands from pickin' and stealin'? I'm ashamed on yer askin' me to do such a wicked thing, Smiffield. If I was to give you a bit it 'ud choke yer."

"You agreed that we should go whacks in everything," I pleaded, appealing to his sense of justice, since I could not succeed in touching his generosity.

"So I meant it; so I means it now," replied Mouldy; "but you wants your share o' the puddin' wirout doin' your share o' the priggin', which it hain't wery likely you'll get. What do *you* say, Rip?"

"P'r'aps he didn't quite twig our game, Mouldy," replied Ripston, who, without doubt, was the most kind-hearted of the two. "P'r'aps if we'd ha' told him wot we was up to, he would ha' done different. Would you, Smiffield?"

As Ripston began to speak, he gave me the last remaining little piece of his second lump of pudding, and I just swallowed it in time to answer him. What a mouthful that was! Never in all my life, at Blinkins's or elsewhere, did I ever taste anything like it. So warm, so savoury, so comforting! And there still reposed upon the cabbage-leaf, on Mouldy's palm, a smoking piece that would have yielded ten such mouthfuls at least.

"*Would* you have done different, Smiffield?"

Just as he repeated the question, Mouldy was in the act of raising the last slice to his lips; but, nudged by Ripston, he paused—with his mouth open.

Should he eat that pudding or should I? It was plain that my answer would decide the momentous question. Excepting the scanty supper I had bought with that twopence the night before, I had eaten nothing since yesterday's breakfast.

"You are right, Ripston," I replied, loudly and boldly; "I *would* have done different."

"Ah! but, now you *do* know, *will* you do different?—that's the question."

"I will," I answered.

"When?" asked Mouldy.

"Now—as soon as ever I find a chance."

"Then, that'll do," observed Ripston; "give him that lump of puddin', Mouldy; he do look awful hungry."

"Don't you be in such a precious hurry," answered Mouldy. "Here it is; *I* hain't a-goin' to eat it," (here he slipped it into his roundabout pocket;) "but, afore he haves it, he's got to earn it. He's got to show us that what he ses he means. Come on."

"Come on where?" asked Ripston.

"Back to Common Garden."

Keeping close to the pudding side of Mouldy, I kept pace with my companions, with a certainty of the sort of business that was expected of me, and, as I am bound to confess, with but a faint disposition to shirk it. Arrived at the skirts of the market, we halted, and Mouldy took a survey.

"Come here, Smiffield," said he, presently.

Bold as brass I responded.

"You see that first stall atween the pillars— the one where the man with the blue apron is, and the baskets of nuts are standin' all of a row?"

"Yes, I see them."

"The first basket at the furder end is almonds. Off you goes; we'll wait here."

This was all Mouldy said, but his meaning was plain enough. I was to go and steal some almonds out of the farthest basket. That the pudding in Mouldy's pocket should be mine, I had steadfastly made up my mind; how to get it was all that remained to consider. Mouldy pointed out the way, and without hesitation, but with my heart going "bump! bump!" I set off towards the nut-stall.

This side the stall was one piled with cauliflowers and rhubarb, and as I approached, I saw at a glance that my best plan was to get round to the back of the cauliflowers, by which means I might reach the almond basket from behind. There is a saying that the devil is seldom ill-disposed towards his young friends, and certainly the saying was verified in my case. Between the cauliflower-stall and the nut-stall there was a narrow passage, through which nobody but the stallkeeper had any business to pass; but, shutting my eyes to the danger, I walked in as though I lived there, and, crouching behind the cauliflowers, saw the nut merchant, whose back was towards me, talking to a customer. The cauliflower woman had her back towards me too, and was not likely to shift her position just at present, for she was sitting on a chair, taking her dinner off her lap.

There was the brimming nut basket, and nobody was looking. I dipped once—twice—thrice, filling my trousers pockets, and then started out at the passage, and made towards Mouldy and Ripston, who were lurking behind a pillar.

"Come on, Smiffield!" exclaimed Mouldy, as I approached, and speaking in a voice quite different to that in which he had before addressed me; "come along, old boy! I've seen quite enough to tell me the sort of cove *you* are! *You* a green hand! You tell that to fellers as don't know what's o'clock. Here, ketch hold of the puddin'; I wish it was double as big."

I didn't think I had done anything like a clever thing till Mouldy made such a fuss about it; and that he was in earnest was certain, more from his manner than his speech. As I walked by his side, he scarcely once took eyes off me the whole time I was devouring the pudding, but kept on jerking his head as though his admiration was too deep to be expressed in words.

"I couldn't have done it half as clean—nor yet a quarter," said Ripston.

"*You!*" replied Mouldy, laying a stress on the word which must have been very hurtful to his friend's feelings; "you ain't bad in your way, Ripston; but when you sets up to be a quarter—ah! or a half a quarter—as clever at nailin' as Smiffield has showed hisself, it on'y shows what a bounceable sort of cove you must be. Why, *I* couldn't have pinched them almonds as clean as Smiffield did—not if you give me a week to practise in! Not but what there *are* things," continued Mouldy, afraid, I suppose, that he might lead me to think too much of myself, "which I dessay I could beat his head off at."

CHAPTER XVI.

IN WHICH MOULDY TALKS LEGALLY, AND EXPLAINS
FOR MY COMFORT THE DIFFERENCE BETWEEN
"THIEVING" AND "TAKING."

IT was all very well while the daylight lasted,
and the comfortable inward sensation derived
from a bellyful of pudding continued to make itself felt, (the almonds that I stole fetched twopence of the man in Coal Yard;) but when
night set in, and I once more found myself lying
in the dark van with nothing to do but to go to
sleep, I began to feel most acutely the stings of
conscience consequent on my evil behaviour
through the day.

I was now a thief! There was no use in endeavouring to evade or mitigate the terrible truth
—I was a thief! I had deliberately stolen a pint
of almond nuts—stolen, run away with, sold
them, and spent the money they fetched! Mouldy was "pillow" on this occasion, and as a tribute, I suppose, to my skill, I was allowed to
"pick my part;" so I lay with my head on Mouldy's breast, whilst Ripston occupied his legs'
end.

But despite this great advantage, I couldn't
sleep. All my pulses seemed to beat to the
mental utterance of that dreadful word "thief!"
Thief! thief! thief! thief! My heart, my temples, my hands and feet equally complained of it,
and I could get no rest at all.

"A thief!" I at last involuntarily whispered.

I had thought that Mouldy was asleep, but he
was not.

"Who's a thief?" he asked.

The abruptness of the question startled me
considerably, but I was too full of the woeful
theme to be started away from it; indeed, in my
bitter remorse I think that I felt rather glad than
otherwise of an opportunity of accusing myself.

"I'm a thief, Mouldy," I answered.

"Well, who said that you warn't?" replied
Mouldy, snappishly.

"But I am, Mouldy; I am."

"'Course you are. No need to be so jolly
proud on it, Smiffield. You are a thief, if it's
worth while callin' such jobs as we seed you doin'
to-day, thievin'; which I don't."

"But I never was a thief before, Mouldy," I
replied, earnestly. "I never was; and that's as
true as I'm layin' here alive. It's that wot makes
me so precious miserable."

"Gammon!"

The word was uttered by Ripston, who, it
seemed, like Mouldy, was lying awake.

"It isn't gammon, Rip; it's quite true," I sor-
rowfully replied. "I wish it was gammon."

"You're afraid to say 'Strike me dead if it
is!'" said Ripston.

"I am not," I replied. And I said it.

"'Course he can say it," observed Mouldy;
"and so he can say 'Strike him dead if he is,'
even now, if anybody asks him."

"I should be afraid of bein' struck dead if I
did, Mouldy," I replied.

"Why would you?"

"Because now I am a thief."

"Oh, no, you hain't," said Mouldy, shaking his
head, as though his opinion on the subject was
deeply rooted. "What you did to-day wasn't
thievin'; not by a werry long ways."

"'Course it wasn't," chimed in Ripston, with
equal earnestness.

"Well, then," said I, "what was it?"

"Well, I don't know 'zactly what it's called;
all I knows about it is, that it ain't reg'ler out-
and-out thievin'."

I shook my head doubtingly, and I suppose
that Mouldy felt the movement.

"Don't believe me; arks the law," he continued. "When did ever you hear of a case like
yours bein' put in the newspapers?"

"That's how to look at it," pursued Ripston.
"When did anybody ever hear of a cove bein'
took afore the beaks at Bow Street for it? It's
the beadle wot settles it. And wot's a beadle
when the law looks at him? Why, he's frightened of a p'liceman hisself. 'Taint likely as the
law would let a beadle settle thievin' cases—now,
is it?"

"Then what's the beadle put there for?"

"What for? Why, I've told you what for.
To settle things—things wot ain't right, to come
to the rights on it—and wot ain't thievin'. That's
wot he carries that cane for."

"Takin' what ain't yours is thievin'; at least
that's what I've always heard say," I replied.

"I knows all about that," replied Mouldy, raising his head on his hand, the more conveniently
to discuss the interesting subject; "they do say
so, but that's their iggerance; they never tried
it, so they can't be 'spected to know any better.
Look here, Smiffield, it lays this way—If a cove
walked into one of them shops in Common Garden
market, and helped hisself out of the till, and
they caught him a-doin' of it, that 'ud be thievin';
if he dipped his hand into the pocket of any lady
or gen'lman wot come to buy flowers and that,
and they caught him a-doin' of it, that 'ud be
thievin'; and so the beak as you was took afore
'ud jolly soon give you to understand. But if a
feller—a hard-up feller, don't yer know—as has
been tryin' to pick up his 'a'pence in a honest
sort of a manner, if he is found with a few apples
or nuts as doesn't happen to belong to him, the
salesman wot they do belong to gives him a clout
or a kick, else he calls the beadle, and he lays
into him with his cane, and then lets him go.
Why, if the beadle was to take one of us afore
the beak, he'd get pitched into for takin' up the
beak's waluable time, and p'r'aps get the sack."

Without doubt, Mouldy spoke as though he
meant what he said; or if he did not, it was very
kind of him to pretend so earnestly in order to
make my mind easy. It was equally kind of
Ripston for so heartily backing him; but, somehow, all that they said didn't lift the new and
strange weight off my conscience. It may have
padded it a bit, so that it sat easier; but lift it
off it certainly did not.

"Well, if takin' things—nuts and that—isn't
stealin', what is it?" I asked of Mouldy.

"Oh, all sorts o' things: prowlin', sneaking,
makin'."

"Pinchin' findin', gleanin', some coves calls
it," put in Ripston; "but, Lor'! wot's the odds
how yer call it?"

"'Spose now a p'liceman was asked," I urged,
"what name would he give it?"

"Oh, ah! who'd think of arstin' such jolly
liars as wot the perlice is?" replied Ripston.

"Fact is, Smiffield, you're funkin'; that's what
you're a-doin' of," said Mouldy. "The 'greement

was, that you wouldn't funk; and here you are, chockful of it."

"Not exactly funkin'," I replied. "If it ain't thievin', it's all right. I thought that it was."

"Bless you, when you gets as old as I am, you'll know better 'un to take fright at words," said Mouldy. "Why, when I was a kid, and lived at home with my old 'oman, I've set and I've heerd the old man a-readin' the newspaper to her; and you wouldn't believe how jolly careful even such artful coves as lawyers are 'bliged to be about the names they give things. Unless a chap is bowl'd out in right down reg'ler priggin', they dursn't call him a thief. They comes it mild, and calls it ' 'bezelment,' or 'petty larsny.' Why, it's no wus than petty larsny if a cove nails a loaf off a baker's counter; and as for 'bezelment!—my eyes, Smiffield!—if you calls sneakin' a handful of nuts thievin', I suppose you'd call what the law calls 'bezelment, highway robbery! 'Sides, s'pose it *was* as bad as 'bezelment, what 'ud you get for it? Ripston 'bezeled a milk-can once, and on'y got fourteen days for it. Didn't you, Ripston?"

"Ripston don't want *that* chucked in his face," waspishly replied the person alluded to. "If we comes to rakin's up of private histories, p'r'aps I might know coves wot had got more 'un fourteen days, not to speak of private whippin's. Howsomever, I won't mention no names. If the cap fits the cove I means, he'd better hold his jaw; that's all I've got to say."

Mouldy was evidently the "cove" hinted at, for he only further made some muttered remark about Ripston being a disagreeable beggar, and then, after a little commonplace conversation, (during which Mouldy and Ripston became reconciled,) my two partners dropped off to sleep.

But, as on the preceding night, I had a bad time of it before I could get to sleep. The arguments used by my companions had failed to convince me. Besides, the abrupt termination to our discourse on the matter, and the nature of the remark that had induced it, was not lost on me. Private whipping and imprisonment for a fortnight was never visited on boys whose ways were as simple as Mouldy and Ripston would make me believe theirs were. True, I didn't know anything of the fine distinctions of the law, and it was very probable that snatching a few nuts was *not* a felony. Anyhow, I was quite satisfied to admit the probability; but, come what might, I would never do anything of the kind again. What I *would* do, I couldn't quite make up my mind. I must get my living somehow. I must tell Mouldy and Ripston in the morning that I meant to be quite honest, to avoid all acts of that sort, and live by picking up jobs in Covent Garden market; and that if they didn't like to keep my company, I couldn't help it. I got so well into my mind that this was what I would do, that presently I went off to sleep quite comfortable.

And that, I am sorry to tell, is all the good that came of my penitent thoughts of that night. I woke in the morning chilly, and dirty-feeling, and wretched—much more miserable than on the morning before. My teeth chattered; my inside seemed all of a shiver; and I felt as though I would have given the jacket off my back for a drink of hot coffee. Mouldy had the price of it in his pocket. Just as we were about to turn out of the Strand the night before, Mouldy had

held a horse for a gentleman who went into an oyster-shop, and earned sixpence. Fourpence we had spent, and there was twopence left. Had the sixpence turned up early in the evening, we should all three have gone to the gaff in Shoreditch with it; but, as it was, we bought some bread and fried fish for supper, and saved twopence for some coffee in the morning.

"What sort of morning is it?" asked Ripston of Mouldy, who was looking out.

"A precious bad 'un," was the answer; "it's a-rainin' hard; I can see the drops bobbin' in the river."

"What will we do now, then?" said I.

"What d'yer mean?" replied Ripston.

"We shall get wet through if we go out in the rain."

"Did yer ever hear such a cove?" exclaimed Ripston, laughing. "Here, Mouldy, s'pose you goes on fust, and borrows a top coat or a silk umbrella for Smiffield! Why, yer jolly young fool, the rain will make your hair curl! Come on."

And out we went, shivering over the wet pavement, and splashing in the mud. It wasn't a sharp rain that was falling, but a steady, close rain; and long before we got to the coffee stall, I could feel my shirt sticking to my shoulders, and my trousers to my knees. I hadn't forgotten what I had made up my mind to do last night—indeed it came into my head the moment I woke—and I had been trying to screw up my courage to tell 'em what I meant all the time we had been plodding through the rain; but how *could* I screw my courage up? Here I was—bitterly cold and hungry, wet through to the skin, and with nothing in the world to fall back on, if I fell out with Mouldy and Ripston!

"Two pen'orth of stunnin' hot coffee—in three cups, Mister," said Mouldy to the stallkeeper.

It was all over. Had it been any one else's coffee, it might have put heart in me to have up and spoke my mind; but as it was Mouldy's coffee, it warmed me towards him as I drank it, and made me think that, after all, he wasn't a bad sort of chap, and that it would be a shame to turn round and snub him with his ways of living. If I didn't hold with the said ways, certainly I had no business to let him stand treat to me out of 'em. Besides, there didn't seem much danger of anything very wrong being done to-day; for though it still wanted a quarter to six by the market clock, there was plenty of bustle and running about, and before we had finished our coffee, Mouldy said—

"Come, look alive, you two; we oughter do werry tidy this mornin'. Don't you know, Smiffield, that them as don't mind doin' their own fetchin's and carryin's when it's dry, would rather pay than do it when it rains?"

And so we found. From six o'clock till ten—it raining all the time—we were never once waiting for a job; and when the trade fell off, and we found time to talk together, it turned out that we had been doing splendidly. I had earned elevenpence; Ripston, one and three-halfpence; Mouldy, ninepence halfpenny. I felt a deal more proud of having earned more than Mouldy this morning, than I did yesterday, when he told me that I could crib things off a stall better than he could. Indeed it was so nice to hold that handful of coppers—all hard earned, at a penny and a halfpen-

ny a time—that in spite of being wringing wet to
the skin, and of having a nasty cut under my big
toe, through treading on a broken bottle, I should
have been happier than ever before in my life if
it had not been that those almonds haunted me so.
I was all the happier, too, to find that, having
been able to earn enough for their wants, neither
Mouldy nor Ripston had taken so much as an
apple. I was half afraid it would have been
otherwise, and was glad to hear Mouldy say, when
we had given him our earnings, (he was money-
holder always,)—"There, now, that's jest what I
calls a werry respectable mornin's work."

"Better than gettin' things wrong, and sellin'
'em ; eh, Mouldy ?" I took courage to remark.

"'Course it's better," he replied; "there's
more on it."

"I wish I was 'bliged to work, and not—not
do t'other," I said.

"Don't know about bein' 'bliged to do it," replied he; "it's werry well while it lasts, but the
wust on it is, it don't last; and then, if you was
tied to it, and couldn't turn your hand to nothink
else, you'd find it rather a pinch at times. Take
things as they comes; that's my motter."

Ripston said it was his "motter" too; and so
we went to a soup-shop in Long Acre, and all
made a very hearty dinner—and there then being
enough in hand for supper, and sixpence over,
Mouldy kindly proposed that that should be spent
in buying me a pair of boots; and Ripston agreeing, in the course of the afternoon we took a
stroll to Petticoat Lane, and for the sixpence
bought a largish, but very decent pair of high-
lows.

CHAPTER XVII.

WHICH TOUCHES ON SUNDRY OF MY ADVENTURES
AS A MARKET PROWLER, AND LEADS UP TO A
CERTAIN SUNDAY NIGHT WHEN I FALL ILL, AND
GIVE PROMISE OF GROWING WORSE.

IT was my original intention to have presented
the reader with a day-by-day chronicle of my career as a market prowler; indeed, to this end I
had covered at least fifty sides of writing-paper,
and there they now lie on my table, cancelled,
and doomed to be converted into pipe-lights, for
which their crisp, smooth nature admirably adapts
them.

And I believe the reader will agree with me,
when he is made acquainted with the reason, that
these fifty pages are very properly abandoned.
The fact is, each page, representing a day, is so
much like another, that, except for trifling dif-
ferences, there is no telling this from that, and,
goodness knows, I have enough to tell without
boring the reader by insipid repetitions. The
days of my market prowling were curiously alike;
at least, the weeks were. From Monday morning
until Saturday we rose in the morning by daybreak, made our way to Covent Garden, peram-
bulated the self-same beats in search of the self-
same jobs, and carried the same sort of loads;
or, trade being slack, we pilfered from the self-
same baskets, and carried the result of our depre-
dations to the old rascal that lived in Coal Yard,
Drury Lane, and afterwards dined according to
the quality of our luck. As Mouldy had truly

observed from the beginning, "sometimes it ran
as high as roast pork, and sometimes it was not a
lump of bread from mornin' till night." Still,
and as I before remarked, come Saturday, to review the luck of the week would be to find that
there was scarcely a penny's difference between
it and the week before—the same amount of
roast pork or its equivalent, the same dearth of
bread, the same amount of cane at the hands of
the market beadle, the same average of nights
with and without straw in our van.

In a worldly sense, an experience of five months
as the partner of Mouldy and Co. found me pretty much as when I started. As the reader will
perhaps remember, my stock of wearing apparel
at the last-mentioned time was not extensive;
consisting, indeed, of one pair of trousers, one
shirt, and a ragged old jacket. Now, I still had a
shirt and trousers; and the jacket falling to
pieces, its place was supplied by a coat—not
much of a coat, although there was a great deal
of it; but still, quite as good as the jacket. As
at starting, I was shoeless, the sixpenny high-lows
being worn off my feet, and the profits proving
insufficient to warrant a renewal of such luxuries
—a circumstance highly significant, as showing
how seldom we lighted on elevenpenny days.

It was about the middle of May when I joined
Mouldy and Ripston; and now, with the reader's
permission, we will let those fifty pages I was
speaking of lie undisturbed, and make a skip to
October of the same year. Apart from business,
little had happened to me worth recording. In
the course of the five months I went seven or
eight times to the "gaff" in Shoreditch, and enjoyed it very much. Once I was locked up all
night at Bow Street station-house, on suspicion
of having stolen a little dog. It was a little slate-
coloured dog, with long hair hanging over its eyes.
I never had a thought of stealing it. It followed
me one Saturday from Covent Garden down to
the arches, and rather than turn it away we gave
it a lodging in our van that night and all the next
day—which was Sunday, and always a pinching
time with us—and gave it some of our bread.
The police found it in our van when they came
round that Sunday night, and being informed who
brought it there, hauled me off there and then,
and no doubt I should have been sent to prison
had not Ripston—between whom and myself there
had sprung up the fastest friendship—bestirred
himself in the matter; and, ascertaining to whom
the dog belonged, went boldly to the house—a
great house it was, in one of the west-end squares
—and gaining admittance by saying he had
"come concerning that little dog," told the lady
all about it from first to last, which not only led
to my honourable acquittal, but to my receiving
a reward from the lady of five shillings. Two
half-crowns! Throughout our whole partnership,
never had we at one time possessed nearly as
much money. It was decided that we should enjoy ourselves on it. We dined at the cookshop,
having veal and bacon and green peas for dinner,
and half a pint of beer each when we came out,
which was rash, inasmuch as, not being used to
it, it excited us to such a pitch of extravagant
jollity, that nothing would suit but that we must
take the roof of the twopenny omnibus to Shoreditch, Ripston and Mouldy smoking a three-halfpenny cigar each, and Mouldy being so ill that we
were all turned out of the "gaff" before the piece

was half over, and had to walk home, penniless, in the rain.

One morning—this was about five weeks after I ran away from home—I met a man in the market who lived somewhere near Fryingpan Alley, and who knew my father. I had seen them together dozens of times. As soon as he saw me, he made a run at me, and it was only by dodging round a cabbage-waggon that I was able to avoid him. Knowing that my father sometimes worked in the market, I always kept a good look-out, assisted by my partners, who, from my description, were well aware of the sort of man my father was.

On the morning following that on which I encountered the man, however, we all kept our eyes open sharper even than in ordinary, and, as it turned out, not unnecessarily. About seven o'clock, Mouldy, who though engaged on a job of summer cabbages, was vigilantly on the look-out for the enemy, suddenly uttered a warning whistle, and directed my attention towards two individuals coming from the fruit-market.

In an instant I recognised them—the man who the day before had so nearly caught me, and my father. He was very white, as was invariably the case when he was in a great passion, and he carried under his arm an old donkey-whip, which, as he had no donkey of his own, I might fairly assume he had borrowed of a friend for the occasion.

He was looking about him very eagerly, and it unfortunately happened that, owing to the manner of his approach, if I ran away, it would be right across the open vegetable-market, and he could not fail to see me. There seemed no escape for me; and as, hiding behind Ripston, I caught another glance at his pale face. my knees trembled and my lips tingled.

"He'll have me, Rip; he's sure to ketch me. Oh, s'welp me, Rip! on'y look at him and that whip."

Without replying, Ripston began to step back, giving me a dig with his elbow to do the same while I remained in his rear. In this manner we approached a great pile of empty gooseberry-sieves; and getting to the back of the pile Ripston pulled away half a dozen, signed for me to squeeze myself into the hole thus made, and, when this was accomplished, he piled back the baskets a-top of me, and took his seat on the edge of a bottom one. And barely was my hiding completed when, as I lay crouched in my hole, I heard my father's voice—

"He won't run agin for one while if I *do* ketch him. Stay a minnit; let's ask this feller if he has seen him; he seems like one of his own kidney."

So saying, he came straight up to Ripston, who was coolly scraping and munching a carrot.

"I say, Jack," said my father, "d'ye happen to have seen a kid in a old corderoy jacket and trowsis lurkin' about the market this mornin?— kid about so high?"

To show how high, he placed his hand against the basket heap, within a foot of my face. I could see plainly through the chinks.

"Soft-face-lookin' kid; no cap; hair wants cuttin'," continued my father.

"Wot's the name on him?" asked Ripston, curtly, getting on with his carrot.

"Jim."

"Well, I knows a Jim," replied Ripston, after a moment of apparent reflection; "he ain't altogether like the cove wot you're a-arstin arter, but he might have altered since you see him last. How long has he been missin,' mister?"

"Over a month," replied my father.

"Then the Jim I'm a-speakin' on is werry likely to be the one. Coves do alter werry quick, don't yer know? The one as *I* mean is a short, thick-necked cove; spitted with small-pox; fightin' weight, 'bout nine stun four."

"Get out! it's a boy I mean," replied my father, impatiently, though evidently completely taken in by Ripston's gravity; "quite a little feller."

"How old?" asked Ripston.

"'Tween seven and eight," spoke my father's friend.

"'Tween seven and eight!" repeated Ripston, musingly, and scratching his ear with the remains of the carrot. "Sure his name was Jim?"

"'Course I am. Jim Ballisat—that's wot his name is, cuss him!" replied my father.

"Oh—h, Jim Ballisat!" replied Ripston, as though a sudden light had dawned on him. "Now I knows who yer means. Now I come to hear it agin, that's wot he said his name was. We calls him Rouser. That's where the mistake was, don't yer see, mister?"

"Yes, yes; but where is he? Butcher him! I'd give a penny to have hold on him just now. You seem to know wot he's called and all about him. Where shall I find him?"

"Lived up Cowcross way, didn't he?"

"That's him. Where is he?"

"Father a coster, or summat in that line?"

"Lord's truth! yes. Well! where is he?"

"Cruel cove, ain't he?—cove as very often larruped Jim with his waist-strap?"

"Oh! he said so, did he? D——n seize him! That's his gratitood, the young willin!"

"Got a thunderin' old cat for a stepmother, as tells lies about him, and drinks like a fish, and who——Well, don't get in a pelt with me, Mister! I'm only tellin' you wot he told us."

"Where is he?" roared my father, shaking Ripston by the collar so vigorously, and so close to the baskets, that they were in momentary danger of being overturned.

"Leave go, and I'll tell yer; not afore."

And, from Ripston's tone, I really thought that he was about to betray me.

"Now, out with it!" said my father.

"Well, if you *must* know, he's gone a ballastin'."

"Where? When?" asked my father.

"I dunno where he's gone, and I don't care," Ripston surlily replied. "All I knows about it is this—Yesterday arternoon he meets a cove wot I knows, and the cove ses to him, 'What cheer, Rouser? What's a-takin' you over Wesmister Bridge? Ain't there nothin' doin' in the market?' So ses Rouser, 'No more markets for me,' ses he; 'my old man is on my tracks, and I'm off.' 'Off where?' asks the cove. 'Well,' ses Rouser, 'I knows a bargeman as lives down Wan'sworth way, and I'm goin' with him a-ballast-gettin'.' There, now you knows as much about it as I knows."

"The thunderin' willin!" ejaculated my father, who was completely imposed on by Ripston's statement. "Did he say when he was likely to be back again?"

"Dunno no more perticklers," replied Ripston

"but *I* shouldn't wonder if he never did come back."

"Why shouldn't you wonder?"

"'Cos he was alwis talkin' about goin' to sea," replied Ripston; "and when he gets on the river, and sees the ships and that, he'll be off."

"Oh! *that's* it, is it?" remarked my father, with an air of great disappointment, at the same time tucking the donkey-whip under his arm. "Come on, Jack; it's no use of us huntin' any longer. Fact is, Jack, he took fright of seein' you yesterday."

"Werry likely," replied Jack.

"Come on. Let him go a-ballastin'. Let him go to blazes, beggar him! What call have I got to go funkin' arter a butcherin' little whelp such as he is?"

And to my great delight, having said this, my father turned about and walked off with his friend, while the mendacious Ripston, tickled off his legs nearly by the force of the joke, helped me out of hiding.

After that, during the remainder of the time that I haunted Covent Garden Market, I never once set eyes on my father or his friend.

On the last Sunday in October, following the May when I met Mouldy and Ripston, I fell ill. Although I had kept about, and made no complaint, I had not been really well for several weeks; which, when I come to think on my way of living, seems not at all surprising. It happened that that summer was a particularly rainy one, and sometimes for several days together my clothes would be wet, or at least damp, and I had no opportunity to dry them, or even to take them off at night. Sore throat and pains between my shoulders were chief amongst my ailments. Once I suffered from toothache through a dreadful fortnight. It was horrible. I was obliged to soak my bread in water before I could eat it; and no matter how hard the times, I dare not avail myself of what may be called the natural advantages that belong to a young market prowler. When hard pressed by hunger, a raw turnip, or even a juicy cabbage-stump, is not to be despised; but during that fortnight of torture, my throbbing mouth revolted against all such cold and stringy food, and there was nothing left but to bear with my misfortune until a lucky wind wafted us to the baker's or the pudding shop. I used to sit the whole night through rocking myself in a corner of the van, to the great annoyance of my partners, who, though, as will presently appear, not at all harsh towards folk plainly ill, could never be brought to understand that there was any necessity for making such a fuss about such a little thing as a tooth. At last an old man who played the fiddle about the streets, and who slept under the dark arches, mercifully extracted the tormentor by tying a bit of catgut round it, and giving it a haul.

But what ailed me on the Sunday evening in question was neither sore throat, nor pains between the shoulders, nor toothache. The summer was fading, and, somehow or other, matters were growing less and less satisfactory at Covent Garden. I say "somehow or another;" but I knew the reason well enough. In ragamuffin slang, the market had grown too "hot" for us. I got to be known there—we all got to be known there, and in a manner that was not at all to our advantage. Our luck seemed dead against us; we could neither get work, nor the worth of a penny without work. Never a day passed but what one or other of us was made to feel the weight of the beadle's cane, or the cruel foot of some salesman. This latter punishment was not so bad when met with under the arcade, because the shopkeepers wore light boots, and sometimes mere slippers; but out in the open, where the waggons and carts were, and the owners of the goods with which they were laden wore boots of the toe-cap and clinker school, it was agonising. One time we had Mouldy down with a kick so bad, that he couldn't do more than just creep one leg before the other for three days.

Everybody was set dead against us—shopkeepers, beadle, salesmen, every one. They didn't wait till they caught us doing something wrong; soon as ever they saw us, they were down on us with a kick or a cuff—until we were that savage and hungry, we were ready to risk almost anything. About this time Ripston found a way of getting into a cellar in which carrots were stored for the winter. This was indeed a stroke of good fortune—at least, so we thought at the time; but alas! in the course of a very few days we discovered that carrots, although of a very refreshing and relishing nature, are not the sort of things to subsist on entirely. I believe that that week's feeding on carrots had a great deal to do with my illness.

I had been very dull all the afternoon, but that was not much to take notice of. The dark arches always are very dull on Sundays; for though you are very welcome to wander about in your rags, and grub for a living as best you can on week-days, the police and the street-keepers in the neighbourhood of the Adelphi don't permit anything of the sort on Sundays. "Get out;" "Move off, young gallows." It's all very well to give the order, but it isn't everybody that can "move off" —that is, right off—for they don't *live* anywhere. They have only got lodgings, and when they go out in the morning, the door is shut against them till night.

For this, and other reasons into which it is not worth while here to enter, the arches were never without plenty of company all day on Sunday. The company was not of a comfortable sort—or rather there were two sorts,—and unless you belonged to one or the other, you were, in a manner of speaking, as much alone as though you had all the arches to yourself. One of these comprised the miserable and moping ones, who came to the arches for no other purpose than to hide and wear the day out, and who lounged about by themselves, smoking the bits of cigars they had picked up in the morning, if they were men, while the females of the same tribe huddled together in twos and threes, and dozed or talked in whispers. The men and women of the other sort were livelier, certainly, but scarcely as pleasant, being blackguards and petty ruffians of the worst class, who swore, and gambled, and got sport out of ill-using the quiet and miserable ones. With this last-mentioned ruffianly set, I am happy to record that neither myself, nor Mouldy, nor Ripston ever had any dealings. On Sunday afternoons, if the weather was fine and the tide favourable, we three usually took a walk on the shore, (the policemen didn't interfere with us there,) and early in the evening we retired to our van, (it belonged to a greengrocer who lived in Bedfordbury, and the man who drove it gave us permission to sleep in it,) and there passed the time in telling stories until we fell asleep.

This was the way in which we spent the evening of the Sunday on which I was taken ill. Mouldy and Ripston had been out as usual in the afternoon; but I felt not at all inclined for walking, and stayed in the van until they came back. We had been lucky enough to pick up a few halfpence the night before, and had a half-quartern loaf and a pennyworth of treacle for dinner; that is to say, Ripston and Mouldy so dined; but for my part, I had no stomach for bread and treacle; indeed, I had eaten nothing since Saturday at dinner-time. I was hot and shivery; my tongue was dry, and my eyes smarted with a burning pain. I had had headache before, but never as now; it throbbed as though it was being tapped with hammers; or rather—for I very well remember the sensation—with door-knockers about which a bit of wash-leather had been tied by way of dulling the sound. There was a little straw luckily left in the van the day before, and, with more consideration than might have been expected in them, my companions let me have it all to myself. But I could get no comfort out of it. It was no use shaking it and punching it up; my head was so heavy, that as soon as I laid it down every bit of spring was taken out of the straw instantly.

As it grew later I grew worse. It was my turn to be "pillow;" but Ripston kindly offered to take my place, and Mouldy, with an equal show of good-nature, insisted on my taking Ripston's body part, although the choice was fairly with him, he having been "pillow" the previous night. They even went to bed an hour before their usual time, in order that I might lie comfortably.

But Ripston couldn't stand it. My head, he declared, scorched him through his jacket and waistcoat, and made his ribs too hot for him to bear; besides, I shook so as to cause his legs to move, and to disturb Mouldy. Although a very fair-tempered boy in the day-time—indeed, whenever he was awake—when he was half-asleep he was about as nasty-tempered a chap as can well be imagined. He gave the calf of Ripston's leg a severe and sudden punch.

"Wot's that for?" inquired the naturally indignant Ripston.

"I'll show yer wot it's for if you don't lay still—jiggin' yer leg about as if you was practisin' a hornpipe!" replied Mouldy, savagely.

"Well, jest you hit the right 'un next time," said Ripston. "It ain't me jiggin' at all; it's Smiffield."

"Wot's the matter, Smiffield?" asked Mouldy. "Hain't you warm enough?"

"I should rather think he was," said Ripston; "warm ain't the word for it; he's blazin' hot."

"Then wot's he a-shiverin' for?" Mouldy fiercely demanded.

"How should I know? Jes' you keep your hands to yourself, and arks him if you wants to know."

"Wot are you shakin' about in that way for, Smiff?"

"'Cos I'm so cold," I answered. "I'm as cold as ice, Mouldy."

"Jolly funny sort of ice as ain't colder than you. Just you feel of him, Mouldy," observed Ripston.

Mouldy did as requested, putting his hand up to my cheek.

"Take that, for tellin' lies!" said he, savagely, at the same time giving me a cruel back-handed slap; "and now begin to snivel, and I'll give yer another."

Although I had struggled hard to conceal it, I had been very nigh to crying all the evening; and this unkind act of Mouldy's set me off. I think I must have wanted very much to cry. No doubt that the slap on the cheek that Mouldy had given me would have drawn tears from my eyes at any time, but for no longer a time than the smart lasted; but now, although I scarcely felt the smart at all, I felt choked with sobs, and the tears fell faster than I could wipe them away. I couldn't leave off. I seemed bereft of all power to try even. It was as though I was full of sorrow, and must be emptied of it. It wasn't sorrow of the bellowing sort; for as I lay with my face to the waggon-floor, if it had not been for the sound of my sobbing, neither of my companions would have been aware that I was crying.

It was one of the oddest fits of crying that ever happened to me or any other boy, I believe. Ever since that day when I had seen my father and his neighbour looking out for me in Covent Garden Market, I had resolved to think no more about home, but go on free and easy as it were, and taking matters just as they came. When on the night of the day on which I had seen him from between the chinks of the gooseberry sieves with the donkey whip in his hand, and heard what he had to say about me, when I lay down in the van that night, I reckoned up the whole business, and, as I at the time thought, settled it for good and all. "Now look here," I said to myself, "you've seen your father and you've heard him, and there's no sort of doubt as to what you'll get if you goes home. Are you going home? Certainly not. Very well, then; that's a settler. If you are not going home, you've got to do as other people do; and it's no use funking, and making yourself miserable about them that don't care a pin's head about you, and are only waiting to lay hold on you, to whack you within an inch of your life. So let's have no more snivelling and whispering, 'Good night, father, and little Polly,' and saying your prayers to yourself like a sneak, and all the while pretending to listen to the jolly good story Mouldy's telling." From that night my heart seemed set to freezing, as one may say, and it had been freezing ever since; so that, until and within the last day or two, any moderate weight of rascality might slide over it smooth and slick, and without the least danger of breaking in at a soft part. It was frozen over strongly enough almost to bear anything. Now, however, there was a thaw. The rain had come, and the frost was broken up completely. The thaw seemed to begin right at the core, softening my hard starved-up little heart, setting it free, and swelling and heaving in a manner that was altogether too much for me.

Likewise it was too much for Mouldy. True to his word, that if I set up a snivelling he would give me another, he once more flung up his open hand and caught me a harder spank even than the first one. Ripston immediately fired up with a degree of pluck that did him honour.

"The gallus brute!" he exclaimed, meaning Mouldy, who, as I before have said, was a bigger and a stronger boy than either of us—"the gallus brute! to punch a poor cove wot's littler than he is, and ill too! Don't lay there, Smiffield, old boy! get up and help us; we'll jolly soon give him wot he wants."

And without waiting for my assistance, Ripston turned back his cuffs and began dancing round Mouldy with a determination that seemed fairly to stagger him. But I was in no mind for fighting, and tried to make matters up between them, assuring them that I was not crying because of the slap on the face; that it had not hurt me at all. I was crying because I felt so ill. I was glad that I did take this course, for as soon as poor Mouldy was sufficiently awake to understand the true condition of affairs, he expressed himself as penitently as a boy could. He owned that he was a precious coward, and offered me the satisfaction of hitting him on the nose as hard as I chose, while he held both his hands behind him—an offer which Ripston urged me to accept. Finding that I would not, however, he was determined to make it up somehow, so he insisted on my having his cap to lay my head on, and his jacket to cover me. Ripston's heart was good to do as much; but only the day before, while running away from the beadle, he had lost his cap, and the blue guernsey which served him for shirt as well as jacket, was, except his trousers, the whole of his wardrobe, and I could hardly expect him to oblige me to the extent of stripping himself.

But although the boys did their best to make me comfortable; letting me have all the straw to myself, and tucking me up as nicely as the bed-clothes would permit, I did not feel any better. That is to say, I was hot and cold as before, and my eyelids pressed heavy and burning on my eyes, and my tongue was parched, and my breath came short and laboured. I *did* feel better though, somehow, since I had got over my crying fit; I felt lighter, and more inclined, if I may so express it, to go easy with my illness—to lie still, and let it do just as it pleased with me.

CHAPTER XVIII.

IN WHICH I BID FAREWELL TO MY PARTNERS AND THE DARK ARCHES, AND AM CONVEYED TO THE WORKHOUSE TO BE CURED OF "THE FEVER."

IT was easy to see that each minute Mouldy and Ripston grew more and more alarmed at my condition. After they had spread the jacket over me and made me comfortable, they did not lie down again, but went and sat in the corner of the van that was farthest from me, talking in whispers.

"P'r'aps it's on'y a cold," whispered Ripston. "When a cold does reg'lar ketch hold on you, it do make you feel precious bad; don't it, Mouldy?"

"Umph!" was all the answer that Mouldy made.

"It *is* a cold; don't you think it is, Mouldy?"

"It's summat, I s'pose," replied Mouldy, vaguely, and in so low a whisper that I could scarcely hear it.

"If he don't get better in the mornin', we'll have to get him some physic, Mouldy."

"Yes."

"Mustard plasters is good for wheezin's at the chest; ain't they, Mouldy?"

"Werry likely."

"I recollects havin' one on when I was a kid. I wonder how much mustard he'd take, Mouldy? A pen'orth 'ud do, I should think; he ain't got a werry big chest."

Mouldy was strangely inattentive to his companion's conversation. To Ripston's last observation he made no reply at all. After a pause of a minute or two's duration, said Ripston—

"He seems to get wheezin's wuss and wuss; don't you think he do, Mouldy? Think it 'ud be any good tryin' it on to beg that mustard to-night, Mouldy?"

"Not a bit; the shops is all shut up, 'cept the doctors'—they keeps open on Sundays, don't you know?"

"They on'y sells pills. P'r'aps pills 'ud do him more good than mustard—eh, Mouldy? The wust of pills, they've got such precious rum names that a cove don't know what to arks for."

"Pen'orth of pills—that's what *I* should ask for."

"And s'pose the cove behind the counter said, 'What sort of pills, my man?'"

"Then I should say, openin' uns," replied Mouldy, after a little consideration.

"I never thought of that. I s'pose they all are openin' uns?"

"I never heard of a sort that different was expected on," replied Mouldy, with the same sort of indifference in his tone as had distinguished his manner from the first. He seemed all the while to be thinking of something else.

"Then that's agreed on," continued Ripston; "the fust penny we ketches hold on in the mornin' goes for pills for Smiffield. What say, Mouldy?"

But Mouldy said nothing; and both boys were quiet for full a minute. I, too, remained quite quiet, for the purpose of hearing the whispered conversation going on between them. Not that I felt anxious about it. I didn't feel anxious about anything. I didn't care what they talked about, only I liked to hear them. It appeared as though Mouldy's reserved manner of speech presently roused Ripston's suspicions.

"Mouldy!" said he, suddenly, "if it ain't a cold, what *is* the matter with Smiffield?"

"Who said it warn't a cold? How should I know what's the matter with him mor'n you?" snapped Mouldy.

"Well, you know, Mouldy, you've been in the 'orspital, and you might have seen what the matter was with a good many coves," explained Ripston. "Don't you recollect anybody's case as was like his'n?"

"You hold your jaw!" replied he, in an impatient whisper. "How do yer know as he's asleep?"

"Sure he is. Don't you hear how reg'lar his wheezin's is?"

"Yes; and I hears summat else, too," said Mouldy, moodily.

"What else?"

"I hears the straw as he's a-layin' on raspin' together. If he *is* asleep, he's got that precious shiverin' on him." And then, in a still lower whisper, he continued, "I wish I hadn't lent him my jacket, Rip. Jigger the cap wot he's got his head on; but I do wish I hadn't lent him my jacket."

"There you are agin!" replied Ripston, reproachfully. "I never see such a feller as you are. Greedy beggar! He'd ha' lent you his jacket, I'd bet a shillin', if you wanted it."

"Lent it be jiggered! It's as good as givin' it; that's wot I'm a-lookin' at."

"What d'yer mean? You can have it back in the mornin' can't yer?" demanded Ripston.

"'Course I can," answered Mouldy. "Oh, yes! I can have it back, Rip, and I can have summat with it, Rip, which I don't pertickler want, thanky."

"Can't you open your mouth, and tell a feller what you mean?"

"Hush! Here, put your head over the side, 'cos he mightn't be asleep arter all, you know, and it might frighten him."

So they both rose softly, and leaned their heads over the side of the van. Somehow, however, my hearing was particularly sharp that night, and I could make out all that they said as plainly almost as though they had stooped down to whisper it.

"Was you ever waxinated, Rip?"

"I was so, and got the places to prove it. But wot's that got to do with Smiffield?"

"Well, you see, Rip, I never was waxinated, so I shall stay up at this end of the wan till the mornin'. You're all right, old boy, and may sleep along with him if you likes; bein' waxinated, you won't catch it."

"Catch what?"

"Why, the fever. That's what Smiffield's got, and that's what I don't want," replied Mouldy, impressively.

"Send I may live! You don't mean it!" said Ripston, in a tone of great alarm. "Then he'll die—won't he, Mouldy?"

"Next door to sure."

"Sudden, Mouldy? Will he die sudden?"

"Not werry sudden; leastways, they don't in general," whispered Mouldy. "They does a good deal to 'em afore they dies of fever—shaves their head, and that."

"What's that for, Mouldy?" asked Ripston, in an awful voice.

"'Cos they goes cranky, and tears all their hair off if they don't," replied Mouldy.

"Lor'! jes fancy poor Smiffield dyin'!" said Ripston, after a few moments' silence. "Poor old Smiff!"

I could scarcely credit my ears, but there could be no mistake about it—Ripston was crying.

I wasn't alarmed—I wasn't even surprised—to hear Mouldy say that I had the fever. Nor did my indifference arise from ignorance. I felt as ill as possible; and "the fever," being the very worst complaint I had ever heard of, seemed to be exactly the proper name for my ailment. "The fever" was very common in Fryingpan Alley. It was never spoken of any other way than as "the fever," and when it once made a settlement in the alley, a good time for Mr. Crowl was sure to follow. But even when I thought on my ailment as one which commonly killed those whom it seized—and for an instant the awful, gaping bullfinch, with his spears, appeared to my mind's eyes—I felt in no dread. I wanted nothing, but to be let alone—not to be moved, or touched, or spoken to. I was glad to hear both Ripston and Mouldy moving to the other end of the van.

Crouching down together, they went on whispering; but I didn't try to make out what they were saying; I didn't care. Besides the buzzing of their voices, I could hear all the other sounds,—the laughing, and talking, and swearing of the lads tossing and playing cards; the dull tramping of feet; and the flapping of waggon tail-boards and the clinking of the chains as the lodgers climbed up to their roosts. By degrees, however, these last-mentioned sounds grew less and less, and presently ceased altogether. Still I could hear the low buzz, buzz, of the two boys, and knew that they were not asleep. I was glad of it, for within the last half-hour or so I had grown terribly thirsty, and sorely wanted a drink of water. I called Mouldy.

"You awake, Mouldy?"

"All right, old boy! we won't go to sleep," he answered.

"Could you get me a drink of water, Mouldy?"

"There!" whimpered Ripston; "what a jolly fool you are, Mouldy! Now you've started him. Why didn't you do as I nudged yer to, and pretend to be asleep?"

"Could I get you a drink of water, Smiffy! How could I, old boy?" replied Mouldy, soothingly. "Where am I to get it from?"

"Couldn't you get us a drop from the pump out in the strand, Mouldy—jest a little drop?"

"Cert'in'y I could go to the pump, Smiffy; but what's the use, when I ain't got nothink to carry it in—no mug nor nothink? You keep quiet till mornin'—about five, don't you know—when the waggon cha . . . [illegible] . . . their horses out; you shall have a precious lot then—as much as ever you can drink."

"Oh, I can't wait till five, Mouldy. I can't wait at all. I shall go out of my mind if I have to wait ever such a little while. I feel all scorched up for a drink. Don't say wait till five, Mouldy."

"Well, I don't want to say it if you don't like to hear it, Smiffy; it's true—that's wot made me say it."

"What's the time now, Mouldy?"

"It's about one. Don't you think so, Ripston?"

"Jest about. It's high tide at one, and I can heat it beatin' agin the wall. Don't you hear it, Smiffield?"

I was terribly thirsty; and listening, I could make out the noise of the rising river striking with a full, cold sound against the wall at the bottom. It was a delicious sound. I did not think of the river at night, black and muddy, and bleak, as it really was. I could hear the plashing, and my fevered mind conjured up the picture of the river as I had seen it on the morning following my first night under the dark arches,—the sunshiny, rippling river, with the hay barge lazily floating along. To go down to the brink of it and drink was the consuming thought that suddenly possessed me. Why not? I knew my way, and wanted neither cup nor jug. I could lay down on the wall of the wharf, and bending my head over, drink, and drink as much as I pleased. I got up, and began climbing over the waggon side. It was so dark that my companions could not see me; they could hear me, however, and by the time I had got one leg over the side, Ripston had clutched and was clinging to the other.

"Why, Smiffield!" he exclaimed, in a

ened and half-crying voice, "Hallo, old matey! where was you goin' ?"

"To get some water."

"But there ain't no water. Oh, jigger the not bein' waxinated, Mouldy!" cried poor Ripston. "Come and ketch hold on him—there's a good feller! There ain't no water, Smiffy."

"Yes there is," I replied, struggling to get away from Ripston; "you said so. You said that it was high tide; and I'm goin' down to the river."

"Oh no, you ain't!" whimpered Ripston, tugging frantically at my leg. "You ain't a-goin' arter water; you're a-goin' down to the river to drownd yerself! You're a-goin' out of your mind, just like Mouldy has been sayin' you would; and you wants to chuck yourself into the river. Do come, Mouldy! Ketch hold on his hand with a bit of my guernsey, if you are frightened; on'y do come, and help me to make him lay down agin."

But Mouldy was not to be persuaded. It was evident that he thought a great deal either about not being vaccinated, or about the possibility of my being mad, and capable of doing him an injury by biting. Anyhow, he kept his position at the further end of the van, from whence he addressed me:—

"Wot are you up to, Smiffield? D' yer want to rouse up the whole arches an' set 'em agin us? D' yer want to bring the peelers, which 'll be here directly, pokin' an' pryin' about our wan to see wot's the matter?"

"I only want some water, Mouldy."

"Well, and who said as yer shouldn't have any? leastways, I cert'n'y said so myself, but I didn't mean it, Smiffield. I will get yer some. You lay down as Ripston wants yer to, an' I'll go an' get yer some water."

"Oh, ah! I knows yer!" exclaimed Ripston, suddenly suspicious of Mouldy's motives. "You're a-goin' to hook it, that's what you're goin' to do. It's all rubbish about your goin' to get water; you're a-goin' to leave me to look arter him best way I can."

I must say that I was much of the same opinion as Ripston; but we both misjudged the honest fellow.

"You wait jest a minnit, an' you'll see all about my cuttin' away an' leavin' yer," said he, dropping over the side of the van.

"But what have yer got to fetch water in?" Ripston called after him.

"It's all right, I tell yer. You lay down, Smiffield, and I'll fetch yer a drink in my cap; there!"

I was willing enough. I have thought many times since, that both Mouldy and Ripston no doubt thought that I had a narrow squeak of doing a very horrible thing, and were very thankful in their own minds that they were able to persuade me from going down to the river. True, the cold wind off the water blowing on me when so full of fever might have caused my death as surely as drowning. Then again, I might, while groping in the dark, have slipped in; and if I had, it would have been all over with me, for when the river is full there is enough water under the wall there to have drowned me had I been ten feet high instead of barely four; so, considering everything, my thanks that I am still in the land of the living

may be due to my two poor little ragamuffin partners, after all.

Mouldy kept his word. I lay down on my straw again; and he took the cap my head had been resting on, and presently could be heard picking his way towards the river. It was a good step in the day, and when you had a glimmer of light to help you, and to save you from stumbling over things; but now, in the pitchy dark, it was as good as double as far, and more than ten times as dangerous, for the carts and things were not put in in a very regular way, and you might come full butt against a wheel where you expected to find a clear passage. Mouldy was, however, lucky enough to get along with very little bungling, and in what Ripston said was less than three minutes, (it seemed twenty to me, I was so eager for him to come back with the water,) we could hear his steps shuffling quicker and quicker, lest what he had been to fetch should dribble all away before he got it home. However, he managed very well; the cap, though an old one, was sound, and so greasy as to be nearly waterproof, and when he gave it up to Ripston over the side there must have been fully a pint in it. In about five long gulps I drank it off, and then lying down again fell into a sleep so full of little bits and tags of dreams that it was like being awake, and lost in a crowd in a foreign country, and which lasted till Ripston roused me by shaking me, and told me I must turn out, as the carman was getting the horses out of the stable.

I tried to do as Ripston asked, but couldn't. I could sit up, but when I tried to use my legs I couldn't get any stiffness into my knees, and I slid down again, grazing my elbows.

"Now then, young fellows," said the carman, "tumble out; I ain't got no time to waste, I can tell you."

"Please, sir, here's one as can't tumble out," said Mouldy, who, rather than come near me, was peeping in through the rails at the back of the van.

"How d' ye mean, can't tumble out?" asked the carman.

"Well, he might tumble out, guv'nor, and that's about all he's ekal to. I'm jiggered if he can climb out!"

"What the d—l do you mean?" asked the carman, locking the stable door, and coming forward in a mighty hurry with his lantern. "Why can't he get out? He got in, didn't he?"

"He complains of his legs bein' nummy, sir, and he can't stand," observed Ripston, pleadingly. "Would you mind givin' him a lift out, if you please?"

"Yes, I'll thunderin' soon give him a lift out —such a one as he won't forget in a hurry, I promise you."

And so saying, the gruff carman, with the lantern in his hand, leapt into the van. "Out you come, you lazy young whelp!" said he; but just as the words were out of his mouth he flashed the lantern light on to my face, and he immediately altered his tune.

"Lor' A'mighty, young 'un!" he exclaimed. "Why, how long has this been?"

"It's been a-comin' on since yesterday arternoon," replied Ripston; "we didn't know as how it had come on as strong as that, though, mister; 'cos we couldn't see him."

"Where does he live? You must get him home somehow," said the carman.

Where was the use of telling him? "If I could only collar hold on him, he wouldn't run away agin for one while," were among the last words I had heard my father say; and was it likely that he would feel more tenderly disposed towards me now? It would have been bad enough to have been collared hold of when I was well, and could get out of the way of the whacks a bit; but, now that I couldn't even so much as stand, it would be ten times worse.

"D' ye hear, young 'un?" repeated the carman; "whereabouts do you live when you're at home?"

But I made no answer, pretending not to hear him.

"Don't either of you chaps know where he lives?"

There were no secrets between us. Each one knew where the other's home was, together with the full particulars of his reasons for abandoning the same; but we were bound by the most terrific oaths never to split on each other. A suspicion, however, that mine might possibly be regarded as an exceptional case seemed to occur to Mouldy, and as the carman asked the question, he directed at me an inquiring glance to that effect. But I returned his look with one of a sort that made him comprehend my wishes on the subject instantly.

"He lives here," Mouldy replied.

"Yes; but where does he come from?"

"He lives here, and he grubs here, and he sleeps here, same as we do—same as all on us," persisted Mouldy.

"I know all about that; but where's his home? where does his father and mother live? Come, now."

"He ain't got no home of that there kind that ever I heard tell of; did you, Ripston?"

"No, nor yet no father nor mother," replied his confederate; "he's a horfen, that's wot he is."

"Poor little beggar," said the carman, looking down on me pityingly; "well, he'll die if he's left here, that's certain; he's more than half dead now, I believe."

"Wouldn't a couple of pills set him right, don't you think, mister?" inquired Ripston, solicitously; "a couple of good strong openin' uns? If as you would be so kind as to lend us a penny to buy 'em with, we would give it you back"——

"What stuff! he's past pills by a very long way," interrupted the honest carman. "'Tain't no business of mine, of course, but I haven't got the heart to leave him here. Shall I take you to the work'us, young 'un?"

I didn't care where—anywhere but home to Fryingpan Alley. I felt too weak to speak, so I nodded "Yes" to the carman's question.

"I'm jolly well sure to get a bullying from the work'us for my pains," continued he; "never mind—they can't refuse to take you. Here, Toby," (he always called Mouldy "Toby," not knowing his other name,) "unbuckle the cloth off the near side mare, and chuck it up here."

Mouldy did as he was desired; and the good carman, first taking the precaution to light his pipe, and take half-a-dozen good pulls at it, wrapped the great warm horse-cloth tenderly about me. Then going to his horses' heads, he led them out of the arches, Ripston sitting down beside me as I lay in the van.

As for Mouldy, afraid as he was of the terrible "fever," he couldn't leave me without a parting friendly word. I heard him hauling himself up at the tail-board, and looking that way, saw his dirty sympathising face peering sadly between the rails.

"Good-bye, Smiffield," said he. "Mister," (this to the carman,) "there's a jacket wot he's covered over with; it's mine; tell the work'us to take care of it for him 'ginst he comes out. Lord bless you, old Smiff! Cheer up, old son!" And he suddenly vanished.

Ripston remained in the van until we turned out of the arches into Hungerford; then he gave my hot hand a squeeze, and with his lips pressed tightly together, looked at me, and nodded in a very meaning and hearty manner, tucked the horse-cloth about me, and without a word dropped over the tail-board, and was gone.

————◆————

CHAPTER XIX.

IN WHICH, WITH THE ASSISTANCE OF DOCTOR FLINDERS, I MANAGE TO CHEAT THE WORMS. I QUIT THE WORKHOUSE WITH MUCH LESS CEREMONY THAN I ENTERED IT.

MY good friend the carman was not far wrong in his anticipations that his interference in my behalf would not be gratefully regarded by the workhouse authorities.

Objection met him at the gate. He dared not admit me without an order, the porter said, and intimated to the carman that his best plan would be to take me back to where he had found me; at the same time broadly hinting his disbelief in the story from first to last, and his opinion that I was the carman's own boy, whom he found it convenient to get rid of. Goaded by these insinuations, my friend expressed his determination to leave me on the workhouse steps, and go about his business. But to this course the policeman demurred, and threatened to take the carman to the station-house, and impound his waggon and horses if he attempted so to desert me.

After half-an-hour of this sort of sparring, the master of the workhouse made his appearance, and overwhelmed the unlucky carman with perplexing questions. Did I belong to that parish? Did the carman bring me on his own account, or on account of his master, whose address the van bore? My friend informed the great man that he had brought me on no one's account, but purely out of humanity, and detailed as much as he knew of me—how that his master's van was placed at night under the Adelphi dark arches, and how that, to his knowledge, I had slept in the same for several months. But this explanation, so far from simplifying matters, made them worse. It was clear, the master said, that my occupancy and tenancy of the carter's van or premises gave me a claim on the parish in which the said carter resided and paid poor-rates; that the master was bound by the acts of his servant; and that if I was admitted, it would only be on agreement that the Bedfordbury carter paid for my maintenance.

"Very well, then," replied the bewildered carman, "I shall take him back to the dark arches, and lay him in a corner." On which the mob which had collected cried shame on the carman for an inhuman brute, and the policeman began to push him about. By God's mercy, however, just at this time up came the parish doctor, and my case was advanced a step by his ordering the van to be drawn into the workhouse yard.

Finally, after the carman had been detained—despite his plea of being due at a moving job in the Whitechapel Road at half-past seven, and that the hire of the van was half-a-crown an hour—for fully two hours, and his master and one of the parish guardians had been sent for, I was carried out of the van into the workhouse, and stripped, and washed, and put to bed.

And there I lay. Everybody said that I was very bad; so I suppose that I was. But I didn't feel bad. I was very snug and comfortable, and in no sort of pain. Indeed, had anyone asked me whether I would rather be well under the dark arches, or have the fever and lie here, I should have decided in favour of the latter without the least hesitation. It appeared quite stupid to argue the matter. What was there to be sorry for? The fever didn't hurt. It wasn't a quarter, no, nor a twentieth part so painful as that spell of toothache I had had in the van. I was there to be waited on. The bed was nice and soft, the physic not particularly nasty, and the arrowroot and mutton broth lovely. And yet everybody looked grave—even the doctor—and came softly up to my bed, and spoke in a low, kind voice, as though they thought that it must be very bad for me to lie there in such pain. Upon my word, I thought more than once that I might possibly be there by mistake, after all—that what ailed me was *not* that terrible fever, of which I had heard everybody express such dread; and accompanying this suspicion would come a dread that presently they would find out that there was little or nothing the matter with me, and turn me out.

I thought so on the second day after my admittance; on the evening of the third day I thought so more than ever. Besides the matron of the ward—a fat, cross-grained, sharp-speaking old wretch, whom all the patients very properly hated—there were two or three nurses; motherly sort of women, who, being paupers, and knowing something about the treatment of the sick, were allowed to exercise their skill and patience as a set-off against the bread and gruel they consumed. On the evening in question, Mrs. Dipple, one of these nurses, came up to my cot, and after making my pillow comfortable and wiping my forehead, said she—

"Master Smithfield, did you ever know anyone that died?"

"Yes, ma'am, lots," I replied.

"Do you ever think about dying, Master Smithfield?"

"No, ma'am; what's the use? I think about living. I don't want to die."

"But little boys do die, you know," continued Mrs. Dipple, kindly. "I had a little boy just about as old as you, and he died. He died, and went to heaven; where you'll go, if you are good."

"What was the matter with your boy, ma'am?"

"He was drowned. He went to sea, and was drowned," said Mrs. Dipple.

5

"Oh! well, you wasn't surprised, then. If a boy's drownded, of course he'll die. He can't help it. If I was goin' to be drownded, I dessay I should think about dying."

"But boys die other ways than by drowning. Some die of fevers—of fevers such as you have got. You know that, don't you?"

"I know lots of boys that died on it," I replied; "but then they had it reg'lar bad."

"They never had it worse than you, to be alive, my son," said she, shaking her head. "Of course, you may be spared; you may be spared, or you may die to-night. You may close your eyes, and never open them again until the Judgment-day. If I were you, I should say my prayers—if I knew any. Do you know any?"

"I know a good bit of 'Our Father,' ma'am," said I, beginning to be impressed by her serious manner; "would that one do?"

"I've got a beautiful book full of prayers for people who mayn't have long to live," replied Mrs. Dipple; "I will fetch it and read you something out of it, if you like."

"Thanky, ma'am; I think I should like."

So away she went to fetch the beautiful book; but the fact is, I had said that I thought I should like to hear her read out of it just to please her. I didn't want to hear anything more about it. Why did she want to come talking to me and making me uncomfortable! As soon as her back was turned, I shut my eyes and pretended to be asleep. Presently I heard her gently calling me, and at the same time I heard the voice of old Mrs. Brownhunter, the matron.

"What the dickins do you want to rouse him for, you stupid old fool?" said she.

"I beg your pardon, missus," replied the nurse; "but you heard what the doctor said this afternoon, didn't you?"

"Of course, I did. What of it?"

"You see, missus, I was thinking that he wasn't a baby, who couldn't have anything wicked to answer for at the Judgment-seat, and so I thought I'd just"——

"Stir him up and set him howling, eh? Be off with you and your Judgment-seats, you old Methodist, you! Gracious me! When they *will* go off quiet, let them, I say. Lord knows, they're trouble enough one way and another, without putting a lot of rubbish into their heads."

"But, missus, I am a mother myself, and"——

"Fiddlesticks!" interrupted Mrs. Brownhunter; "what's that to do with it! You're a pauper here, and I'm matron. *I* know what's good for patients, I suppose; and I'm answerable to the Board. You mind your own business."

I heard this conversation, every word of it; but I was such a dreadfully ignorant boy, that what either the nurse or the matron meant, I could not entirely make out. The allusion to the Judgment-seat was quite lost on me. By "letting 'em go off quiet," I thought the matron meant letting them go off to sleep quiet; and for once I quite agreed with her. Clearly, it *was* better to let a tired person go off quiet, than to stir him up and set him howling.

Next morning I awoke, feeling more like myself—my old self—than ever since I had been ill—evidently very much to the astonishment of everybody about me. Mrs. Dipple, as she gave me my breakfast, quite spoilt it by her talk about snatchings from the grave; and presently, when fat Mrs. Brownhunter waddled past, she paused an instant to exclaim, sneeringly—

"*You*'re a nice article to read prayers to!"

But Doctor Flinders was more surprised than anybody.

"Hey-day, young fellow!" exclaimed he; "you never mean to tell us that you've weathered it through!"

"Yes, sir," said Mrs. Dipple; "he's cheated the worms, as the saying is."

With that the doctor felt my pulse, and had a good look at me.

"You are right, ma'am," said he, laughing, and patting my cheek; "upon my life, I believe that he has. It is wonderful. Last night I would have backed a penny rushlight against his life; and now, I'll undertake to say that he has at least as good a chance of living as of kicking the bucket. He'll do, ma'am. I'll warrant we have him hearty and on his legs again before his hair grows long enough to need cutting."

It was the last part only of Doctor Flinder's speech that caused me surprise. What he had said about my chances of living caused me no amazement; for, as before observed, I never once thought that I was in danger of dying. What did astonish me was his observation on the probability of my being set up hearty and on my legs before the time when my hair needed cutting. I have not before had occasion to mention it; but since I had been an inmate of the workhouse, my hair had been cut, and my head shaven as smooth as a pumpkin. Why, it would be ever so many weeks before my hair could grow long enough for cutting; and shouldn't I be well before that? Doctor Flinders must make a mistake.

So he did; but, what was worse, so did I. My hair grew but slowly; but I was *not* hearty and well by the time it wanted shearing. To be sure, the rules of the workhouse at which I was staying were particularly stringent as regarded boys' heads, and didn't allow of the hair growing an eighth of an inch longer than the scissors could be made to bite at; still, starting with no hair at all, and the weather being cold, the remainder of October and the whole of November passed before my crop infringed the workhouse laws; nevertheless, the barber had to come to me, in consequence of my being still too weak to go to the barber.

Unfortunately, too, my illness did not terminate with the fever. Indeed, as far as feeling miserable and in pain goes, I may truthfully say that my real illness began just about that time when Doctor Flinders prophesied that I should be hearty and on my legs. True, I *was* on my legs, in as far as I was compelled to get up and dress myself, and walk about the ward. But if any one imagined that I was "hearty," they never laboured under a more perfect delusion. As regards feeding, I was hearty enough. I was more than hearty—I was wolfish, and any day could have eaten four times as much as the stingy dietary scale awarded me, which, of course, was a certain sign that my health was mending. But if I could have had my choice, I would sooner have had the fever all along, because then I should have been allowed to lie snug in bed, and been waited on, which was ever so much better than being neither up nor down, as one may say, and setting my sore bones on hard forms and the sharp edges of bedsteads, and being in every-body's way; and having this week my feet so swollen that I couldn't get my shoes on; and next week the ear-ache; and the week after, bad eyes, so that I had to wear a great green shade over them; and all the while feeling snappish and being snapped at, and getting the creeps every time the ward-room door swung open—all of which I suffered, and a great deal more, which, though it would appear foolish were it written down, was dreadfully hard to bear, and made me sick and tired of the workhouse, and longing for the time when I should be well, and they would give me my clothes and let me go.

For, without doubt, that was what I expected they would do. I thought it likely that they might make up what I was short of, and give me a shirt and a cap, and perhaps a pair of boots—indeed, I very much wished that they might help me so far; and that when I desired it, I had only to say to them, "I'm very much obliged to you for curing me, and now I think I'll go," and they would open the door and let me go. *Where* I should go, seemed just as much a matter of course, — back to the dark arches ; back to Mouldy and Ripston, whom I longed to see again, and who, I had no doubt, would be delighted to see me! It might be supposed that, having enjoyed such a long spell of comfortable feeding and lodging, I should not be able to think of being obliged to return to my market and dark-arches life without dread. Nothing of the sort; I only thought of the jolly larks we used to have, and how we used to rove about, earning our money and spending it just how we pleased. Besides, what was the world to me without Mouldy and Ripston?—an empty world, with not a single soul to speak to, or make myself at home with. Of course, there was Fryingpan Alley; but Fryingpan Alley was now cut altogether out of *my* world, and might as well have been in the moon, as far as I was concerned.

Only that I was so very sure in my own mind as to what I should do, I might have found out the true state of the case several weeks before I did; for in the same ward with myself were other boys who had lived nearly all their lives in the workhouse, and knew all its ways. They were a foolish sort of boys, though; and I never talked to them much—never about my own affairs. That was my secret. The master himself knew no other than that I was an orphan, and hadn't a friend in the world, (as the carman had told him;) and it wasn't likely I was going to let out anything to the boys which might lead to my father being sent for.

At last, there came a day—it was in February, and the snow was lying on the ground pretty thick—when Dr. Flinders came round, and ordered myself and another boy named Biles, who had been sent up to be cured of the scarlatina, to be discharged from the sick ward on the following day. When the doctor was gone, Biles said to me—

"Let's see, Smithfield, you're an orphan, ain't you?"

"I'm a orphan," I replied.

"Then war-orks to you!" said Biles, grinning.

"What do you mean? Why war'orks to me?"

"Stop till you gets to Stratford, and then they'll show you," answered Biles; "all orphans goes to Stratford, don't you know? What with the walloping, and the skilly, and the blackhole, it's a awful place. I know a boy—a orphan, just like you—wot they killed."

"What did they kill him for?"

"'Cos they caught him climbin' over the high wall, with the spikes a-top, tryin' to get away," replied Biles. "At least, when I say they killed him, I on'y tell you what everybody says. They caught him a-gettin' over, and they pulled him down and shut him in the dark hole; he was never seen any more! What d'yer think of that?"

"I think he was a jolly fool for goin' to Stratford," said I.

"He didn't go; they took him in the conwayance—like they'll take you," answered Biles.

"No, they won't," said I; "let them go to Stratford that's got a mind to. When the master comes round by and by, I shall ask him to give me my own clothes, and let me out to go where I like."

"That's right!" grinned Biles; "you ask him; he's sure to do it, and I dessay he'll give you a tanner to pay your omblibust!"

But I didn't mind what Biles said. I always thought he was a fool, and now I was sure of it. Was it likely, since I had had so much trouble in getting into the workhouse, that they would mind my going out? It stood to reason that they would be very glad to get rid of me.

The master went through the wards every night at nine, to see that everybody was a-bed. When he came through ours that night, and was near my bed, I called him. Everybody in the ward lifted his head off his bolster and stared with surprise. I didn't know what a daring thing I had done. The master could hardly believe his ears.

"Did you call *me*, sir?" asked he, turning about, with his hands under his coat-tails.

"Yes, please, sir; I wanted to ask you to get my old clothes and put 'em down here, so that I may put 'em on when I get up in the mornin'. I'm goin' off in the mornin', please, sir."

The master's eyes quite blazed behind his spectacles as he looked at me; then, turning to the matron, he calmly asked—

"Is that boy right in his head, Mrs. Brownhunter?"

"Quite right, sir—as right as he'll ever be, the owdacious little rascal!" replied she, meekly.

"And can you account for this extraordinary behaviour, ma'am?"

"On'y that he's just as wicious as he always has been," replied Mrs. Brownhunter, spitefully.

"Very good," said the master, taking out his pencil and pocket-book; "let us see—he's one of the lot that goes away to-morrow, and his number is"——

"Three-forty-seven, sir," put in the matron, blandly.

"Thank you; I shouldn't be surprised, three-forty-seven, if you hear of this little affair again." And glaring at me once more, he went on his way.

Here, indeed, was a discovery! It was not till many minutes after I had buried my head under the bedclothes that I could bring the fact fairly before my mind; but there it was. I was *not* free to leave the workhouse! I was a prisoner, and to-morrow would be removed to that frightful place Biles had told me of—to be placed in the black-hole at once, no doubt, for my insolence to the master!

What ever should I do? Which way could I escape from the dreadful fate that awaited me? Even if I found a chance to run away, there were the clothes! Not, I am ashamed to be obliged to confess, that I felt any scruples about running away in clothes which had only been lent to me, but they were such queer-looking clothes—a sort of green baize, with brass buttons; the coat being a bob-tail, and the breeches being corduroy, and coming no lower than the knees, and finishing off with blue worsted stockings, and shoes with brass buckles. Where would be the use of running away in such a rig? Anybody would know me a quarter of a mile off! Still, it was but a very little way from the workhouse to the dark arches; and if I could only reach them in safety, and find my friends Mouldy and Ripston, they might manage somehow to help me out of the mess.

But how to get out of the workhouse was the difficulty, and one that kept me awake hours after all but the nurses were asleep. There was one way—only one—and that not very promising. There was a young woman in the ward, a sort of helper to the nurses—not a regular nurse, but a poor young woman who was a pauper, and who got no more liberty than the other paupers. She was a very pleasant and good-looking young woman, and somebody used to send her letters; sly letters, which the gate-keeper used to take in. Sometimes she used to slip down and take the letters of the gate-keeper herself, but more often she would send one of us boys down, and as she always got us an extra slice of bread and butter for our trouble, we never told of her. The gate-keeper used to get something too, I suppose, for he never told of Jane, but used to keep her letters as artful as could be. I think it was money for tobacco Jane used to give the gate-keeper, for the last time I had gone down to ask him if any letters had come, he gave me one, and said, "Give Jane my respects, and tell her I ain't had a pipe of 'bacca since yesterday." My poor chance was to go down without being sent to the gate-keeper, ask him for a letter, and tell him that Jane wanted me to slip out on a little errand for her, and that if he would let me, I was to buy him some tobacco, and bring it in with me. It certainly was a lame sort of plan, and required enough of lying and artfulness to work it out, to make my prospects at Stratford dismal indeed, if it miscarried; but I could think of none better, and resolving to try it in the morning, I went to sleep.

The morning came. Half-past seven was the breakfast-time, and it was the eight o'clock post which generally brought Jane's letters. I didn't flinch from my plan; indeed, if my resolution had flagged when I awoke, it would certainly have been spurred to its firmest by the jeers and grins that beset me on every side. How beautifully I should catch it when I got to Stratford! was the only subject of conversation throughout the breakfast-time.

At a quarter-past eight, having managed to stow my cap under the upper part of my trousers, I stole quietly out of the ward, and down the stairs. It was a single flight, and at the bottom was a long passage which led into the yard, at the farther end of which was the gate and the gate-keeper. The window of the sick-ward overlooked the yard; and looking up, there was Jane looking down, and looking, too, as though she couldn't make out what on earth I did down in the yard at that time in the morning. But I took no notice of her, and marched bravely up to the lobby in which the gate-keeper sat.

"No letter," said he, as I came up.

"I know, sir," answered I ; "but, please, Jane says would you mind me just runnin' round the corner for her, to fetch some writing paper, and she says"——

"Cert'n'y *not*," interrupted the gate-keeper, fiercely ; "and you may tell Jane from me that she's a-comin' it a great deal too strong in askin' such a redicklus thing."

He looked up at the window as he spoke, and there was Jane shaking her head as hard as she could.

"Ah ! it's all very fine, you makin' signs—Don't stop him. I'm bound to stop him. I ain't a-goin' to risk my place, just because"——

"And, please, sir," I broke in, hurriedly, seeing how my chance was failing—"please, sir, Jane said that I was to bring you in half an ounce of 'bacca."

"Ah ! that's all very fine, too !" said the gate-keeper, his tone becoming more civil, while at the same time he gave another glance up at the ward window, where Jane still was with a very red face, and evidently with a strong suspicion that mischief was brewing, shaking her head this way and that, in the most bewildered manner. "I ain't to be bribed by Jane buyin' me 'bacca ; if I wants 'bacca, I can buy it. Give us hold of the three-ha'pence. Cut away with you, and if you are gone as long as a minute, see what you'll catch."

Give him the three-ha'pence and cut away ! Leave to go—the road open and free before me, and the whole business to be baulked for the want of three-ha'pence ! Such a cruel thing was *not* to happen. The Father of lies stuck to me in my extremity.

"I haven't got the coppers, till I get change, sir," I said ; "I was to bring you tobacco out of this sixpence which Jane gave me ;"—and I fumbled at an imaginary sixpence in my trousers pocket.

"Be off, then," said he ; "you've been standin' a-jawin' long enough already, to have gone there and back again."

He slipped back the bolt of the little wicket, and I was free ! I should have liked to run my hardest from the instant I set my foot outside the workhouse gate, but for fear anybody might be watching, had to content myself with trotting at a moderate pace till I reached the first street corner. Then I set off at top-speed. It was a bleak bracing morning ; the frosty road was hard as iron, and I felt as light as a cork. The neighbourhood was not strange to me ; I knew all the short cuts, and in about six minutes had reached the alley in the strand that led down to the dark arches.

———◆———

CHAPTER XX.

IN WHICH, DRIVEN BY STRESS OF WEATHER, I ONCE MORE MAKE SAIL FOR TURNMILL STREET—BREAKERS AHEAD.

As I turned into the alley in the strand that led *to the arches*, St. Martin's Church chimed half-*past eight.*

The sound brought me to a standstill. I had never once given it a thought as I came along—Mouldy and Ripston would not be at home ; they would have been gone to work an hour and a half since. It could hardly have been a more awkward time for me. They certainly would not return until dusk, and I must pass the interim in the best way I could.

It couldn't be helped ; but it certainly was vexing, and quite damped the triumph of my escape from the workhouse. To see Ripston and Mouldy was, of course, the first and most important business—every other hinged on it, indeed. No doubt they were to be found hanging about the market ; but, putting the question of prudence quite aside, how could I go and seek them ? A pretty figure *mine* was to be seen hunting through Covent Garden ! No ; it wasn't to be thought of. I must stow away under the arches, and amuse myself somehow until they returned.

With this resolve, I made my way down the familiar flight of dark, slippery steps, and presently found myself in that quarter of the "arches" where our van used to stand. But, somehow, the place did not appear half so familiar to me as I expected to find it. It had about it an air of desolation that the absence of our van did not account for, and seemed altogether a hundred times darker and lonelier, and drearier and bleaker, than ever before. My footsteps, light and cautious as they were, echoed from the reeking walls ; the cobblestones were slippery as glass ; while the faint light showed the icicles webbed about the green bricks in every direction.

I hunted about in search of some vehicle in which I might stow away for a few hours ; but the only cart I could find was an old water-cart, and that down towards the river end. The water-cart was one of the common sort—a square box with a hole in the top part of it, into which, when in use, the water is pumped ; and very pleased I was at finding a hiding-place so snug and sheltered. But it turned out not so nice as I had hoped ; a goodish drop of water had been left in it, but it had frozen—not hard enough, however. It seemed firm to the touch ; but as soon as I sat on it, it began to thaw, and to soak through the seat of my smallclothes. So I got out of the box, and lay along the top of the cart in the lee of the driver's perched-up seat as much as possible, so as to avoid the wind.

But it was one of those winds it is impossible to avoid—a whistling wind, keen as needles, and curiously capable of winding round corners without abating in power. It came full blast in at the narrow arched entrance, and with such force that it was still full blast, and laden with splinters of icy snow it had picked off the shore and off the barges, when it reached the water-cart, peppering the shallow partition behind which I was crouched. Of course, much allowance was to be made for the time of year and season now, and when I had last visited the arches ; but the fullest allowance I could make did not account for the terrible way in which that wind served me. Every succeeding gust of it converted my flesh into "goose-flesh," from my forehead to my heels. It nipped my ears, it glided down my back between my collar and neckerchief as though it were no thicker than a knife-blade ; and if I raised my head a little to avoid the unpleasant sensation, it whipped in at my mouth and routed about within me, producing noises as though I were an empty bottle. I was compelled to hold on my muffin cap with both my hands, until my fingers smarted with cold as though they had been burnt. Half-an-hour of such treatment was as much as I could stand. It was quite a treat to get up, and with my hands in my breeches pockets, to run up and down, stamping over the slippery cobble-stones to take the numbness out of my toes.

But, with the reader's permission, I will make short work of describing how I spent that melancholy February day. There occur in every one's lifetime days that are nice to remember—"red-letter" days, as they are called; likewise, there are days that cling not the less tenaciously to the memory on account of their ugliness. I don't know if these ugly days have a special name—lead-colour, or other; but the day in question—the February day—is as much part of my old remembrance as though it had been notched in my brain, as Crusoe used to notch his days in the pole. How cold I was! how empty, and shivery, and downhearted! I think there was not a quarter of any one hour of the many I passed in that dreadful place that was spent like the preceding. On the cart—in the cart; daring everything to escape the horrible wind, until I had thawed and soaked up nearly every bit of ice it contained; hopping round the water-cart, skipping over its shafts, and going down on to the bleak, oozy river-bank to play a solitary game at duck-stone.

Towards the afternoon I was so hard driven that I resolved to attempt to make a fire. There were bits of coal enough to be picked up on the shore, as well as bits of wood; but what I wanted was a lucifer-match. How to procure one was the great difficulty. Outside, on the river, there were plenty of coal-barges and men at work on them, and some of the men were smoking. Easy enough it would be to beg a lucifer-match of one of these, if I durst ask; but how could I, rigged as I was in that muffin-cap and swallow-tail? They would be sure to ask me questions; to talk about me amongst themselves, or to other people, perhaps, and so lead to my apprehension. The only way to obtain the match, and, at the same time, to avoid such danger, was to divest myself of part of my workhouse attire, and begrime my face and hands, so that I might pass for a mud-lark.

It was a terrible operation, simple as it may seem—all the more terrible, no doubt, because of my still being qualmish and shaky from my long spell of illness. Mudlarks never wore shoes or stockings; so these had to be pulled off, leaving me on my tender feet, (they were very tender, as I recollect,) smarting on the icy stones. Mudlarks never wore caps nor jackets; off they came. Mudlarks were muddy to the knees—to the elbows; their faces were smeared with mud. With my naked legs and white feet to walk directly into the river slush was my next job—slush black as ink, and with a thickish rind of ice to break through to get at it—to dip my arms into it, and with my muddy fingers smear my face. Mudlarks invariably carried an old saucepan to put their gleanings in as they collected them; luckily enough, there reposed an old saucepan, its handle just peeping up out of the mud, under the stern of a coal-barge.

So set up, I walked boldly up to the coal-heavers, and in a civil way asked one of them if he happened to have a lucifer-match about him that he could spare. The person asked, by way of reply caught up a clinker and threw it at me, cleverly hitting the knuckles of the hand that grasped the filthy old saucepan, and causing me to drop it; whereat the jolly coal-heavers, much amused, set up a laugh, and pelted me with bits of coal until I was glad to run—squelch—squelch—through the mire, and take refuge in the lee of a barge, aboard which there was nobody but one old fellow pumping water out of the vessel. As he saw me approaching, he ceased his occupation, and, catching up a boat-hook lying handy, ran to the head of the barge, and, stooping over, began fiercely poking at me with it. Luckily, it was too short to reach me.

"Out you come, you warmint!" he exclaimed. "Out you come, you awful young prig! Jest out of prison, and at it again directly—hey? Out you come!"

"I hain't out o' prison, mister," I replied, beginning to cry; "I never was in prison."

"Not out o' prison, you awful young liar! Why, look at your hair! If that ain't a gaol crop, what is it?"

"It's the work'us," I answered, completely breaking down. "I've been in the work'us, and had my head shaved 'cos I had the fever; and I've run away from the work'us; and all I asked them coves for was a lucifer to make a bit of fire, 'cos I was so cold; and then they began to pelt me. See here!"—and I held up my knuckles to show him how they were bleeding.

Sprawling on the barge, with his white head craning over the black prow of it, the old fellow regarded my up-turned, muddy, tear-stained visage searchingly, and, as it seemed, found enough of truth in it to shake his previous suspicions.

"You are such a awfully artful crew, that there's no believin' one o' you; howsomever, since it's only a match you want, here it is, and welcome. Here's two, 'fear one goes out."

And to land them to me dry and sound, he stuck them into a crack at the end of the boat-hook, and lowered them down to me.

But, alas! my endeavours were fruitless. I had half stripped and begrimed myself—I had borne the pelting of the brutal coal-heavers—all in vain. I had coals, and I had wood, and I had a bit of paper; but the whole were damp; and with deep sorrow I saw my two lucifers one after the other expire, leaving no result behind them. I looked out on to the shore, and though the jolly coal-heavers were still at work, the barge on which the friendly old man had been working was now quite deserted. Therefore there remained nothing for me to do but to go down to the water's edge and wash the mud off my arms and legs and face, leaving them to dry in the wind for want of a towel. Then I put on my stockings and shoes, and my cap, and my swallow-tail coat, and, by way of promoting the circulation of my blood, performed several walking matches, from one end of the arches to the other, against the quarter chimes of Saint Clements Danes.

At two o'clock, or thereabouts, it began to snow steadily and heavily; but so far from being sorry to see this, I was delighted. Thought I, it will soon be all right now; they can't stand much of this; they'll soon be home. But though I sat on the bottom step of the flight down which they always used to come till I was chilled to the bones, they didn't come. Other people did—some whose faces I knew, and others who were strange to me; but I kept in the dark. I didn't want a mob round me, asking a lot of questions as to why I didn't go home to the workhouse.

I waited till dark—till the churches chimed seven—but neither of my old friends made their appearance, and I was dead-beat and heart-sick. I was beset every way—by hunger, (I was too full of my plan to eat much breakfast,) by disappointment, and by anxiety to make up my mind what to do.

And now it was made clear to me—if I had not known it before—how completely my plans were centred in making up to Mouldy and Ripston once more; for now that they had failed me, I was all adrift. All I had done—all I had risked, and dared, and overcome—had gone for nothing. What could I possibly do, but —— go home?

I had been working up to this decision for hours; since, indeed, the setting in of the heavy snow which should have driven my friends to the arches, and did not. The idea had come forward with wonderfully short and shy steps. When it first just began to whisper, it was whistled off—stuff and nonsense! rubbish! the last thing to be done!—but as my hopes of the two boys coming home fell away, it edged in bolder and bolder, and now took tight hold of me, and would let me think of nothing else.

And, after all, it was not such a dreadful thing to think of. More than nine months had passed since I had set eyes on anyone at home, and how did I know but that they would be very glad to see me, or, at the very worst, that my father would let me off with a good talking to? Besides, I was a bigger boy than when they had last seen me, (I had grown wonderfully while I was ill,) and knew how to seek work and to set about it, so that it wasn't as if I meant going home to be an encumbrance.

So I tried to screw up my courage. Nevertheless, when I got out into the Adelphi, (it was still snowing at a tremendous rate,) I lingered round about, and at last ran as far as the market to take just one last look round for Mouldy and Ripston; but they were not to be found, and I set my face towards Fryingpan Alley.

My resolve at starting was to march into the alley without stopping or taking notice of anyone; since I had got to face my father, it had better be done at a dash. But by the time I reached Smithfield, and turned into Cowcross, I found myself walking slower and slower, till, by the time I reached the distillery wall, I pulled up altogether, and began to question myself whether, considering the sort of man my father was, it would be safe to approach him at a dash. It was Tuesday, and Tuesday was generally a good day with him. Would it not be better to wait till he came out of the "Dog and Stile?" He was never so soft-hearted as when a little gone in liquor. I would not go to the house; I would hang about the alley till I saw my father.

Unless my father's habits were altered, he would go home to his supper a little after ten, and now it was nearly nine. It was a very dark night, and I was able to get pretty close to the alley without any great risk of being seen. I stood on the opposite side of the way. I find now, that Fryingpan Alley is faced by a boarding hemming in the new railway; but at the time of which I am writing there were houses, and courts, and alleys, as on the other side, and it was just inside the entrance of one of these alleys that I took my stand.

The thought of seeing my father, and wondering what he would do and say to me, kept me up, and saved me from feeling either cold or hungry; but I waited and waited till it was ten o'clock and past, and he didn't come, and then I began to be afraid either that for once in a while he had taken his pipe and his pint indoors, or else that he was at the public-house getting very drunk, in which case he would be harder to deal with than if he were quite sober. I began to feel cold, and hungry, and faint, and all the rest of it, when these thoughts came into my head, and I must needs go as far as the "Dog and Stile," and, creeping cautiously up, take a peep through the chinks of the swinging door.

But a very small portion of the bar of the "Dog and Stile" could be seen in this way; and, as it happened, my ears were better served than my eyes by approaching the door so closely. There was a row in the tap-room. I could plainly make out Mr. Piggot's voice, and an Irishwoman's voice, and many other voices, all swearing and laughing, and threatening and persuading, at one and the same time. All in a minute the Irishwoman's loud abusive clacking became a screech of rage and pain; there was a staggering of the people quarrelling towards the door; and I had barely time to get out of the way before it was swung open, and a woman was pushed out.

She had a child in her arms, and, as might be seen by the light that shone through the windows of the public-house, her clothes were slouched about her, and tattered and bedraggled in a shameful way. She had long red hair, all touzled and hanging about her eyes, and her lips were cut and bleeding. There was no mistaking her—she was my stepmother; and the child in her arms—a poor little dirty-faced thing in an old bed-gown, and with a rag of a shawl wrapped about her—was my own sister Polly.

Evidently Mrs. Burke was drunk, or as near that state as was in the power of intoxicating liquor to reduce her to. It was a man that had thrust her out of the "Dog and Stile," and so vengefully that she was sent tottering into the gutter, and only by great exertion saved herself from falling on her face there. She was not defeated, however. Gaining her legs, she reeled back to the door, and hammered at it with her bony fist, (how well I knew it!) shrieking out in horrible language for her bonnet. She would have her bonnet or she would smash every blessed and beatific window in the angelic house—send her to heaven if she wouldn't!—and as she spoke she aimed a shoulder hit at a square of glass, and drew back her red fist through the jagged hole. This brought the man who had thrust her out once more to the door; he had a ragged bonnet in one hand, and he clapped it, wrong side in front, on her fiery head, and, raising his other hand, would have given her a frightful blow in the face had not some one behind caught him by the waist and jerked him back just in the nick of time.

"Come, that's enough of it, Jim Ballisat," exclaimed Mr. Piggot. "My house ain't goin' to be made a randywoo for this sort o' caper. What d'yer mean by it, Jim? Wallop her at home, can't yer? You're more like a devil than a man!"

As before observed, despite Mrs. Burke's rags and dirt—despite her tangled hair and disfigured face—I knew her as soon as I set eyes on her; but I didn't know my father, and when Mr. Piggot addressed him as Jim Ballisat I was very much amazed. *This* my father! True, he was in his shirt-sleeves, and never in my life had I before seen him out of the house without his flannel jacket, so that doubtless made all the difference in his appearance; but then his shirt-sleeves were torn, and filthy dirty—not at all like the shirt-sleeves I had been accustomed to see about his arms. Moreover, this man had not my father's face. It was altogether a different face. My father, as I knew him, was a smartish man, and by no means indifferent to personal appearance. When the work of the day was at an end, as soon as he had finished his tea, he would have a bowl of warm water, and taking off his jacket and waistcoat, tidily unbutton his shirt-front, and tucking it under his braces, have a good wash, and brush his hair, putting plenty of oil on it to soften and take the obstinacy out of it, and tie on his silk neckerchief, and all this with no more important business before him than to go round to the "Stile" and smoke a pipe with his chums. When he has been going to the play, he was so fastidious as to black and shine his ankle-jacks and go to the expense of new laces. On such occasions I have seen my mother spend a good half-hour curling his hair with bits of hot tobacco-pipe. But here Jim Ballisat, as Mr. Piggot declared him to be, was a very different figure—a man with an un-washed, bloated face and puffy eyes, with a head of hair that evidently had not known a brush or comb since that distant period when his face was last washed, with a beard a week old at least, and his thick hairy throat all bare. Tall hats, I think I have mentioned, were an abomination against which my father, in common with every other decent male inhabitant of Fryingpan Alley, most resolutely set his countenance. Now, however, cocked a-top of his uproarious hair was a hat of the tall sort, dirty-white and dreadfully battered. There he stood on the snowy pavement, yelling horrid oaths and flourishing his great fists, and threatening to stave Mrs. Burke's jaws in if he could get hold on her; while she, depending that those who held him would keep him tight, stuck the arm that was not engaged a-kimbo, and wagged her hideous bleary face within two yards of him, shrieking defiance. I do think that if he could have got at her he would have murdered her. If one blow of his fist would have done it, I am sure it would have been done had they given him the chance. However, with persuasion and pulling they got him to come back into the house, and shut the door.

"You go home, marm," exclaimed a well-meaning bystander. "You take my advice, and make yerself scarce."

"And what for, may I ax?"

"You'll have him at yer again if yer don't."

"And indade I'll not go home!" screeched Mrs. Burke, tearing from her head the bonnet, about the safety of which a minute before she had expressed so much anxiety, and dashing it into the gutter, and demoniacally jumping upon it. "Whirroo! Is it me that's to be frightened by the likes of a dhrunken, dirthy bla'gard baste sich as him?" (Here she plucked a hair-pin from her "back knot," and allowed the full shock of fiery hair to fall about her bruised and bloody face.) "Don't I owe me ruin to the schoundhril? Hasn't he sowld out of me dacent home the bits of shticks me own first dear man—the man as you ain't fit to clane the shoes of, Jim Ballisat—lift me? Doesn't he dbrink ivery pinny he can borry or shtale, and lave me to sbupport the brat in me arms, which, Hiven be praised, is none o' mine, but of the shthrumpit as consoorted wid him afore he pershwaded me to have him? Don't I work me fingers to the bones for the lazy shpalpeen? Don't I"——

What else Mrs. Burke did for my unfortunate father the attentive mob was cheated of hearing, for at that moment a policeman came up and unceremoniously pushed her off towards Fryingpan Alley.

CHAPTER XXI.

IN WHICH, BY A MIRACLE, I ESCAPE MY FATHER'S JUST VENGEANCE, INCURRED BY BRINGING DISGRACE ON "HIS AND HIS'N."

I FOLLOWED my stepmother and the mob as far as Fryingpan Alley, and saw the policeman, who seemed to know very well where she lived, hustle her unceremoniously into the arched entrance.

Now, what was I to do? Clearly, it was no use following Mrs. Burke any farther. Had she been the same Mrs. Burke I had known of old, the experiment would have been sufficiently dangerous; but now it was altogether out of the question. Young as I was, it was quite apparent to me that she was a greater fury than ever; and how she was likely to receive me, were I rash enough to make myself known, was plain from what I had heard her say about my little sister Polly. Poor little thing! Grievous as it was to see her in such a deplorable condition, to see her at all lifted a great weight from my mind. Not only was she alive, (and, judging from Jerry Pape's singular behaviour and my father's lasting malignancy, I very often had doubts about it,) but from the hasty view I had been enabled to obtain of her, she was not in the least maimed or disfigured.

Were my chances of finding a friend in my father any better? It did not seem so. He had become a drunkard, and, as I had heard them say, more like a devil than a man. I had seen him drunk many a time, and observed what a spiteful and dangerous man he was under such circumstances; but never before had I seen him so drunk as he now was. Yet, if I went away, where should I go? I was starving with cold and hunger. I durst not go back to the workhouse. The dark arches, now that they were deserted by my old friends Mouldy and Ripston, were no longer inviting. I was as much alone in the world as though there was no other living creature in it. After all, my father *might* take compassion on me. No doubt Mrs. Burke had done her best to set him against me, and had kept his wrath hot for me. Now, however, she was out of favour. Perhaps my father had found her out, and would be even glad to take me back again, were it only to spite her. Reckoning affairs up in this miserable manner, I crept slowly back towards the "Dog and Stile," the door of which, now that the misance had been removed, was once more open, and business progressing the same as usual.

The taproom window faced the street, and I stooped down under it and listened. The company were singing. "This day a stag must die!" was the song of the moment, and presently it was completed amidst the "brayvos" and hammering of pewter pots on the tables.

"Who d'yer call on for the next harmony, Sam?" somebody asked.

"I calls on Nosey Warren."

"Nosey Warren be butcher'd! I'm a-goin' to sing."

"Never mind him. Pipe up, Nosey."

"I'll see him butcher'd fust, and then he shan't! I'm a-goin' to sing *my* song, I tell yer; and them as don't like to jine in the chorus can do the t'other thing."

And then the speaker struck up "The death of Nelson." I knew the song, and I knew the voice that was singing it. There was a water-spout attached to the wall by the side of the tap-room window, and I climbed up it and peeped in. It *was* my father. It gave me quite a thrill of delight to hear him—he was singing it so like himself, and so unlike the dirty, blear-eyed man who had bundled Mrs. Burke into the gutter. He *looked* more like himself, too, and stood upright, waving his hand, and pointing out the enemy with his forefinger, exactly as Lord Nelson did it. Perhaps it was being in such a dreadful passion that had made him look so different. He seemed all right enough now; indeed, he seemed especially tender-hearted, so that when he came to "At length the fatal wownd," his voice quite failed him, and he passed the sleeve of his shirt across his eyes before he could proceed any further. Should I go in and make myself known to him? It was no use shillyshallying about it. If I meant to do it, I had best do it at once.

I pushed open the door, and made my way to the tap-room. My father had just finished his song, and the company were "knocking it down" in the most complimentary manner. As I stood at the tap-room door, gulping down my lingering remnant of hesitation, the potman came behind me with some pots of beer in his hands.

"Now, then, in you go, young feller, if you're goin'!" said he, at the same time urging me forward with his knee, so that I was pushed against the door, opening it; and in I went.

The room was tolerably full of company; but, looking round, I failed to see my father, which was no wonder, as, having concluded his song, he had dropped his arms on the table before him, and his head on his arms, so that the battered white hat being still on his head, that and the dirty shirt-sleeves were all that was visible of him.

Awaiting the fresh supply of beer, and having nothing at the moment to engage their attention, the company generally favoured me by turning their inquiring glances in my direction.

"Well, work'us!" observed the potman, "what are *you* arter?"

"Please, sir, isn't my father here?"

"Well, that's a good 'un, arstin' me! ain't yer got two English eyes in yer head?"

"He was here just now; I saw him."

"What sort of a cove is he?"

Now I caught sight of the white hat.

"There he is!" I answered, pointing towards *him, with my* heart in my mouth, as people say.

The potman, (who was a stranger to me, and a new hand at the "Stile,") seemed much tickled at my answer, and laughed and winked at the company.

"Lord's truth! Carrots ought to be here now," said he; "it 'ud be as good as a panter-mine to see her slip into Jim—wouldn't it?"

"What's the name of your father, my boy?" somebody asked.

"Mr. Ballisat, sir."

"Strike me blind if I didn't think so!" replied somebody, and whom I now knew to be a hare and rabbit-skin man living in our alley. "I thought I know'd him soon as he showed his head inside the door. Hi, Jim! Wake him up, some on yer. Jim! wake up, old man. Here's your boy come back agin." And being a lame man, and having his crutch with him, he reached over, and gave my father a tap on the head with the handle of it.

"You go to ——," growled my father, rubbing his head without raising it. "You keep your stick your own side, or p'r'aps I might get rusty."

"But look up, Jim. Here he is, a-standin' before you."

"Gammon!"

"Speak to him, young Jim," said the man. "He'll know your woice, I'll wager."

"It is me, father," said I, laying a shaking hand on his arm. "It is me. I've come back again."

Slowly raising his heavy head off the table, my father gave me a scowling glance that made me back a yard or so away from him. He remained so long with his eyes fixed on me that I grew hopeful. I knew his passionate nature, and it seemed to me certain that if he meant to ill-use me he would have started up at once. I actually began to indulge in the blissful expectation that he would presently extend his hand to me, and tell me that I was forgiven.

He did nothing of the kind. As he looked at me, his eyes grew steadier; and taking his arms off the table, he deliberately arose and came round to where I was standing. Taking all my collars at a grip, and hurting my throat cruelly with the knuckles of his big fist, he thrust me down upon a form.

"Now I've got yer! B—t yer young eyes! now I've got yer!"

And still holding me tight with one hand, he proceeded to unbuckle the terrible waist-strap with the other.

"Why, what are you a-goin' to do with him, Jim?" asked the lame hare and rabbit-skin man; "you're a-hurtin' his neck, Jim. Let go on him; he's a-goin' quite black in the face!"

"He'll be black somewheres else besides his face, and green and yaller too, afore I've done with him," replied my father, with awful coolness, as his hand, less sober than his head, fumbled at the buckle of the waist-strap.

"Why, you wouldn't go a-latherin' of him—would you, Jim?" exclaimed the potman.

"What have you got to say agin it?" asked my father, fiercely.

"Oh, it's no odds of mine, of coorse; on'y when a kid comes and chucks hisself on your mercy, as one may say, it seems gallus cruel to take advantage on him."

"Let him go, Jim; you was a kid yerself once, reccoleck."

"Ay, let him go; let him go, Jim! he seems more'n half dead now," said the company.

"Now I've got yer," repeated my father, as the buckle-tongue at last yielded, and he whipped the strap off with a flourish. For a moment he hesitated as to which would be the most convenient posture to place me in while he flogged me, and then lifting me up by the collar, he flung me flat with my face on to the table. He thus obtained a full-length view of me, and, as it seemed for the first time, noticed the strangeness of my attire. With a grunt of scorn he took the bagginess of my breeches between his finger and thumb, and so turned me over on to my back.

"Why, what d'yer mean by wearin' this Bartlemy Fair rig? Where did yer get it from?"

I was so full of terror that I couldn't answer him a word.

"D'yer hear, yer young cuss? What game have yer been up to? Who's been a-dressin' of yer up in this style?"

"It's summat like the Penitensherry," some one suggested.

"Refermatery, *I* think," said another; "the cut o' the hair is werry much like the Refermatery."

"Can't yer open yer lyin' young jaws?" exclaimed my father, giving me a shake; "*is* it Penitensherry?"

"Penitensherry be blowed!" observed the potman; "they ain't that, and they ain't t'other crack-jaw word; they're work'us, that's what they are."

"What! work'us!" and, in the extremity of his horror, my father withdrew his hand from my throat. "It's a lie," roared he; "they're Penitensherry togs, that's what they are."

"No, father; they're workhouse clothes," I ventured to explain; "they're the clothes what they gave me when I was carried to the workhouse with the fever."

Had he suspected that "the fever" still lurked in the green bob-tail or the smalls, my father could not have regarded them with greater consternation. He actually shrank away from the table, thus enabling me to assume a less ignominious position.

"Here's trouble for a cove!" he exclaimed, in a voice tremulous with emotion, and looking round appealingly on the company. "He comes and he tells me to my head that he's bin and disgraced me and mine by chuckin' hisself on the union! Penitensherry would ha' been a corker; but work'us! work'us!" and he took to weeping. "You heard him, all on yer, didn't yer? Ain't it enough to make a feller werry nigh bust hisself with his feelin's? He goes off arter werry nearly killin' our other kid, and I goes a-losin arternoon arter arternoon, and can't find no tale or tidin's on him. Werry well; that I shouldn't so much ha' minded; but what does he go a-doin' next? Why, he goes and ketches fevers, and chucks hisself on the parish, purpose that he might come here and show hisself off in pauper togs, and make me look little! Yet all on you set on me and say, 'Let him be.' Yes! I'll let him be. Cuss him, I'll make a jelly on him."

"Not in my house you won't. I've had enough of you, what with broken winders and bisness upset, for one day."

It was Mr. Piggot that spoke. Attracted by the loud tone in which my father was speaking, and dreading a revival of the quarrel so recently quelled, he had left his bar to peep into the tap-room and see what the row was about. As luck would have it, he entered the room in the very nick of time to do me a service—just in time to catch the buckle-end of the strap as it was whirling in the air. But father had hold on the other end of the strap, with a turn of it round his hand, so that Mr. Piggot was unable to snatch it away, and only got his knuckles rapped by the brass buckle for his pains. This made the publican savage.

"Out you go, you big, bullying coward, you," he exclaimed; "I tell you, you shan't ill-use the boy in my house;" and as he spoke he rashly laid a rough hand on my father's shoulder. Next moment, there were heard the sounds of a smart spank, and then of a dull thud—the first being caused by the sudden visitation of my father's fist to Mr. Piggot's face, and the second by the consequent banging of Mr. Piggot's head against the tap-room door.

My father was in a terrible passion, and stood sparring with his great fists, and glaring and mouthing, like the mad drunkard he was. One good came to me through the landlord's interference: to enable him to spar, my father was obliged to quit his hold on me, and I was not slow to avail myself of it, and to shuffle from the table to the ground.

"Fetch the police, Peter," said Mr. Piggot to his potman.

"Fetch 'em! fetch forty on 'em, you infernal old rotten gin-tub," roared my parent. "Look here; he's my child, and I'll do jest what I like with him. I tells you, old Piggot, and I tells every man in this room, that I'm just a-goin' to begin to welt that young wagabone jest as long and jest as hard as wot I've a fancy to. Now, which one of yer is it as says that I shan't?" And as he spoke, he dealt the table such a tremendous blow with his clenched fist as fairly made even the full quart pots leap.

There was a tremendous stir by this time, and the tap-room door was half open, with half-a-dozen people looking in. I was still crouching under the table, where I had crept out of my father's way, when the friendly potman stooped down and dragged me out behind the men's legs; while my father was too busy defying Mr. Piggot, the police, and all the rest of the world, to take notice.

"Now, you cut home as fast as your legs will carry you, young feller, and think yourself lucky to get off so easy."

And with that, he pushed me out into the street, closing the door after me.

CHAPTER XXII.

IN WHICH I MAKE THE ACQUAINTANCE OF TWO JEWS, AND AM SCANDALOUSLY FLEECED BY THEM.

IF any one had observed me as I turned away from the "Dog and Stile," not knowing the peculiarities of my case, they never would have supposed that I was escaping from some tremendous danger. People escaping from great perils that may easily pursue and overtake them naturally run. I didn't run. Where was the use? Where was I to run to? If ever there was an outcast boy, surely I was that one. Without a home; without a single friend in the world; with an empty belly, and clothed in worse than rags—inasmuch as the livery I had on was not mine, and fettered my free going almost as much as if the corduroys on my legs and the linsey-wool-seys on my arms had been fetters and handcuffs. "Think yourself lucky to get off so easy," the potman said. Lucky! In what way, I should like to know? It was all over with my hopes and schemes. I was regularly in for it, and didn't care a button what happened next. I was so altogether cast down, that if, as I skulked along Turnmill Street, I had heard my father coming raging after me up the street, flourishing his waist-strap as he ran, I don't think that I should have hurried myself in the least to avoid him.

It was by this time fully half-past ten o'clock, and the shops were being closed. Which way I was going was not worth thinking about. All ways were the same to me now; so, with my hands in the pockets of my parish breeches, I went slouching along through the pelting snow, taking the streets as I came to them, as a homeless dog might.

In this manner I jogged along for a quarter of an hour or so, until I found myself in Hatton Garden, with my face towards Holborn. Facing Kirby Street, in that locality, there is another street leading into Leather Lane. This street is not a long one, and is made up of shops. All the shops, however, except one, were closed. The exception was a baker's shop, and the baker was putting up his shutters.

The shutters were all up but one, and through the bit of corner window yet visible, there was exposed to view a heap of twists and rolls and other sorts of small-sized fancy bread. Had my legs been suddenly deprived of use, I could not have been brought to a more complete standstill. It seemed that my doggish jogging through the snow was not aimless, after all; this was what I was in search of—this bread! One or two of those new and crusty little loaves — the twists preferred, on account of being flat and easy to bite at. How many of those lovely twists could I eat? Which would I choose? That one at the bottom for one, because it was so brown and crispy, and that other one leaning against the window, because——

Whiz! up went the last shutter, shutting in the beautiful bread and the light, and leaving the baker's shop only one more to add to the dark and dismal row.

It was like waking out of a dream. Since the morning, I had felt no desire for food; I had not even thought of it; but now a sudden sense of faintness beset me, and an indescribable numbness pervaded my inner parts, awakening my stomach and setting it aching for food. I *must* have something to eat. The painful craving roused my wits, and I was no longer dull and sluggish, but as broad awake as ever I was in my life.

Some food MUST be got.

But how? Should I beg?

Who of? Hatton Garden and Leather Lane are no places for gentlefolks, nor indeed for any *other sort of folks,* in any number, at eleven o'clock at night. How could I beg, dressed as I was in workhouse clothes? Who would give me a penny and pass on, as that good gentleman in Smithfield had done, on the first day of my running away from home, without asking questions as to why I was out so late at night, and why I did not make haste back to the workhouse? Besides, there was no time for begging; by the time I had begged a penny there would be no way of spending it.

Was there anything I could steal?

The only open shop in sight was a gin-shop; the only foot passenger in sight a policeman. At least so it seemed, as I glanced up and down the street; but the snow was so blinding that I could scarcely see twenty yards before me. But, presently, I heard footsteps and laughter coming from towards Hatton Wall, and presently could make out two young gentlemen, with cigars and walking-canes. They were so merry, that it seemed quite like Providence sending them this way that I might beg a penny of them. Stealing from them, I declare, never came into my head; nor was it likely that it should, for, as I said before, both young gentlemen carried walking-sticks, and the policeman was as yet in sight.

The closer the two young gentlemen approached, the higher my hopes grew; that they were real rich gentlemen seemed certain, for on the hand that held his cigar each of them had a ring, with a more brilliant stone in it than I had seen since my uncle Benjamin's time. " P'r'aps they'll give me a penny a-piece," thought I; " or, perhaps, if one of them has got a loose sixpence, I shall get that." It seemed so lucky, too, that one of them should stop at the very doorway where I was to relight his cigar.

"Please, sir, have you got a copper to spare?" I asked this one.

"Ask my friend," he answered, laughing, as though he thought it rather a good joke. " Barney, give the poor lad a shilling."

He didn't say it quite like I have written it down, because (as I knew as soon as he took his nose out of his comforter and began to speak) he was a Jew. " Give the boor lad a shillig!" My heart was in my mouth.

But it didn't remain there long—no longer, indeed, than it took the other young gentleman to get *his* nose and mouth free; then it sank to the very bottom of my empty belly, for, observed the young gentleman—

"Hold out your hand, then."

I did so, and he spat in it!

" That's the sort of shillings I give to cadgers," said he.

"Ha! ha!" laughed the other young gentleman. " You are the rummest feller that ever *I* come across, Barney."

For an instant I felt sick with passion, and would like to have clutched Mr. Barney's nose as Mrs. Burke had often clutched mine; but my craving for money to buy bread with was so fierce that it would let no other consideration stand in its way. I wiped off the spittle against the wall, and said, civilly—

" *Now,* if you please, sir, won't you give me a penny?"

" Be off!" said Mr. Barney. " You've got hold of the wrong customers. We are gentlemen, we are, and don't want to be bothered by cadgers."

" Will you give me a ha'penny, then?" I pleaded.   "I wouldn't ask you if I wasn't so hungry."

"Give *you* a ha'penny, you artful young bla'-guard!" replied Mr. Ike.   "Why, you are better dressed and got a sounder pair of boots on your feet than half the honest boys that run about. Half as good a pair would be good enough to beg in.   What's your opinion, Barney?"

"My opinion is, that he's one of them saucy whelps that one mus'n't be in the least familiar with, but they at once begin to take liberties," replied the gentleman who had honoured me by spitting in my hand.   "We'll give him in charge of the police if he doesn't take himself off, Ike."

It was what Mr. Ike had said, however, that made most impression on me.   He was quite right.   My boots were bran new boots—given to me only the morning before, that I might go well shod to Stratford.   A pair only half as good *would* be good enough to beg in; no boots at all would be good enough—better, at least, than an empty belly, such as mine was.   I felt almost as much obliged to Mr. Ike as though he had placed ready money in my hand.   I would sell my boots. They were not mine according to law, it is true; but then—agreeably to Mouldy's doctrine—it was not according to law that a boy should want a lodging and go hungry.   Further, I have no doubt that Mouldy would have argued that the boots were given to me for my comfort, and that if I could get more comfort out of them than by allowing them to remain on my feet, the intention of those who had given the boots to me, so far from being frustrated, would be accommodated beyond their most charitable anticipations.   The boots should go.   Field Lane was not very far off; and though I never had any dealings with the shopkeepers there residing, I had heard it frequently mentioned, by lads who slept under the dark arches, that the Jews there kept open late for the convenience of their customers, and, moreover, that they were never oversqueamish about what they bought, or in asking questions as to where the goods offered for sale came from.

"Thanky!" said I, to Mr. Ike; "I forgot all about my boots."   And I at once knelt down and began to untie them.

"What d' yer mean—forgot all about 'em?" asked Mr. Barney.

"I forgot the sort of boots they was—how good they was.   I wouldn't have your penny now, if you was to offer it to me.   Keep your pennies to yourself, and your spit too, or p'r'aps you might get half a brick at your head."

"Come on, Barney," said Mr. Ike, who was apparently about seventeen years old, while his companion was possibly a year older ; "if he annoys us, we'll give him in charge."

"Stop a bit.   Don't be in a hurry, Ike."

"What's the good of stopping?"

"But see what the young beggar's doing! He's pulling his boots off!"

"P'r'aps he's going to shy 'em at us, like the prisoners in the docks sometimes do," laughed Mr. Ike.   "What are you taking your boots off for, young un?"

"I'm goin' to sell 'em."

"Goin' to sell 'em—eh?   Why, you won't find anybody to buy 'em to-night.   Where are you going to take 'em to?"

"I shan't tell yer.   It ain't no bis'ness o yourn."

"That's more than you can tell, my boy," replied Mr. Ike, in a kinder tone than he had yet used, and at the same time dabbing the fire out of his stump of cigar against the wet wall, and pocketing it.   "If you're goin' to sell 'em there'll be no harm in my having first look at 'em. Come over to the light of the lamp-post, my lad."

I had taken off my stockings, (they were new, and made of blue worsted,) and stuffed them into the boots, which I had tied together by their laces, and slung across my shoulder.   Taking me by the arm, Mr. Ike led me to the light of the street lamp, and there he took one of the workhouse boots in hand in an astonishingly business-like manner, looking at it closely, bending its sole, and inquiring carefully into the condition of its welt.

"How much?" asked Mr. Ike, when his inspection was at an end.

"How much what?" I answered, never dreaming that the young gentleman was disposed to buy my boots.

"How much money?—what do you want for 'em?   You said that you wanted to sell 'em—didn't you?"

"I don't want no more of your larks," said I, still incredulous that he could be in earnest. "What odds is it to you what I want for 'em?"

"Do I look like larking, my lad?" asked Mr. Ike, looking at me in a way that was meant to be convincing.   "I mean bis'ness.   Put your price on 'em, and I'm a buyer."

I could no longer disbelieve him; yet his question came so sudden that I didn't know how to answer.   How much *did* I want for the boots? I recollect my mother giving two-and-ninepence for a pair not half as good at the shop facing the churchyard on Clerkenwell Green.   The boots under discussion were such warm, comfortable boots!   and standing on the stones with the snow melting under my naked toes, they seemed more valuable than ever.

"I want eighteenpence for 'em," I said, at last.

"How much?—eighteenpence for a pair of boots and stockings like these?"

"No; eighteenpence for the boots without the stockin's."

Mr. Ike looked at Mr. Barney, and Mr. Barney returned the look, and then both young men fell to laughing as though I had told them the funniest thing they had ever heard in all their experience.

"Come, come!   a joke's a joke; but we shall never do business unless you talk serious.   What *do* you want for 'em?"

"Eighteenpence—not less—not a penny less. If you don't know the worth on 'em, I do."

And truly I did.   Each moment, with the cold creeping up my legs, I grew more and more alive to their great value.

"Will you take sixpence?" asked Mr. Ike.

"I'll take eighteenpence, or I'll have 'em back.   Give 'em here; I don't want you to buy 'em."

Mr. Ike tossed his head with the air of a person compelled to submit to an imposition, and tucking the boots under his arm, made a plunge at his trousers' pocket and took out some money.

"Here you are," said he, putting the money into my hand; "and now cut your lucky, before I alter my mind."

He gave me sevenpence—sixpence and a penny; and linking his arm in Mr. Barney's, was moving off. I caught hold on Mr. Ike's cloak, and dragged at it.

"*Now* what do you want?" said he, looking round with affected astonishment.

"I want another elevenpence, or I want my boots and stockin's back," said I.

"Why, you must be out of your mind!" exclaimed Mr. Barney. "We can buy 'em bran now by the gross for less money."

"But there's the stockin's."

"Ah! I overlooked the stockings. Let's have a look at 'em."

I did not set much store by the stockings, never having been used to such luxuries since I had worn boots, until I went to the workhouse; but they were very good ones. Mr. Barney examined them closely, and then folded them up and put them in his pocket.

"Now, look here!" said he; "we don't want a bushel of words over the bargain. I see now that you are a deserving lad, and we'll make a rise on our first bid. We'll give you a shilling for the lot."

"Too much," observed Mr. Ike.

"I shan't take it. Here, take back your sevenpence. I don't mind throwin' the stockn's in—eighteenpence the lot. I wouldn't take that if I wasn't so precious hungry."

The two young gentlemen had continued walking along while we were discussing the matter, and presently they turned down a street leading towards Saffron Hill. Just as I spoke about being so very hungry, we came up to a little, dingy chandler's shop, not yet shut up, and in the window of which was a cold-boiled cushion of bacon and some loaves of bread.

"It's only your gammon about being hungry," observed Mr. Barney.

"Well I hain't eat a mouthful since seven this mornin'," I replied. "I don't know if you call *that* being hungry."

"Hungry as all that, and won't take a shillin' when it's offered to him!" said Mr. Ike.

"Ain't had nothing to eat since seven o'clock this morning!" observed Mr. Barney, halting before the window of the chandler's shop. "So awful hungry he don't know what to do, and yet refuses money, a quarter of which would get him a regular blow out! Oh! it's all crammers—it *must* be. Why, for about fourpence he might buy half a loaf and a whole lot of that bacon!"

There are few things more tempting to a sharp-set and not high-bred appetite than a plump boiled cold cushion of bacon. This one happened to be a particularly plump cushion, perfect only for a little wedge cut out of it just at the knuckle part. I felt as though I could have eaten every bit of it. I itched to take the shilling, but it *did* seem a shame to let the boots and stockings go at such a miserable figure. I turned my eyes resolutely away from the bacon!

"*I must* have eighteenpence," I said.

"Oh, well! since you want eighteenpence so bad, p'r'aps you've got something about you as would tell up to the value of it. Got a handkerchief?"

"No."

"Got a pocket-knife?"

"No."

"Got nothing at all in your pockets? Feel."

"It's no use feelin'; I ain't got nothink but jest what you can see—just what's on my back."

"Oh, well. I don't want to know anything about your private affairs, either on your back or off your back. All I know is, that I buy anything that anybody offers me."

And as the young Jew spoke he looked meaningly up and down at me, from my Scotch cap to my knee-breeches.

"Anything," repeated he, "I can buy, you know, if it's to the amount of eighteen shillings—let alone eightpence—if it comes to that. So long as I can see my way to turning an honest penny, it makes no difference to me what I buy—not the least."

What was Mr. Barney driving at? Did he mean that he would buy my whole suit of clothes, and give me eighteen shillings for it? If I might judge from the wretched price he had given me for my boots and stockings, I could hardly hope so. I would have been glad to sell them for half the money; and it seemed that there could be no mistake about his being willing to buy the lot at *some* price. How the sale could be accomplished was altogether a puzzler; I only hoped that it might. Of all things—after getting something to eat—it was necessary that I should get out of the tell-tale bottle-green bobtail and smalls.

"Well, if you've a mind to deal you'd better look sharp about it," said Mr. Barney, rattling the money in his breeches pocket.

"But we—we can't deal out here."

"Oh, yes, we can! I've reckoned 'em up all but the shirt. I s'pose there is a shirt—isn't there?"

"Yes; but I ain't a-goin' to pull it off out here, so don't you think it."

"I didn't ask you to. All I asked you was to put a price on it," replied Mr. Barney.

"Haven't you got a shop or anythink?" I asked.

"Well, not exactly a shop—more of a ware'us, ours is."

"Ah! let him come home; that'll be best, Barney," spoke Mr. Ike.

And so saying, with my stockings in his pocket and my boots tucked under his arm, Mr. Barney and the other young gentleman began walking sharply towards Saffron Hill, while I kept just behind them. Presently, on arriving at the dingiest part of the "Hill," they paused before a private house, of which Mr. Ike had the key, and in we all three went, along the dark passage, and up a flight of creaking stairs to a back room on the second floor.

"Hold hard! I'll strike a light," said Barney.

He did so, and lit the wick of a tin oil-lamp, with a reflector at the back of it, that was nailed against the wall—enabling me to see the sort of place Mr. Barney's "warehouse" was. It was exactly like a rag-shop, without the bones and bottles, and the brilliant pictures and verses about "Mrs. Saveall and Mrs. Wasteit;" and another, much in vogue at that time, entitled "The Contrast," in which were pictured a lean and ghastly wretch leaning against a workhouse wall, on the one hand; and on the other, an elegant swell, with rings on his fingers and varnished boots on his toes, lounging on a seat near the Serpentine river in Hyde Park, in company with a splendid female creature, the feathers in whose bonnet alone must have cost a mint of money, and a tremendous run upon that fleet and valuable bird, the ostrich; while the verses under the picture informed you that the gentlemen above pictured were brothers and that the sole reason for the wide difference in their worldly condition was, that one "had hoarded his bones and saved his fat," while the other had been less prudent.

These badges of the regular rag-shop trade were missing from Messrs. Ike and Barney's establishment; but there were old hats heaped in a corner so high, that the crown of the topmost crushed and battered beaver reached to the ceiling, nearly; while in another corner was a heap of old boots and shoes, blue and mouldy, and of all sorts and sizes, from the patent-leather to the clayey, scouch-heeled, long-tongued ankle-jack of the navvy. Hanging from pegs driven into the four walls, and piled on a long board that stood on trestles, was a pile of every conceivable article of male and female attire, thrown together pell-mell, and emitting a sickening odour of encroaching mildew and mustiness.

But, for all that, it was a living-room. The hat heap, and the boot heap, and the bunches of old breeches and coats swelling out from against the walls and the piled-up bench, left a clear space of about six square feet before a fire-place and a fire-grate, (before which was suspended a great, closely-woven fire-guard;) and this was where the two young gentlemen "lived"—where they ate and drank and made merry. It was evident that it was so; for on the mantle-shelf there was a gridiron but recently used, as might be seen by the trickling tears of grease that extended from it, and hung suspended from the shelf-edge; if you wanted further evidence as to its being a living-room, there it was, before the fire-place—a tea-tray on an extended camp-stool, and, set out thereon, two dirty cups and saucers and a coffee-pot, a scrap of butter on a cabbage-leaf, and three-parts of a loaf. It was a sleeping-chamber, besides; if a bed-like bundle tied in a patchwork quilt, and protruding from under the bench, went for anything. Just above the bench hung a little looking-glass; and on a mite of elbow room at the corner of the bench, and under the looking-glass, there was a ragged comb and a hair-brush to match, some heavy finger-dented hair-grease in a gallipot, and one dirty "dicky" and a collar, showing how and where the two young gentlemen had got up the splendid appearance that had so imposed on me when I first beheld them in Hatton Garden.

What chiefly attracted my attention, however, was the part of a loaf on the tea-tray. I took it up.

"May I eat this?" I inquired; and as I asked, my ravening hunger overleaping my manners, I bit a big piece out of it.

By way of an answer, Mr. Barney caught me a whack on the knuckles with the tin match-box he still held in his hand, and sent the bread rolling amongst the mouldy boots and shoes. My will was good to scramble after it, but so was Mr. Ike's; he pounced on and secured it with the agility of a terrier after an escaping rat.

"Quite enough of that, young feller," said he, rubbing the dirt off the bread on the leg of his trousers; "if you're a thief, the sooner you get out of this, the better. A pretty feller you are to ask up into a place where there is property lying about!"

And he cast an anxious eye over the valuables strewing the room, and was about to put the precious loaf on a high shelf out of my reach, when Mr. Barney, licking his rosy lips and winking at his friend, took it out of his hand. After regarding it anxiously for a moment, and weighing it on his palm, said he:—

"Now, look here, young work'us; there's no mistake about it, you are hungry, and it goes to my heart to see it. I won't be hard on you—I couldn't. Here you are. Now, don't say another word about them rubbishing boots and stockings of yours. I don't mind being soft-hearted and foolish, so much as I mind being put in mind of it. Good-bye! Never mind about gratitude and all that sort of thing."

And as he spoke, he took a shilling out of his pocket, and laying it a-top of the half-loaf, pressed the lot on my acceptance. If I hadn't tasted the bread, I believe that I should still have held out; but, as it was, I was powerless to refuse so tempting an offer. I took the shilling, and putting it into my breeches pocket, was deep in the loaf in an instant.

"That's all, isn't it?" observed Mr. Barney, with the room door open and the door-knob in his hand, as though anxious for me to go, now that the bargain was completed.

"That's all, as far as the boots and stockings go," I replied, through a mouthful of delicious bottom-crust.

"What do you mean? What does he mean, Ike?" asked Mr. Barney, innocently.

"Ain't you goin' to buy the coat and things?" said I; "wasn't that what you meant when we was in the street, just now—when you said something about eighteen shillin's?"

"Eighteen shillings!" repeated Mr. Ike, taking up one of the bobtails and snapping the material between his finger and thumb to test it; "why, you'd never be such a young fool as to take eighteen shillings for a suit like that, would you?"

He spoke so seriously, that I thought to be sure he meant it; and a spasm of alarm twitched me, to think what a daring scoundrel I must be to run away with so much money's worth.

"Yes," I replied; "give us hold of the money. I don't mind takin' it. I don't think the clothes becomes me; that's what I want to sell 'em for."

Mr. Barney fumbled at his pocket.

"Well, since you are ready to take such a little price for the suit," said he, "of course, it ain't for me as a buyer to offer you any more. Here you are."

He held out some money in his hand—eighteen-pence.

"That isn't eighteen shillin's!"

"Eighteen grandmothers, you young fool! what do you take me for!" laughed Mr. Barney, derisively. "That's the price; take it or leave it."

"If I bought 'em, I should buy 'em in the scale," said Mr. Ike; "they're on'y fit to tear up for land rags. Institootion rubbish! Shouldn't buy 'em at all if I was you, Barney."

My heart, which was just now at my throat, as people say, at the prospect of becoming the possessor of the enormous sum of eighteen shillings, sank again heavy as lead with this cruel disappointment.

"You ought to buy 'em, after you said you would," I said.

"I'll stand to my word," replied Mr. Barney, tossing the shilling and sixpence in the air and catching it again.

"What's the use of eighteenpence? I shall have to buy some more clothes if I sell these; I couldn't buy 'em for the money."

Barney once more took me in hand, and closely examined the quality of my breeches and my waistcoat and my bobtail; he unbuttoned my waistcoat, and plucking out a handful of my shirt, examined that too.

"Oh, don't let's be hard on him," said he, appealing to Mr. Ike; "we shan't be no poorer a hundred years to come, Ike. Don't you see how it is, Ike?—the lad's clothes fit him a little too tight, and he wants to get out of 'em."

At this joke both gentlemen laughed tremendously, and as by this time I had eaten nearly all the bread, and felt courageous, I laughed too.

"Oh, well, as long as you understand each other, I don't care. It's all very fine about not being hard on him, Barney; don't you be too hard on me. I've got to stand half the loss, don't you know?" said Mr. Ike.

"Nobody was ever the poorer for doing a good action, Ike; that's what I believe," replied Mr. Barney, who straightway began to overhaul the pile of tattered garments on the bench. After some searching, he fished out a large-sized pair of fustian trousers—wretched-looking things, tattered fore and aft, and black with greasy wear.

"There's a bit of stuff, now!" he exclaimed, finding a comparatively clean inch or two of the fustian, near the waistband, and holding it up to the light of the lamp; "never was bought under four shillings a yard! They're the sort of trousers now to do you service, if I could afford to let you have 'em, eh?"

"But they ain't like that all the way down; look at that great hole—look how they're tore!"

"They're second-hand, of course. You didn't think I was going to find you a suit that was bran new, did you?" asked Mr. Barney, reproachfully.

"But they're too big."

"Too big!—where?"

"Here," I replied, extending my arms down the length of the trousers as Mr. Barney held them up; "and this way, too."

"Not too full, as they wear them now. It's fashionable to wear them full now; isn't it, Ike?"

"I'd be sorry to wear a pair as tight as they are," replied Mr. Ike; "I should expect to be laughed at if I did. If there's anything to be said against 'em, it is that they may be a trifle too long for you; and that's easily altered."

"Try 'em on," said Mr. Barney, taking up a pair of shears; "try 'em on, and all that hangs down below the leg, we'll cut off; they're sure to fit then."

To try them on, it was necessary to take off my waistcoat and coat, as well as my trousers, owing to an economical arrangement of buttons and button-holes in the parochial attire. As I took them off, Mr. Ike secured them, and stowed them out of sight. The fustian trousers certainly were full. They seemed to touch nowhere, except where they bore down; and the waistband came *up so high under my arms*, and lapped over so *much, that the buttons* were of no use at all.

"There, I told you so; a pair half the size 'ud be big enough."

"Why! what's the matter with 'em?"

"Look at the buttons! This one ought to be in the front—not under my arm."

"You wouldn't get a nigher fit unless you was measured. What odds about right buttons and wrong buttons! They ain't dress trousers, don't you know; they're workin' trousers."

"They're jolly uncomfor'ble."

"Enough to make 'em, when you've got your shirt all bunched up round your waist," exclaimed Mr. Ike, pausing in his occupation of lighting the fire. "Take it off, Barney; we'll try and find him a thinner shirt, presently."

Mr. Barney took the hint, and whipped off my shirt in a twinkling.

"That's better," said he; "here's a hole that'll catch this button, and here's another one that'll catch *this* button. There you are! *Now*, what have you got to find fault with?"

"They come up so jolly high, I shan't be able to wear a waistcoat with 'em."

"Of course you won't; them sort of trousers are made high on purpose to do without 'waistcoats,'" replied Mr. Ike, smiling pityingly at my ignorance; "why, you don't suppose they would make 'em so full as that if they didn't have a meaning for doing it? I only wish that I may be able to find you a jacket that will suit you as well. What's that one close by your elbow, Barney?"

"This one? oh, this is nearly a new jacket—at least, it can't have had a month's wear; a pen'orth of hartshorn would make it look quite like new. We can't afford to let him have that."

"Oh, give it to him, poor lad," said Mr. Barney; "here you are," and Mr. Barney assisted me on with it.

It wasn't a bad jacket as regards soundness; the worst of it was, it was all hard and stiff with paint, as though it had last belonged to a paper-staining boy.

"That's the ticket; that's warm and comfortable for you," observed Mr. Barney, as he adjusted the top button of the jacket; "here's your cap; now go."

"But I haven't got any shirt; ain't you goin' to give me my shirt, or another one?"

"What! as well as the jacket and fustian trousers? I wonder you've got the face to ask such a thing," replied Mr. Barney.

"And ain't you goin' to give me some money? My clothes are worth a jolly sight more'n these."

"Now, what do you think of that, Ike?" exclaimed Mr. Barney, turning to his companion, as though his feelings were terribly shocked. "I gives him an inch, Ike, and now he wants an ell! There, be off with you, do; I'm quite ashamed of you!"

And wagging their heads, as though my ungrateful behaviour had quite upset them, the two young Jews hustled me out of the room, and down the stairs, and gently thrust me into the street, shutting the door.

CHAPTER XXIII.

IN WHICH I DISCOVER THE EXTENT OF THE SWIN-
DLE PUT ON ME BY MESSRS. BARNEY AND IKE.
MY LAST APPEARANCE AT COVENT GARDEN. I
BECOME A PUBLIC SINGER, AND MY PIPES ARE
PUT OUT BY AN OLD FRIEND.

THE church clocks were chiming midnight as the door of the Jews' house closed at my back, and I scudded through the soft cold snow towards Holborn.

My mind was in such a state of confusion concerning my late transaction with Messrs. Barney and Ike, that it was some considerable time before I could bring myself to a deliberate consideration of my position. Had the two Jews reason for charging me with greediness and ingratitude? They certainly looked perfectly serious when they accused me, and their manner was exactly that of persons who consider that their good nature has been abused; still I could not forbear thinking that, after all, they had very much the best of the bargain.

How had I come out of the business? At starting I had a pair of warm stockings, and a sound pair of boots to my feet; now I had neither the one nor the other. At starting I had an entire suit of clothes to my back; now I had but half a suit. At starting I had a shirt; now I had none. On the other hand. At starting I had a hungry belly; now that defect was repaired by a tolerably abundant meal of bread. My present suit was not entire, but it covered me completely; and though not so new as the workhouse suit, it was quite as warm, to say nothing of the immense advantage I derived from getting out of a livery that made it impossible for me to appear in public with any degree of safety during daylight. I had no shirt, and, coming out into the cold after being so long used to one, I missed it very considerably; but I should soon get over that trifling inconvenience. Two months out of the five that I kept company with Mouldy and Ripston, I had been without body-linen, and was none the worse for the deprivation. At starting I had not a farthing in the world, and now I had a shilling.

Had I?

Had the pavement immediately before me fallen away, leaving a fathomless gulf, I could not have halted more abruptly. The pockets of the manly fustians were wide and deep, so that I had to stoop my shoulders to reach the bottom of them. I *did* reach the bottom, and with despairing avidity poked about the corners.

The shilling was not there!

In a terrible fright I plunged my hands into the outer pockets of the jacket.

No shilling!

With the speed of lightning came the blissful recollection that I had observed an inner pocket in the jacket, and in my eagerness to search it, I tore off the button that secured it a-top.

Empty, save for some bread crumbs the paper-staining boy had left in it! Oh, Lor! oh, dear! what had become of it?

I had never brought it away from the Jews' house. When I had taken the bread and the shilling in exchange for my boots and stockings, as I now very distinctly remembered, I had slipped the money into the pocket of my corduroys; and when I had taken them off to fit on the fus-

tians that I then had on, I had forgotten to remove my money! It afforded me tremendous relief to recollect so patly how the mistake had occurred; and without stopping to button my disarranged jacket, I retraced my way to Saffron Hill as fast as my legs would carry me.

It was easy enough to find Saffron Hill—to make my way to that part of it which I had so lately quitted; but there arrived, I was brought to a dismal standstill.

Which was the house?

Every house was numbered, but what was the number of that in which the two Jews lived, I had not noticed — there was no reason why I should notice, or remember a moment afterwards if I had done so. The houses were all of a pattern, painted alike, or rather without paint alike; the doorsteps, the scrapers, were exactly similar. Whether I had passed the right house, or whether it was farther on, it was impossible to say.

I looked sharply about the thresholds of each door, to see if anything could be made out of recent footsteps on and near any one in particular, but the snow was falling so fast that I could find no footmarks but those I had made since my return. I looked up at the windows, and to my great delight found one — the only one with a light shining through it—a second-floor window! By jumping up at the knocker, I managed to reach it and give a loud knock.

I waited at least a minute, and finding that nobody answered, I knocked again—twice this time, and louder than at first. The window with the light in it was opened, and an old man thrust out his head adorned with a night-cap.

" Who's there?"

" Please, sir, is this the house where the Jews live?"

" Where *who* live?"

" The Jews, please—Mr. Ike and Mr. Barney, please? I won't keep 'em a minute; I only want "——

" I wish I was down there, —— you. I'd give you what you want."

And without waiting to listen to another word, he slammed down the window in a manner that convinced me that I had knocked at the wrong house.

Now what was to be done? It would never do to knock at any more doors on the chance of finding the one I wanted. It was nothing less than throwing away a shilling to go away. Without doubt, it was no one's fault but my own that I had come away without my money. It was a foolish blunder of mine, that might be remedied as soon as I could see my two friends—there could be no doubt of that, or they would not have been so cut up at what they conceived to be my unjust behaviour. They would be glad to give me back my money when I explained to them where I had left it. The best thing to do would be to wait till the morning, and look out for the young gentlemen as they came out to go to business.

So, by good luck, I discovered a deepish doorway nearly opposite to the house in which I was almost sure the two Jews resided, and there made myself as comfortable as under the circumstances was possible. Dozing, or lying awake thinking, I passed the night till about seven o'clock in the morning, when the shopkeeper on whose premises I was trespassing opened his door and drove me off.

I took care, however, not to go far, and somewhere about nine o'clock I had the satisfaction of seeing emerge from the house I suspected two young fellows, with black bags hanging over their arms. They were dressed altogether different from the two cigar-smoking, swaggering young men I had met on the previous night; indeed they were of almost shabby appearance, having coarse old great-coats on, and greasy caps. Nevertheless, I felt so sure the one was Mr. Ike and the other Mr. Barney, that I made no scruple of making straight up to and accosting them.

"I say, sir," said I, touching the one whom I took to be Mr. Barney on the arm, "I left my shillin' in the pocket of them corderoys. I wish you'd give it to me."

"Eh! what shilling? what corderoys?"

"The ones I sold you last night, you know; the ones you bought along with the bobtail and that. It's quite right what I say; just you go back and feel if you don't believe me."

The young man I took to be Mr. Barney stared at me in comical surprise.

"What does he mean?" he exclaimed, turning to his companion; "do you know the lad, Mr. Wilkins?"

"Never saw him in my life till this moment," answered Mr. Wilkins, who, however, was wonderfully like the gentleman who last night had spit in my hand.

"It's all a mistake, you see, my good lad," observed Mr. Barney, blandly. "What is the name of the person you want?"

"I didn't hear their full names," I answered; "but one was Ike and the other was Barney. I thought *you* was Mr. Barney."

"Barney, my dear boy? oh, no. My name is Wilkins—William Wilkins," replied Mr. Barney, trying to speak like a Christian, but utterly failing; indeed, his reply as it above stands, is by no means as he gave it. What he said was—"Bardey bi tear boy! oh, doe. Bi dabe is Wilkids—Wilyab Wilkids."

"Do you mean to say that you ain't the two as bought my work'us things last night?" said I, more and more convinced that I was not mistaken; "do you mean to say that you don't live in that house, and that you ain't got a ware'us full of old hats and old clothes?"

"I mean to say that you're a very impudent lad to ask such questions," replied Mr. Barney. "Me and my friend know nothing about old clo'; we're in the French-polishing line."

"It's all gammon," I cried, driven to tears by rage and bitter disappointment; "you've got my shillin', and I mean to have it. Here comes a p'liceman—I'll talk to him about it."

There was a policeman at some distance down the street, and he was coming towards us. Finding it was so, the two French-polishers glared at me in a very savage manner, and were for moving off at a brisk walk.

"Come on; what's the use of stopping to listen to that young beggar's cheek," observed Mr. Ike, as they were hurrying away.

"You'd better stop—I'll call 'Stop thief!' if you don't. You give me my shillin'."

"I'll give you a clout over the head if you don't hook it," exclaimed Mr. Ike, pale with rage. "What do you want following us? Why don't *you beg of* them as can afford it? Give you a

shilling, indeed! Here's tuppence—now be off before you're made."

"I shan't be off," I replied, taking the twopence and pocketing it; "I'll have the lot, or else I'll tell the perlice."

"What'll you tell the police?" inquired Mr. Barney, suddenly facing round, as though suddenly inspired with a bright idea.

"I'll tell 'em that you bought my clothes, and cheated me out of the money," I replied.

"What sort of clothes?" said Mr. Barney, his eyes twinkling.

"My work'us clothes—all my workus' suit, and my boots and stockin's."

"Oh, indeed! that's it, is it? You've been running away from some work'us, and selling the clothes you ran away in. Come on; you shall have enough of the police, since you're so fond of 'em."

And so saying, Mr. Barney collared me by the jacket as though it was his honest intention to drag me off to the police-station straight. It was a brilliant stroke, and worthy of the cunning rascal who had tempted me with the hunch of bread the night before. My defeat was sudden and complete. With a desperate wriggle I released myself from his grasp (he didn't hold me very tight) and ran away, never stopping until I reached the Bagnigge-wells Road. My escape, however, cost me my cap. As I ducked under Mr. Barney's arm my cap came off, and giving a hasty look round to see if I was followed, I saw the blackguardly young Jew pick it up and say something to his companion, with a grin, as he stuffed it into his bag. If the observation he made was not "That makes that tuppence square," I'll wager it was one that carried the same meaning.

Looking back to that time, it is always a wonder to me that I did not feel more miserable than I did. Surely, no boy ever had more cause to feel completely wretched—with twopence only in my pocket, twopen'orth of rags to my back, and nobody in the wide world that cared a button for me. It may appear an odd sort of argument, but I have no doubt of its truth, that the last-mentioned fact—the being without a friend in the world—kept me up under the circumstances rather than otherwise. If I had known anybody who cared for me, I should naturally have cared for them, and fell to funking and grieving as to what would be their feelings if they came to know my deplorable plight; as it was, however, I had nobody but myself to care for, and this I did to the full extent of my ability. Availing myself of the shortest cuts, I made my way out into Holborn, and so through Great Turnstile and Drury Lane into Covent Garden Market, where I invested my twopence in bread and coffee at the old familiar stall.

The remainder of that day I spent in and about the market, searching high and low for my late partners, and with a sharp eye for a job. But in both respects I was quite unsuccessful. Mouldy and Ripston were not to be found. I made myself known to one or two of my old market acquaintances, and was by them informed that neither of the lads I inquired after had been seen or heard of since the frost set in about Christmas time—now nearly two months since. Work there was none to be obtained. I had hoped that, dressed altogether differently from when I last plied in the market, and being thinner and taller, I might pass as a stranger, and do very well—the market men preferring to give jobs to strange boys rather than to old and artful hands; but, to my great disappointment, wherever I showed my face it was remembered. "What! you out again, young gallus? Be off, you young hound. I recollect you; take your gaol-crop somewhere else, or you'll be made." They all mistook it for a gaol-crop, and, owing to the unlucky loss of my cap, it was fully exposed to view. I couldn't earn a single ha'penny. It didn't snow that day; but the frost was sharp, and the wind bitterly cold.

I plied the market all day, hanging on and off as it were, until it grew dusk, and the shopkeepers in the arcade began to light up. My firm resolution in the morning was to *work*, and to keep my hands from picking and stealing, though even of so mild a character as my old partners had declared fruit and nut-snatching to be. But at the time the good resolution was made, I was in the enjoyment of the warmth and comfort conferred by a cup of coffee, and filled with hope. Now, alas! I was empty of both. There is much truth in the proverb that "a hungry belly has no conscience." I was *all* hungry belly, and I had no conscience. I came out of Tavistock Street about five o'clock, fierce as a wolf in winter, with a steady determination to walk once more through the market—once only—and not to come away empty handed. Two minutes afterwards, I was scudding towards Drury Lane with a booty of a magnificent pineapple.

Pineapples at that time were not nearly so plentiful nor nearly so cheap as they now are. The one I had become the possessor of had been one of a row of six, and I had heard the shopkeeper say to a gentleman who had asked the price of them, "All in that row, half-a-guinea, sir." Although perfectly astonished to hear such a tremendous price set on the fruit, I was glad that I had heard it, otherwise Bogey Simmons (the old gentleman in Coal Yard, who dealt in market pilferings) would have derived from my ignorance a most unfair advantage in the transaction; for it was Bogey's way to insist on those who dealt with him setting a price on their goods; and in the matter of the pineapple, had I been left to the guidance of my own judgment, I should have thought fourpence—at the outside, sixpence—a stiffish sum to ask for it. As it was, I resolved to ask him two shillings; and made so sure of the money, that, on the road, I settled in my mind how I would spend tenpence of it—sixpence in a comfortable supper, and fourpence in a lodging; for, owing to the miserable manner in which I had passed the preceding night, I yearned for the comfort of a bed almost as much as for something to eat.

Bogey Simmons lived at a house in Coal Yard, the kitchen of which was in the occupation of a cobbler. The cobbler's stall was approached by a flight of steps in front of the house, and the cobbler being on good terms with Bogey, allowed people who came to transact business with the latter to pass through his stall out through a door at the back, and so up to Bogey's room above. As I approached the house, I was delighted to find that it was all right—a light was burning in the stall, and over the top of the yellow curtain that screened the half glass door could be seen the cobbler's hands rising and fall-

ing as he pulled at his wax-ends. The cobbler knew me well enough; so, without hesitation, I went down the steps and tapped at his door—having first, however, taken the precaution to stuff the pineapple into one of the ample pockets of the fustian trousers.

The cobbler opened the door. I could see by the glance he gave me through his spectacles, that he at once recognised me; but, to my great astonishment, he affected to regard me as though I had been the most perfect stranger.

"Well, my boy, what do you want?"

"It's all right; let us come through. I'm goin' up to Bogey."

"What do you mean 'let you come through?' Who's Bogey?"

"Bogey Simmons; him as buys"——

"He don't live here," interrupted the cobbler; "he's gone away. And that's what *you*'d better do, unless you want to bring the police poking round my place again. I thought I had seen the last of your crew."

Evidently there was a screw loose. This was apparent even more from the cobbler's manner than his words. When he referred to the police, he did so with considerable nervousness, and a fidgety glance this way and that up and down the alley.

"Where has Bogey moved to? Do tell us, mister; I wants to see him pertickler."

"He ain't moved nowhere's yet; he's laying at Colbath Fields a-waitin' to be tried," replied the frightened cobbler, pushing me gently up the steps. "Do go, that's a good lad; they're a-watchin' the house now for all I know. Be off; it's no use you stoppin here."

"But look here—you might as well buy it as Bogey;" and I began to haul the pineapple out of my trousers' pocket. "You shall have it for a shillin'—ninepence!—there."

"Put it back! put it back!" cried the cobbler, trembling with excitement, as he squeezed back the pineapple into my pocket with his waxy hands; "*will* you go? Stay here another moment and I'll cut your throat." And as he spoke, he snatched from off his work-bench a bright old knife, ground down at the point to almost needle sharpness, and made at me so furiously, that I took the steps two at a time, and ran for my life.

It really did seem as though the fates were against me. Bogey Simmons was the only person we three partners had ever dealt with. There were other "dealers," whose names and places of abode I had heard tell of, but I could not think of one now; and so there I was as badly off as though my pockets were empty. Confound the precious pineapple! Had I taken three or four pears or oranges instead, I might have gone out in the Strand, and held them out for sale at the edge of the pavement. I might have gone round to the gallery door of the Adelphi or the Olympic—it was just the time—and disposed of them in a twinkling, but how could I offer a pineapple for sale in that way? If I did, I should find myself where Bogey Simmons was in a very short time.

There was only one course to pursue—a most extravagant course, and one that I resigned myself to with bitter regret—I must eat the pineapple—I had never tasted the fruit, and had no particular desire to; I would have exchanged it for its weight in bread with the greatest of pleas-

6

ure. But there was no choice; I *must* eat something. And so, presently arriving at a mews somewhere near Bedford Square, I got into a cart I found there, and crouching down out of sight, ate up my half-guinea's worth, body and bones. *If* I had had a knife I should have peeled it like a turnip, but being possessed of no such handy implement, I just bit off the top-knot, and ate it fairly down to the stump.

The result was that it didn't agree with me. I was dreadfully sick, and so ill that I had scarcely power to move. I stayed in the cart until near the middle of the night when my limbs ached so with cold, that I sat up to rub them. As I did so, I spied a stable-heap at a little distance off, smoking bravely, and crawling out of the cart, I bedded comfortably among the warm litter till daybreak.

How I passed that day I could scarcely relate if I tried. I only know that I went aimlessly moving about, (I did not dare approach Covent Garden, the reader may be sure; though, indeed, I well might for all the good it had yielded me,) up one road and down another, feeling more benumbed than hungry, and neither seeking nor finding relief. I was too benumbed to think, somehow.

Then came the evening once more, and I was in Gray's Inn Lane. There was a little mob of people blocking up a part of the pavement, and when I came up I found that they were listening to a boy singing in the road. I always liked singing, and the boy's song happening to be one I very well knew—it was one of Mrs. Burke's favourites—I found heart to stand and listen. "Erin-go-bragh" was the song. His voice was not a bad one, but it did not suit the song—at least it did not suit it so softly well as did Mrs. Burke's voice. However, it suited the people very well; and when the boy had finished the song, and came round with his cap, the halfpence went "chink, chink" into it in a way that made me stare again.

It opened my eyes, did that boy's song and its results, in more ways than one. It opened them so on one special object, that for a while I could see nothing else, or hear anything. It engrossed me entirely. The eyes of my mind were so completely fixed on it—on the object in question—that the mob dispersed and the singer went his way, and still I remained standing on the path as when I had first taken my stand there.

The object in question was that of a boy—not a boy in a black jacket and trousers, and with boots to his feet, such as he whom I had just listened to, but a boy in a tremendous pair of fustian trousers and a slouchy jacket smeared and daubed with paint—a shoeless and capless boy singing "Erin-go-bragh" in the road. I could see the boy as plainly as though just off the path-kerbing a looking-glass was fixed; I could hear him singing the Irish song with a true Irish flavour in its tune—the flavour that Mrs. Burke put in it, as I well knew from hearing it so often, and having so often practised it. There was a larger mob listening to the second boy than to the first, and the circumstance of his having no cap did not stand in his way when the song was finished, and he came round pulling a spray of his front hair in a civil way.

A brewer's dray, lumbering past, smashed the *looking-glass* in which I had seen the second boy so plainly reflected; but there was I, the original, with my eyes as wide open as ever, on the pavement. What was to hinder me? Why *shouldn't* I step into the road and do as the other boy had done? What could be easier? It was quite an honest way of picking up a few halfpence, (my conversations with the Methodistic old Mrs. Dipple at the workhouse had made me think much more about honesty than of old—" as was instanced in that little affair of the pineapple," may occur to the cynical reader; but consider, my dear sir, how hardly I was driven!) and there was not the humiliation of "cadging" about it. People were free to stop and listen, or pass on; they were free to listen and pass on afterwards, without paying their halfpenny, if they chose. I wasn't a greedy and grasping boy; if only one in ten, ay, or in twenty, gave me a halfpenny, I would be satisfied. And without a moment's further consideration over the matter I walked into the road, and after going a little way to get the song and the tune in order in my mind, I presently stood still and piped up.

It was at the corner of Liquorpond Street where I made my stand, and there was then, as there is now, at that spot, a public-house. When I first began the song I was disappointed to find that it attracted scarcely any attention. But this was easily accounted for. I thought that I had pluck enough for almost anything—for things twenty times more daring than singing a song in the street; and doubtless had it been simply singing a song in the street for my amusement, I could have accomplished it heartily enough, not caring a button who heard me. But now I *did* care who heard me, and that made all the difference! and, for the first time in my life, I discovered that I was possessed of the quality of bashfulness. I seemed to be afraid of the sound of my own voice; and when presently two little girls stopped to look at me and listen, I affected to be in fun, and made a grimace at them, (although my ears were tingling, and I could feel my face turning red,) and ceasing to sing, took to whistling, and to hopping on and off the pavement as though I was merely a boy out at play. At the same time I felt very much ashamed of my weakness, and screwed up my courage to the resolution that, as soon as the two girls were out of earshot, I really would strike up in earnest.

And so I did. I stood my ground firmly before the public-house window, and fixing my eyes intently on a placard in the window, concerning "old vatted rum," began my song. First a boy stopped, but I did not flinch; then an old man and woman; then a servant-girl, with a beer jug in her hand. I thought to myself concerning this last one, "You are sent on an errand and ought to be in a hurry. If *you* stop and listen I should say that things looked promising." She *did* stop. She didn't stare at me as the old man and woman did, but she stood against the post, half turned from me, and I could see she was softly marking the time of the tune with her door-key against the beer jug. I was very much obliged to her—it would be difficult for me to explain how much. I turned away my gaze from the " old vatted rum " placard, and sang my song *to her*, my confidence increasing each moment.

Before I was half through with the second verse of "Erin-go-bragh," my audience had increased to a dozen at least, exclusive of a man in a cart, who drew up just behind me. In less than a minute the dozen was increased to twenty, including three Irish bricklayers' labourers, who came out of the public-house, and I wished that they had passed on, for they came and stood right between the servant-girl with the jug and myself, very much to my distress.

The song at an end, I raised my eyes, and to my great delight found three or four hands stretched out towards me, each one with a penny or a halfpenny in it, and gratefully enough I gathered them in. The heartiest hand of all, however, was one with nothing in it, and belonged to one of the Irish labourers before mentioned. It would be presumptuous, perhaps, to ascribe his behaviour entirely to the effects of my vocal talent; but it is a fact that that, acting on some previously imbibed influence, quite unmanned the poor fellow. His very legs bowed to the overwhelming power of his emotion, and he stepped staggeringly towards me, grasping my hand with a fervour that quite hurt my knuckles.

"'Melia murther! but it does the heart of an Irishman good to hear that swate song. That's Irish music, ye spalpeens!" continued he, turning to the people, "music as you don't mate in this dirthy counthry ivery workin' day in the week. Shure you couldn't uv been payin' dacent attintion to it, or you wouldn't be so shparin' av your dirthy coppers. Sing it agin, alanna! sing it agin, an' its mesilf that'll go round wid me hat at the ind of it."

Three or four more halfpence was the result of my Irish friend's exhortation, and the crowd—now quite a mob—laughed, and cried, "Sing it again, boy; sing it again."

Nothing loth, I began the song again, the tipsy Irishman still holding my hand and steadying himself by it, wagging his head with his cap off as solemnly as though it were a hymn I was singing. This second performance was a tremendous success. True to his word, the Irishman went round with his cap, and presented me with a big handful of coppers out of it. Just, however, as I had pocketed the money, and was turning about anxious to escape from the crowd, a hand was placed on my shoulder, and a woman's voice addressed me.

"What! is it you, little Jimmy? Goodness gracious, child! What on earth do you mean by it?"

There was only one woman in the world whose voice I dreaded, and this was not that one. It was a kind voice, and one with which I was familiar. It was Martha's voice—Martha, Mrs. Winkship's niece, whom the reader may remember my having made mention of.

———◆———

CHAPTER XXIV.

IN WHICH I AM BEHOLDEN TO AN OLD FRIEND FOR SUMPTUOUS FARE, AND FLANNEL AND FRILLED LINEN. THERE IS A PROSPECT OF MY BECOMING A CHIMNEY-SWEEP.

NEXT to Mrs. Winkship herself, there was nobody for whom I entertained so much respect as for her niece, Martha.

She was, as I think I have before mentioned, an extremely plain young woman—so much so,

indeed, that, standing as well as she did with her aunt, who was an influential person, and able to set up any matrimonially-disposed and likely young costermonger handsomely in business, no one thought it worth his while to pay his addresses to her. Whether this was lucky or unlucky for Martha, is impossible for anyone to say; it was not much to be wondered at, however. She was not even called by her proper and womanly name, but by an appellation suggested by her cruel visual deprivation, "Boss-eye!" By this name she was spoken of and spoken to. When a costermonger came to hire a barrow, he said, civilly enough, "Give us the key of the shed, please, Boss-eye." If he was more than commonly intimate with her, he further nicked the nickname and called her "Bossy." I believe she was no more regarded as an eligible object to make love to than the cast-iron face that formed part of Mrs. Winkship's door-knocker. I don't believe that she ever expected to be made love to. She found quite enough to occupy her mind in keeping the barrow-books, and marketing and cooking for Mrs. Winkship. She was a kind-hearted creature, however, and always pleasant.

She always had a kind word for me, and many and many a time, in the old starvation days at home with my stepmother, something more substantial; and it is one among the few gratifying recollections of my childhood that I never called her Boss-eye. Mrs. Winkship invariably addressed her as Martha, and, proud to follow so good a woman's example, I called her Martha as well. I was the only boy in Fryingpan Alley who did so, which may in some degree account for her marked partiality to me.

"Gracious goodness, Jimmy!" was her exclamation, as she discovered me endeavouring to extricate myself from the mob of my own raising, "What! brought down to this? Oh! come along, you wretched little boy; come along this instant, and tell me all about it."

Had I not known Martha of old as a firm and trusty friend, I should have doubtless resented her grasp on my shoulder—especially as, at the same time, she urged me in the direction of her house, which, as the reader is aware, was unpleasantly close to my own.

"Tell you all about what, Martha?" I asked, as she hurried me down Liquorpond Street. "I don't want to come any further this way. I don't want to go near the alley any more. I had enough of goin' near there the night afore last."

"I know; I know all about it, you poor starved-lookin' little mortal," replied the kind-hearted young woman. "Aunt knows all about it, too. Only this mornin' she was speakin' about it. 'If ever there was a poor boy drove out to ruin, Martha, he's the one,' said she. 'If I was like another woman, and had legs to go about on, I'd walk a good five mile to fall across that boy, if it was only for his mother's sake.' And here I find you, and how do I find you?" And Martha wiped her eyes on her apron.

"Thunderin' hungry, Martha—starved a'most." And I cried, too, and we stood just opposite the brewery near Leather Lane, crying, one against the other.

"Come on," suddenly exclaimed Martha, taking hold of my hand; "come on; I can't, as a Christ'an woman, let you go. Aunt said she would like to fall across you, and so she shall."

" Come on where ?"

" Home, of course,"

" What! to Fryingpan Alley? Not if I knows it." And I held back resolutely.

" Come on, you'll be all right. I'll go first and see that the way's clear. Not that there's much occasion," continued she, casting a pitying glance over my tattered and narrow length; " nobody'll know you. *I* shouldn't, only for your voice."

So, after a little further persuasion, I was induced to accompany Martha; and when we approached Fryingpan Alley, she left me at a dark and secluded part of Turnmill Street while she went on to see that the coast was clear, and to announce my coming to Mrs. Winkship.

Martha was gone so long—so it seemed to me —that I began to think that she had possibly over-estimated Mrs. Winkship's regard for me, and that the good lady was not, after all, so anxious for an interview with me as her niece had thought herself justified in inferring. To comfort myself under the disappointment that this reflection brought me, I took to counting the money I had earned by my singing; and, to my great astonishment, found that it amounted to the handsome sum of fourteen-pence-halfpenny. Earned in less than half-an-hour, too! To be sure, the largeness of the sum was partly due to the interposition of the friendly Irishman; but, suppose I deducted half—three-quarters even—from the total on that account, there still remained threepence-halfpenny. Threepence-halfpenny a half-hour was sevenpence an hour—one-and-ninepence for three hours—for the three hours of dark between tea and supper-time! Whew! And I looked anxiously towards Fryingpan Alley, more than half inclined to hope that Martha might *not* be coming.

She did come, however, and at a brisk rate, too, and with something bulky under her shawl.

"It's all right, Jimmy," said she, as she came up to me. "It wasn't safe to come before, as your stepmother was out in the alley, rowing with Nosey Warren's wife. She's gone indoors now."

"But s'pose she comes out agin? s'pose she should come out agin, and I should run up against her? I don't think I shall chance it, Martha; thanky all the same. I think I'll be off another way."

"No, you won't, Jimmy; you've been off too long as it is," replied Martha, firmly, spreading herself before me so as to pen me securely in the doorway in which I was lurking. "You come home with me, that's a good boy. No fear of her knowing you, even though she did run up against you, if you put these on. Look here."

And as she spoke, Martha produced from under her shawl an old cloth cloak that she probably used herself to wear when she was younger, and one of her old bonnets; and in a twinkling she had the one on my head and the other on my back, and, linking her arm in mine, right-about-faced with me and marched me off towards Fryingpan Alley, with a kind determination there was no resisting.

Had Mrs. Winkship been my nearest relative —my own mother, even—she could not have manifested more dismay at the appearance I pre-*sented when divested of* the cloak and bonnet.

Martha introduced me to her comfortably enjoying her hot rum-and-water before a jolly fire in the back parlour.

" Here he is, aunt. Did you ever see such a pictur ?"

To judge from the astonished—almost appalled —look with which Mrs. Winkship, with both her hands raised shoulder high, regarded the said "pictur" as it stood framed in her doorway, it might fairly be said that she had seldom or never seen such a one.

" *This* him! This the bright little feller as used to be the image of the poor dead gal as bore him! Good Lord above us! what a spectacle! And all through *you*, you carneying, two-faced Irish vagabond!" continued the indignant barrow-woman, shaking her fat fist in the direction of Number Nineteen. "All *your* bringing about, you drunken, draggletail carroty scoundrel! Hang you! if I had you here this minute I'd pummel you, if they gave me a month for it. Come here to the fire, you poor, starved-looking miser's cat! Have a sip of this, my poor chap. Why, I declare to goodness, Martha, he hasn't got so much as a bit of shirt on! The lies they've been tellin' about him! Why, it was only the night afore last that we heard of him in a work'us rig, all warm and comfortable; and now here he is without "——

How Mrs. Winkship finished the sentence I do not remember. Cold and famished as I was, the sudden heat of the fire affected me with a strange tingling and giddiness, and I felt myself sliding down on to the hearth-rug.

I must have remained some time in my fainting-fit—or, at least, have crept very slowly out of it—for when I came to myself, certain alterations had been made in my condition, of the progress of which I had been profoundly ignorant. There was a sofa in the back parlour, and I was lying on it. My filthy jacket and trowsers were removed, and replaced, as regards the latter, by what I suppose was a pair of the late Mr. Winkship's flannel drawers; and, as regards the former, by two articles—the one a flannel waistcoat, (probably the property of the same lamented gentleman,) and an item of linen apparel, with frilled cuffs, and a frill down the open front of it, and so ample that it wrapped under my feet with a full yard to spare. Bless her kind old heart! if it wasn't one of Mrs. Winkship's bed-gowns, I am very much mistaken.

I still felt rather swimmy in my head (for which, by the by, a strong flavour in my mouth of Mrs. Winkship's favourite liquor may partly have accounted) as I raised it from the pillow, (so clean and white—whiter even than the bolster-cases at the workhouse,) and for a few moments looked wonderingly about me, at a loss to know where I was and how I had come there; but presently making out through my hazy eyes the familiar figure of stout Mrs. Winkship bending over the fire-place and stirring something in a little saucepan, the real condition of affairs was made known to me. Martha was not in the room when I awoke, but presently she came in, and placed on the table three magnificent mutton-chops, the bare sight of which drew me up to a sitting posture. I believe I should have got right off the sofa to indulge in a nearer inspection of the tempting meat, only that the mysterious muffling of my legs checked the movement

My suppressed exclamation, however, drew Mrs. Winkship's attention towards me.

"Halloa, old chap! so you've come to life again!" exclaimed she, cordially, as she waddled over from the fireplace, and shook hands with me as though I had fainted off so long a way, that I wasn't expected to return just at present. "Why, cheer up, old chap! What d'yer mean by goin' on like this?"

By "goin' on like this," she meant, what did I want to cry for? But that was her fault; she shouldn't have kissed me. She didn't kiss me on the mouth, but on the forehead; and whether it was that the sensation of being kissed was so foreign to me, (I had never been kissed since that night when my mother died, and my father and I lay in young Joe Jenkins's bedroom,) or that I was in that weak condition as to be unequal to sensations of any kind, is more than I can say. I only know that there ensued immediately on receipt of the motherly old woman's kiss a tingling of my blood as when I had fainted just before, only that it was a hot tingling instead of a cold one—a tingling with life instead of death in it, and resulting, as before stated, in a wholesome fit of tears.

Judiciously leaving me to lay my face on the pillow and have my cry out, Mrs. Winkship, assisted by Martha, bustled about to get supper ready; and in a few minutes there arose from the bright little Dutch oven suspended before the bars of the grate a fragrance that went very far towards consoling me and reconciling me to the novel situation in which I found myself.

"Are you ready, Jim?"

"Quite, thanky, mum!"

"I had a little chicken biled for dinner, my dear," said Mrs. Winkship, evidently delighting in treating me as a "patient," and lifting me in her mighty arms from the sofa to a chair between the fire and the supper table; "and I've just hashed up what was left in the broth for you. You eat that—every bit of it, mind!—and then by that time the chops will be done to a turn."

I needed no further pressing. The hashed chicken was very nice, I dare say; but it wasn't the sort of thing to peg away at. It was a downright shame to treat a delicacy so rudely; but for that my wolfish hunger, rather than my proper self, was responsible. I regarded the savoury mess—there was a considerable quantity of it—rather as an enemy than a friend—an enemy that barred the way to a real and substantial enjoyment, and whom it was desirable to exterminate as speedily as possible. It took me so short a time to dispose of the hash that I almost believe Mrs. Winkship held her breath in amazement throughout the entire process. I think it must have been so, or she would never have been able to produce the tremendous sigh that accompanied her emphatic exclamation—

"Well! that ever I should have lived to see the like of that! It was like a drink of water to him."

That was exactly what I felt it to be like, but I didn't like to tell her so; indeed, when she asked me if I could eat any mutton-chop, I sacrificed my feelings for hers to the extent of replying, "Just a little bit, ma'am," all the while yearning for every chop in the Dutch oven, and a jolly thick round of bread to sop the fat up with. My eyes, however, were more ravenous than my stomach, (which was scarcely to be wondered at, considering the brief opportunity at present allowed the former for feasting,) and after consuming one chop—the biggest—and a few fried potatoes, I felt myself fully satisfied.

"And now," said Mrs. Winkship, when Martha had cleared away the supper-things, and the sofa was wheeled round to the fire, and we all three were seated comfortably on it, and a stiff jorum of hot rum and water, for the good old woman's comfort, was conveniently placed on the corner of the mantelpiece—"now, then, Jimmy, tell us all about it."

And I did. I faithfully related to her every one of the most important events that had happened to me since that morning when I ran away from Mrs. Burke, after inflicting that savage bite on her thumb (I was wicked enough not to be very sorry when I was informed that she was compelled to wear it in a sling for more than a week afterwards.) I told her all about my partners, Mouldy and Ripston; how I fell in with them; how they offered me a share of their sleeping-place; how I had joined with them in their market pilferings. I don't think I should have ventured to have told her about this could I have foreseen the effect of the revelation. Once more the old lady broke out against Mrs. Burke, wishing that she had her there at that moment, and hoping that she might taste of the gaol she had so nearly driven me into.

"But they don't send people to quod for nailing things in the market, ma'am," I explained; "it's the beadle that settles them sort of cases; that's what he's there for. Mouldy told me so."

"Mouldy was a lying villain, then," responded Mrs. Winkship, "as you would, sure as eggs, have found one day, Jimmy. It was a mercy that fever fell on you, Jimmy, since it put a stop to your thievings. It did put a stop to 'em—eh, my boy?"

"Oh, yes, 'm! it quite put a stop to 'em," I replied; and as at this point of interruption I had got no further into my story than that part where I was carried to the workhouse, I resolved to say nothing about the pineapple. I have thought since that it was odd she should make such a fuss about my dishonest market practices, while she seemed to treat my misappropriation of the workhouse suit almost as a joke — as something to laugh at till her fat sides shook, at all events. She didn't laugh, however, when I got a little further into the story, and told her how the two young Jews had served me. She grew as furious concerning them as she did at Mrs. Burke's behaviour; and when I got to that part where the young "clo'" dealers so cleverly contrived to swindle me out of my shilling, she had not the patience to sit on the sofa and listen, but stood up, with flashing eyes, and her hands on her hips, in a tremendous rage. "Devil take 'em for a pair of beauties, I say!" exclaimed she. "Rot 'em! the shabby curs," (here she stamped her foot;) "if I was a man instead of a woman, I'd spend a week in laying wait, but I'd catch 'em. If I knew a man I could trust with the job, I'd give him a pound, poor as I am, to find 'em and give 'em a twistin'."

"The Lord be thanked it's no worse!" exclaimed she, piously, as I finished my narrative. "It's bad enough for Polly Barnard's boy to turn up as a beggar—more disgrace and shame to the man who killed her and took in her place an Irish riff-raff not fit to clean her shoes—but it might have been worse."

"How do you mean — a beggar, ma'am? I didn't turn up beggin'. When Martha found me, I was singin'. You don't call that beggin', do you?"

"Cadgin', then; it's about the same, I reckon," replied Mrs. Winkship. "If one ain't as bad as the other, there ain't much difference that I see."

I may here remark, that amongst people of my born grade no one is so contemptuously regarded as he who is known as a "cadger." The meaning they set on the word is not the dictionary meaning. The "cadger" with them is the whining beggar—the cowardly impostor, who, being driven, or finding it convenient to subsist on charity, goes about his business with an affectation of profoundest humility, and a consciousness of his own unworthiness; a sneaking, abject wretch, aiming to crop a meal out of the despising and disgust he excites in his fellow-creatures. The ordinary beggar—the fellow who knocks at your door and says, "Will you kindly spare a copper to a poor fellow hard-up?"—is regarded as quite a superior person compared with the "cadger." My opinion of the cadger naturally was the popular one; and when Mrs. Winkship stigmatised street-singing as cadging, I felt so ashamed that I could not look her in the face.

"If I had known it was beggin', let alone cadgin', you wouldn't have caught me at it," I replied. "Anybody may have that fourteenpence for all that I shall touch it. Where is it, ma'am?"

"Never you mind where it's gone; you don't want that sort of money, Jimmy. As money it's right enough, and much good may it do the poor creetur as it was sent to; but it ain't good money to spend by the one as gets it. What did she say about them dirty rags that you took as well, Martha?"

"Bless you! she was up to her eyes in thankfulness about 'em. She set to cuttin' 'em down at once, to make little Billy a pair."

What did this mean! What "old rags" did Mrs. Winkship allude to? To what old rags could she allude but to my dirty old fustian trousers, since the woman to whom they had been taken "at once set about cutting them down to make little Billy a pair." Good luck to little Billy! he was quite welcome to 'em, as well as to the jacket, and to that disgraceful one-and-twopence-halfpenny into the bargain. Where was the good-natured barrow-lender's kindness going to end? Certainly, not at ridding me of the wretched garments for which I had swopped away my workhouse clothes. The flannel shirt and drawers she had dressed me in were perfectly warm and comfortable, but scarcely fit to appear in publicly. Perhaps, however, I might, after all, be mistaken as regarded the "old rags" discussed between Martha and my benefactress. It would be better to know the truth at once. Whilst wondering in my mind what would be the best way to gain the required information without asking bluntly for it, I spied a biggish-sized button lying on the mantelshelf.

"Do you want that button for anything pertickler, ma'am?" I asked of Mrs. Winkship.

"Not very particular. Why?"

"Because it 'ud jest do to sew on my jacket; the top button has been off ever since I first had it."

"Drat the dirty thing, and every button on it," replied she. "You'll never see that any more, Jimmy."

"Never see it any more, ma'am!" I exclaimed, (little hypocrite!)—"shan't I? I hope I shall, though. Cert'n'y, it wasn't much of a jacket! but it was better than none."

"Don't you trouble; you shall have a jacket," replied the good soul, patting my head kindly. "I wish that was the hardest part of the business, Jimmy."

And having so mysteriously expressed herself, she took a pull at the hot rum-and-water, and afterwards, instead of setting it on the mantel-shelf again, sat nursing it on her knee, looking into the fire thoughtfully. Martha, who was busy darning a stocking, was quiet too.

"What is the hardest part of it, ma'am?" I asked, after enduring the tantalising silence for fully a minute; "do you mean the trousers?"

The question seemed to tickle the old woman's fancy immensely, and she chuckled over it so that the spoon tingled against the glass she held on her lap.

"No, it ain't the trousers either, Jimmy," she presently answered; "it's what I'm to do with you. Something must be done with you, you know. You ain't to go to ruin, because them as ought to know better turns their backs on you."

It wasn't the words so much as the way in which she said them—holding my small hand in her jolly fat one the while—that affected me. I was very young and very ignorant; but I must have been a natural-born ruffian to have remained unmoved after a declaration of such a character.

"Thanky, ma'am," I replied, with tears in my eyes, at the same time gratefully grasping as many of her fingers as my fist would contain; "you always was a good sort towards me, ma'am."

"The question is, what can I do? You can't stay here, you know. There'd be a pretty Bedlam if they found you along o' me."

"No, ma'am, I mustn't stay here," I promptly responded; "I should be afraid to."

"That's the thing. You see you are such a little chap to go on your own hook, else I might set you up with some sort of a stock, and put you in the way of sellin' it."

"There's that barking bis'ness you was speakin' of one time, ma'am," I suggested; "p'r'aps you might know of somebody as would take me at that."

But she shook her head.

"There's plenty as would take you at that," said she; "but what 'ud be the good? You'd be found out in a week."

"Something of a trade would be the thing," quietly put in Martha, as she sat darning her stockings; "if we knew anybody with a trade, now, as would take him, aunt?"

"Ah! if we did," answered her aunt, stirring the remains of her grog testily; "how many 'ifs' go to a bushel, Martha?"

"Well, I was a-thinking, aunt — but I s'pose you wouldn't call that a trade?"

"What?"

"Chimney-sweeping. There's cousin Belcher at Camberwell, you know, aunt, *he* keeps boys."

The suggestion acted like magic on Mrs. Winkship. For an instant regarding Martha with a glance of gratitude and admiration, she emptied her glass with a relish, and clicked her finger and thumb.

"That's it!" exclaimed she, triumphantly; "that's the identical ticket. Just like my thick head, leading me forty miles round to find what's just under my nose. We've hit on the right think at last—eh, Jimmy?"

I dutifully answered, "Yes, 'm," though, in truth, I was not so dazzled by the brilliancy of the notion as Mrs. Winkship was. Chimney-sweeping might be a trade; but, decidedly, it was not one I should have hit on had I been free to choose. My thoughts on the matter might have been different had it been put to me a few hours back—about this same time the night before, for instance—when, famished and ragged, I huddled down in the stable heap in the mews; but, to a boy who had supped off chicken hash and mutton-chops, and who sat on a soft sofa, tucked up in soft flannel and clean frilled linen, the prospect of climbing up a chimney was not particularly enticing.

"Drat it all! I'm so glad the thought should have popped into your head, gal," continued Mrs. Winkship, evidently liking the idea more each moment; "it is worth a Jew's eye. It perwides for the case all round, just as if it was made for it. Fust of all, it's a trade, and one that it's easy to learn and follow, and money to be made at it. You know Dick Belcher was quite as poor as this boy when he started, Martha; then, it's a good way off, and in a part where nobody would think of looking for him; besides which, it's a bis'ness of which the very natur on it is to disguise and make look different, so that your own parents might pass you by in the street and never know you! That settles it. Make us another jorum, Martha; the last didn't do me a bit of good—it never does when I'm worritted in my mind; and, if you like, you may mix yourself and Jimmy a thimbleful, just for a night-cap. Fust thing in the mornin', Martha, you take the omlibus over to Camberwell, and bring Belcher back with you."

CHAPTER XXV.

IN WHICH I AM INTRODUCED TO MR. BELCHER; LIKEWISE TO MRS. BELCHER; LIKEWISE TO SAM, AND HIS FRIEND "SPIDER."

NOTWITHSTANDING the many inducements to comfortable repose provided by my good-natured friend the barrow-woman—the soft bed made on the sofa before the fire, the luxurious sheets and blankets, to say nothing of the spirituous "night-cap" I had at her recommendation imbibed—it was some considerable time after she had bade me good-night and carried off the candle ere I could get to sleep.

The fact is, the more I pondered on the probabilities of my becoming a chimney-sweep, the less I liked them. Nor were my objections purely whimsical. As long as I could remember, a sweep had resided in Fryingpan Alley, and he had two boys—not his sons, but apprentices—and a more wretched pair it was hard to imagine. I

say that Mr. Pike—our sweep—had two apprentices, and so he had invariably; but not invariably the same two. Six or seven months was the longest they ever lasted. Either they ran away, or the workhouse people (they were parish apprentices) fetched them back to the "house" again, or they died, and were carried off in a shell in the dusk of the evening to lie in the parochial bone-house until the next convenient burying-day.

Unless, however, you had private means of information, and knew of these repeated changes in Mr. Pike's establishment, you would never have suspected them. If Bob died on Tuesday, Jack, who took his place, would by the following Saturday become his exact counterpart—just as grimy, just as ragged, just as weak-eyed, and addicted to winking and blinking in the sun. He would not at present, perhaps, have acquired the sore knees and elbows that, previous to his demise, distinguished Bob, the dead one; but that difference could not be discovered by the casual observer. The sore knees and elbows were sure to appear in the course of a few weeks, however, as well as the cough and the half-gagged voice, which sounded as though it proceeded from a throat loosely stuffed with wool.

Mr. Pike was popularly believed to be a cruel brute. The boys were for ever begging bits of old rag of the women in the alley to tie about their poor knees, and save them a little of the cruel chafing against the sooty chimney bricks; but so sure as Mr. Pike discovered them so bandaged, off would come the rags at one ruthless snatch, and the boy would be taken down into the cellar to have his wounds dabbed with brine for half-an-hour, to "harden" them. It was currently reported amongst the juvenile inhabitants of the alley that Mr. Pike's method of teaching a boy to climb a chimney was as simple as it was efficacious, and consisted in his tying one end of a cord round the boy's tongue, the said cord extending up the chimney and hanging over the edge of the chimney pot; then Mr. Pike would mount to the roof of the house, and, grasping the end of the cord there to be found, the lesson would begin. If the boy climbed satisfactorily, (which, being altogether new to the business, was not at all likely,) all very well; but if he halted or bungled, Mr. Pike would give his end of the cord such a jerk as speedily brought the climber to his senses. It was an ordinary joke of Mr. Pike's to light a handful of shavings, sprinkled with pepper, in the grate of a chimney in which a lad of his might be idling. Once he sent a boy up a chimney, and he never came down any more; and the only way to account for his disappearance was, that Mr. Pike had fired so many shavings that the poor lad was entirely consumed. Either this, or that he had escaped out at the chimney-pot. Indeed, the latter supposition, on account of the boy being seen in Shoreditch a fortnight afterwards, was admitted by the least romantic of the inhabitants to be the most probable.

I lay awake so long regaling on the above and similar horrors, as to hear the Dutch clock in the kitchen strike twelve, and one, and two. Then I fell asleep, and slept until the same clock was striking ten, which, after all, was not so very long a sleep, considering that I had had scarcely any rest at all through the two nights preceding. Mrs. Winkship and her niece, however, must have been up at their usual time, which, as I knew of old, was an early time—time sufficient to have prepared and finished their breakfast; time sufficient to have made a journey to some ready-made clothes shop and back again, for there lay the result of the journey across the back of a chair by the bedside—a stout cloth jacket and waistcoat, and new corduroy trousers; while under the chair reposed a bran-new pair of boots—nicer-looking, even, than those Mr. Barney cheated me out of—and a pair of comfortable socks. On the chair was a shirt, and hanging to the knob at the back of the chair was a cap. There could be no doubt that the suit was mine, so I at once jumped up and dressed myself in it; and then, putting my head out at the door, and spying Mrs. Winkship enthroned on the coke measure at the street door, I called out to her, bidding her good morning.

I don't know how much my suit cost, but if the sum exceeded the value of the gratification the good old woman evinced at my appearance, it must have been something immense. She brought me some warm water to wash my hands and face, and with her own hands, and with her own brush, brushed my hair and anointed it with her own pomatum. "Now look in the glass," said she. "What do you think of *that?* Why, you're as fine as fust-o'-May, Jimmy!"

"They ain't much like a sweep's togs—are they, ma'am? I shan't like to go up a chimnbly in these," I remarked, eyeing myself proudly, and indulging in a glimmer of hope that her views on the chimney-sweeping subject might have changed.

"I should think *not,*" replied she, sharply. "Any rags is good enough for that sort of work. You must keep these for Sundays, Jim. I daresay that Belcher will be able to find you a suit good enough to wear o' work-a-days. Martha has gone over to Camberwell now, and I daresay she will be back, bringing Belcher with her, by the time you have finished your breakfast."

Soon after breakfast, however, Martha returned without Mr. Belcher, and with a message that he was engaged until the evening, when he would drive over in the pony-cart. I got considerable comfort out of the mention of the pony and cart. It was substantial proof that Mr. Belcher was not such a poor beggar of a sweep as Mr. Pike, at all events.

For safety's sake I kept close within doors all day long; and shortly after dark there came a knock at the door, and Mr. Belcher made his appearance. He wasn't a bit like a sweep, being white instead of black, and wearing a smart hat and a drab overcoat. He was a tall, strong-looking man, middle-aged, and with a stoop in his shoulders; he was pitted with small-pox, too, as badly as Martha was, and was pale and cadaverous-looking; and his mouth was an ugly-looking mouth, the yellow teeth of his upper jaw projecting over the lower, and being for the most part exposed to view. I didn't like the look of him a bit.

"Well, Jane, what's the pertickler bis'ness?" he asked of Mrs. Winkship. If he was in no other way like a sweep, he was in his voice, which was of the husky, muffled sort, just like Mr. Pike's.

It seemed that Martha had been charged not to tell him what he was wanted for; and now that his sister-in-law, in a few words informed him of her wishes as regarded myself, it appeared to me *that he didn't look best pleased.*

"That the youngster?" he asked, looking at me.

"That's him. Stand up, Jimmy."

"He's a tall 'un. How old is he?"

"Under nine—eight last birthday. That isn't too young—is it?" said Mrs. Winkship.

"Lor', no!—too old, I was thinkin'. Nothing like beginnin' with 'em when their bones is lissum," replied Mr. Belcher; and then, after turning me about a bit, he shook his head, as though not perfectly satisfied with the survey.

"Pity to make a sweep of him, ain't it?" said he—"nice, decent-looking boy like he is?"

"Well, p'r'aps it *is* a pity; but it's the best we can do, take my word for it, Dick. You'll take him—won't you?"

"Trade's wery slack, replied Mr. Belcher, dubiously; "sides, that blessed Act o' Parlyment, wot's just passed, has quite cut up the boy-trade. I sacked a boy o'ny last week."

"I know all about the Act o' Parlyment," said Mrs. Winkship, testily; "and" (perceiving that her relative was inclined to hang back from her proposition) "likewise I know that you still keep climbers, because you told me so the last time you was here."

"Ah, that's for the shaft-work, Jane," Mr. Belcher replied. "I question if he's narrer enough for shaft-work."

So saying, he took a rule from his pocket, and placed it across my shoulders.

"He'd find it a squeedge," observed Mr Belcher, at the same time passing his hands over my chest and back. "You see, Jane, he ain't like a lad with flesh on him, what might be pulled down to the proper dimensions. I shouldn't be able to allow him to get another ounce of flesh on him if I took him; it 'ud be wicked to allow it; he'd be sticking in the middle of a flue, or somethink, if I did. Why, there was just such a case at a saw-mills shaft—ninety-eight feet high it was—up Bermondsey way; there the poor lad stuck, just half-way up, and there he had to stay till "——

"Humbug, Dick!" interrupted Mrs. Winkship, in a pet; "if you don't want to take him, say so. Don't stand there sending your soul to Old Nick with a bushel of lies. You didn't find *me* humming and hawing, and making tuppeny excuses, when you came over here askin' favours of me, remember. But never mind."

From the bottom of my heart I wished that Mr. Belcher, with his awful talk about boys sticking in sawmill chimney-shafts ninety-eight feet high, would get in a pet too, and take himself off as he came; but this he evidently was not disposed to do. Whatever the nature of the favour conferred, once upon a time, by Mrs. Winkship on her sister's husband, her allusion to it was enough to make him alter his tone.

"Who said I wouldn't take him?" said he. "'Course I'll take him. What I meant was, that it's a pity that he's just goin' into the trade when Acts o' Parlyment and machinery are risin' up to knock it over. He's welcome to come along o'me and learn the trade, such as it is."

After this declaration of Mr. Belcher, (which had the effect of completely mollifying his sister-in-law,) there ensued between the contracting parties a long conversation, all concerning me, but in which I took not the least interest. It was enough for me to know that I was to be made a sweep of; that the man with the white pock-marked face, and the yellow overhanging teeth, was to be my master; and that I was not to be allowed to gain an ounce more flesh than now covered my bony frame, to make me perfectly miserable.

"Then that settles it," observed Mr. Belcher, after a while. "When will he be ready to come?"

"He's ready now—as ready as ever he'll be," replied Mrs. Winkship.

"What! now—to-night, do you mean? Take him off with me to-night?" inquired my future master.

"I should take it as a favour if you would take him off to-night. The sooner he goes the better."

"Just as you please; one time's as good as another, as far as I know. Put your cap on, boy."

There was no use in making a fuss over what couldn't be avoided; besides, when it came to this, I felt a little spiteful towards Mrs. Winkship that she should have been so very anxious to pack me off at once; and I am ashamed to confess that my response to her tearful "Good-bye" was not so cordial as it might have been. Mr. Belcher's pony and cart were waiting at the end of the alley, in charge of a boy who stood at the pony's head. And here occurred an illustration of how the artfullest plots and schemes may be frustrated in a single instant, and that by a means least expected. The boy at the pony's head was one that Mr. Belcher had promiscuously hailed from among a dozen loitering about the alley; it was my old enemy, Jerry Pape. As good luck willed it, however, that treacherous scoundrel was too intent watching Mr. Belcher, with an eye to halfpence for holding the pony, to take any heed of me; and so we drove away.

It was growing quite late by the time we reached Camberwell, and that part of it where Mr. Belcher resided. It was in a little dirty street, close by the canal. From what I could see of the houses in the street, they were of the poorest sort; but Mr. Belcher's house figured amongst them brilliant as a new toy on a dust-heap. It was the richest house as regards bright brass that ever I clapped eyes on. The door, shone on by the lamp that overhung it, was absolutely dazzling: it had a brass knocker; number twenty-six in bold brass figures; a brass key-hole; a brass plate with the inscription "Belcher, Chimney-Sweep," in red letters on it; and a brass bell, big as those attached to a Piccadilly mansion, with "Belcher" in more red letters on the knob of it, and "Sweep's Bell" in bright green on the flat part round the knob. Inside the parlour window was a wire blind, blood red, and deeply edged with shiny brass; and on the blind was an effective representation of Buckingham Palace with one of its chimneys on fire, the pot splintered into a hundred fragments, and the flames mounting to the heavens; while her Most Gracious Majesty Queen Victoria, wearing her crown as a night-cap, leant out at a bed-room window, with affrighted eyes and dishevelled hair, beckoning imploringly with her sceptre to Mr. Belcher, who, loyally responding to the call of his sovereign by waving his brush and scraper, was hastening across the park to the rescue as fast as his legs could carry him. The name of "R. Belcher" appeared on the cap the running sweep wore, as well as on his brush and on his scraper; but in order to obviate the possibility of any mistake as to his identification, the sentry at the palace gate was seen to be shouting,

(the words were carefully preserved in a band just in front of his nose,) "Come on, R. Belcher! We thought you wasn't coming, as the Prince of Wales, who has been over to your place, said that you was gone to another job." "So I was—at the Duke of Wellington's," replies R. Belcher; "but at the calls of my Queen I left it blazin'—and here I am."

A boy about my own age, and as ragged and black as either of Mr. Pike's boys, hearing the sound of the cart wheels, made his appearance from the side of the house, (it stood at a corner,) and took the pony by the head. Mr. Belcher got out of the cart, leaving me in it, and applied himself to the brass knocker.

"Let me help you out, young sir," said the little sweep, obsequiously addressing me; "or p'r'aps you'd better, gov'nor. I might spoil his togs if I touched 'em."

"Young sir be——," Mr. Belcher observed, with a laugh; "he ain't a sir, you young fool; he's a new boy."

"A new boy, eh! Why, you must be ravin' mad, Dick! What the deuce do you want another boy for?" This observation was made by a female, who responded to Mr. Belcher's appeal to the brass knocker—a fat, blowsy female, with a shrill voice, and a cap with plenty of brilliant flowers in it perched atop of her untidy head of hair, and earrings in her ears as flashy as the brass knocker, but who was, nevertheless, unmistakably Mrs. Winkship's sister.

"Want! Yes, I wanted him a lot!" I heard Mr. Belcher growl; "it was either have him, or offend your blessed sister, and that wouldn't do, you know. Be off in, and I'll tell you all about it." Then turning to the boy, he threw him the reins. "Take him" (meaning me) "round to the kitchen with you, Sam; I'll call him when I want him."

Never once removing his astonished gaze from my face, Sam did as he was bid, and led the pony round to the back of the sweep's premises, where there was a large yard, the end of which was open to the Surrey Canal; and at that part of the yard nearest the back of the house was a long black-looking shed, with two doors to it, as could be seen by the light of the lantern Sam carried.

"Out you come, my tulip," exclaimed he, with an insolent familiarity which I suppose he thought he was entitled to as some compensation for the former civil speech he had been inveigled into wasting over me; "out you come; that there's the kitchen. Don't you make too much noise goin' in, or you might wake the cove wot's asleep there, and then you might get a hidin'. I'll be with you in a minnit, soon as I've bedded the pony down. No 'casion to knock; shove—it'll come open."

The door I was requested to shove was exactly the same in appearance as that which by this time Sam had opened, and which showed the place to be a stable. If there was any difference, indeed, the "kitchen" door was the ugliest and dirtiest door of the two. It came open with a slight push, and I entered. The place was very dark, except for a coke fire that burnt redly in a skillet perched on a bit of paving-stone in the middle of the shed, and at first I could see nothing but the fire; but in a few moments my eyes grew more accustomed to the gloom, and I could make out, close by the fire, a little table and a couple of stools, while on the other side of the fire, and lying against the wall, was a black shapeless heap, from which proceeded a sound of snoring, and plainly denoted the whereabouts of the person asleep hinted at by Sam. I did not advance many steps into the shed, nor did I make much noise; enough, however, to rouse a little dog that was lying with its master on the black heap. The dog growled and barked, and the boy awoke.

"What do you want a-teasin' of him, Sam? he ain't hurtin' you, is he?" asked a figure black as the heap it rose from, except for the white eye-balls which the light of the fire revealed. "Shut the door, will yer? Ain't my rhumatiz bad enough, beggar you, but you must set the draught blowin' in upon me? *Will* you shut that door, cuss you?"

I couldn't tell whether it was the voice of a man or a boy, it was such a strange-sounding one —half gruff and half whistling, and trembling with rage. Looking intently at the figure, I could now see that it had risen to its hands and knees, and looming in the ruddy duskiness, it certainly looked big enough for that of a man. As the figure raised its voice, the dog raised its; so that there was all at once a considerable uproar.

"You make a mistake," said I, edging back towards the entry; "it ain't Sam—it's me."

"Cuss you! Now shut the door!" and at the same moment something that looked like an old Wellington boot shot past my face, and banged against the door-post just behind.

CHAPTER XXVI.

IN WHICH I MAKE FRIENDS WITH THE "SPIDER," AND ENGAGE WITH HIM IN A QUEER SORT OF CONVERSATION, THAT MAY OR MAY NOT LEAD TO IMPORTANT RESULTS.

IT wasn't likely that I was going to shut the door, at least, from the inside, and so trap myself in with such an ugly customer. I, however, had no objection to shutting it from the outside, and this I was about to do when up came Sam, the light of his lantern showing his grinning face.

"Halloa! I thought I seed you go into the kitchen a little while ago," said he; "why didn't you shove the door open, like I told you?"

I briefly explained to Sam the events of the last few minutes.

"Come on back," said he, laughing, and grasping one of my hands in his paw, black as ink; "there ain't no call to fear Spider; it would take him as long crawlin' off his bags as far as the door, as you might to get as far as the turnpike."

"It wasn't the dog I was frightened of," said I, "it was the man what was layin' by the fire."

"Well, *that's* Spider," replied Sam; "that's what his name is. 'Man' you calls him! I never seed such a man. Come on; the guv'nor said you was to sit in the kitchen, don't you know?"

Sam pushed open the door and went in, and I followed, taking care this time to give the figure on the soot-bags no excuse for shying his other boot at me.

"Who was that that was here just now, banging and slamming and letting in the wind, enough to blow a feller's bones out of their sockets?" *demanded Spider, in* the querulous voice of one

who has long lain an invalid; "did you see him? Who was it, Sam?"

"Who was it? Why, a young swell, Lord Fluffum's youngest son, come to ask arter you, and bring you some jint ile. Tell you what, Spider, you'll get yourself into a row one of these days chuckin' them boots of yours about; you're alwis at it."

"Oh! my poor bones!" groaned Spider, whining like a dog in pain; "then why don't they shut the door after 'em, Sam? How would *they* like the wind let into 'em, if their jints was all of a screw, like mine is? Who did you say it was, Sam? I didn't hit him, did I?"

"Not werry hard; he's one of them swells as don't holler for nothing, as it happens, and so he ain't werry angry with yer. Here he is."

And he stepped aside and held up the lantern, that the cripple might have a fair view of me. By the same means I got a fair view of him, poor fellow. He couldn't have been more than sixteen or seventeen years old, judging from his size; but, attired as he was in black rags, and crouching on his knees, with one hand resting on the soot-bags that were evidently his bed, and the other performing the double service of lifting his hair from his eyes and shielding them from the glare of the lantern-light, he might have passed for a decrepit old man of seventy.

"I begs your pardon, sir," said he, humbly; "it's my pain as gets over me, and makes me forget myself at times. I hope I didn't hurt you, young gen'lman?"

Before I could answer, Master Sam burst into an explosion of mirth.

"That's beautiful, that is! that's rippin'! He took *me* in, Spider; but not so much as that. Why, he ain't no young swell, you jolly fool; he ain't nobody. He's on'y a new boy wot's a-comin' 'prentice or somethin' here; that's right, ain't it, old flick?"

"Yes, that's right," I replied; "I've come to learn the trade of bein' a chimbley-sweep."

"Come *here* to learn the trade!" repeated the Spider, the expression of pain momentarily vanishing from his puckered face in his astonishment. "Well, that's a rum start."

"Hain't it? it's the rummest start as ever *I* heard on," giggled Sam.

"How do yer mean?" I asked; "why can't I learn it? 'Course I ain't goin' to set about it in my best clothes. Mr. Belcher's goin' to find me some common sort of togs to work in."

"Oh, there's no fear of spiling your togs!" observed Sam, whom the whole business seemed to highly amuse.

"It mightn't spoil *some* sort of togs," I replied, with a scornful glance at poor Sam's wretched rags. "I shouldn't like to get the soot over *my* clothes wot I wears of Sundays, so I tell yer. I'm going to have another suit to follow my trade in."

"But there ain't no trade here to foller," said the perplexed Spider. "Since the Act o' Parly-ment the trade's all fell to nothink. You can't learn to be a chimbley-sweep without chimbleys to practise on—don't yer know?"

As the reader may imagine, although this rather puzzled me, I was not at all sorry to hear it.

"Oh! well, I ain't perti ckler," I remarked; "any sort of work'll do for me. What do all the other boys work at?—what do you two work at?"

"Spider don't work at all—he's past it," explained Sam; "he'd ha' been sacked when the the others went, on'y he was bound for seven 'ears, and the parish would not take him off the guv'nor's hands. There used to be eight on us; but they're all gone 'cept me and Spider."

"But *you* sweeps chimbleys, sometimes, don't you?" I remarked to Sam; "you looks as though you did."

"No, I don't," returned Sam, grinning; "I goes about a bit, of mornin's, with Ned Perks and the guv'nor to machine jobs; but that ain't nothink. It's night jobs wot keeps the concern goin'—night jobs down in the country. I goes with the gov'nor and Ned, and minds the cart."

"What sort o' jobs is them country jobs?" I inquired; "is it climbin' up factory shafts?"

"I don't know what it's climbin' up," replied Sam; "fact, I don't think it's climbin' up anythink—do you, Spider?—'cos they take the machine and things with 'em."

"And they don't bring home no sut! It's a rummy go to me altogether," replied poor Spider, who, being at that moment seized with a fresh rheumatic pain, wriggled back to his bed, and there lay groaning and making whistling noises through his closed teeth.

Before poor Spider could sufficiently recover from his rheumatic twinges to continue the conversation, (which had begun to grow very interesting to me,) the voice of Mr. Belcher was heard calling on me to come into the house; and, directed by Sam, I found my way to a back door, and was from thence conducted by my new master to the parlour.

The same fat, blowsy woman whom I had rightly conjectured to be Mrs. Belcher was there, and on the table was a spread of bread-and-cheese and onions. The lady's reception of me was not cordial.

"Here, young what's-yer-name?"

"Jim, ma'am."

"There's some supper for you, if it's good enough. 'Taint the fat o' the land, with applesarce, such as some people have been feedin' you on, I'll be bound; but it's the best you'll get here."

"Thanky, ma'am; I'm werry fond of bread-and-cheese, 'specially with a ingun," I replied, in as conciliatory a tone as I could assume.

"And of all other sorts of wittles, I'll go bail. As if it wasn't enuff to have one lazy hound eatin' our 'eads off, but that that stuck up marm must"——

"There, that'll do," growled Mr. Belcher; "quite enough said. How should *she* know how we was sitiwated? If things was as they used to be, one boy, nor two boys, would have made any difference. P'r'aps you'd ha' liked me to ha' told her?"

"I'd be werry sorry," responded Mrs. Belcher, with peculiar emphasis, "I'd sooner suffer starwation than she should know."

"It seems so when you sets on cacklin' at this 'ere rate afore he's been in the house half-an-hour," replied Mr. Belcher, sneeringly. "You get your supper, Jim. The missus is the least bit cross to-night. It's arter her time for settin' up, and she's tired."

Acting on this hint, I made as short work as possible of the liberal hunch of bread-and-cheese, and in about five minutes was able to announce that I was done.

"Then toddle to bed as soon as you like," said Mr. Belcher. "Can you find your way back?"

"Back to where, sir?"

"Back to the kitchen. That's where you've got to sleep; that's where all my boys sleep. You'll find it wery warm and snug. Sam'll show yer how. Mind you have a bed to yourself, Jim; two in a bed ain't 'ealthy. There's sacks enough for all on yer. Good night. You've no 'casion to get up in the mornin' till you're called."

"Has he got his workin' clothes?" sleepily asked Mrs. Belcher, who by this time had composed herself for a doze in her great easy-chair.

"I was forgettin' them. Here they are," replied my master, giving me a black bundle from a corner. "The shirt you may as well keep on; likewise the boots; as for the rest, you'd better double 'em up careful, and bring 'em in here in the mornin'."

Taking the bundle, I bade my master "Good night," and found my way back to the "kitchen." The fire was still burning, and the lantern suspended from a nail in one of the roof-beams, so that I was able to see pretty well about me; but I couldn't see Sam. I could see Spider, curled up with his little mangy-looking, dirty-white dog, (recognising me again, he uttered but the smallest of growls;) but Sam was nowhere visible. This was perplexing, and I was still looking about, when a voice right at my elbow exclaimed, in a sleepy whisper—

"Last into bed puts the candle out, don't yer know?"

It was Sam. He was in bed. He was lying atop of a heap of soot-sacks—lying *in* the top one, indeed—with a soot-sack doubled up under his head as a pillow, and his sooty cap pulled over his ears; so that, as I turned to see from whence the voice proceeded, all that was visible of Sam was his white teeth and his eyeballs.

It is astonishing how rapidly one acquires the weakness of fastidiousness. The night before last, whilst shivering in the open cart in Bedford Mews, had anyone said to me, "It is just six miles from here to Camberwell; but if you choose to trudge the distance, you will find there a snug shed with a jolly fire in it, and any number of sacks—sooty, but soft—to bed on, and all at your disposal," I should have thanked my informant in the heartiest manner, and started off there and then, my only fear being that matters might not turn out to be so brilliant as was promised. But since the night before last I had enjoyed the luxury of a comfortable couch; and the result was, that the snug shed, and the jolly fire, and the heap of soft sacks all ready and at hand, so far from filling me with satisfaction, caused me a pang of something very like disgust.

"Which is my bed?" I inquired, in a melancholy voice, of Sam.

"You may have part of mine, if you like to, which it'll save you the trouble to make one," replied Sam, generously. "All you've got to do is to fetch two sacks off that heap—one to get into, and one for a piller; on'y be quick, and don't make a row so as to wake Spider, 'cos if you do, he'll begin to cough, and the cough shakes the rheumatics into his legs, and then it'll give you the mis'rables all night to hear him groanin' and crunchin' his teeth."

It was departing somewhat from the letter of Mr. Belcher's injunction to accept Sam's proposal, but after all, since we slept in separate sacks, it was no worse than only sleeping two on a bedstead; so, gulping down my repugnance, I undressed by the light of the coke fire, and putting on the grimy trousers out of Mr. Belcher's bundle, I prepared a pillow and a sack ready for slipping into, and then, blowing out the candle in the lantern, next minute was bedded on the black bags, snug and warm, at any rate, and not particularly uncomfortable, only for the overpowering odour of soot. It was an odour, however, with a soothing effect, and, combined with the fumes of the burning coke, sent me to sleep in a very little while.

It was not yet daylight when, awoke by the barking of Spider's little dog, I found that Sam was getting up to go to work, having been roused by Ned Perks, who, in spite of poor Spider's complainings and entreaty about the wind and its disastrous effects on his joints, persisted in standing with the shed door wide open, giving directions to Sam.

"It'll be the death on me, I'm sure it will," whined Spider, sitting up to cover up his tortured legs with more sacks. "I wish it would. I wish it would come all of a bust, and be the death on me."

"And a —— good job too, for all the good of sich hawful!" (offal, I think he meant,) growled Ned Perks. "It's 'bout time you was sent to the knacker's, you precious snivillin' bag-o'-bones! You might be worth a flimsy then, and that's mor'n you are now."

So saying, the brute went away, taking Sam with him, and banging the door.

Bearing in mind Mr. Belcher's intimation that I need not get up until I was called, I lay still, and presently I heard Spider stirring.

"You're like the rest on 'em," said he, presently, and in an impatient tone; "here you lay, just as though it was the middle of the night, instead of five o'clock in the mornin.' Your jints is all right, ain't they? hang you! What do you care whose jints ain't, and who warnts a fire and who don't?"

I thought to be sure that Spider was addressing himself to me, and was about to tell him that if he wanted me to get up and light the fire he might at least have asked me in a civil manner. Before I could speak, however, he began again.

"Don't get a-lickin' me. I don't want none of your lickin'. It's easier to lay here a-lickin' than to go and do what's wanted of yer, ain't it? You won't get up, eh? P'r'aps that'll make you, you lazy beggar! Ah! I thought it would."

It was plain that Spider was talking to the little dirty-white dog previously alluded to as occupying part of his couch, for simultaneous with the sound of a smart thump a sudden whine was heard, and then a scampering, and a scratching at the kitchen door.

"That's havin' the use of your jints!" groaned Spider, in allusion, as I suppose, to the activity displayed by his canine friend. "I wish I was ekal to it. I wouldn't lay here wishin' myself dead, and everybody wishin' the same." And then, as I could hear, he shuffled off his sacks,

and crept tediously and with many pauses after the dog.

"Oh, yes! you're in a great hurry, ain't yer? It's all werry well a-boundin' to the door and makin' a show of bein' willin', you wagabone! but how can I trust yer? How did yer serve me yesterday, you willin? Didn't yer go a-hookin' it off and leavin' me without a fire till nine o'clock a'most? How do I know but as how you're arter servin' me out agin just in the same way? Don't lick me, I tell yer. I shan't b'lieve yer a bit the more for them sneakin' ways. If you warnt to make friends, there's other ways of doin' it, 'sides being a sneak. Here, smell o' this. Now go, and be quick back agin; if you don't, I'll just about smash yer. I'm always promisin' to smash yer, but if you don't mind yerself this morning, I'll do it, I will, swelp me goodness! Now be off."

Hearing the cripple talk in this strange way, I peeped cautiously over the edge of the heap of sacks on which I was lying to get a peep at him; but the place was so dark, and he was so black, that all I could make out was his dim figure crawling all fours towards the door, and the little white dog dancing and whining about him, and running to and fro between his master and the door, expressing, as plainly as a dog could, his anxiety to be off. When Spider said, "Smell o' this," he held something out to the dog, though what it was, although I tried very hard, I could not possibly discern. He had dragged a sack along with him to the door; and when he had pushed it a little way open to let the dog out, and swiftly pulled it to again, he rolled himself in the sack, and squatted on one side to wait.

He waited, and waited, uttering no other sounds but those expressive of his rheumatic pains, for fully a quarter of an hour, and until the daylight began to show through the dingy skylight in the roof of the shed. Then he began to grow fidgety and grumble under his breath, and once or twice he opened the door just a little way, and peeped out.

"I wish I was behind him, cuss him!" exclaimed he presently, in a whining whisper; "I'd make him move hisself a little quicker. He's larkin'—that's what he's doin.' What does he care? His jints is all right. He's met with some other dawg, bust him! that's wot it is; and he's foolin' away his time while I'm layin' here freezin' to my marrer a'most. Cuss him! I wish I was behind him. All right! stop till he does come home. I'll give him one of my three slices for his brekfus, won't I? Oh yes! I'll give him the lot, bust him! I'll—— Here he comes, at last!"

As Spider spoke, first a swift pattering of canine feet, and then a scratching at the door was heard; and on Spider pushing open the door a little, in ran the little dirty-white cur, bearing in his mouth a clean shank of mutton bone. Such I saw it was instantly; not so poor Spider, whose vision was defective. The dog bolted past him, and made for the other end of the shed.

"Come here! D' ye hear? Ain't yer had foolin' enough? cuss yer!—bein' gone all this while after a single stick. It's a good thick un, I think, though, and new: dropped out of somebody's bundle, I dessay. Here, Pinch! Pinch! good dawg! bring it here, Pinch."

But Pinch didn't seem inclined to obey. He had retreated into a corner, and there he lay with his treasure. Poor Spider was furious. Finding that Pinch wouldn't come, he set out at a good all-fours' pace to rout him out and inflict summary vengeance on him; but before he had made three yards, control of his faithless "jints" failed him, and he slipped with one side of his face to the floor. Then, moved by rage and pain, he fell to abusing Pinch in terms so terrible, that had he been anything better than the conscienceless vagabond his master made him out to be, he would have been consumed with remorse. But the dog's timidity increased in proportion with the cripple's fury, and he wouldn't stir a peg. Strengthened by his passion, Spider got on all-fours again, and reaching the corner where the dog was hiding, made a fierce grab at it, (which the animal was lucky enough to avoid,) and the next instant, had Spider been canine himself, and rabid, he couldn't have made a madder noise.

"Hang you! cuss you! bust you!" he roared, catching up three different articles—to wit, a boot, an old earthenware jug, and a lump of coke—and hurling them along with each anathema at the retreating cur. "It ain't wood at all; it's a bone. You'll bring bones home when I sends you arter wood, will yer? Jest let me lay a fist on yer!" And he began to shuffle and wriggle along after the unlucky tyke with all his might.

There was such a noise that it was useless for me to pretend to be asleep any longer; so I sat up and inquired of Spider what the row was about.

"I'll show him when I ketch hold on him;" replied he, still making after the dog, with the bone of contention in his hand. "I'll kill him with it. I've often threatened to smash him, and now I'll do for him. Hold him, that's a good feller!"

"What's he been doin'?" I asked, as the delinquent bolted past me, and I made a pretence at stopping him.

"I'll tell you what he's been doin'," gasped Spider, quite out of breath with his tremendous exertion at the last five minutes. "He's been makin' a fool of me. He knows werry well that I can't make a fire until he has gone and got me sticks enough. Werry well he knows that—cos it's his job every mornin', so there's no 'scuse for the beggar—and what does he do? Why, yesterday, he goes and gets about three bits, and all on it as wet as muck; and then he steps it off, and comes back when he likes. Well, I looks over that, and I send him agin this mornin', lettin' him smell a good wholesome bit of wood 'cos there shouldn't be any mistake; and agin, what does he do? Why, instead of thinkin' on what he's sent arter, and doin' what he's told to, he goes on his own hook, a-huntin' arter bones to pick; and he's got the cheek to bring 'em home, and 'spects he's goin' to pick 'em while I'm a-sittin' without a bit of fire till Sam comes home—which p'r'aps it'll be ten or eleven o'clock—and me all of a ager, and and not a still jint in me."

Here the poor fellow's rage became subdued in grief, and he began to cry and rub his eyes on his sooty cuffs.

"Cheer up, matey! We'll soon have a fire," said I, quite touched at sight of the poor helpless wretch's emotion. "I'll help yer."

"How can yer? How can yer help me till that greedy 'umbug goes out and picks up some wood?"

"How? Why, I'll go and ask Mr. Belcher for some. He'll let us have some, won't he?"

"It ain't him; it's her. She's the one that won't let you have it," replied Spider, sinking his voice to a whisper. "Bless yer! if she know'd that I lit a fire more than a quarter of an hour afore brekfustime—which is ten, when the boys comes in from their mornin' sweepin' (leastways, that was the laws when we had boys to come in, and it's the same now there's on'y young Sam)—she'd think no more of crackin' me over the head with the copper-stick or the fust thing that come handy, than she would of drinkin' a glass of gin. That's why I'm 'bliged to be so artful about gettin' in my wood, don't yer see?"

Now, it happened that before I came away from Mrs. Winkship, the night before, she had slipped a sixpence into my hand.

"You tell me where there's a shop open, and we'll jolly soon have a fire," said I. "I've got a a'penny."

"What! do yer mean to say you're good to stand a a'penny bundle?" said Spider, so near a prospect of a fire lighting his dull eyes with joy.

"Oh! I'll tell yer where, sharp enough: it's a chandler's shop just round to the right, outside the gate. I say"——

"What?" I inquired, seeing that Spider paused.

"You don't 'appen to have another a'penny 'sides the one for the wood, do yer?"

"Yes, I have got another, why?"

"Wouldn't you like a drop of hot coffee, young un? Hot coffee is so lovely when yer jints feel all of an ager. I've got a pot we could boil it in; you can get half-a-nounce for a a'penny."

Had the price of the half-ounce been the five-pence halfpenny remaining when the wood was bought, I don't think I could have resisted the beseeching look that accompanied his suggestion; so off I went, and in ten minutes returned, and in five times ten minutes afterwards the iron skillet was a cheerful spectacle: Spider gratefully crouching at one side of it, and I at the other, sipping our coffee, I from the bottom part of the yellow earthenware jug which was fractured when Spider threw it after his dog, and he from an old iron spoon, with which he dipped the comforting beverage from the bubbling coffee-pot as it stood on the fire—hot enough, I should think, to scare away the most obstinate ague that ever settled in poor mortal's "jints" to plague him.

If it did not scare away the demon that tormented poor Spider, it at least charmed it quiet for a time, and he grew quite chatty. He told me how that being an orphan, and an inmate of the workhouse as long as he could remember, four years ago he was bound 'prentice to Mr. Belcher, the parish paying the person the liberal premium of seven pounds ten, in consideration of which the master-sweep agreed to instruct him, Tobias Chick, in the art and mystery of chimney-sweeping, to clothe him suitably, feed him liberally, and cherish him in sickness. For fully a year, trade being brisk, and Tobias proving industrious and active, (indeed, it was his marvellous agility in mounting a chimney that had earned for him the title of "Spider,") Mr. Belcher had faithfully fulfilled his terms of the contract, till there came an unlucky day in the depth of winter when Mr. Belcher was applied to to clear out a long disused steam-engine boiler, and being of a handy size for such a job, it fell to the lot of the Spider to descend into the great boiler through the man-hole, and pass the greater part of the day lying his full length on the icy cold iron, scraping away at the furred interior. The result was that rheumatism made such a firm settlement in the poor fellow's legs, that in the course of a few months he found himself quite unable to stand on them, and he was of no further use as a chimney-sweep. Since that time until within the last few months, Mr. Belcher, unwilling that the disabled Spider should fall an easy prey to that "old man of sin," whose delight it is to find "mischief still for idle hands to do," installed him in the "kitchen" to wait on his numerous flock of boys, in the fulfilment of which office he prepared the coffee for breakfast, and the gruel for supper; and he devoted himself to the promotion of order and harmony generally. With the decay of Mr. Belcher's business, however, and the passing of that ruinous anti-chimney climbing Act of Parliament, Spider's occupation as cook and housekeeper came to an end, and here he was. Mr. Belcher didn't want him, and offered seven pounds ten to take the burden off his hands, but the parish was much too wide-awake to do anything of the sort; with three years yet unexpired of the term of the apprenticeship contract, and the tolerable certainty that poor Spider would die within that period, and require burying, they preferred that Mr. Belcher should go on cherishing Tobias Chick in sickness as he promised to do.

"Do you get plenty of grub?" I asked him.

"Well, cert'ny, not so much as I *could* eat; but Lor', it ain't for me to grumble, bein' a dead weight, and not so much as earnin' my salt, don't yer see? not, as far as I can make out, and from what Sam tells me, there'd be much for me to do if I was ever so hearty. Why, Sam tells me as how sometimes they don't take a pound among 'em all the week through. That's bad, you know."

"I s'pose it's them night jobs in the country that tells up," I remarked.

"Yet, I'm jiggered if I can make it out," continued Spider, not heeding my observation; "here's only a pound bein' earnt, and yet there's new drab coats, and new sating gownds, and a pony not enough but there must be a new horse bought, 'not a knacker's sort of horse, mind yer, but a regler clipper; a chestnut; goes like steam, Sam sees it do.'"

"Well, I s'pose be don't keep the horse for a ornyment; I've heard of people makin' a werry tidy thing by having' horses and carts."

"Ah! but s'pose they keep 'em and don't work 'em," said Spider, lowering his voice to the softest of whispers; "s'pose they keeps their horse shut up in the stable all day?"

"Then, I should think they had nailed it."

"Give thirty pound for it. Sam see it paid for."

"And never wor' it?"

"Never in the day-time."

"What do you mean, never in the day-time?"

"It's night-time when the big brown horse is put in harness, never on'y at night-time," observed Spider, with an impressiveness that showed the subject of the brown horse's nocturnal excursions to be one that he had pondered. "Hush! Don't *you say that I spoke a word about it.*"

"Why not? it ain't no secret that there is a brown horse, is it?" I asked.

"It ain't no secret that there is a brown horse; oh no, that's right enough," returned Spider, with the same air of mystery.

"Then, what is the secret?"

"Where he goes to," whispered Spider solemnly, from behind the bowl of his coffee-spoon.

"He goes to them night jobs, what pays so well, don't he? didn't you just say that he did?"

"Yes! them jobs what pays so well; them country chimbleys wot so werry often want sweepin', and which ain't got no soot in 'em—not a common sort of soot anyways," returned Spider, chafing his sooty nose with the spoon-bowl, and shaking his head dubiously. And at this moment, Sam came in, putting an end to the queer conversation.

CHAPTER XXVII.

IN WHICH SAM ENLIGHTENS ME AS TO THE SECRET OF THE MYSTERIOUS SOOT.

It was not long before I discovered that Spider and Sam had told me nothing but the truth, when they said that my opportunities of learning the trade of chimney-sweeping would be but few.

There was really next to nothing for me to do. It seldom happened that there were more than half-a-dozen jobs for Mr. Belcher and Ned Perks to divide between them, and Sam went with one, and I with the other. My work was over by ten or eleven o'clock in the morning, nor was it of a sort to tire me, consisting as it did in nothing more arduous than carrying part of the machine as we went from one house to the next, handing the sticks at a job to Mr. Belcher to be screwed one into the other, taking them from, and bundling them up as he unscrewed the end sweeping up the hearth when the job was at an end. Certainly it would not have cost Mr. Belcher half-an-hour's extra trouble a-day to have dispensed with my services altogether. After breakfast-time I was free to amuse myself in any way I chose; and as my food was regular, tolerably good, and plentiful, the dearth of trade did not cause me much anxiety.

Better still, it appeared to cause Mr. Belcher no anxiety. He seemed to have quite as much work as he cared about, and did not trouble himself to get more. More might have been got, I am sure, and by a no more troublesome process than bawling "sweep" in the streets as we went along of mornings. But this, although prompted by a knowledge of my small utility to my master I more than once suggested, he would by no means allow. It wasn't respectable, he said. There was his house, and there was his bell, free to anyone to pull that had occasion to pull it; if people did not like to pull it, they might do the other thing. He always had plenty of money in his pocket, and was accustomed to partake freely of rum and milk with Mr. Perks early in the morning, and use the parlour of the George and Dragon in the evening, drinking glass after glass of gin and water, and smoking a long parlour pike.

That is, he so beguiled his evenings when business did not engage him. After about six weeks in his service, I found that the "night jobs in the country," previously mentioned, happened on an average about twice a week. Sam wished they happened more frequently, because, before starting on these country jobs, Mr. Belcher always had something very nice and hot for supper, and Sam always came in for a share, as well as for a drop of rum to keep the cold out. They generally started about eleven o'clock — the brown horse being harnessed in the cart. They—Mr. Belcher and Mr. Perks that is — never went "dressed," but in their working clothes, and with black faces and hands, conveying with them the sweeping machine, (the brush end of it resting over the back of the cart and plainly to be seen;) besides the machine they took (so Sam informed us) a long sack with certain tools within it, of the nature of which, further than that they "clinked" when the sack was lifted, Sam was ignorant. They likewise took with them a lantern, (not the stable lantern, but one with a round glass with a slide, like a policeman's lantern,) and something good in a bottle.

Their time of returning was uncertain. Sometimes it was as early as two o'clock, and sometimes not before four. Sometimes—according to Sam—Mr. Belcher, after going many miles to a sweeping job, found that it couldn't be done, or by a mistake somebody else had done the job, or the fires were unexpectedly wanted that night, and the job must be put off till another time. It was not to be wondered at that at such times Mr. Belcher was out of temper all the next day. How would any man like to be kept out of his bed half the night, driving his horse four or five and twenty miles, so that when it came home and stood still in the yard you could not see it for the smoke that reeked from its wet hide? It was a great shame, and enough to make milder men than Mr. Belcher, or his man Perks, swear. "I alwis knows when they've had a disappintment before the ''ts up to the cart," said Sam, "'cos of 'em car' ; only one sack—that one with the tools in. ن they've got two sacks, the little un with the tools in it, which the guv'nor carries, and the long un with the soot in it, wot Ned Perks carries—a puty heavy load it is gen'lly—then I knows that it's all right, and there's a drink out of the bottle for me, and not afore it's wanted, standing shivering out in the cold for nigh on an hour sometimes."

In one respect, however, Mr. Belcher showed himself considerate of Sam's tender age, and of the impropriety of keeping him out of his bed a moment longer than was necessary after one of these midnight journeys. Soon as ever the brown horse entered the yard, Sam was dismissed.

"You go to bed, my lad; me and Mr. Perks will look after the traps, and the nag," he would say. And so they would, finding so much to do that—as we could plainly hear through the thin partition that parted the stable fr.· the kitchen —they were occupied sometimes for an hour or more. There was nothing strange in this, however. Mr. Belcher's horse was a valuable one, and it was only natural that he should spend a little extra time in rubbing it down, and making it comfortable before he left it. The strangest part of the business was—what became of the soot that was brought home from these country jobs?

After the conversation I had with Spider, as already narrated, no more was said between us on the subject. He was not a communicative young fellow, as a rule, and seldom opened his mouth for speech except as related to his affliction. Certainly I did not take the matter very much to heart, but now and then in idle moments I had broached the subject, and was invariably cut short by being advised to mind my own business, and not poke my nose where p'r'aps it might be snapped off before I was aware of it. Nevertheless, the mysterious fact remained. According to Sam, who could have had no interest in making a false statement, the soot from the country jobs was put into the cart by Ned Perks, was driven home to the yard, was carried into the stable—and that was the last that was ever seen of it. True, Ned Perks did not live at Belcher's, but had a house of his own in the New Kent Road, and that being a good step from Camberwell, it was a common thing for him, when they returned from these late jobs, to put the pony to the light cart and drive home in it, bringing it back in the morning; but of course it was absurd to suppose that Ned, who did no sweeping on his own account, carried away the soot: why should he?

Connected with this part of the business, too, was a circumstance of so singular a character, that looking back on it I cannot help feeling surprised that it excited so little of our attention. Ned Perks did not invariably ride home on the above-mentioned occasions, but stayed at Mr. Belcher's; and when such was the case, although being very sleepy, the noise of harnessing and getting out the pony may have escaped us, we were always made aware of it by Spider's dog Pinch. Whether it was the peculiar odour of that uncommon soot in the stable that disturbed the dog's repose, or whether, having a deep dislike for Mr. Perks, his delicate organ of scent made him aware of his enemy somewhere about the premises, and consequently caused him uneasiness, was not clear; anyhow, the little dirty-white dog was uneasy whenever, having returned from a country night job, Mr. Perks, instead of taking himself off in the pony cart to the New Kent Road, stayed the remainder of the night at Belcher's; moreover, his mode of expressing his uneasiness was peculiar. The whining noises he uttered were only prevented from becoming downright howls by his master grasping his muzzle in his hand, and on three several occasions we were all awoke by frightful noises, Pinch having escaped when his master dropped to sleep, and being discovered scratching up the earth close to the stable partition with a ferocity altogether foreign to his weak nature.

"He smells a rat," said Sam; "good dawg! fetch it out. There is rats in the stable, don't you know, Spider; that's what he's arter."

Spider crawled off his sacks, and securing Pinch brought him back to bed, and after much threatening and coaxing got him to lie still.

"It ain't rats; rats don' come now and then, they comes regler when they comes at all," observed Spider, in a frightened whisper. "Lord send I could get away from here, that's all I've got to say."

Presently Spider spoke again.

"Did you hear Perks go, Jim?"

"He ain't gone yet; leastways, I didn't hear the pony being put to."

"I knowed it," whispered Spider, "that's wot it is, Perks ain't gone, and what's more, he ain't goin' to-night. It's awful to lay here and know that — that Perks ain't gone home, ain't it, Jim ?"

"It's on'y awful 'cos it makes your dawg kick up such a jolly row ; that's all the awful I can see about it."

"He's a-tremblin', Jim, jist as though he'd caught my ager and his jints was goin'. Poor Pinch ! I got yer, Pinch. Jim, do you know anything about dawgs ?"

"'Bout the breed on 'em ?"

"No, 'bout the natur' on 'em, Jim ?"

"Well, *that's* the breed on 'em ; ain't it ?"

"No, the breed means all about their coats and their markin's, Jim ; don't yer know, the natur' on 'em is summat what's inside 'em and makes 'em knowin', don't yer understand ?"

I was sleepy and Spider was growing profound, so I simply answered, "Ah."

"They're knowin'er than we thinks, dawgs are, Jim."

"I've known one or two knowin' uns," I answered, gaping.

"Have yer now. What's the knowin'est thing you ever knew on 'em, Jim ?"

It was quite evident that Spider (as was frequently the case) had a wakeful fit on him, and wanted to keep me awake, too, for company's sake. Spider wasn't the sort of chap one could downright like, but I am sure I felt a great deal of pity for him. So I thought of two or three stories of knowing dogs I had known or heard of in my time, and told Spider about them, one after the other.

"Ah ! they're knowin'er than all that, sometimes, Jim," he answered, when I had exhausted my budget ; "they've got a summat—a power in 'em a jolly sight more curious than what makes 'em kill rats and nail things off counters. Do you know anything about sharks, Jim ?"

I did not.

"Sharks is rummy things ; if there's a sailor what's dyin' in a ship, they'll foller it till he *does* die, so as to get him for supper when they chucks him over."

"Oh ! come, I don't want to be told any of them sort of stories. I wants to go to sleep ; what do you want to give a feller the creeps for ? I don't mind layin' awake a little while talkin' about dawgs if you wants me to, but I ain't goin' to talk about dead people."

"I was on'y tryin' to make you understand what I meant 'bout that power in dawgs what I was speakin' about," observed Spider, apologetically. "It's the same thing in dawgs as what it is in sharks, Jim."

"Werry likely."

"On'y dawgs is more dreaded of it than glad ; 'course, you can tell in a minute that they *are* dreaded of it by their 'owlin, whenever they gets a scent on it."

"Gets a scent of what ?"

"Now, what do you want me to say it agin for ? What was I just speakin' about the sharks, and "——

"That'll do, I tell yer, I don't want to talk no more to you. Good-night ; I'm goin' to sleep."

Next day, while out with Mr. Belcher, although I trust not given to "telling tales out of school," something was said about sharks, and being on easy terms with my master, I told him the shark story I had heard from Spider. He laughed.

"What brought that story up then ?" he asked ; "what was you and Spider talking about before you began to talk about sharks and dead sailors, Jim ?"

"Oh, we was talkin' about dawgs." And then, never dreaming of the injury I was doing Spider. I told Mr. Belcher all about Pinch's strange behaviour, and Spider's remarks thereon. Mr. Perks was present, and they looked at each other in a queer sort of way, and presently afterwards sent me off. Spider's dog Pinch never came home that night. To his master's quenchless grief, he never came home any more.

I had been about six weeks with Mr. Belcher, when one Saturday night Sam came into the kitchen with the astonishing news that his mother had that day come up from Dorsetshire on Mr. Belcher's invitation to consult with him on very important business, the upshot of the consultation being that in consideration of certain moneys handed to her by the master sweep, Sam's indentures were to be cancelled, and Sam was to go home with his mother on Monday morning.

"So *you'll* be all right now, Jim," said Sam ; "it'll be your job to go with the guv'nor and Ned on them country jobs o' nights. Now I'm a-goin', I don't mind lettin' you into a secret which ain't no further use to me. Every time you goes out with the brown horse, there's sixpence for yer. Leastways that ain't the secret, that's what the guv'nor gives you every time for keepin' of the secret."

"Very well, I don't mind," I replied, mightily pleased at the change in my prospects, (I always envied Sam those night rides ;) "I'm used to keepin' secrets. Is it a werry hard secret the guv'nor wants keepin', Sam ?"

"Easy as nothink," whispered Sam, (it was in a corner of the kitchen, and out of Spider's hearing, that our conversation took place ;) "the guv'nor 'll tell yer."

"No, you tell me, that's a good chap ; then I can go on practisin' the keepin' on it agin he asks me to."

"You won't tell Spider ?"

"'Tain't likely."

"Nor ever open your mouth about it to any of the coves you plays with on the barges ?"

"No fear."

"Well, then, it's about that soot what they brings home in the big cart of nights, and what we've often talked about. Here, come outside ; old Spider's a-prickin' his ears up I can see."

We went outside.

"What sort of soot do you think that is now, Jim ?"

"What sort ? I on'y knows one sort, it all comes out of chimbleys, I s'pose, don't it ?"

"Out of some sort of chimbleys cert'ny. Put you ear close, Jim. The sort what we brings home is out of church chimbleys."

"I never knowed that churches had chimbleys," I replied, not very awe-stricken by the " secret " that Sam made so much fuss about.

"Course they have, ain't there the flues what keeps the church warm—ain't there the fire in the westry ?"

"Ah ! I s'pose there is now you come to speak on it. Well, what cn it ? Why shouldn't a church chimbley be swep ?"

"Hu—sh, that's what *I* said when fust the guv'nor told me. It's a studyin' the Acts o' Parliament that puts you up to these things," replied Sam, "and accordin' to the Act there *is* a werry good reason for not sweepin' the church chimbleys, leastways for keepin' it dark if you do do it. It's agin the laws. I don't know 'zactly what laws, but religion's got something to do with it. War'orks to yer if they caught yer at it. You'd be ex—execum — well, the guv'nor did tell me."

"Executed, I know; tucked up at the Old Bailey: I've seed 'em."

"Executed be jiggered; forty times wuss than that. Crossin' the roads, with a pinted stick drove through your stomack is a part of the sufferin's I know, but there's ever so much more on it. That's why the job's got to be done at night, when nobody ain't lookin'. If you was to see how they go creepin' in the shadders and hidin' when they hears anybody comin', just when they're goin' to start off with the machine and the bag, you'd know in a minute what a tickler it was."

"And s'pose they was to ketch the boy what went with 'em to mind the horse?" I inquired; "would they make *him* cross the roads with a pinted stick in his stomach?"

"Lor' bless yer, he's right enough; it's on'y when they ketches you in the hacshal fac, that they exy — what's-o-names yer. You must be took in the church or else the churchyard with the soot on yer, afore they can prove it. Sometimes arter doin' the sweepin' job, and you are comin' away with the soot, you're 'bliged to drop the lot and run for it. Three weeks ago we were served that werry trick down at Barnet."

"Well, it's a rummy sort of law what says to a feller, 'Come down here and do a job for us, but don't let us catch you at it, cos' if you do we shall shove a pinted stick into your stomack!' Sure you ain't got hold on the wrong end of the stick, Sam?"

"I've got the end of it what the guv'nor give me, that's all I knows about it," replied Sam. "Don't you see, Jim, it's this way as far as I can make out. It's the minister hisself what's bound to do the job by Act of Parlyment, and he turns it over to the clark, and the clark turns it over to the beadle, and it's the beadle wot writes to the guv'nor on the quiet. 'You come down,' says he, 'sich and sich a night, and I'll have the key in the church-door, and the money for doin' the job you'll find on the westry mantle-shelf.' I don't say that's how it is exactly, but it is summat like it, I know. It's the same at hangin's, as you may have heerd, Jim. It's the Lord Mayor as the judge makes believe what's goin' to hang a feller, but the Lord Mayor don't care about the job, and tells the next cove, which is the top-sheriff, to do it, and he turns it over to the next cove, which is the bottom-sheriff. 'All right,' ses the bottom sheriff, 'I'll tuck him up at eight o'clock to-morrow mornin' without fail;' but he doesn't do it, he writes on the quiet to Jack Ketch, and he comes and does it, and stands something to the other coves for settin' him on to the job, which so long as it's done the judge don't care; and so they makes it comforble all round. I dessay the guv'nor tips the beadle a trifle out of the sweepin' money—which is a 'ansom sum I'll be bound—and that makes *that* comforble all round. Course it *oughter* be a 'ansom sum," continued Sam,

"considerin' the trouble, and the soot bein' nothink in your pocket."

"How do you mean, nothink in your pocket? it's as good as any other sort of soot, ain't it?"

"But you musn't use it as sich," returned Sam, impressively; "it's agin the laws—so the guv'nor hisself told me—to deal in soot what comes out of a church, so they makes him take a hawful oath that he won't deal in it, but'll take it away and bury it. That's Ned Perks's job; *he* takes it away and buries it in his back garden. There, now you knows all about it, from fust to last. That's the secret what you'll have to keep—what you'll get sixpence a job for keepin'."

All this Sam told me with an air that was convincing of his perfect belief in the "secret" he had so long and so faithfully kept, and I accepted his statement unhesitatingly. It *was* a secret! I had been the holder of secrets before, but never of one of such magnitude as this—no, nor anything like. It was like something acted at the "gaff" in Shoreditch. As we shortly afterwards turned into bed, I could not, on account of the presence of Spider, ask Sam any further particulars on the subject; but I couldn't get a wink of sleep until daylight for thinking about it, and when at last I did close my eyes, I fell into a delightful dream, in which, as I lurked with the swift brown horse under the churchyard wall, several "exy — what's-o-names," in shape of ghosts, took possession of the cart, crouching down and hiding in it, waiting for the guv'nor and Ned Perks to come out of the church with their burden of sacred soot, and holding me spellbound against warning them of their frightful peril by voice or gesture. I saw the guv'nor carrying the sweeping-machine, and Ned staggering under a tremendous sack-load, coming up the churchyard-path towards us, and endured tortures from my inability to leave the horse's head and run to them. On they came. "Now we're all right, Ned!" said Mr. Belcher. "Now, my brave comrade, we may defy the 'exy—what's-o-names' and all their works. Ha! ha! Let down the tail-board, Jim, and we'll have it in in a twinkling." And, still unable to give him any hint of the impending danger, I let down the tail-board, and instantly out swarmed the "exy—what's-o-names"— three of them—each armed with a pointed stick, sharp as a needle, and as stout and long as a laundry clothes-prop, and falling on us with hideous yells, they spitted us all three through the middle of our stomachs, and so shouldering us, made at a swift pace for the tombstones.

Frightful as was my dream, however, it by no means turned me from my hot desire to become Sam's successor; nay, on the contrary, I think it rather stimulated my yearning, and my only fear was that Sam's surmise might after all turn out to be incorrect, and that it might be Mr. Belcher's intention for the future to do without a horse-minding boy, or that perhaps he would insist on Spider's going. Spider couldn't walk, but he could sit upright on the cart-seat and hold the reins, and that would be quite sufficient for the purpose. This last reflection rendered me a miserable boy all through that day—which was Sunday. I would have questioned Sam further on the subject, but he was away all day with his mother. I did put a fishing question to Spider—

7

"I wonder who will go with country-cart o' nights, when Sam's gone?"

"Who! why, you of course, who else can go?" replied Spider, who seemed not a little astonished that I should entertain any doubt whatever about the matter.

"I thought p'r'aps they might take you," said I.

"Me! what use should I be? why I couldn't get into the cart without bein' lifted in. Whew! a nice cove *I* am to take a night-ridin'; why, I should be dead in a week. No, whoever goes, it won't be me, Jim; you may be precious sure o' that."

But I couldn't bring myself to the same opinion. I had known Mr. Belcher, and his foreman Mr. Perks, long enough to know that consideration for poor Spider's health would not be allowed to balk any business design they might entertain. Spider was nothing but a dead weight on the firm. Was it possible that the whole was a scheme for polishing Spider off, and making an end of him?

To my great joy, however, I was spared another night of tantalising speculation and dreams, for in the course of the evening Mr. Belcher called me into the parlour, and after a little friendly chat on common-place matters, introduced the subject I had so deeply at heart, and formally announced his intention of taking me altogether in Sam's place. He didn't go so deeply into the "secret" as I could have wished, merely alluding to the country night-work as "pertickler and private bisness," concerning which it was confidently expected of me that I should hear and see, and say nothing, "which it'll be made worth your while so to do," said Mr. Belcher. "All masters wot keeps 'prentices, Jimmy—and that's wot you are, in course, though there ain't no writin's to show for it—all masters has their secrets. I've got mine, and one of 'em I'm a-goin' to let you into, and perwided you keep it as tight as wax, it'll be none the wuss for you. Look at Sam; he's had that there secret to keep, and he's none the wuss for it, is he? Sam's a boy wots never been without a tanner in his pocket; he's a boy wot knows the taste of lots of wittles and drinks, wot boys whose masters carn't put confidence in never gets a smell on. In course you understand, Jim? A nod's as good as a wink to a blind horse, hey?"

"Quite as good, guv'nor, and better, too," I replied, delighted at Mr. Belcher's confidence, and none the less at Mrs. Belcher's kindness and condescension, who was present, and more than once handed me her gin-and-water to sip.

"On the tother hand," continued Mr. Belcher, "s'pose Sam had cut up rough? S'pose havin' been trusted with the secrets of his master's trade, he had kept 'em loose—gone about blabbing, you know; do you know what I should ha' done to Sam?"

Such a scowl sat on his long white face as he said this, that I didn't know how to answer him.

"I 'spect he'd ha' ketched it pretty hot, and serve him right, too," I replied.

"Hot! I b'lieve yer; hotter than ever a boy ketched it yet," responded Mr. Belcher, laying both his hands on my shoulders, and looking hard into my face the while; "if arter I'd trusted Sam with my trade secrets, he had gone about whisperin' and blowin on me, I b'lieve I should ha' killed him. I *know* I should. I should have felt in such a drefful rage when I heerd on it, that my first hact would have been to have took his —— young windpipe, so, and have choked his —— young life out on him. Don't you think that's wot I should ha' done, missus?"

"I haven't got the least doubt on it," emphatically replied the lady appealed to.

Neither had I the least doubt of it. When Mr. Belcher said, "I should have taken him by the windpipe, so," he slid his hands up from my shoulders, and so embraced my throat with them that the first knuckles of both his thumbs met and pressed me with a movement that at once convinced me of the ease with which Mr. Belcher could have strangled Sam, if, by his treacherous behaviour, he had merited that punishment. The expression of his eyes while he went through the pantomime of strangling a boy was alarming. It alarmed me, I must confess, although I knew that we were on friendly terms.

"'Course," said he, "i t's a thing I shouldn't like to be drove to, and I dessay I should be werry sorry for it arterwards; but that's how I should ha' served him, to a dead certainty, if he had aggrawated me. But he *didn't* aggrawate me; he was a sensible, wide-awake sort of a boy, just such another as you are, and so he got all the ha'pence and none of the kicks. Enough said. I ain't a-goin' to let you into the trade secret now; there'll be time enough for that when you sees what it's like, which'll be to-morrow night—*unless the moon shines.*"

Here the subject dropped; and after regaling on a better supper than had fallen to my lot ever since I had been in Mr. Belcher's service, I was dismissed to the kitchen with a parting injunction to breathe no word of our conversation to Spider.

How I passed the next day is not worth while here to describe. Decidedly it was the longest day I ever experienced, not forgetting that memorable time when having escaped from the workhouse, I beguiled the hours of daylight under the dark arches, waiting for Mouldy and Ripston. But one thought beset me—would it by and by be moonlight? It was dark enough last night, but the night before and again the night that preceded it was bright moonlight. Of the moon's changes I was of course ignorant. I knew about tides as well as any waterman on the Thames, but of the moon and the laws that govern that luminary, I was as much in the dark as I most devoutly hoped her ladyship herself might that night be. It was all chance it seemed to me. Perhaps the moon would shine and perhaps it wouldn't; just as it took it into its head. Since Mr. Belcher's trade depended on the moon, it was only fair to infer that he knew as much of her ways as any man, and according to his own declaration, it was quite a matter of uncertainty.

I ate no breakfast that day—no dinner. At the time, however, a gleam of comfort warmed my appetite. It came from Spider, and consisted in a single exclamation—"Ah, my jints! my jints!" exclaimed he; "there's a change in the weather a comin; it'll rain afore dark, I'll lay a farden."

And while the poor fellow whined and moaned in firm belief in his prognostication, I was thrilled with delight, and knowing of old how true a prophet he was, took heart, and went at my tea with a relish.

CHAPTER XXVIII.

IN WHICH I STARTED ON THE WISHED-FOR JOURNEY. I OVERHEAR A CURIOUS CONVERSATION CONCERNING THE "QUICK" AND THE "QUIET." I AM MADE WISE AS TO THE IMPORT OF THE SAID CONVERSATION.

WITH the dusk the rain began to fall, and before nine o'clock—it was May now, be it remembered, and the evenings were long—the night was as dark and dismal as even I could desire. A little later the consummation of the great event was assured beyond a doubt by Mrs. Belcher calling me into supper, (I was not out of earshot, the reader may depend,) just as she had invariably called Sam in before the start on a night-journey. The meal was plentiful and splendid, consisting chiefly of a honeycomb of tripe fried in butter, and mashed potatoes. There were present Mr. and Mrs. Belcher, Ned Perks, and myself.

When the fried tripe was finished, Mr. Belcher, who appeared in the best of spirits, observed,

"Now, my dear, we'll have jist one pipe and a stiff glass, and then we'll be off. Mix the boy a drop all to his own cheek, missus. He'll want it. We've got thirty miles afore us, in and out, and if it ain't set in for a all-night soaker it's werry strange to me."

Graciously enough Mrs. Belcher mixed me half-a-tumbler of grog, hot and strong, and of which, although it made my eyes water, I partook manfully, as became a person about to engage in a dare-devil adventure such as ours. Presently, Ned Perks, having finished his glass, disappeared for a few minutes, and then returning, announced that he was quite ready to start when the guv'nor was.

"I've put a couple of extra sacks beside the long 'un into the cart," said he; "we shall be glad of 'em to kiver over us, as its a-comin' down like cats and dawgs."

In the yard we found the brown horse already put to, and presently we set off, Mr. Belcher and Ned on the cart seat, each with a sack worn hood-wise over his head, and I snugly ensconced in a corner of the cart, covered by the tarpaulin that was used to throw over the horse when he was standing still. Besides ourselves the cart carried the sweeping-machine and the other tools in a sack, which Sam could only describe as "clinking," and which, as I lay in the bottom of the cart with my arm resting on them, was exactly all I could make of them, though I was curious enough to endeavour to feel their shape through the thick sackcloth that covered them.

I had not the least idea which road we were travelling, which rather heightened the romance of the business. Lying in the dark with the mysterious jingling tools under my elbow, we were whirled along at a tremendous pace by the strong brown horse, whose hoofs could be heard plash, plash on the miry highway, bound on a mission against which mighty Acts of Parliament protested, and daring the vengeance of the terrible "exy—what's-o-names," and the frightful torture of cross roads and pointed sticks that inevitably awaited our non-success! Talk about the pieces they brought out at the Shoreditch "gaff!" When ever did they bring out a piece like this? And this wasn't a piece, it was *real!* The hot-and-strong Mrs. Belcher had mixed for me may have had something to do with it, but the longer I thought on how delightfully desperate our errand was, the better it pleased me, till I began to half wish that while I was minding the cart, a young "exy—what's-o-name"—one about my own age and size, and with not much of a stick in his possession—might venture to attack me. I wouldn't run, I'd stand to it. There were three or four dodges in the boxing art that Mouldy had put me up to, and it was not impossible that I might be able to astonish my young "exy—what's-o-name." Pooh! if he would only lay aside his pointed prop, I'd take him one hand, and give him a licking he wouldn't get over in a hurry.

By the time I had worked myself up to this valorous pitch we must, at the rate the brown horse was going, have accomplished fully ten miles of our journey, and as I could hear by the sharp "pit-pat" against the tarpaulin that covered me, it was still raining fast, and Mr. Belcher drew up by a wayside horse-trough to give his animal a drink.

"I don't know how you are, Ned," said he, "but I'm like a drowned rat; reg'lar sopped through to my shirt. S'pose we have a drain?"

"We'll want it wuss by 'nd by maybe," said Mr. Perks, his naturally growling voice not improved by his ten miles' soaking, "else there's nothink as I'd like better. Pity we didn't bring a drop more in the bottle."

"But we can take a swig out of it and have it filled again here, can't we?" suggested Mr. Belcher.

"Is it safe, d' ye think?"

"Safe enough if we sends young Jim in for it, nobody ever see *him* afore. We'll chance it anyhow; anythink's better than ketchin' a wilent cold, which is easier ketched than got rid on."

Mr. Perks was nothing averse to the last-mentioned proposition, and after drawing a short distance past the horse-trough, (which stood before a roadside public-house, the shutters of which were, on account of the lateness of the hour, partly raised,) the bottle brought from home was brought out, and first Mr. Belcher and then Ned Perks took a long pull at it.

"I reckon we shan't get a drop of stuff like that here," observed the latter gentleman, smacking his lips.

"Carn't be expected, so we had better take as much of t' other as we can carry. How much is left in the bottle, Ned?"

"Not a quarten, I should say, by the shake of it."

"Better finish it, then. Let's have another toothful each and give the boy wot's left. A fellar might drink a pailful a night like this without feeling any the wuss for it."

It was something more than a toothful that was left in the bottle when Ned Perks handed it to me, and it was brandy, but with the possibility before my eyes of having a "exy—what's-o-name" to encounter shortly, I made no scruple of tilting it all down my throat.

"You see that pub, Jim? Hop in there and get a pint of best brown. Don't kiver the cloth over your shoulders, then you 'll pass for a boy wot's livin' in the nabrood."

I suppose I did pass as Mr. Belcher hoped I might. There were several late lingerers at the bar, and I was served with my pint of brown brandy without exciting any particular notice.

"How far d' ye call it from here to Romford,

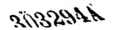

mister ?" asked a customer, as I for a moment paused between the bar and the door to adjust the cork of my bottle.

"Not a great way," answered the landlord; "three miles—p'r'aps three and a half."

"Is it straight ahead, mister ?"

"Straight as you can go." And as he spoke the landlord inclined his head in the direction he meant. That direction was the one that the brown horse faced; so that it seemed we were going to Romford.

The bottle held just a pint, so that the two men had primed themselves pretty well—especially considering the extra good quality of the liquor. I got into the cart, and was about to make myself comfortable in my old corner, when Mr. Belcher remarked—

"Stop a minute, young feller; s'pose we turn about a bit. You lay under the seat, you'll be quite dry enough; and hand me up that tarpaulin to put over my shoulders."

I dutifully did as requested.

"I wish we'd ha' brought another sack," growled Mr. Perks, "I'm pretty well satter-ated."

"Well, there *is* another sack, ain't there, Ned ?"

"On'y the long 'un."

"Well, won't that keep the wet out as well as a short un ?"

"It'll keep the wet out, but"——

"But what ? Are you afeared that the party what it's for'll ketch cold ?" remarked Mr. Belcher, with a laugh.

"No fear of that," replied Ned Perks, and laughed too. "Give us up that 'ere sack, Jim." And putting it across his shoulders, we set off again at the same rattling pace as before.

Whether it was that the brandy had loosened the tongue of Mr. Belcher and his man so that they talked louder and with less caution than during the previous portion of the journey, or that lying as I now was, close to them, and with my ears uncovered, I was better able to listen, is more than I can say. I only know that previous to our arrival at the horse-trough, I had not noticed them talking together at all, and that now I could hear them engaged in a conversation of a spirited nature; not plainly, because of the noise of the cart-wheels, and the hoofs of the high-trotting brown horse, but now and then when we came to a soft bit of road it was easy enough to make out what they said, though, owing to the excessively slangy shape the talk took, by no means easy to understand it. The brandy had whetted my yearning to learn all I could respecting the secret, and so I did not scruple to place my ear as high up as possible.

"He won't get it for no less," remarked Mr. Belcher, "thunner me ! if a squeaker's worth five quid, a full-grown 'un's worth a tenner; why, it ain't orspital price. So I told him. 'Jes you consider the size and weight on it,' ses I, 'and the orkardness on it; 'tain't like a kid,' ses I, 'as you can carry in a pocket hankercher a'-most.' "

"Werry good ! what did he say to that ?"

What "he" said to that I couldn't catch, for at that moment we got on to some stones, and Mr. Belcher's voice was lost in the noise. When the stones were past, Mr. Belcher was in the mid-*dle of a sentence.*

" ' ——'tain't in my line,' ses I, 'it's all werry well you a pintin' out the difference betwixt quick and quiet, but a head is a head, and a neck is a neck, and I ain't ashamed to say I ain't got the nerve on me to do it.' 'Humbug,' ses he, 'I'd as soon do it as cut a slice of bread; or a leg or a arm either; I s'pose you don't set up as bein' a cove of refinder feelins as wot I am ?' ses he. So when it come to that I cut it short, and ses I, 'I don't want to argy; a subjik *is* a subjik, and a head *ain't* a subjik. Cutten orf heads ain't in my line, and subjiks is, and as such I am at your service, but not at t'other. Warn't I right, Ned ?"

"In a bisness pint of view 'corse you was right, not as I'd mind a mag if I had a tool what was sharp enough," answered Mr. Perks, " and if they'd act square and honest with a feller, in course it's easy to see the trouble wot it 'ud save. But s'pose we humoured 'em—what 'ud be the consekents ? Why the trade 'ud be spiled; it 'ud be as easy to get the head or the pertikler jint wot they wanted, as though it was butcher's meat"——

"My sentiminks to a air, Ned," interrupted Mr. Belcher, emphatically.

"And what would be wuss," continued Mr. Perks, "they'd be warntin to deal with us coves just as though we was common butchers and kept shops with weights and scales."

"But he alwis was a stingy feller, don't yer know," observed Mr. Belcher; "don't you recollect just when we first jined in the purfession, when he warnted that carrawan giant down at Bexley for a subjik, what a doose of a job we had with him benden him over at the knees and"——

More stones.

"——wouldn't hold it, bein' short in the length morn'n a foot. I've heered my uncle tell the story a hundred times," (Mr. Perks was speaking now) "so what did they do but they sticks it up agin the side of the cart, and puts a old hat on its head and a short pipe in the mouth, and just as they got through Brentford pike up comes"——

More stones.

" ' ——better give him a lift out,' ses the pleceman, 'and let me take him to the station, he looks werry bad,' ses he, 'he looks as much like a dyin' man as ever I see.' 'Oh, he's all right,' said Spifler Wilkins, 'he ain't a good colour naterally, and when he get's a drop it's sure to fly to his kumplixshon.' Well, he'd ardly got the words out of his mouth, when the beggarin' cart-wheel—they was a walkin' the mare, don't you see, all the time, and the bobby was a follerin' at the tailboard with the light of his bull's-eye throwed into the cart—he'd hardly got the words out of his mouth when bump goes the wheel into a ruck, and the dead 'un pitched forward on its face, and"——

Not stones this time, but a man with sheep, and a brute of a sheep-dog yelp, yelping after them, so that Mr. Perks's voice once more became quite inaudible.

"—— rash thing for Spifler to do, wasn't it ?" (This remark by Mr. Belcher.)

"Well, Spifler Wilkins had the name for bein' rash, yer know, he never could go to work till he was half mad with rum. It was a werry lucky thing for the pleceman that it was the butt-end of the auger instead of the pint of it that Spifler hit him with. As it was, it laid him in the road flat as a flounder."

"And Spifler made the best of his time, as a matter in course, and bolted?" observed Mr. Belcher.

"What, and leave the dead 'un as had rolled out laying in the road? Not he. 'What's the use of fightin' if you comes away without yer winnins?' ses he, and he makes his pal get down and help him left the dead 'un in agin. Best of the lark was, Mr. Bobby, findin' the ugly customers he had to deal with, warn't so much hurt as he was playing possum, and when Spifler had got his dead 'un packed away all comforble, he goes and has a look at the pleceman; 'Tell you what, Soapy,' ses he to his pal, 'jiggered if I don't think that crack on the head croaked him; 'spose we lift him in as well, it'll save his friends the expense of berryin' him;' but he'd no sooner said it than the pleceman gives a holler, and rollin' away from Spifler, got up and cut away as though the old gen'lman was arter him."

There was something in this story of Ned's, the scraps of which, as overheard by me, are above recorded, that tickled Mr. Belcher very much, and for full a minute afterwards he did nothing but laugh at it, in fits and starts, as he recalled the raciest bits to mind. I, however, saw nothing in it to laugh at. The picture of the policeman shamming dead, and wriggling to his feet and running away, was funny enough in an abstract sense, but what was the story about in its entirety? What was it about the "dead 'un"? Was the "dead 'un" a dead man? It would seem so from the circumstance of their putting a hat on his head and a pipe in his mouth. How came he there then? How came he in Mr. Spifler's cart?

How about the conversation which preceded the story of Mr. Spifler?—about cutting off heads, and which was not a story as it seemed, but a recent and personal experience of my master's? Was it in allusion to cutting off somebody's head when Ned Perks spoke of "not caring a mag about doing the job if he had a tool sharp enough"? I couldn't make it out at all; but in a state of frightful bewilderment, crouched under the cart-seat, the sweat trickling down my face. Where were we going now? Who or what was the "party" the long sack was for—the sack that Ned Perks had over his shoulders—and who wasn't likely to catch cold because the said sack was wet? Soot couldn't be called a "party." My master and his foreman went on talking, but I had no ears to listen to them. My valour had all oozed away, and my knees smote the cart flooring as the suspicion stole into my mind that all that Sam had told me was wrong, that sweeping church chimneys formed no part of Mr. Belcher's midnight missions, and that the Secret was nothing less than *murder*.

It was still raining steadily, when, pulling rein, and gently whispering "whoa, lass," to the brown horse, Mr. Belcher brought the vehicle to a standstill, and after a few moments spent in looking about him, called on me to get out, and screwing up my courage I obeyed. It was lucky that it was so pitchy dark, or Mr. Belcher would have seen enough in my face to have convinced him that something was amiss with me.

"There, now we're here I'll let you into a bit of the trade secret I was speakin' on," said he. "You see that church over there?"

I peered through the darkness in the direction he indicated, and could dimly make out the gray shape of a church spire, and between it and us there were other low standing gray shapes, which could have been nothing but tombstones.

"Yes, sir," I replied; "I see the church."

"Well, we're a-goin' there to sweep the chimbleys," whispered he. "I ain't got no time to go into particklers now, on'y to tell you that sweepin' church chimbleys is a job wot's got to be done quite on the quiet. D'ye understand?"

"Ye—s—s, sir," I answered, timidly, for at that instant I set my foot on the sack with the "clinking things" in it, and Ned Perks's observation about what he would do if he had a tool sharp enough, flashed into my mind. "Ye—s —s, sir; I understand."

"Why, what's the matter with yer?" asked Mr. Perks, laying a hand on my shoulder. "He's a-shiverin' like a haspin."

"He's been to sleep layin' under the seat— that's what it is—and he's just fresh woke. Ain't that it, Jim?"

Thankful enough, for more reasons than one, that my master made the suggestion, I answered him promptly that it was just as he said.

"Have a little suck at this," said he; "it'll set you right in no time." And as he spoke, he held the brandy-bottle to my mouth.

The sip of brandy revived me wonderfully—as, strange to tell, did the sight of the tombstones and the church spire. There was at least a show of truth in Mr. Belcher's assertion that he was going to sweep the church chimneys.

The men got out, and leading the horse a little way to some trees that stood opposite a wicket-gate, there halted.

"Now, you get out, Jim," whispered my master, "and stand at the mare's head while we go and do the job. We shan't be very long about it. Hark; that's the church chimin' twelve; before it chimes half-arter we shall be back agin, and there'll be a tanner for yourself. You're awake and all right, now, ain't yer?"

"Yes, thanky, sir; I'm all right." And so I was: that last nip of brandy had quite set me on my legs again, and I felt almost ashamed of the babyish fears that had beset me in the cart.

"You ain't got no fear of tombstones, and that?"

"Not I, sir!" And I laughed a little laugh, to convince him how lightly I held such nonsense.

Ned then lifted the tools out of the cart, while Mr. Belcher lit the lantern. They did not go off immediately, however. They halted by the wicket, and Mr. Belcher took from his pocket a piece of white paper with lines drawn over it, as I could plainly see by the fierce light from the bull's-eye lantern that was directed full upon it. The paper they laid on the top bar of the wicket, and consulted it closely, tracing the lines with the tips of their fingers, and now and then looking towards the church, with their eyes shaded from the pelting rain with their hands, as though to see if something there tallied with the tracing on the sheet. Doubtless this was what they were looking for. It was a plan of the church flues they were consulting! Sam, after all, was right, and I was a fool to get into a funk about nothing.

"It's all right, I s'pose," I heard Mr. Belcher say, as he folded up the paper and closed the bull's-eye slide; "on'y I wish it was this side of the church instead of the 'tother."

Ned made some reply, but what I did not hear, as they went through the wicket and up the church path, and were almost instantly lost in the darkness.

And there I waited, holding the brown horse by the bit-rein, with the rain pelting down and wetting me to the skin, (for the tarpauling was now put to its proper use, and covering the brown horse's tender loins,) with nothing in sight but the little gray shapes in the churchyard, showing hazily through the blackness of the night, and the tall, gray shape beyond and above all, that showed where the church steeple was; and nothing to be heard but the dismal pit-pat of the rain on the leaves over my head, against the cart panels, against the protecting tarpauling on the horse's back. I didn't mind it much however; I had been in a few queer situations in the course of my young experience—situations even more dismal than my present one, and apparently hopeless. It wasn't pleasant, standing in the pitch dark, close to a churchyard, all alone, at midnight; but it wasn't for long: they would be back with the soot very soon now, and I should get my sixpence, and the horse would put his best legs foremost for home, and I should get to my warm bed, and it would all be very jolly to think about.

So I comforted myself until the church bells chimed the quarter past twelve, informing me that as yet not more than half the time I should have to wait had expired—not half the time; for after Mr. Belcher had called my attention to the fact that it was striking twelve o'clock, a good five minutes were spent in examining the plan at the wicket. I began to grow fidgety. Of course there *were* no such things as ghosts! True, Mrs. Dipple, at the workhouse, said something about the "resurrection," and, not knowing the meaning of such a hard word, I asked her, and she explained that it meant rising out of the grave; that everybody—good as well as bad people—would have to rise out of their graves; but what did she know about it? No doubt she was an old fool, as good Mrs. Brownhunter had called her; still, it was a great satisfaction to pat the brown horse's neck, when I called her "good lass," as Mr. Belcher did, to hear her whinny and scrape the gravel with her hoof in a natural and commonplace manner.

The church bells chimed the half-hour.

"It's all over, now, then," thought I; "I don't think I've stood it bad, considerin'; they'll be back in a minute."

And for a minute—two, three, four minutes— my eyes were fixed towards the church path, in the momentary hope of seeing brave Ned Perks staggering along under his load of soot. But he didn't come; nobody—nothing—came. My teeth began to chatter, and the old feeling of funk rapidly stole over me. I patted the mare, and called her "good lass," and several other endearing names, but she made no response, and stood as still as a tombstone. "The bad, as well as the good," was what Mrs. Dipple had said; then I suppose the bad were the "exy—what's o-names," who came with pronged props after people they caught near their abode. Flap! flap! flutter! flutter! hoo—hoo—hoo! An owl, no doubt; but at that moment an "exy—what's-o-name" of *the largest size stalking* through the branches overhead—causing me to cry out with fear, and grasp the brown horse round the neck, and the brown horse to snort, and give herself an uneasy shake that made her harness rattle with a very frightful sound.

I could stand it no longer. Were Mr. Belcher and Ned never coming? I would go a little way up the path, and listen if I could hear them. This I did, first taking the precaution to grope amongst the gravel for two big stones to skid the wheels, in case the brown horse should take it into her head to bolt.

I could not see three yards before me up the path, and I was obliged to go scraping along with my feet, to make sure that I did not stray off the flagstones that made the pathway. Every few steps I took I paused and listened; but no sound, except the pattering rain, was to be heard. I ventured a little further, bearing in mind Mr. Belcher's remark, that he wished it was *this* side of the church, and not the *other*. I was not near the church yet. Creeping along, step by step, my foot presently struck against something that made a swishing sound, and instantly brought me to a standstill. It was nothing alive, for it did not attempt to get out of the way when I kicked it. Finding it so, I mustered pluck to stoop down and feel it, when, to my unutterable surprise, what should it turn out to be but the chimney-sweeping machine! There was a tree close by, and the machine was lying as though it had been placed against the tree, and fallen as I had found it.

My first fear was, that my master and Ned Perks must be in the immediate neighbourhood; that perhaps Ned was only resting a little from his load of soot; and that I should be presently discovered, and very properly get into a row for leaving the horse and cart; and full of this fear, I crouched down and listened with all my might. I could make out no sound, however—not the least; and while I was peering my hardest through the darkness on every side, I suddenly caught sight of a gleam of lantern-light over by the church. It was but a momentary flash, and extinguished at once; but it lasted long enough for me to perceive that it was coming towards me; so without more ado, I scudded back along the path, unskidded the wheels, and took my place at the mare's head as though nothing had happened.

So long a time elapsed before anything occurred to justify my suspicion that the light betokened Mr. Belcher's return, that I began to hope or fear (it would be hard to say, in my utter confusion of mind, which it was) that it was a false alarm, when suddenly I made out the two figures coming up the path, and much closer than I would have thought they could have approached without my being aware of it.

"I always know when they've had luck, by Ned Perks coming along bending under his sackful, and the gov'nor carryin' the tools." So Sam had said; and judging therefrom, they *were* in luck. Ned *was* bending under his sackful, and Mr. Belcher was carrying the tools, including the sweeping-machine, which he must have picked up as he came along. They halted at the wicket, and, in a cautious voice, Mr. Belcher inquired—

"Is it all right, Jim?"

"All right, sir."

"Nobody been past—nobody spoke to yer?"

There was the "exy—what's-o-name," but strictly speaking, it had not addressed itself to me; besides, I was in no condition of mind for conversation, so I shortly answered, that since they were away, I had seen or spoken to no one.

"That's the sort, Jim. Let down the tailboard; and soon as we've lifted the soot in we'll have a wet a-piece, and be off like winkin'."

I let down the tail-board, and the two men lifted in the soot—a great load of it—such a load, that they were compelled to rest the part where it was tied on the ledge of the cart, and shove it in, both of them pushing at the bottom of the sack. They turned on the light of the lantern a little while they did this, and, to judge from their appearance, you would have thought they had been doing a job at brick-making rather than chimney-sweeping—they were so soiled with clay. Their hands were smeared with it, as were their boots as high as the ankles; even the ends of Ned Perks's black silk neckerchief were as though they had dabbled in clayey water, and the soot-sack was daubed with clay-stains from top to bottom. When the soot-sack was comfortably stowed, out came the brandy bottle, and they both took a drink out of it, and gave me a drink.

"Drink hearty; it won't hurt yer, my lad," said Mr. Belcher, kindly; "and take this, cos you've been a good boy—considerin' it's the fust time, a werry good boy; the usual is a tanner, but there's a bob for you."

And he gave me a shilling, while Mr. Perks showed his appreciation of my good behaviour at a cheaper rate by kindly patting my head.

"How shall we manage 'bout the ridin'?" asked Mr. Perks. "The boy had best sit atween us, hadn't he?"

"He'll be drier squattin' down in the corner, like he did comin' along, I should think," replied Mr. Belcher.

"I don't mind the rain, sir," said I; "I'm as wet now as I can be; it won't hurt me, sir." Somehow, I felt full of a strange dread that was proof even against the preposterous quantity of brandy I had been persuaded to imbibe since we started from home. I didn't want to sit at the bottom of the cart.

"Ay, ay; but I've got one at home now wot it has hurt; I don't want another laid on my hands with rheumatiz, I can tell yer," replied Mr. Belcher.

"Think it's as well for him to sit at the bottom?" asked Mr. Perks.

"Squat down, Jim," said Mr. Belcher, by way of reply. "There you are. We'll put the tarpaulin' over our knees, so that you can kiver over your shoulders with a corner of it." And he pushed me down into the corner of the cart I had previously occupied.

"Don't you get restin' your head on that soot-sack," observed Mr. Perks; "cos it's wet through, and you'll get a ear-ache."

And having taken their seats, Mr. Belcher whipped the brown horse, and away it sprang, as though delighted that it was allowed the use of its chilled limbs.

The strange dread that had beset me since I made the singular discovery in the church path increased more and more. Clearly, sweeping the church flues was *not* the purport of Mr. Belcher's visit to Romford: he had not even taken the machine with him to the church, but only a little

way up the path, and there left it. He had only carried it with him in the cart and towards the church as a blind. No chimneys had been swept that night, and yet there was the full sack.

Filled with what? "Don't lay you head on it," Mr. Perks had cautioned me. No fear; I was afraid to touch it—to turn my head even towards where it was lying. All the talk that had happened between my master and Mr. Perks about cutting off heads, and the caravan giant of Bexley who was bent over at the knees, and of the "dead 'un" with the short pipe stuck between his lips, came back to my recollection with terrible distinctness, along with Ned Perks's cool avowal, that with him the perpetration of certain horrors was merely a question of having "a tool sharp enough."

What *was* in the sack? My dread decreased nothing; but the longer I dwelt on the subject, the hotter grew my yearning to be released from terrible surmise, and know the truth.

How could I learn it?

Cautiously I put out a trembling foot, and, reaching over to where the clayey sack was, felt at it with my toes. It was soft, and it yielded to the touch. Was it soot after all?

I *must* know somehow, even though I ran a risk, my suspense was so tormenting. I had a clasp-knife in my pocket, and, without pausing to reflect on the rashness of the proceeding, I softly took it out and opened it; and, gently reaching over, slit a hole in the sack with a sudden slash. It would have been a mercy if I had withdrawn my hand as suddenly as I put it forward. This, however, I did not do; and—horror of horrors!—there fell out of the slit, with a lumpish weight, across the hand of mine that still held the knife, a man's hand, cold as ice, and so white that it showed in the dark like a light!

Of the loud cry I gave I know nothing, beyond that it was a noise so loud that the horse gave a startled leap forward; and the next instant I was over the back of the cart, sprawling in the mud, and up again with a sensation as of a bruised face, but with a pair of legs, thank heaven! sound for running. And run I did; and all the faster that presently I heard a man's voice, and the sound of other legs hastening after me.

CHAPTER XXIX.

IN WHICH THERE OCCURS A SCENE THAT BEATS HOLLOW EVERYTHING I EVER WITNESSED AT THE "GAFF" IN SHOREDITCH.

IT was Ned Perks's voice.

"Come back; d'ye hear!" he bawled. "B——t yer young eyes, will yer come back when I call yer? I'll twist yer infernal neck when I get hold on yer, if yer don't shut up your jaws and stop."

How could I stop? I had now no sort of doubt that Mr. Belcher and his companions were murderers; and when Ned Perks said that he would twist my neck, I fully believed him. I ran so fast that I had not much breath to spare for calling out; but to the best of my ability I so exerted myself, crying out "Murder!" as I went running and stumbling and splashing along the muddy country road. I ran so fast as to pletely outstrip Mr. Perks; and, finding that he had no chance of overtaking me, he paused, and gave a whistle, and immediately afterwards I heard the well-known hoof-falls of the high-trotting mare coming in my direction. It was all over now! My speed was no match against that of the horse; so, quaking with fear, I scrambled into the narrow ditch that skirted the road, and lay flat down on my belly. There was water in the ditch, so that I had to rest on my elbows to keep my face out of it. Rank grass and weeds grew on either side so as to overhang me, and, wretched as was my plight, I rejoiced to think that I had a good chance of escaping their observation even if they searched for me.

After Ned Perks had whistled he still continued to run in the direction I had taken, and just when he had reached opposite to where I was concealed, Mr. Belcher came up in the cart.

"Got him?" asked he, eagerly, of Ned, at the same time pulling up.

"He can't be far-off, —— him," growled Mr. Perks, too blown almost to speak. "He's just about here. What the blazes was the matter with him? What did he take fright at, I wonder?"

"We *must* have him, Ned! we're bound to have him or they'll have us. The gaff's blowed!"

"How d'ye mean blowed? who blowed it?" inquired Mr. Perks, in a tone of the greatest alarm.

"Who? Why, that cunnin' whelp. Hunt about, Ned! D—l and all, we must get hold on him: when we do, we must put him past chirpin'. D'ye hear, Ned? What's the use of standin' there like a fool? he'll be a mile ahead by this time."

"It's werry fine to say, 'What's the use o' standin' still,' when a feller's fairly belldst off his legs," growled Mr. Perks. "How do yer know he means blowin' on us? What call have yer got to think so?"

"Come and look for yourself, if yu don't believe me; look here!"

And I could hear Ned put his foot on the cart-step to raise himself, so that he might look into the vehicle, and at the same time a flash of light skimmed along the water in the ditch close to my face, showing that Mr. Belcher had unslid the screen from before the bull's eye that Ned might see what the matter was.

"*Now* what do you think?" asked Mr. Belcher.

Ned Perks jumped down from the cart-step.

"Come on," said he, with a frightful oath; "you're right when you say we've got to ketch him, guv'nor."

"He'll have to have his mouth shet, Ned: it's no use ketchin' him without we shets his mouth."

"Don't you trouble, guv'nor, I'll settle him. You trot the mare and I'll hold on and run behind. He can't have got far; he must have been nearly baked when I left off runnin' arter him, and this ain't a road he's likely to meet anybody at this time in the mornin."

And, to my inexpressible relief, the advice Mr. Perks gave was immediately followed, and next moment I could hear the brown mare's retreating steps.

But what was I to do? If I ran forward, I might overtake them; if I ran towards London, they would speedily overtake *me*. In a pretty pucker of indecision I rose reeking from the *ditch and scrambled* out to the road, and, as I did

so, to my astonishment and alarm a man broke suddenly through a gap in the hedge, and, stepping across the ditch, laid a hand on my shoulder.

"What's the row?" said he, gruffly.

He had a lantern with him, and as he spoke he let the full blaze of it fall upon me. By the same light I was enabled to get a sight of him, and I very much doubt, extraordinary as must have been the figure I cut with my sooty rags saturated with muddy water, and my face all bloody from my scramble out of the cart when I made the dreadful discovery, whether he was more amazed than I was at his appearance, attired as he was in a great shaggy coat, with a slouched hat, and a gun in his hand.

"What's the row, my lad?" repeated he, still with his hand on my shoulder, but in a much kinder voice than he had at first spoken. "How came your face bloody? How came you in the ditch? Did them fellows in the cart put you there?"

My head was so full of horrors that at first sight I thought that the man with the gun could be nothing less than an assassin—a highway robber perhaps—who lurked hereabout to rob and shoot people. A glance at his honest-looking face, however, reassured me.

"They didn't put me in the ditch, sir," said I; "I got there out of their way, sir. Don't let 'em get at me, please, sir. They're a-goin to settle me if they ketches hold on me, as you might have heard them say if you was close enough."

"Well, I thought I heard something of the sort," replied the game-keeper — for such the reader has, of course, made out the man with the shaggy coat and the gun to be;—"but what are you tryin' to get away from 'em, that's what I want to know? What is it that they threaten to settle you for?"

"'Cos I've bowled 'em out, sir. I didn't mean to do it—leastwise, I didn't think that that was what I was a-doin' when I did it—but I bowled 'em out, and they're arter me to settle me 'cos they thinks as I'm goin' to split on 'em."

"Bowled 'em out in what? What game have they been up to? Poaching?"

"Wuss than that, sir," I replied, a new fit of trembling assailing me as a picture of the awful white hand rose before me. "They've been up to murder."

"What!"

"Murder, sir. They've got the man wot they murdered in the cart with 'em; he's tied up in a sack. I seed his hand. That's how I came to bowl 'em out."

The cart was not yet so far away but that in the silence of the night the noise made by its wheels could be faintly heard. The gamekeeper was in a state of tremendous excitement, which was momentarily increased by his indecision as to what was best to be done. His first idea was to run after the vehicle; indeed, he had taken a dozen strides before he saw the uselessness of such a proceeding.

"Got the murdered man's body in the cart, young 'un—you're sure of that? You saw it, you say?"

"I saw its hand. I cut a hole in the sack to see what was in it, and the hand fell out on mine."

"I'm afraid it's true as he tells it," said the perplexed gamekeeper, half aloud, "it sounds true, but blessed if I know what to do." Then, turning to me, said he—

"Since you know all about 'em, you can tell me where they are bound for, boy."

"For London, sir—for Chicksand Street, Camberwell, sir—that's where Mr. Belcher lives, sir."

"How do you make that out?" returned the man, suspiciously; "that last's a lie, anyhow. They're a-goin' right away from London."

"Yes, sir, but they're coming back," I explained. "They've on'y turned round on the road; they was a-goin' to look arter me 'cos I slipped over the back of the cart. They're sure to be back directly, sir. Pray don't let 'em ketch me."

"Coming back, are they? o—oh, that rather alters the look of the case. What you mean to say is, that when they find that you have given 'em the slip, they'll turn about again."

"No doubt on it, sir."

"Then if they'll only be good enough to put off coming back for about seven minutes, I think we can arrange a meetin' with 'em," observed the gamekeeper, delighted at the prospect of circumventing two such scoundrels.

Still keeping hold of my hand he jumped the ditch again, and entered at the gap in the hedge which brought us into a sort of plantation. Here he took a little whistle from his pocket, and blew twice on it in a peculiar manner, and after repeating the signal it was replied to in the same sort, by some one evidently some distance away.

"Tom's over in the Briars, I hoped he wasn't so far off," spoke the gamekeeper, and once more he blew the whistle twice sharply and impatiently, so that Tom in the Briars might understand that he had better be quick.

No answer came to the last whistle, and it was evident from my friend's impatient stepping this way and that, and listening first with his left ear and then with his right as it were, that he was in a tremendous fidget lest the men in the cart should win the race.

"I'll have a slap at 'em if I have to do it single," muttered he, "if they won't stop the horse, I'll bring him up lame." And he handled his gun determinedly.

In a little while, however, his quick ear caught the sound of approaching footsteps through the wood, and the next moment two great dogs came trotting up to where we were standing, speedily followed by Tom. The dogs seemed disposed to treat me as "varmint," and to that end one of them proceeded to possess himself of a mouthful of my trousers, but the keeper kicked him off and he slunk to the rear.

"Now," said the gamekeeper, number one, "just you tell Tom here what you've told me—no more and no less—and be quick about it."

No more and no less I repeated to Tom, what I had previously stated to his companion.

"You're sure they'll come back, youngster?" said Tom.

"Certain—unless there's another road they can go to London by," I replied.

"Then we shall nab 'em, for there ain't no other road," answered Thomas, the gamekeeper.

"Hark!" said I, "they're coming back, I think." My ears were quick enough to detect the approach of the men I held in such terror.

"That's the cart, sure enough. How shall we manage?"

"You keep in the shade ready for a spring out when you're wanted, and I'll stop 'em," replied Tom, hurriedly.

"And the dogs!"

"Ah! confound the dogs, I forgot them, they'll make a mess of it if we don't mind. Here! I've got it. You want taking care of too, young 'un, and we'll kill two birds with one shot. Sit down here."

I sat down.

"Duke! Slot! mind him." And one on either side of me the dogs crouched down with a move-if-you-dare expression in their eyes, it was quite unnecessary for them to repeat.

All these little arrangements did not take so long to make as they do to write, no, nor a quarter the time. Nevertheless, time sufficient had elapsed to enable the brown mare to lessen by at least half the distance that parted us when I first heard her returning. It was plain, that, unable to discover me, my master dreaded the worst, and he was making up for lost time at the mare's top speed. Under any circumstances, to get back to London and home was of the first importance.

From where I was sitting I could obtain an indistinct glimpse of the road through the hedge, and I saw the figure of one of my friends stalk to the middle of the road, and there drop down on one knee right in the path of the horse who came tearing along. The clatter of hoofs and wheels seemed so close that I thought, to be sure, the man in the road must be trampled over, when with awful suddenness a flash of light lit up the dark road, followed immediately by the loud report of a gun.

My first thought was that my friends had adopted no less certain means of arresting the villains in the cart than by shooting them, or at least that they had shot the mare as Joe had hinted that he would; but the dogs being for a moment mazed by hearing the gun, I ventured to raise my head a little, and then the sight that met my gaze was one of a very lively kind. The brown mare rearing her highest, and frightened out of her wits by the flash and the explosion, (just indeed as Master Tom hoped it would happen,) and fighting hard against the grip that one of the gamekeepers had on her bit, the other gamekeeper with his gun in one hand and his lantern in the other, with the light thrown full on the faces of the affrighted sweeps, one of whom, Ned Perks, I think, handled the whip, thong in hand, and swore a string of terrible oaths that if the man who held the mare's head did not leave go, he would smash his brain-pan. Mr. Belcher affected coolness.

"What game's this, mates," he exclaimed, with an attempt at a laugh, "if you must play at highwaymen, you might find somebody to stop better off than a couple of chimbley-sweeps. Take yerselves off now, afore yer gets into trouble. Leave go her head, you sir! She'll be atop of yer else."

"In the name of the Queen, we arrest you," spoke Tom the gamekeeper, in a tone befitting the occasion.

"Arrest us! well that's good, too! What are you a-goin' to arrest us for, now?"

"Murder. For the murder of the man whose body is now lying tied up in a sack in your cart."

The light of Joe's lantern still rested on the faces of the two men, and though I was trembling to that degree as more than once excited a re-monstrative growl from my canine guard, I could see that Mr. Belcher and Perks exchanged glances that could have but one meaning.

"In a sack! in a sack with a slit in it, eh ?—him, I'd give a summat to have him here this minnit," observed Ned Perks, grinding his teeth.

"That's right! in a sack with a slit in it, and the dead man's hand showing through the slit. Tumble out, or make room for us that we may drive you to Ilford; that's where we'd better lodge 'em, eh, Tom ?"

"Have a peep in the cart first, Joe, to make sure," observed the man who still held the head of the mare, who was by this time comparatively quiet.

Joe, acting on his friend's instruction, walked to the back of the cart, and peeping over, threw in the light of the lantern to find, no doubt, things just as I had described them, but he had no time to tell his friend what he saw. While the cart was rocking up and down, and the brief conver-sation was taking place between Mr. Belcher and one of the men, Mr. Perks had slyly provided himself with a long stout iron rod out of the bag of "clinking" tools, and as Joe the gamekeeper peeped over, he raised the rod, and dealt a blow at Joe's head that, had not that person been swiftly warned by a cry of "Mind, Joe!" from his mate, would probably have cracked his skull. As it was, it merely made a big splinter fly from the top rail of the tail-board.

"Run, Belcher! it's all up," cried Ned Perks, and being a nimble fellow, at one spring he vault-ed over the side of the cart, swift as thought. Mr. Belcher, although not a nimble man, was not on that account to be deterred from attempting to make his escape; he stepped in a mighty hurry from the cart, but happening thereby to bring his head within gun-stock reach of Tom, who still held the mare's bit, he received the full benefit of a swinging crack on it from the butt-end of Tom's gun, and dropped like a log into the road.

Ned Perks was more lucky. He still had the iron rod in his hand when he jumped from the cart, and seeing the gap in the hedge fairly before him, he jumped the narrow ditch and made for it; with his head low, he scuttled swiftly along straight in the direction where I was lying in cus-tody, and I verily believe would have stumbled over me, had not the loud cry of terror I uttered pulled him up short.

His fiendish satisfaction at finding me, blinded him for the moment to everything save my hate-ful presence. I believe he did not see the dogs at all; he only saw *me*. He didn't say a word; he only made a hideous face at me, and threw up the iron rod above his head with both his hands. Duke and Slot, however, were obedient dogs, and knew but one meaning for their master's injunc-tion " mind him." They rose on their long legs as the bar was swung upward, and before it had time to descend, they were at him, and plucked him down with his face to the ground, as easy as one could pluck down a stalk of hollyhock.

CHAPTER XXX.

IN WHICH ONE JAIL-BIRD ESCAPES, AND THE OTHER ONE IS SECURELY CAGED. I FLEE FROM THE LAW AND ITS OFFICERS TO AVOID THE EVIL CONSE-QUENCES OF " CHIRPING."

WHILE the dogs still retained their tenacious hold on Mr. Perks, the one to his neckcloth and the other to his right arm just above the elbow, Joseph the gamekeeper, with an alacrity increased, possibly, by the reflection that the ruffian on the ground would have felt no scruples in beating his brains out, whipped a pair of handcuffs out of his coat pocket, and hauling Mr. Perks's unresisting wrists behind his back, there locked them secure-ly together. While he was doing this, he spied an end of stout cord hanging out at the pocket of Mr. Perks's jacket, and of this, without asking leave, he possessed himself, and made fast Mr. Perks's legs just above the ankles; and there be-ing no longer a possibility of that gentleman get-ting up and running away, Joseph made the dogs quit their hold, and went out into the road to as-certain how his mate was getting on. As is need-less to remark, I went with him.

Mr. Belcher was still lying in the mud as when struck down, and Tom the gamekeeper, having made fast the brown mare's reins to a tree, was in the cart investigating its contents by the light of Mr. Belcher's own bull's-eye lantern.

"My man's fast," exclaimed Joseph, bustling eagerly up to the cart; "how do you find things, Tom ? Is he dead ? Are there any signs of life in the poor fellow ?"

"I should rather say not," answered Thomas, certainly with more of disappointment than com-miseration in his tone. "He's dead enough—dead about a week, I should say."

"What! murdered a week ago ?" exclaimed Joseph in a horror-stricken voice. "You don't mean that! Good Lord, what ruffians !"

"Ruffians enough, I'll go bail, but not murder-ers, Joey; leastwise, there's no murder here."

"What then ?" asked Joseph, in amazement, at the same time hauling himself up for a peep at the mystery.

"Body-snatching—that's all; judge for your-self."

"But the boy said it was murder. What made you say that is was murder, boy ?" asked Joseph, reproachfully.

"'Cos I thought that it was," I replied, begin-ning to feel alarmed lest I had altogether put my foot in it, as the saying is; "he wouldn't have let 'em put him into the sack without they killed him first, would he, mister ? Hain't they done no harm arter all, mister ?"

"Harm enough to send 'em to Botany Bay," replied Mr. Thomas; "and that's where they'll go, as sure as they're nabbed. Well, I'm precious glad it ain't so bad as we thought it was," (this might have been his conclusion on cool reflection, but at the time he spoke I much doubt if he was not fibbing.) "See here, Joe, they're old hands at it," continued he, holding open the mouth of the bag in which the " clinking " tools alluded to by Sam were kept; "here's the gimlets, and the boring-rods, and the ropes, and all the set com-plete. My eyes! there'll be a stir in the morning. Lend a hand, Joe; we'll stow the beggars at the bottom of the cart, along with the game they've been fishing for, and drive over to Ilford at once. Got the cuffs on this fellow?" asked Joe, getting down, and speaking in allusion to Mr. Belcher.

"He's got a cuff o' the head that fits him quite tight enough," grinned Mr. Thomas; "you may as well pop 'em on, though, Joe; it'll be as well to go through with the job fair and easy."

Joe went round to the other side of the cart, where, half a minute before, one of the "beggars" in question was lying stunned and bleeding; and, arrived there, he uttered a cry of astonishment.

"Why, he's off, danged if he isn't!"

It was quite true. The blood-letting, combined, perhaps, with the reviving influence of the cooling rain, had restored Mr. Belcher to consciousness; and, having fresh in his mind, probably, the example of the policeman, whose case Mr. Perks had made mention of in connexion with his funny story of Spifler Wilkins, he had crept away and was gone.

The men's first fear was that Mr. Belcher had availed himself of the opportunity to release his companion, and that they had both stolen away together; but, in supposing such a thing, they had given my master credit for much more generosity than was his due, and as the trail he had left behind him in the shape of foot-marks and a few spots of blood showed. The said foot-marks and spots led up to a low wall that skirted the right-hand side of the road, as the hedge and the coppice skirted the left-hand side, and formed the boundary of an extensive park. It was evident that, with a stealth and nimbleness his profession conferred on him, Mr. Belcher had reached and climbed this wall, and was by this time, in all probability, as far away as two minutes' desperate running would carry him. He had not gone empty-handed. The gun belonging to Thomas the gamekeeper had been rested against the cart, while Thomas climbed into the body of the vehicle, to see about the "murdered man," and the said weapon had vanished along with the "resurrectionist." This possibly formed one reason why the men came to the conclusion that it would be better to take care of the fellow remaining in their hands than to attempt the pursuit of the runaway. Thomas's gun was a double-barrelled one, and though one of its charges had been expended in frightening the brown mare to a standstill, the contents of the second barrel remained; and a loaded gun in the hands of a desperate man is a thing to be avoided.

"'Tain't likely he'll take it away for good and all," reasoned Thomas; "he'll drop it when he gets to t'other side of the park and out into the main road. I shall get it back right enough—the name's on the stock—as right as they'll get him when we put 'em on his track."

They crossed the road, and making through the gap, found Mr. Perks exactly as he had been left; at least, the slight change that had taken place in his condition certainly was not to his advantage, the faithful Slot having taken a fancy to rest his heavy fore-paws on the back of Mr. Perks's head, so that the nose of that unlucky wretch was pressed into the moist earth to an extent that threatened suffocation. He was powerless to cry out; all he could do to signal the extent of his distress was to wave the fingers of his imprisoned hands; this, however, he did with an energy that induced his captors to hasten his deliverance.

"Take his heels, Tom, and I'll take his shoulders," remarked Joe. "You carry the lantern, boy, and go first."

"What are you going to do with me?" gasped Mr. Perks, probably imagining that, after the treatment he had already received, it was not unlikely that they intended to deal with him in a violent and summary manner—to take him, perhaps, bound neck and crop as he was, and pitch him into some handy piece of water.

"We're going to do nothing with you, my lad," replied Thomas, "'cept carry you to jail. You'll find somebody there that will do something with you, I daresay."

"They can't hang me, even if they brings it home to me, that's summat," said Mr. Perks, philosophically.

"Lucky for you," remarked Joseph; "you'd have murdered me if you could, you know you would."

"I'd ha' murdered *somebody* if I could, there's no mistake about that, strike me blind if there is. I'd ha' clove his —— head through if it hadn't ha' been for them infernal dawgs as hindered it. That's the whelp I mean."

And suddenly raising his head as he spoke, and catching sight of me going first with the light, he drew up his knees and made a lunge at me that would have hurt me, I don't know how much, had not Joseph perceived his design, and to avert it, let Mr. Perks's shoulders fall unceremoniously to the ground.

"Don't repeat that trick, young fellow," observed Joseph, again catching up his end of Mr. Perks in the coolest manner; "there's two ways of getting you to the cart, you see—carrying you, and dragging you; you know which is easiest."

"You might drag me to ——, if you liked, if you'd on'y let me get one fair swipe at him," growled Mr. Perks, savagely. However, he allowed himself to be carried to the cart and shoved in at the tail-board without further attempting to assault me. When he found that the men were making ready to start, and that, beside the dead body in the sack, no one was to share the lower part of the cart with him, he found his tongue again.

"Where's my mate?" he inquired, in a tone of surprise.

"Where you'd like to be, I'll warrant," replied Joe, with pardonable but indiscreet malice; "he's luckier than you—he's bolted."

"Bolted, and took my gun with him," put in the equally indiscreet Tom.

If, however, they thought to add envy to the tortures Mr. Perks was already enduring, they missed their aim. Ned was a wide-awake villain. It was not the first time he had been "in trouble," and he was properly alive to the advantage of having a trustworthy "pal" at liberty.

"Got clean off, d'ye mean to say?" asked he, eagerly.

"I didn't say that," answered Tom; "he'll be glad to lay that sore head of his down somewhere before he's many hours older, and then they'll nail him, as sure as he's born. Give the boy a lift up, Joe; let him ride between us."

"Can't I run by the side, please, sir?" said I. "I can keep up with you, if you don't drive very fast." I was, not unnaturally, a little afraid of trusting myself so close to the ruffian who had expressed himself so unamiably towards me.

"Pish! you're safe enough," replied Mr. Joseph, bundling me up on to the cart-seat; "he's a cleverer fellow than I take him for if he can so much as move a limb to hurt you or anybody else until we lift him out." And whipping the mare, we started for Ilford, distant about two miles.

We had not gone far, however, when Mr. Joseph was convinced that Ned Perks *was* cleverer than he took him to be, inasmuch as he found means of hurting me in a mental, if not in a corporeal sense, and that without freeing one of his limbs, or even attempting to do so.

"Jim!" he shouted.

"Don't answer him," said gamekeeper Tom.

"Jim, you heerd what they said, didn't yer? The guv'nor's gone, and he's took a gun with him. How far you have chirped, or how far you ain't chirped, I don't know. Don't—you—chirp—any—more."

The concluding words of Mr. Perks's sentence were delivered slowly and deliberately, and in a manner calculated to be impressive.

"Save your breath, you silly fellow," laughed Mr. Tom, turning about in his seat to address the live man lying cheek-and-jowl with the still and peaceful dead man in the cart: "he'll say what he likes, and he'll say the truth."

"Jim!" persisted Mr. Perks.

"Sit down here in front, and hold on to the rail, my boy," suggested gamekeeper Joseph; "you won't be able to hear what he says then, perhaps."

I adopted the suggestion most willingly, as it removed me a little from the man who had expressed his willingness to be dragged to the antipodes of heaven if he were allowed only "one fair swipe" at me, and sat on the butt of the shaft, with my feet on the step, and holding on with both hands to the front rail of the cart.

"Jim!" bawled my persecutor, loudly enough for me to hear had I been on the other side of the road; "you know what the guv'nor told yer; you know what he promised yer if yer ever chirped about his business, or cut up any ways orkard. He'll do it, mind yer. You dare so much as open your jaws to'rds chirpin' more'n you have chirped, and he'll be down on yer—certain. P'r'aps it mightn't be this week, and p'r'aps it mightn't be next, and you might think it was all blowed over. You'll see. When you think you're rightest you'll find yourself wrongest, and then he'll drop on yer. Don't you think as the law'll kiver yer; the law can't be alwis a-lookin', and it wouldn't take the guv'nor a minute to do what he said, don't yer know, and he'll do it. If you was a-bed a hundred miles off, and the door was double-locked, and there was iron bars acrost and acrost the chimbley, you'd wake up and find him stoopin' over yer in the dark, ready to do what he said. So take a caution, my kiddy."

It was hard to resist a caution so conveyed. Discovering the drift of Mr. Perks's address to me, the two gamekeepers did all they could in the way of loud talking and tapping the front of the cart with their feet to prevent my hearing what Ned said; but I heard every word, and was thrown into such terror that it was a mercy I did *not lose my hold and pitch* head foremost under the wheels. It was all very well for my friends to say, "Don't listen to him, my lad; *you're* safe enough if you only speak up when you get before the magistrate. He's only trying to frighten you into telling a lot of lies and getting yourself into trouble to screen him." It was so easy for them to say this, and to believe in it, too; but *they* didn't know Mr. Belcher—they didn't know "what he said he'd do," or how he looked when he said it. My acquaintance with the law up to the present time had taught me nothing of its protective power, but the contrary most emphatically. My gamekeeping friends meant well, without doubt; but they, in their ignorance, regarded me as a boy who had never offended the law and set it against me. To my small mind it seemed preposterous that because of my accidental discovery of Mr. Belcher's nefarious trade the law would turn round friendly towards me—that its terrible instruments, the police, would go out of their way to serve me—to say, in effect, and as regards Mr. Belcher and his vengeance, " Come and stand behind me, my lad; he shan't hurt you; if he attempts to do what he said he would, I'll draw my staff and floor him in a twinkling;" and that the market beadle, if he met me, would shake hands with me affectionately, and inquire how I was getting on. Nay, even supposing that the law was inclined to shield me against my enemy, Ned Perks had very truly said that the law couldn't *always* be looking; and how little time it took to strangle a boy, Mr. Belcher had clearly demonstrated in the course of that memorable conversation I had had with him. Besides, by this time I had come to understand to a certain extent the true nature of the offence of which my master had been guilty, and with the understanding came the suspicion that I had been rather too fast in the business. Stealing dead bodies out of churchyards was a very disgusting and horrid thing to do, (the more horrible because, in my profound ignorance, I could conceive but *one* use—a cannibal one—to which Mr. Belcher could put the bodies he stole,) but regarded as a crime—in such light as murder and burglary are regarded—it after all did not figure before my obtuse vision as anything very enormous. So that, weighing one consideration against another—the two chief being Mr. Belcher's view of impending vengeance, and the law's doubtful protection—by the time we reached the lock-up at Ilford, I was extremely sorry that I had been instrumental in bringing about such a tremendous fuss, and firmly resolved to adopt Ned Perks's advice and "chirp," when I was taken before the magistrate to give evidence, as little as possible.

And this resolution I kept through the remainder of that night at least. I admit that it was a very hard trial. When the first great excitement at the police-station had passed over—when the beadle had been knocked up, and the poor body in the sack conveyed to the parish dead-house—when Ned Perks, (his legs untied so that he might walk,) with his handcuffed hands and dismayed black and white face, and his jacket all torn by the dog's fangs, had been placed before the inspector, and the charge had been duly and deliberately entered against him, and he had been led to the cells at the rear of the station—when this was all over, and I found myself in the police waiting-room seated before the police fire and with a dozen policemen, including the grim inspector himself, all gathered about me, all so agreeable and chatty, and asking questions, and getting me coffee, and some dry clothes to wear, and some sticking-plaister for my forehead, (I had caught an ugly tear on it when I tumbled out over the tail-board of the cart,) it really appeared that the law *was* friendly towards me, and that I might trust it to any extent; but Ned Perks's ominous words, "Don't you think as the law'll kiver yer,—the law can't be alwis a-lookin'," still rang in my ears, and I maintained a guardedness of speech corroborative of the gamekeeper's testimony that all the way coming along the prisoner had been doing his best to intimidate me. What they wanted chiefly to know was where the sweeps lived, (there was no name on the cart.) Joseph the gamekeeper declared that I *had* mentioned an address, but that it had entirely slipped his memory; therefore there was no use in my saying I didn't know. What I did say was that I had forgotten; whereat the law, hitherto so jovial and pleasant, grew suddenly sullen and snappish, and its representative, the inspector, severely intimated that if I didn't open my mouth that night, I should be compelled to in the morning—that was a very certain thing.

I didn't believe it; but, alas! it turned out exactly as the inspector had prognosticated. The gentlemen on the bench, before whom Mr. Perks was taken early next day, were a very different sort of people to deal with from those who had cross-questioned me at the station-house. Evidently the magistrate had been informed of the exact state of the case, and one of them of terrible aspect, with white hair and green spectacles, made a set at me it was impossible for any boy to resist. I foresaw that I was lost the moment he began to tackle me on the subject of oath-taking.

"Look at me, boy!" he exclaimed, rapping the desk before him, with a noise that made me catch my breath. I did look at him, and there he was, unmistakably the law's beak whom I had often heard of, but never before seen. There he sat, with the lion and the unicorn over his head, and the black ruler in his hand, glaring greenly at me, with twenty bare-headed policemen humbly waiting to do his slightest bidding.

"Don't look at the prisoner, sir," repeated the green-eyed one sharply, for Ned Perks, in the dock, had made a sort of coughing noise, and I had instantaneously glanced towards him; "turn your eyes to me, sir—keep them there."

"Do you know what taking an oath means, sir?"

I did. In our conversation respecting the law and its operations—a topic Mouldy was particularly partial to—he had fully explained the matter to me.

"It means kissin' the book, sir, and hopin' as summat 'll happen to you if you tells crammers," I replied, my eyes fascinated by the glaring green spectacles until they watered as though I were looking at the sun.

"If you tell falsehoods—yes. And, pray, do you know what *will* happen to you if you swear in this court to speak what is true, and then endeavour to mislead this court by telling falsehoods?"

"Fire and brimstone, sir; leastaways, that's what I've heard," I replied, taking advantage of the green spectacles being momentarily lowered while their owner blew his nose, to rest my eyes by blinking them repeatedly, and deriving immense relief from the process.

"Fire and brimstone in the world to come, decidedly," responded the beak of the law, bringing the green blazers to bear with, if possible, a fiercer shine than ever. "That, however, does not release you from the responsibility of the act in this world, sir. If you swear to what's false in this court, sir, it is perjury; and perjury is a felonious offence, the ordinary punishment for which is transportation beyond the seas for a lengthy period. Swear him, usher; and you, prisoner, turn your face from the witness while he is under examination."

How could I help "chirping" under such circumstances? He was such a sharp gentleman, that the moment I began to speak of any part of the case under discussion, he seemed to know all about it, and put such questions to me as drew from me the fullest particulars, however reluctant I might be to reveal them. Ned Perks's face being turned from me I have no doubt saved me a great deal of embarrassment; though, as I now and then, as we came to what I was aware were ticklish details, turned my eyes in the direction of his hands, (which were still handcuffed behind him,) I could see by his manner of now clenching them and now twiddling his fingers, that he was striving might and main to make those members of his body serve him instead of the nods and winks he would have directed towards me had I been allowed a view of his countenance. All I knew I was compelled to tell—of my leaving home, of Mrs. Winkship's recommendation of me to Mr. Belcher, of my conversation with Sam about the church chimney-sweeping, of the discourse between Mr. Belcher and Ned that I had overheard as I lay in the cart—everything in fact, up to the moment when, scared by the apparition of the white hand, I jumped out of the cart; the result being, after Thomas and Joseph the gamekeepers had given their evidence, that Mr. Perks was remanded for a week to give the police time to apprehend Mr. Belcher, so that both prisoners might be placed in the dock together.

"As for the boy, he had better be taken home to his parents; and whoever takes him must be particular in impressing on his father the necessity of his being here again this day week," observed the gentleman with the green spectacles.

There was other business for the court to attend to, and when our case was concluded, I followed the police in charge of it and the two gamekeepers out into the high street. The men stood together talking for a little while, and then they adjourned to a tavern hard by, and, scarcely knowing what I did, I went with them. My confusion, however, did not arise from the circumstance of Mr. Perks being remanded to prison, nor was it due to the dazzling effect of the green spectacles; it was the last words of their wearer that had so completely upset me. "As for the boy, he had better be taken home!" This, indeed, was a climax to the ruin I had brought on myself by my stupid meddling in matters in which I really had no concern. Better be taken home! Better be taken back to my father by a policeman who would inform him of my connexion with the body-snatchers, and, worse than all, of my recommendation to them by innocent Mrs.

Winkship! Why, the alley wouldn't be able to hold him from murdering that good old soul, as well as myself, if such news came to his ears, and this after the many acts of kindness she had exhibited towards me. It must not be. Such a terrible catastrophe must be avoided somehow—anyhow—even though I dared the terrible beak of the law and his mandates, and took such prompt measures as should put it beyond the power of the officers of justice to carry me back to Fryingpan Alley.

The only way of accomplishing this was to escape from my present custodians, to make my way out of Ilford, and hide away somewhere in my old haunts at Westminster. I say my custodians, but it really seemed that I was in no one's custody. I tried it by walking in and out of the parlour in which the police and the two game-keepers were sitting drinking beer—into the public bar, into the yard in the rear of the premises, into the street—and found that I might do so without let or hindrance. It certainly appeared as though I was free to go ; but knowing the artfulness of the police, and of their well-known habit of appearing most indifferent to an object they are in reality looking sharpest after, I restrained my itching to be off, and resolved to go back and sit in the parlour a little while, keeping my ears open.

I had not long to wait; indeed, the two policemen seemed to have been talking about me while I was outside.

"Oh! here he is," remarked one of them, as I entered the parlour ; "you'd best keep close by us, young gentleman ; you'll have that chap with the gun after you else."

This was supposed to be a joke, so the other policeman and the gamekeepers laughed.

"You'll be glad to get home again and out of danger, my lad, won't you?" one of the men asked.

It was clear that to express a disinclination to going home would be to increase the anxiety of the police to convey me thither carefully, according to his worship's directions.

"I shall be very glad indeed ; I wish I was there now," I answered. "I'll take jolly good care never to run away again."

"Do you know your way home from here?"

"Very well indeed, sir," I eagerly replied. "Can I go at once, please?"

"You mustn't go till I'm ready to take you," answered the policeman ; "and that won't be till after the court rises at four this afternoon. You ain't obliged to stay here, though. You ain't a prisoner, you know, you're a witness. You can go down to the station and sit down there, or you can walk about a bit, so long as you don't go far."

I could scarcely restrain an exhibition of my delight at hearing the officer express himself in this way. I wasn't a prisoner, I was a witness, and was free to take a little walk !

"Thanky, sir," I replied, and strolled out of the parlour, saying no more, and leaving the police uncertain as to which of the proffered indulgences I intended to avail myself.

Avoiding all appearance of hurry, I walked down the Ilford road, which, as the reader is probably aware, is in a direct line with the principal highway at the east of London, Bow and Stratford lying between. It will be remembered that *on depositing the sack of "soot" in the cart at* the churchyard at Romford, Mr. Belcher had presented me with a shilling, which I had carefully transferred from the pocket of my wet rags to a similar receptacle in the dry and comfortable clothes which were supplied me at the police station. It was my rapidly-formed intention to expend this shilling, or part of it, in feeing the first driver of an available vehicle that might happen to pass that way to give me a lift Londonwards. But by good luck I was spared this extravagant expenditure. I had barely struck into a bend of the road that hid me from the court-house, when there came bowling along at a handsome rate a pair-horse carriage, with a convenient and unspiked splinter-board behind. Such a splendid opportunity was not to be lost, and in half a minute I was seated on the end of one of the carriage-springs, holding on to the board, and whisking along at the rate of ten miles an hour.

CHAPTER XXXI.

IN WHICH I BREAK NEW AND DANGEROUS GROUND, AND FIND MYSELF THE OWNER OF IMMENSE WEALTH.

MY carriage ride continued through Great and Little Ilford, through Bow and Stratford as far as the Mile End Road, and even then it was only brought to a premature close through the malicious conduct of a boy about my own age, who, desirous of a gratuitous lift down the road, and disappointed at finding no room for him at the back of my barouche, appealed to the coachman to "cut me down behind" in so energetic and pertinacious a manner, that at last the coachman (who was engaged in deep conversation with the footman by his side, and not at all obliged, I am sure, to the villain for his interruption) was compelled to hear him, and to act on his suggestion. It was a rash thing for a fugitive to do, but I don't think I could have resisted the satisfaction of punching that boy's head, even if the terrible beak of the law himself with the green spectacles had at the same time appeared coming down the road.

It was yet early in the day, however, (it did not take long to settle with my envious young friend,) and by two o'clock I had reached Whitechapel. It was not until I saw "Whitechapel Road " written up against a wall that I knew where I was, and the discovery gave me considerable satisfaction. Personally, I knew nothing of that part of the metropolis ; but I had, during my Dark Arches' experience, made the acquaintance of several boys who originally came from Whitechapel, and they one and all agreed in declaring it the "slummiest crib anywheres."

A "slummy" place—a hole-and-corner court-and-alley neighbourhood—was exactly the place for me in the position in which I then found myself, my great first and foremost desire being seclusion until such time as the unlucky body-snatching affair had blown over ; and then ——.

Bother about "then"—"now" was the time. In an hour or so the Ilford policemen would be growing uneasy about me, and there would probably be a search that must, if possible be evaded. I turned into Cutler Street, and wound in and out of a dozen of the narrowest and ugliest thoroughfares I could find, and finally anchored at a delightfully "slummy" soup-shop, where I invested fourpence of my shilling in food. The soup-shop keeper let beds at the rate of fourpence each, as I found on inquiry; so, with his permission, I sat in a corner until the evening, when, after having another pen'orth of soup for supper, I was shown upstairs and stowed away for the night.

I was tired enough to have dropped to sleep immediately, and I daresay I should have done so had my mind been as weary as my body, or even had I been beset by only one difficulty, whatever its magnitude. On the contrary, I was in a perfect adder's nest of difficulties. I could not bring myself to believe in the terrible fix I was in, until, by a tremendous effort, I shut the gate of my mind, as it were, on my flock of troubles, and let them in again singly for review; and then they made themselves known to an extent that completely bewildered and stunned me. The most provoking part of the business was, that my difficulties had grown out of my "escapes." I had escaped from the cart in the first instance, and thought myself lucky; I had escaped from Mr. Perks, when with murderous intent he was raging after me, which beyond question was matter for congratulation; I had escaped from the Ilford constabulary in the most extraordinarily fortunate manner; and, after all, how did my run of "good luck" leave me? Worse than it found me a hundred times. My father would be set on my track again; Mrs. Winkship, the only real friend I had in the world, would be justly incensed against me for betraying her; Mr. Belcher was at large, and hungering to catch me and serve me "as he said he would;" and the law—the last refuge for a fellow whom all the world are vengefully pursuing—was provoked against me, and would doubtless instruct its officers to lay violent hands on me wherever I might be met. Well, so things were, and what had best be done? What *could* be done? Nothing, absolutely nothing, but hide as I could, and wait and see.

With this thought I fell asleep, and with this thought I awoke next morning, and went down to the shop and spent my remaining threepence in some breakfast. With no other thought in my mind, I skulked about the live-long day, confining my walks to the lowest and shadiest parts, and avoiding the police with fear and trembling. This state of things of course could not last. So my old enemy, Hunger, suggested when, as the evening fell, he reminded me that I had not yet dined, and wasn't likely to sup.

"It is ridiculous to talk about 'waiting and seeing;' you must *do* something," said Hunger.

"How? How can I move without making matters worse?"

"*Can* they be made worse?"

"Jigger'd if I can see how they can be made much worse; I'm sick of this, anyhow. It's bad enough to be afraid to turn a corner for fear a policeman should grab hold on me, without going hungry all the time. If I was near the market, bless'd if I *would* go hungry, neither. What do I care? Everybody's agin me."

Which simply meant that I was ripe and ready to better my circumstances at the expense of everybody or anybody, as well as I knew how. Had I known how to pick pockets I am afraid that it would not have been any consideration as to the enormity of the crime that would have

stood in the way of my setting about it at once. But I did *not* know how; it was much too tremendous an undertaking for me. It was easy enough to snatch fruit from Covent Garden stalls, while the salesman was too far away to see you, or to catch you should you unluckily be detected in the act before you had time to get away; but the bare idea of going up to a lady or gentleman and inserting your hand in their pocket, take out and make off with whatever it might contain—whew! he must be a much pluckier boy than I was that attempted it. Of course, I knew that it was done—nay, I had had boys pointed out to me, while I lived under the arches, who picked pockets for a living, and I had likewise seen conjurors and people that could throw summersaults and swallow clasp knives, and one was as great a mystery to me as the other. Morality aside, had the two tasks been set before me—turning a summersault and picking a pocket—I certainly should have chosen the former as being the easiest. And reflecting more than ever before in my life on what a tremendous business picking pockets must be, I sauntered out of the slums, and shortly found myself in Aldgate, where the shops were all alight and gay, and the pavement was thronged with people who carried plenty of money with them.

Close by Fenchurch Street there was a grocer's shop. It was a very splendid shop, not only on account of the plate-glass, and the great show of foreign fruits, and teas, and spices, and jars of pickles and preserves, but besides these, there were all sorts of Chinese figures in stoneware and carved and painted wood, such as I had never seen before, and which, indeed, seemed strange to most people, for hardly any one passed but gave a look in, and not a few stopped for a still closer look, so that there was quite a small mob round the window. I just got a peep, and being in no sort of hurry, thought I would wait till the people had cleared away a bit, and then I would see all about it.

There was a lamp-post, just facing the shop window, at the edge of the pavement, and I stood leaning against it, waiting. Among the people round the shop was an old lady whom you could not fail to see, because she was very fat and took up more room than any one else. There was something she wanted to see at the bottom pane, and she had to stoop, and push out a good bit to see it. Keeping my eye on the fat woman, and wondering when she would have enough of it and move off, I presently saw a boy a little bigger than I was, pressing close behind her, and moving as she moved. He wasn't a very well-dressed boy, and I thought he was going to have a lark with the fat woman—to push her head against the window, or something. I thought so till I got a peep at his face, and then I saw that whatever he was after—and that he *was* after something more than was to be seen in the grocer's window, I was boy enough of the world to see at a glance—it was not larking. Then, as I looked harder than ever, I saw him do a thing that made me catch my breath and hold on to the lamp-post as though the risk was my own. He put his hand down by the side of her silk dress, took it away again, and as he did so, somebody shifting from the window caused a streak of gas-light to fall on his hand, and on a purse he held in it, and on a bulge of white money showing through the silken chinks. Then he slipped off, no one taking the least notice of him, while the old woman, having finished her inspection, went the other way smiling and nodding her head as she thought of the funny mandarin in the window, making the whole business seem a little like a lark, after all.

But what a lark for the boy! That lovely silk purse with all that money in it! I had sold my boots and stockings for a shilling and about two pen'orth of bread; and I'll be bound there was at least a dozen shillings in that purse — and that only in the end I had got a glimpse of!

"What a shocking thief!"

"What a lucky chap!"

"Don't I wish *I* had that purse?"

These were the thoughts that came into my stupid head one after the other, and then came other thoughts, which were so sudden, and so powerfully wicked, that they made me look to the right and to the left of me as though I was afraid that somebody might *hear* them.

"How easy!" "While you've been shivering here it might have been done three times over!" "You haven't got pluck enough!"

"That's all very well," said I to myself in answer! "easy enough when a fat old woman, with a pocket in her silk frock, sticks herself out like *that!* Any one could do it. I could! But how long might a cove wait for another such a chance?"

And so it came about that I presently found myself standing against the lamp-post *waiting* for "another such a chance!"

I didn't have long to wait. The "luck" that attended my first pilfer in Covent Garden Market seemed ready at hand. Before I could have counted fifty, a lady—not a stout one nor an old one, it is true, but owning a bead purse and wearing a silk dress—came out of the grocer's. She was fidgeting at the purse, out of which, I suppose, she had paid for the goods she had bought; and just as she reached the door, she shut the snap of the purse and dropped it carelessly into the pocket of her silk gown.

"*You* would be the sort to crowd in among the others round the window," thought I.

And so she did.

She sauntered up to the window to have a look at the nodding mandarins, and I crept softly behind her. It seemed that in wishing that she might go to the window I had pledged myself to a bargain I was bound to go through with if she did so. I did as nearly as possible as I had seen the other boy do. While I looked very hard indeed at the Chinaman, my hand slid between the folds in the silk gown, through which I had seen the purse disappear. In an instant my fingers were touching the slippery bead-work, and in another instant the purse was mine! I was strong to run now, and I *did* run; I ran all the way to Whitechapel Church, and there, in a by-street, and by a light that shone from a little shop window, behind which an honest old tailor sat stitching a coat, I opened the clasp of the purse, as it still lay in the pocket of my trousers, and emptied it. One at a time I took the pieces of money out, looked at them, and slipped them into the other trousers' pocket. I kept count as I went, and found that I had got eighteen shillings and fourpence — two half-crowns, a half-sovereign, three shillings, and a fourpenny-piece.

In all my life I had never had so much money;

no, nor a half, nor a quarter as much. It was an enormous lot of money. But I was not pleased on that account. The largeness of the sum seemed to make the crime I had committed all the more tremendous. The half-sovereign, especially, made the business seem dreadfully wicked. Had it been an old purse, with a couple of shillings—or, at the outside, half-a-crown — in it, I believe I should have got a sort of comfort out of the reflection that it was a great risk, and the money no more than paid for it; but when I saw the rich-looking shining purse, and the gold and the large and small silver, I was in great terror, and fully of half a mind to take some of the weight from my conscience by dropping the half-sovereign down the tailor's area. I did drop the empty purse there.

I didn't quite know what to do; that is, I didn't know what to buy to eat, or where to buy it. "If Mouldy or Ripston was with me now I should be all right," I thought; but, at the same instant, it came into my head that perhaps my old friends would not speak to me *now*, or have anything to do with my money. I was a pickpocket — a *real* thief, such as Mouldy had described that time when he was trying to prove to me that our business at Covent Garden was not real thieving. "I don't call *myself* a thief, I can tell you," said Mouldy; and he spoke as though he would be very sorry indeed to be one. Yet I was one, and Mouldy, if he met me, might turn his back on me. It made me feel very miserable indeed to think of this, nor did I arrive at a more comfortable condition of mind until I had stopped at a hot-eel stall and spent the whole of my odd fourpenny-piece.

After this, I past the greater part of the evening in eating or in choosing what I would eat. My stomach must indeed have been empty! I went again and again to a confectioner's five times, for a twopenny sausage roll, and that after I had bought and eaten a twopenny loaf and some treacle. The last thing I bought was a pen'orth of eating-chocolate, and I afterwards very much wished that I had *not* eaten it.

But after all, I found, on counting up when I began to think of looking for a lodging, that I hadn't spent *very* much — one and sevenpence was all — and even after I had bought a good strong pair of boots, I found myself with something over three-and-sixpence, besides the half-sovereign, which I fastened with a pin in the cuff of my jacket.

And now the reader knows how I came to be a *real* thief. But I didn't mean to repeat the trick. Not I! It was done, and it couldn't be helped; but not a soul in the world beside myself knew it, nor were they likely to; when I got up in the morning I would look about me and see what could be done. There were a hundred ways of getting a living with thirteen-and-sixpence to start with.

CHAPTER XXXII.

IN WHICH I MAKE THE ACQUAINTANCE OF LONG GEORGE HOPKINS, WHO KINDLY OFFERS TO TAKE ME AS AN IN-DOOR APPRENTICE, AND INSTRUCT ME IN THE MYSTERIES OF HIS CRAFT.

So I'll be bound there were a hundred ways of

getting an honest living; but, to my shame, I never tried one of them.

I returned to my lodging at the soup-shop after my tremendous "success;" and, when I set out therefrom next morning, I felt as well-disposed to find something honest to do as, under the circumstances, could be possible; but, since I had run such a risk to obtain the means of setting myself up in the world, nothing could be more foolish than to embark in any business rashly and without giving it deliberate consideration. So I went along, deliberately considering this and that until dinner-time came, and I went to a cook-shop and had a good dinner. After dinner, I strolled through Petticoat Lane, and seeing there exposed for sale a yellow silk neckerchief, spotted with blue, of the fashionable "bird's-eye" pattern, such as my father wore, I bought it for three-and-sixpence, well aware at the time that it was ridiculous extravagance; but trying to fudge my conscience that the three-and-sixpence was invested rather as a tribute to my father than to my own personal vanity. After that I bought a pint of beer to cheer my spirits, which the remembrance of home, conjured up by contemplation of the blue "bird's-eye," had much cast down.

Whether it was the action of the stimulant on my already excited mind, or that the beer of Petticoat Lane was particularly powerful, I can't say; but shortly after disposing of my twopen'orth of beer, my spirits rose to that degree I could scarcely contain them. All dread of my enemies ceased, and I felt full enough of courage to face Mr. Belcher himself, provided he did not have the double-barrelled gun with him. Gazing into a second-hand tool-shop, it occurred to me that an individual against whom all the world were making a dead set was justified in arming himself, so I entered the shop, and purchased a terrible-looking old flint pistol for two-and-three-pence; but finding that it was an awkward implement to carry about in a shallow trouser pocket, I re-sold it at the same shop late in the afternoon for one-and-fourpence. So was my dearly earned eighteen-and-fourpence frittered away, that after pawning the silk neckerchief (I never durst wear the glaring thing; I was not reckless enough for *that*) for eighteenpence, I found myself in the street, on the evening of the third day, as poor in pocket as when I stood against the lamp-post facing the grocer's window in Aldgate; and so——

But the reader can guess what happened next. The ice was broken, and I was in for it. I tried very hard to make myself believe that I was a poor forlorn boy, despised and hunted by everybody, and right-down driven to adopt courses which were so utterly repugnant to his nature that it was the merest turn of a straw with him whether he allowed himself quietly to starve, or consent to yield to the promptings of a hungry belly; but how much less I was to be pitied in my second than in my first attempt is sufficiently shown in the fact that finding but four shillings in the purse, I was much disappointed, and more than ever impressed with the conviction that if ever there *was* an unlucky and despised boy, I was that one.

Whether I had better fortune next time is more than I can recollect. There were so many "times," some good, some middling, and some

very bad indeed. Not that I was allowed to remain for any time in undisturbed pursuit of my new trade of pocket-picking.

Not more than two months. Indifferent as was my fortune within that time, (and it must be plain to the most honest person that the less a pickpocket gets the greater risk he runs, as those are the poorest pockets that are closest kept,) the devil was so good-natured towards me that I was enabled to get rid of the poor clothes the Ilford police had supplied me with in lieu of my wet and sooty rags, and provide myself with decent attire. Moreover, it was not a "bad time" that led to a marvellous and unexpected change in my fortunes, but to the best time it was ever my lot to fall on.

I had shifted from the soup-shop, and was lodging in Wentworth Street, Whitechapel. In the dusk of a July evening I was taking a stroll down Cheapside and the Poultry, (being "respectable," I could make an appearance in respectable places, you see,) and at the last-mentioned place saw an old gentleman busily inspecting the contents of a hosier's shop. He was one of the easiest sort of old gentlemen for a pickpocket to operate on, being so stout that when he stooped his coat-tails hung fairly away from his body. By this time I had been long enough at the "trade" to know that little is to be gleaned from coat-tail pockets. People don't carry valuables there; they may, perhaps, deposit their spectacle-case there, (and if the glasses have gold rims, the catch is, of course, a tolerably good one,) but as a rule, nothing is to be found therein but a pocket-handkerchief, or some little odd and trumpery parcel bought to carry home. · It was seldom after the first fortnight that I ventured to touch a coat-tail pocket, but that of the old gentleman in question looked so particularly tempting—so curiously easy of access—that it seemed a pity to let even so much as sixpen'orth escape in it. Brushing past him, I weighted the tail, and found that it contained, as well as a handkerchief, something hard, and square, and lumpish. This was nothing, however—it might have been no more than a cake of breakfast cocoa. I turned about and dipped, nevertheless, and, to my joyful amazement, pulled out a handsome brown leather pocket-book. I had found purses and loose money, and money wrapped in paper in pockets before; but a pocket-book never. Trembling with delight, I hurried down a by-street, and stealthily unclasping the book, peeped into it by the light of a street lamp, and saw within it some folded bank-notes, and quite a nest of loose gold. I was so completely astonished, that for several seconds after I had made the discovery I stood with the book in my hand and partly concealed up my jacket sleeve, not knowing which way to turn.

The question was decided for me. I could have solemnly declared that no one had followed me out of the Poultry and into the by-street. In momentary dread of pursuit, it stood to reason that I should not be careless in this respect; nevertheless, as though he had sprung out of the ground, a man was suddenly beside me with his hand on my shoulder.

"Don't run; it's no use," said he.

As though it had been something that burnt, I dropped the pocket-book into the gutter, and turned about, fully expecting to find that my captor was either a policeman or the old gentleman on whom I had committed the theft. It was neither one nor the other; to my great astonishment it was a strange gentleman—a tall gentleman, dressed handsomely, with a kid glove on one hand and a flashing ring on the bare hand that held me by the collar. As coolly as though it were his own property, he picked up the book and put it in his own pocket.

"There's no mistake about the saying that the biggest fools have the best luck," he observed, still retaining his hold on my collar, and marching me farther down the dark street.

"Please, sir, I found it; it's no use to me, sir; you can keep it, sir, if you've got a mind to," I exclaimed, in a terrible fright, and scarcely knowing what I said.

"Course you found it; d——n it! you never worked for it, unless you call such bungling as you have just shown a sample of work," sneered the mysterious gentleman.

"You may have it, sir; p'r'aps it's yours, sir; p'r'aps it was you as dropped it, sir," I insinuated, hoping to furnish the gentleman with an excuse for walking off with the pocket-book, and letting me go about my business.

"Who are you working for?" asked the gentleman, abruptly, when we had got well down the street.

The gentleman takes me for an honest errand-boy, thought I. "Please, sir, I works at—at—a box-maker's down Whitechapel way," I replied, endeavouring to look like an innocent box-maker's boy.

"What d'yer mean?" observed the gentleman, in a growling tone I should have thought him incapable of. "Who are you working for, I asked you, didn't I? Are you one of Spendlow's gang, or are you one of Nosey Simmonds's boys?"

I knew, now, that he wasn't a gentleman, and my courage rose. "I ain't neither one nor the t'other," I answered. "You let me alone; that's the best thing you can do."

"Then you come from Tom Martin's?"

"I don't know Tom Martin. Jest you leave go my collar. I don't want the pocket-book, but just you let go, will yer?"

"I'll twist your infernal young neck, if you don't keep still," replied he, giving me a shake. "If you don't work for them I've named, who do you work for?"

"Nobody, if you must know," said I, finding that it was best to be civil to him.

"Nobody! do you mean to tell me that you are working on your own hook?"

"Nobody's else's."

He left go my collar for a moment, and gazed at me as though he more than doubted my assertion.

"Look here, my lad," said he, bending down so as to be able to whisper to me; you may think to gammon me, but I tell you that if you do you will be the first boy that ever did do it. Let's have the truth, now. If you have got a master, why, tell me, and there's no harm done; if you haven't, tell me, and p'r'aps I might stand your friend."

"You ain't a policeman, then?"

"A what?"

"A policeman; you ain't nothing in the perlice? not a detective or nothing in that line?"

The gentleman laughed.

"Don't say another word," said he; "am I anything in the police, indeed! You are a nice sort of chap to try your hand at stilting," (first-class pocket-picking!) "Why, what d'yer mean by it?. How long have you been about?"

"Two months," I replied, perceiving that there was nothing to be gained by concealing my business from him.

"Started green, and been at it about two months—reg'ler working?"

"Alwis workin'."

'Never once been nabbed?'

"Not once."

"Then you're a lucky fellow, that's all *I've* got to say about it," replied the gentleman laughing again, as though he saw something astonishingly funny in my statement. "You ought, by rights, to have been nabbed the first nibble, for you certainly are about the greatest dunce at the trade I ever *did* meet. It's high time that somebody took you in hand. Come along with me."

He spoke as though he was the somebody who meant to take me in hand, and the supposition that that was what he meant caused me an uncomfortable sensation it would be hard to describe. I didn't like the look of him a bit, and somehow I felt almost as much afraid of him as though he had been a policeman. I didn't go so far us telling him so, but what I did tell him was that I was much obliged to him, but that I didn't want taking in hand. He turned on me savagely.

"Never mind what you want and what you don't want," said he. "Well, I'm ——! what next? If you never had a master before, you've got one now, and so you'll find. There's no two ways about me, so hold your tongue and walk by the side of me until we get home; then we'll have a little chat together."

He turned back into the Poultry, and went up Cornhill, and through Houndsditch, and so into Whitechapel, and wound and twisted about through various thoroughfares, until Little Keate Street was reached, I keeping by his side as he commanded.

I have often since wondered why, as I did not like the look of him, I did not run away, seeing that I had plenty of opportunity for doing so; and the best solution I can find is, that had he appeared to have taken pains to keep me close by him, and manifested any anxiety lest I should run away, it is very likely that I might have attempted to escape; but he didn't seem to take the least pains in the world about me; he walked along swinging his silk umbrella with the air of the most ordinary person out for an evening stroll, only once in a while giving a downward glance in my direction. Somehow, he seemed to make sure that I would not disobey him, and, incomprehensible as it now appears to me, if that was his conjecture, it was a perfectly correct one. I did *not* dare disobey him. To be sure he had seen me commit the theft, and he might possibly and after all be *something* in the police way. Anyway, I felt myself powerless to do aught but what he desired.

Arrived at Keate Street, and about the middle of it, he gave a curious little knock at a door, which was opened by a smartly-dressed and very good-looking young woman, who, not at first perceiving me, observed to my companion, "I didn't expect you home so early, George," and kissed him very affectionately.

"I've brought you a new lodger, Suke," said he.

She didn't seem best pleased, I thought, and answered, sulkily, "Well, you know best, of course, George. I should have thought that you was sick of lodgers; he'll last just about as long as the last one did, I suppose."

"You may take an oath he won't last a day longer if he plays any tricks with me," replied George, with an ugly laugh. "Tea ready, Suke?"

"Very nearly. Go in."

We went into the front parlour, which was very nicely furnished, and the tea-things were already spread on the table before the cosy fire. There was a sofa in the room, and on this George threw himself languidly and remained, with his arms under his head and his feet in the air, in perfect and perplexing silence, until the young woman before mentioned appeared with the tea-pot, and a dish of lovely broiled ham, garnished with eggs. Her temper evidently had not improved during her absence. "Out of the way, unless you want to be scalded," said she to me, spitefully, as she came by with the tea-pot; and when she had set it and the dish down she turned about to leave the room.

"Ain't you going to sit down, Suke?" he inquired.

"No, thanky; I've had my tea," she replied.

"Oh, go to ——, if you like!" snapped the irritable and impolite gentleman. "What the devil is it to do with you?"

The young woman deigned no reply, but went out, shutting the door behind her with a decision that unmistakably betrayed the extent and quality of her emotion.

"Had your tea?" he presently inquired of me, rising from the sofa abruptly.

"No, sir," I replied, growing each moment more and more uncomfortable.

"Draw up, then; take that chair against the window."

"Please, sir, I don't want any tea."

"Go without, then," replied he; "I'm going to get my tea. Never mind, sit where you are; I'll eat and talk too, and you take care and keep your ears open."

"Where d'yer come from?" he presently asked.

The question took me so suddenly, that I didn't know how to answer it, even if I had been inclined. Where had I come from? From Clerkenwell, from Camberwell, from Wentworth Street —which should I say? Mr. George, however, relieved me of my embarrassment.

"All right! I don't want to know particular, since you're shy about it," he remarked, not allowing the conversation to interfere with his appetite for the eggs and ham. "Have you got a home to go to—a regular home, with a father and mother? I must know that."

"I've run away, and I daren't go home."

"Why daren't you?"

"'Cos I should be about murdered."

"Because you'd be about murdered, eh?" repeated Mr. George, placidly helping himself to lump sugar; "that's all right. There'll be no occasion for you to go home and be murdered, my lad; you're going to live here in future."

"Live here?"

"Ah! I'm going to take you as an in-door 'prentice; I'm going to feed and lodge you, and you're going to work for me."

"What at, sir?"

"At what you've served two months at, so you say," replied Mr. George, with an incredulous shrug of his shoulders; "at the trade I caught you working at to-night."

"Not that that style of performance will suit me," continued he, after a pause, sufficiently long to enable him to give his undivided attention to pouring out and sweetening a cup of tea; "oh, dear no! I'd sooner board and lodge you, and find you in togs and pocket-money for six months, rather than see you going about your business in such a beastly, bungling manner. Luck's all very well, but a man's a fool who trusts to it. Nobody ever prospered who trusted all to luck, my lad. You've been lucky—lucky to the last, I may say, because if it hadn't been your luck to have met with me, you'd have found yourself behind a grating in less than a month, sure as eggs."

And as though to illustrate the aptness of the simile, he whipped the last remaining egg in the dish into his mouth entire, and this bringing the meal to an end, he leant back in his chair, and, taking a pretty little toothpick from his waistcoat pocket, proceeded to use it, while he further enlightened me as to his intentions as regarded myself.

"What I've got to say," said he, "may be said in a very few words. You're a lad in want of a master—devilishly in want of a master—and I'm a master not particularly wanting a lad, but happening to be open for one that suits me. At present you're a muff—you ain't worth your salt; but I've took a sort of fancy to you, and if you've a mind to go into the thing all right, and square, and earnest, why, I'll make a man of you. I can do it. My name is George Hopkins—Long George Hopkins, I'm called. You, being a muff, may never have heard of me; but I'd lay a matter of twelve to one that the first policeman you meet has. 'Know him? Ah! I should rather think we did,' he'd say; 'he's one of the cleverest trainers in London.' I've got it in print to show in a dozen newspapers." And he ran the fingers of his unoccupied hand through his curls, and, tilting his chair, continued to pick his teeth gracefully, allowing me full half-a-minute for silent admiration of a man who had earned for himself such wide-spread reputation.

"I'm going to train you," continued he, presently, in a patronising tone, and with his thumbs hooked in at the arm-holes of his waistcoat.

There was no use in contradicting him, and, seeing that I was expected to say something, I replied, "Thanky, sir! if you're a-goin' to do me any good, I'm werry much obliged to you."

"Do you good! it's a chance that a dozen boys in this street would jump out of their skins for. You'll see. You think yourself a wonderfully clever chap, no doubt; kids always are conceited —I was. Now I'll warrant, in less than a month, to bring you along so that you won't be able to think of a job like this" (here he tapped the pocket into which he had placed the pocket-book I had stolen) "without feeling downright ashamed of yourself. That's saying something, isn't it?"

I began to feel more at my ease with Mr. Hopkins, and I answered that I thought it was saying a great deal.

"Exactly; it's saying everything. In fact," said he, taking out a meerschaum pipe from a handsome case, and filling and lighting it, "it's caying ten times more tin, and twenty times less risk in getting it. It's as plain as A, B, C. 'It's a wretched life, and you'd better turn your hand to honest ways,' say the Johnny Greens, who know no more how to lighten a pocket than they do of well-boring; and they're right enough; as they find it, honesty *is* the best policy, no doubt. What's your name?"

"Jim Smith"——

Wishing to conceal my real name from Mr. Hopkins, I was about to give him the one that Mouldy and Ripston had conferred on me, but having doubts as to how he would take it, I hesitated when I had got thus far.

"Very well, Jim Smith, so far so good; now let us go a little further into the business. You haven't been doing by any means first-rate, now, I'll wager, in spite of all your good luck?"

"Well, as for that"——

"You've no need to tell me; I know all about it," interrupted Mr. Hopkins, waving his hand. "It's always the same; meat to-day, banyan to-morrow— no certainty; never a regular half-crown in your pocket, eh?"

"Nor a reg'ler shillin' either," I answered. "How can it be reg'ler when you're 'bliged to take it as it comes, and when you can get it?"

"Of course, it can't be regular. Well, well, it's the light of other days, with all that sort of thing, if you will only mind yourself, as I told you before. I teach you your business—I provide you grub and bub, while you're learning it, all free and without charge—and, when you're knowing enough, you work for *me*. You understand? You work for me, and I dress you as handsome as any young gentleman in the land. I feed you on the best; I lodge you like a duke. Slack times or busy shall make no sort of difference to you; there's always a good dinner, and if you want a crown to spend of evenings, all you've got to do is to ask for it. How do you like the offer?" And Mr. Hopkins grinned to see the expression of astonishment and incredulity that, naturally enough, was visible on my countenance.

"I couldn't be off likin' it," I replied; "but what's it all goin' to be done on the strength on? that's what I want to know."

"On the strength of your going to work, and bringing me home all your earnings," answered Mr. Hopkins.

"You mean, bring home all I can—can—get?" I observed, taking much more kindly to the generous fellow now than at first.

"Just so," nodded he, puffing out a mouthful of smoke.

"Oh, well! I don't think there need be any hagglin' over it," said I eagerly, and only afraid, either that he might be joking or presently see cause to alter his mind, "I'm quite willin'; it's just the sort of place as'll suit me, I think."

"No doubt of it," replied Mr. Hopkins. "That's one side of the picture; now let's have a look at the other side. You heard what Mrs. Hopkins said when we first came in, didn't you?"

"''Bout you bein' back sooner than she"——

"Pish! no, stupid head; about you not lasting longer"——

"Longer than the last lodger? Oh, yes, sir! I remember."

"*You* didn't know what she meant, of course?"

"*Course not.*"

"Well, I'll tell you. Our last lodger—about two years older than you he was, and as clever a little fellow as ever turned his hand to diving— he lasted as a lodger of mine only nine weeks. He's lodging now at Coldbath Fields—getting up the stairs without a landing. Three months of it, and twice privately whipped. Bad for him, isn't it?"

When Mr. Hopkins spoke of "the stairs without a landing," he rose for a moment from his chair, and gave a correct imitation (according to the imitations I had seen of the same process as given by the boys under the Dark Arches) of the working of the prison treadmill.

"Should say it jest *was* bad for him," I answered. "How did he come to get to Coldbath Fields?"

"Because he was a swindling young whelp, who thought he could give me a chalk in the game I had taught him," replied Mr. Hopkins, savagely. "It's like this, Jim Smith. The boys who come to lodge here, and don't stay, are the boys I trust, and who cheat me. It's a foolish game for 'em to play, 'pon my word and honour, Jim, it is. You see there's no mistake about me. To the boy that sticks to me, I'm a brick. Not only do I do by him as I've already told you, but if he *should* be so unlucky as to get hampered, he still finds a friend in me. I get him bail, I get him a lawyer to defend him, and if love or money'll do it, I get him off. If he can't be got off, whatever can be done for him while he's laying by I do, and I'm a father to him the moment he comes out. Only don't let him fancy that he is cleverer than I am. Money does wonders, you know, Jim. So sure as a boy of mine takes to fiddling, I'd manœuvre him into quod before he sleeps that night, if I paid five pound an oath against him."

"And serve him right," said I, earnestly.

"That'll do, then. I've nothing more to say— at present, at all events. Now you can go for a walk, or to the play—whichever you like—till eleven o'clock. Have you got any money?"

"I've got a fourpenny-bit, sir."

"I've some loose silver somewhere. Ah? here's three-and-sixpence. We mustn't be extravagant, you know, until we see our way a bit clearer. Be off. Don't be later than eleven."

———◆———

CHAPTER XXXIII.

IN WHICH I MEET WITH AN OLD FRIEND IN A NEW CHARACTER, WHO GIVES ME SOME STARTLING INFORMATION.

As Mr. Hopkins gave me his parting injunction not to stay out later than eleven o'clock, he shut the door of his house on me, leaving me free to wander whithersoever I pleased.

I never felt so utterly bewildered in all my life as, fingering the three-and-sixpence he had presented me with as it lay in my pocket, I made my way by various short cuts known to me towards Shoreditch Church. I didn't know what to make of Mr. Hopkins. He seemed earnest enough, else why had he taken the trouble to show me where he lived?—why had he given me three and sixpence? He had revealed enough to me to convince me that he was a rogue—in deed, it was enough for me to remember his un-scrupulous appropriation of the pocket-book to convince me of that; but if that was all he wanted, why didn't he be off with it and leave me, as I so broadly hinted to him that he was at liberty to do? Clearly it was *not* all he wanted; he wanted me.

But on what terms? I was to be dressed like a young gentleman; I was to be fed on the best; lodged like a duke; and only have to ask for five shillings to be sure of getting it! For what? For doing what I had already been doing for nearly two months, and had grown quite used to. For doing, with all ease and confidence, inspired by the comforting reflection that, come the worst, all that money could do would be done for me, that which I had never yet done without fear and trembling. Why, all the pull was clearly on my side, and it would be a very foolish thing not to take him at his word. There couldn't be any harm in sticking to him, at all events, while he acted up to the proposed terms; if he ceased to do so, what was to hinder my running away? I could scarcely forbear laughing outright in the street. What a fool Mr. Hopkins was, with all his wise words and knowing winks!

I had permission to go to the play, if I chose. By the "play" no doubt Mr. Hopkins meant a regular theatre, but I had never been to a regular theatre. There was a "gaff" near Whitechapel turnpike, and since I had been "on my own hands" I had been there several times; and though the acting there certainly did not come up to the acting at the Shoreditch gaff, it was very good, and I stood still for a moment pondering whether I would go there to-night. It was a long way, however, and I mightn't get home in time. "I'll have a turn at the old crib," I suddenly resolved; "the second performance begins at half-past eight, and it wants full a quarter to that now. I'll go there, and I'll go in the boxes. I'll take some sausage rolls and some oranges in with me, and I'll enjoy myself reg'ler. What odds if it *does* cost me a couple of shillings? I can afford it; I can have five shillings whenever I like to ask for it."

It was a very short distance from Shoreditch Church to the gaff, and within five minutes from when I made up my mind to go there I had bought the sausage rolls and the oranges, and treated my-self to half-a-pint of sixpenny ale, and was in the thick of the throng pressing about the gaff wait-ing for the doors to be opened for the second per-formance.

The mob was an uncommonly large one, by reason, as I presently discovered, of its being a benefit-night in behalf of Mr. Roshus Fitzherbert, the principal tragedian. Besides singing and dancing, there was a new piece out—"The Seven Steps to Tyburn"—and Mr. R. Fitzherbert was announced to play the part of the leading char-acter. Boys, big and little, were crowding on all sides of me, and just before me was a boy in a corduroy jacket, who stuck his elbows out in such a way that I could feel the pocket in which my sausage rolls were squeezed flat to my breast. I took the liberty of giving him a gentle kick, at the same time informing him of the amount of damage he was the cause of.

"Jigger yer sossidge rolls!" replied he. "Why didn't yer eat 'em comin' along, then they couldn't ha' got squeezed?"

He spoke without turning his head, but I knew his voice immediately; and, with a joyful exclama-tion, I laid my hand upon his shoulder.

"Why, you don't mean to say as how it's *you*, Ripston?"

"What, Smiffield! Lord's truth! this is comin' to the gaff for summit!" exclaimed my old friend; and, in utter disregard of the personal discomfort of his neighbours, he wriggled round to shake hands with me. The movement, however, cost him his forward place towards the gaff-door, and we were hustled and elbowed until we found our-selves out of the crowd, and, by the light of the great lamp attached to the gaff, we had an oppor-tunity of viewing each other.

"Well, this *is* a stunnin' meetin'!" exclaimed Ripston, absolutely collaring me in his excess of gratification. "Why, I've been a-thinkin' on yer as bein' dead lots and lots of times, old Smiff, since the last time we seed you, and here you are dressed rippin' and all half a head bigger, if you're an inch! What a jolly swell you are, too, Smiff. You've bin a-crackin a tidy crust since them 'Delphi times I should think, good luck to yer!"

I wasn't much of a "swell." I had a sound suit of clothes to my back, and sound boots to my feet, and a decent cap on my head, and that was all; nevertheless, my appearance, compared with what it was just at the time when I fell into that fever, had doubtless changed to a degree to justify Ripston in his eulogium.

Ripston was *not* a swell. His trousers were of the same material as his jacket, and both were grimed with dirt. His face, too, was smutty enough to show distinctly the tracks of perspira-tion, brought on by his eager struggles in the mob to secure the chance of a front seat. But what struck me most was his hands. They were as dirty as they ever were, but they were corned as they never were in my recollection; and as I regarded them so heartily laid on the collar of my dandy black jacket, I felt a thrill such as is seldom felt in the course of a long life.

"Why, what's the matter, Smiff? Ain't yer glad to see me?" asked Ripston, suddenly drop-ping his hands from me. And then, after regard-ing me for a few moments, he suddenly broke into loud laughter. "I knows what it is now; I didn't think of it afore," he exclaimed; "you've got 'spectable, Smiff, and you don't like mixin' with me. 'Course you didn't know I was changed; how should yer?"

This explanation did not comfort me, however; on the contrary, it made me wish that Ripston was a hundred miles away. I knew well enough what he meant; nevertheless, I asked him.

"Changed from what? What do yer mean to say that you're changed from, Ripston?"

"Why, same as *you're* changed—changed from them old ways of pickin' up a livin'," whispered Ripston. "I'm a greengrocer's cove now—carries out coals, and taters, and all that, don't yer know? Comfor'ble crib it is; eighteen-pence a week and all my wittles and lodgins. I've been at it this seven months."

"How's Mouldy?" I inquired, not without the wicked hope that my guilty conscience would re-ceive comfort in the intelligence that Mouldy had turned out a consummate ruffian—a burglar, or highwayman, perhaps.

"Mouldy's dead," replied Ripston, shortly.

"Dead?"

"Dead since last boxin'-day. Come on, the doors is open; we shan't get a seat in the gallery if we don't shove in."

"I ain't goin' to the gallery, I'm a-goin' to the boxes, Rip. You come to the boxes too, Rip; then we can sit together and have a jaw between the pieces."

"Boxes is fourpence; a penny is every mag I've got."

"Never mind, I'll stand a box for you; I've got some money; I've got more'n a shillin'."

I was ashamed to say that I had nearly three.

"More'n a shillin'! my eyes! you *have* been a-gettin' on. *You* ain't got a crib at a coal-shop. If I was to guess, I should say that you was a linen-draper's cove. Are yer?"

"You've just guessed it," I replied, much relieved that Ripston had found an occupation.

"And you've bin a savin' up, and you're come out for your holiday. Ain't I right?"

"You alwis was a stunner at guessin'," I answered, vaguely; "but come on, Rip, or we shan't get a seat in the boxes neither."

We did, however, get a tolerably good seat, and, being in a select and expensive part of the house, besides two young girls and an old lady, we had the box all to ourselves. The performance had not yet begun, so I produced my mash of sausage rolls and invited Rip to partake of it; I further showed him the oranges I had bought, which quite confirmed his opinion—if confirmation was necessary after my tacit acknowledgment—that I was out for a holiday.

"Mouldy dead, eh?" I remarked, as Rip was knuckle-deep in flakey crust and sausage meat.

"Had a haccident, and killed hisself the day arter Christmas-day," answered Ripston, taking a fresh mouthful of the pasty, and shaking his head in a melancholy manner.

"What sort of haccident, Rip?"

"Fell off from a roof. Arter lead he was. Yer knows that old ware'us wot faced the river, wot was to let when you was down there—that 'un where the crane was wot we used to have a lark on?"

"I knows it."

"That was where he got his haccident, then," said Ripston, inclining his head to mine, and sinking his voice to a whisper. "You knows how things was goin', Smiff, when you got the fever and was took away. Well, they got wuss and wuss. We lost the wan wot we used to lodge in, and nobody 'ud let us have a share of ther'n, for fear that we might have your fever on us, and they might ketch it; so we had to get into a corner and sleep on the stones—*you* knows the bird-limey sort of stones there is under the 'Delphi, Smiff? That was our luck at home, and that it was the same as though it was cut out of the same stuff. Market coves down on us, pleecemen agin' us, no jobs; and, as for makin' a little in the old way, don't yer know, yer might as well 'have tried to nail the buttons off the beadle's coat wirrout his knowin' it, as 'tempt such a thing. Then come the weather—*you* knows the sort of weather it was, Smiff, perishen', orful sort of weather, 'specially when your wittles was chiefly wegetables. How we got through them two months, blest if *I* know. Then there come Christmas-day. A cove nat'rally 'spects a bit of grub *on a Christmas-day*, if he don't get any any other time; but it was no use our 'spectin' it. Nothin' but a 'Swede' for brekfus', and Mouldy so down on his luck on account of chilblains that there he sat nussin' his feet, poor feller, and goin' on, enough to make yer mis'rable. They keeps Christmas down the 'Delphi, don't yer know, Smiff? much jollier than might be 'spected. They gets the money somehow—clubs together, I s'pose—and has a fire, and summat to warm 'em and smokes and sings songs reg'ler like a party. We jined in the Christmas afore, but we couldn't jine this time, and there we stopped in our corner, a-shiverin' one agin' the other, without a mite to eat arter that Swede till it was bed-time. I never seed poor Mouldy so desp'rit. He was alwis a good 'un at his wittles, yer know, Smiff, and the sound of the frizzin' and fryin', and the smell of the steak and inguns and that, was too much for him. 'This is the last day I'll have of this, Rip,' said he; 'if the luck won't turn of itself, I'm jiggered if I don't turn it; it's their time to have steaks and inguns to-night—to-morrow it shall be ourn, Rip, and no mistake.' Well, yer know, I thought he was on'y sayin' so because he felt so savage. I never dreamt that he meant anything serious, so I jest said 'All right,' and went to sleep without takin' any more notice of Mouldy or enythink else.

"Well, next mornin', when I woke Mouldy was already up and off. He never did go anywheres without tellin' me, and I couldn't make it out. I asked the coves wot I knowed if they had seed him that mornin', but nobody had. I went and hunted round the market—never dreamin' of the words he had said afore he went to sleep last night, mind yer—but no Mouldy; and then, 'bout ten o'clock, I come home agin, and jest as I got down the steps a feller ses, 'Well, how is he?' ses he. 'How's who?' ses I. 'Why, your chum, Mouldy,' he ses. 'Ain't you bin to see him, or wouldn't they let yer in?' ses he. It took me so sudden that I couldn't get my words out what I wanted to speak; so, ses the feller, 'Mouldy's gone to the 'orspidle—you knows that, don't yer?' 'Gone to the 'orspidle!' ses I; 'what's he gone there for?' 'Broke both of his legs, and a whole lot of his ribs,' ses he, 'tryin' to nail lead off a roof down by the waterside; and he's gone on a stretcher to Guy's. The gutter wot he climbed up by he was a-climbin' down by, with the lead on him, don't yer see, and the extry weight on it made the spout give way, and down he come a reg'ler buster. He's dead afore this, I dessay.'"

So completely engrossed was Ripston in the recital of his friend's melancholy end, that the stage-curtain had positively risen without his being aware of it. True, the opening performance was merely a *ballet*, an entertainment of a light and trivial character, and in which a boy of Ripston's high dramatic inclinations could scarcely be expected to take delight. When he had progressed so far with his story, his emotion compelled him to pause and wipe his eyes, after which he gave but a single glance towards the stage, and proceeded.

"Well, I wasn't long a-gettin' to Guy's, you may lay your life, Smiff; and goin' up to the cove what stands at the gate, ses I, 'Please, I come to see my brother,' ses I. 'What name?' he ses. 'Mouldy,' ses I; 'he's got both of his legs broke, and a whole lot of his ribs.' 'I know,' ses he; 'he fell off a house, or somethink. You're a 'spectable sort of visitor!' ses he; 'but never mind, you are the on'y one as has come to inquire arter him, so you may go through. Ask for sister 'Melia's ward,' ses he; 'that's where they've took him.'

"So I did; and when I gets to the door, there was sister 'Melia, and I asks her civil if she'd show me the way to the boy Mouldy. 'Is your name Ripston?' ses she. 'Yes, mum,' I ses. 'Come along,' ses she; 'that's all he keeps saying on, "Where's Ripston?" He ain't long for this world, poor boy!' ses she; 'you'll be in bare time to see him alive, I'm afraid.' Well, there he was, Smiff. They'd washed him, and they'd put him on a white shirt; and he did look so orful white, and his eyes looked such great 'uns—blue eyes Mouldy had; blest if I ever know'd he had blue eyes till that time, Smiff—that I was reg'ler frightened. A gen'leman wot was a parson, I think, was talkin' with Mouldy when I got up to the bed; but when the poor cove see me, he put his hand out for me. 'What cheer, Rip? I'm so jolly glad you've come,' he whispered; 'I thought I was a-goin' to die without never seein' on yer agin, Rip. Shake hands, old son,—don't yer squeedge.' Blest if I could answer him, Smiff; there was a summat stickin' in my throat that come up higher when I went to open my mouth, and I couldn't say a word. 'Mister,' ses Mouldy to the gen'lman wot was a parson, 'Mister,' ses he, 'would yer mind talkin' to Ripston a little wot you've been a-talkin to me?' 'All right,' the parson says; and he did, while Mouldy ketched hold of my hand. All about bein' honest and that, the talk was; but, in the middle on it, Mouldy give my hand a sudden squeedge, and was took wuss. He couldn't speak, but he looked at the parson werry hard, and then he looked at me and nodded his head, and then he died."

Here Ripston once more evinced serious symptoms of an outburst of grief, seeing which, I dexterously pressed on his acceptance my largest orange, which he instantly commenced to suck with a vigour that showed the tremendous strength of the emotion that I had so happily been the means of diverting.

"Reg'ler struck of a heap I was, I can tell yer, after that talk, and seein' of poor Mouldy turn his toes up," continued Ripston, throwing the orange-peel into the pit, with a sigh. "I was good to change, don't yer see, like Mouldy asked me to; but how can a cove change when he's got nothink to change on? This was wot I thought on when I come out of the 'orspidle; and I thought on it a good bit, till at last I made up my mind that I would stop about the gate till the parson come out, and ask him how a cove wot had a mind to change had better set about it. By and by he comes out, and just as he was a-gettin' into the carridge, I up and arst him. I forgets all his questions he asked me; but the best on it was that he winds up by givin' me a shillin', and where he lived 'rit on a card. 'If you're in the same mind to-morrow mornin' as you are now, come to me,' ses he, 'and I'll see what I can do for yer.' I was in the same mind sharp enough, never fear; and it was the luckiest mind as ever I made up. He give me some togs, and then he went along with me hisself to the cove wot keeps the tater shop in Spitalfields, and he gets me the place; and that's where I am now, and where I means to stick. There, now yer knows all about

my changin'; which I'd ha' done long afore if I'd on'y ha' known how easy it was. Didn't you find it easy, Smiff?"

I couldn't trust myself to answer Ripston's embarrassing question verbally, but I nodded my head in a manner intended to convey to him that I found "changing" the easiest thing in the world.

"Well, yer see, I dessay you found it easier than we did, yer didn't have so much to change from as wot me and Mouldy had," continued Rip. "Yer never got reg'ler hardened to it, like. Lor'! well I recollecks what larks it used to be for me and poor Mouldy to watch yer in the market, sometimes, when yer thought we wasn't lookin', and see the funky way you had of doing things. You'd never ha' made a out-and-out regular prig, don't yer know; you never had pluck enough, Smiff; leastways, not pluck; it ain't, it's summat wot's like pluck—like pluck wot's gone bad, like a speckt apple; it's the shape of pluck, but it's rotten. Why, I don't b'lieve, Smiff, that you'd ever ha' knowed wot nailin' even was, if we hadn't ha' put yer on it so jolly close as wot we did."

"P'r'aps I never should,"I replied, giving Ripston a look that must have been to him altogether incomprehensible.

"Well, you didn't go werry deep—leastways not nigh so deep as me and Mouldy did; that's a comfort, ain't it?"

"Course it's a comfort."

"I say, Smiff, ain't it rummy that we should come acrost each other, both changed?"

"Rather. That's a pretty sort o' dance, Rip."

"Jigger dancin', it's jolly rubbish; that's wot I calls dancin'. It wouldn't ha' been half so rummy if one on us had changed and the t'other one hadn't. Lord, Smiff! I wonder what I should ha' thought if I'd ha' been carryin' on the old game, and come acrost you to-night lookin' so jolly 'spectable! I wonder what I'd ha' done if you'd spoke to me, as werry likely you wouldn't? I'd ha' hooked it away, I think. Yet I dunno; it's werry likely I should ha' cheeked it out—p'r'aps made larks 'bout yer bein' a draper cove, and dressin' like a toff. I should ha' pretended not to b'lieve about yer havin' grow'd 'spectable, and gone in for aggrawatin' yer by callin' yer swell-mobs, and that."

All this while Ripston had talked to me in whispers, and with his head inclined to mine, so that it was impossible for the old woman who sat to my left, or the two girls in front, to hear a word of his discourse. I had never seen him so sprightly in all my life—never known him so chatty and communicative; but, as may easily be imagined, his talk had anything but an exhilarating effect on me. His every word and gesture was a reproach to me. Hard usage and studied neglect had corned my conscience so that it had lost its fine susceptibility, and was not easily pricked to wakefulness; but here was Ripston assailing it butt and bayonet, as it were. My acquaintance with the two boys had been of a peculiar sort—of a sort more likely than any other to beget friendship the most durable. The news of Mouldy's death, and of the manner of it, had given me a terrible twisting. That alone was enough to make me cast down and miserable; but when my old friend Rip, whom I had always liked even better than Mouldy—Rip, turned honest, talking honest, *looking* honest unmistakably

—took to gouging the wound, to stabbing and re-stabbing it so unmercifully, and yet so innocent-ly, I felt ground down to the earth in shame and remorse. That I looked almost as bad as I felt I could not but be aware, and the dread lest Rip-ston should presently, by this means, detect me, increased each moment. The dread was not groundless. Rip's natural shrewdness had not suffered in his conversion to honest ways. When he had finished drawing his funny picture of our meeting under other circumstances—him still a little prig, and me, as I was, a respectable linen-draper's boy—he was convulsed with glee, in which, by a poke in the ribs, he invited me to join. Not I. At that moment I would have giv-en very much more ready money than I was in possession of to have been able to have forced a laugh, though never so lame a one. But I couldn't laugh or smile even. I could only look hard be-fore me, as though I didn't hear him, with my lips squeezed tight together, and my brow lower-ing. Ripston broke off short in the midst of a promising chuckle, and, with a face turned sud-denly grave, laid his hand on my arm—

"What's the matter Smiff? I say, Smiff, it's all right, ain't it? *You* ain't purtendin'? You *are* a draper's cove, ain't yer?"

To my great relief, at that very moment the stage-curtain drew up on the first scene of the "Seven Steps to Tyburn;" and, to hide my con-fusion, although the stage was a mist to me, I clapped my hands, and cried "Bravo!" with the noisiest.

———◆———

CHAPTER XXXIV.

WHICH IS DEVOTED ENTIRELY TO A DESCRIPTION OF THE THRILLING DOMESTIC DRAMA ENTITLED "THE SEVEN STEPS TO TYBURN," AS PERFORMED AT THE "GAFF" IN SHOREDITCH.

THERE are a few people, acquaintances of my ragamuffinhood, with whom, before all others, I should like now to meet, that I might, as far as lay in my power, discharge my obligations to them; and, without doubt, the talented author of "The Seven Steps to Tyburn" is reckoned amongst the number. Should this meet his eye, if he will call on the publisher he can obtain my address, and I cordially invite him to come and see me. If, since he produced the celebrated domestic drama in question, the world has dealt kindly with him, and he is now prosperous and wealthy, (I have a faint suspicion that I detected the limnings of his masterly pen in a three-volume novel, entitled, "The F——— of the F———," recently published,) I have a bottle of "comet port" it will give me great delight to share with him. If—and such, alas! is the common fate of genius—he is still the threadbare man—altered only as regards the colour of his hair and the plumpness of his features—who, napless hat in hand, appeared before the curtain, responsive to the demands of a delirious audience, on the mem-orable evening of my visit to the Shoreditch gaff, why, then, if the small matter of ten pounds or so is of service to him, I am very sincerely his to command.

As my mind dwells on the events of that night, I am straight translated to that fourpenny box, *and I can see Ripston*, with his dirty face and his mouth a little ajar, so rapt, that he positively for-gets to breathe in the ordinary way, and resorts to irregular and stertorous gasps and grunts in the unavoidable performance of that operation of nature. I can see the rat-tail plaits of hair of the two young women that occupied the seat in front of us hanging below the blue "curtains" of their straw bonnets. I can see—and I swear I never have seen its like since—the pattern of the gown the old woman who sat on my left-hand wore, the three plain rings on her "marriage finger" when she clapped her hands, and the mangey-looking old boa she wore about her neck, although it was hot enough to make the ham-sandwiches the young men brought round along with the play-bills and the ginger-beer, uncomfortably limp and clammy. I can see the audience, and the stage, and the orchestra, with its two performers, a harper and a fiddler; and I can see the play from first to last. In the modest hope that the readers who have taken an interest in my fortunes and misfortunes up to this point will not be averse to know some-thing of the drama that so opportunely influenced them, I have been at the pains to set down the most salient features of "The Seven Steps to Tyburn."

In the first and second steps it is difficult to make much of the hero of the piece; indeed, as regards the first stage, he can scarcely be said to take a "step" at all, being a mere babe in arms. However, as every one knows, whatever direction they may take, the seven "steps," or "stages," or "phases," or "ages," of human existence must date from the mewling and puking period, and so long as the delineator does his best to meet any difficulty such an immutable ordination may bring upon him, nothing can be said about it.

The gifted playwright in question encountered this difficulty, and provided for it with a neat-ness and adroitness that is not the least amongst the remarkable features with which the drama abounds. The father of the hero is by trade a costermonger, and by name Harry Wildeye. His wife is Ellen Wildeye, (daughter of a reduced gentleman who, smitten by Harry's manly appear-ance as he delivered his wares at her father's house, gave ear to his passionate vows of ever-lasting adoration, and became his bride,) and their offspring in arms is christened Frank. The ris-ing of the curtain showed the home of Harry Wildeye, clean as scrubbing-brush could make it, but scantily furnished, its sole contents being a bottomless chair, two inches of candle stuck in a ginger-beer bottle, and an empty bread-tray. It was night, and the besotted wretch had just returned from his tavern orgies. Harry Wildeye is an irreclaimable drunkard, and in dumb show (there was no speaking allowed at the Shoreditch "gaff") he took care to make the audience un-derstand beyond the possibility of mistake as to his condition, by staggering and reeling across and across the stage, and applying a gin-bottle he carries with him to his lips, and keeping it there long enough to imbibe, at least, a pint of the in-toxicating spirit. His wife, with dishevelled hair, and a hectic flush on her cheeks, evidently at the very last stage of a galloping consumption, was at the farther end of the room with her infant (the future Stepper) in her arms, kneeling at a rusty grate, in vain attempting to kindle a fire to warm her shivering babe, with no more promising ma-terial than two old shoes (she is barefoot) and a stay busk;—the busk of the very stays which at that very moment encircle her agonised bosom, as an artfully dislocated button of her gown body unmistakably reveals.

So intent was she on her occupation, that despite the noise her tipsy husband makes in staggering to and fro, she failed to hear him—she remained, indeed, innocent of his hateful presence while he sang "Jolly Nose," and being vociferously encored, sang it again. Having politely bowed his acknowledgment of the compliment conferred on him, he deliberately crossed over to where his wife was, and by way of reminding her that he had come home, approached her from behind, and drew her for a short time about the stage by her dishevelled hair, she screaming the while, and hugging her babe in a way that was heartrending to behold. Presently, however, he flung her from him, and turned all his pockets inside out, to show that he had no money, and then he slapped the gin-bottle significantly, that she might understand what it was he wanted a little money for. Having struck this posture—empty pockets, extended and solicitous left hand, and gin-bottle grasped in right, exactly *as* promised on the bills outside—he retained it, while his unfortunate wife, still kneeling, first clasped her hands despairingly, and then, plunging one of them into the pocket of her gown, withdrew therefrom a handful of pawnbrokers' tickets, and placing them in the empty bread-tray, which happened to be lying handy, and suddenly raising her face and regarding him like Ajax defying the lightning, held out the lot, and offered it to him as a significant reply to his inhuman demand. This was *her* attitude as promised on the bills, and having struck it she stuck to it, thereby completing the picture. The effect was tremendous, and for quite a minute the gaff resounded with stamping and kicking of feet, and whistlings, and shouts of "brayvo" and "hencore." The old lady beside me was so deeply affected by the harrowing spectacle, that she pulled out of her basket a scent-bottle of curiously large size, and turning away as though ashamed to exhibit so much weakness, took a long and hearty nip.

Exhilarated by such unmistakable signs of popular approval, the drunkard proceeded to fresh acts of barbarity. He dragged his wife three times round the stage by her hair, and then once more furiously renewed his demands for pecuniary assistance, stamping his foot and holding out his hand. By way of answer she shook her head until her hair obscured her vision, and showed him *her* empty pockets. Laughing derisively, he kicked her four times heavily with his hob-nailed boots, and then, plucking a pawn-ticket from the bread-tray, dashed it contemptuously in her face, at the same time shaking her gown-sleeve between his finger and thumb, thereby plainly enough indicating how she might raise a trifle if she were so minded. Then, with a wild, despairing cry, *she* resorted to the bread-tray, and selected therefrom two other tickets, on which were respectively inscribed, (in rather larger characters than is commonly met on such documents,) "Flannel petticoat, ninepence;" "Stuff petticoat, and small things, fifteenpence;" thus graphically intimating to him and the audience that, willing as she might be to oblige him, as in wifely duty she was bounden, womanly pride, as well as the dictates of common decency, made it imperative on her to decline his suggestion.

Although much exasperated by her refusal, he neither pulled her hair nor kicked her this time, but vented his rage by turning from her and facing the company, rolling his eyeballs, and grinding his teeth, while he brooded further schemes for her persecution. Suddenly he smote himself violently on the forehead with his open palm, and clicked his finger and thumb, as much as to say, "I've got it!" and then turning to his wife, he pointed the way to the street, and took to walking up and down the stage with the mincing air of a young lady waiting for somebody. The action was simple, even to unintelligibility, to the audience at large, but the outraged, down-trodden wife appeared to discover something in the ruffian's gestures at once curiously exasperating and strengthening. With a cry of indignation and scorn she suddenly regained her legs, and stood before the monster erect as a police-inspector, and after regarding him with flashing eyes for fully a minute, she delivered fairly on the bridge of his nose a sounding right-handed hit from the shoulder, and down he went like a log, while she stood over him, and taking from her bosom a scroll of paper, and unrolling it like a charity boy's Christmas piece, displayed it to the audience, neatly inscribed with the words, "Woman's Virtue is her Brightest Jewel."

This was another decided hit, and the applause that greeted it, if anything, exceeded that which was called forth by the exhibition of the pawn-tickets in the empty bread-tray, and continued until the drunkard put an end to it by suddenly starting up and flooring his wife by a single blow of the gin-bottle. The applause that followed this feat was not uproarious, but a deep murmur went through the house that plainly showed that this touch of real life, melancholy though it was, was recognized and appreciated by the beholders.

"How do you like the piece, Smiff?" inquired Ripston, as the curtain fell on this the first step.

"I think it's a stunnin' piece," I replied, with a sigh, and thinking of my own mother, and that time when she turned on my father on account of his observation about Turkey, and he up with his fist and knocked her down over the fender.

"So do I. I think it one of the stunninest pieces I've seen for this month," answered Ripston, emphatically; "if there's a fault to find with it, it's too cuttin'."

"It *is* cuttin'."

"It'll be cuttiner as it goes on, or it's werry strange to me," observed Ripston, shaking his head sagely. "It's the kid wot's in its mother's arms as goes to Tyburn in the Seven Steps; leastways I reckon so; don't you, Smiff?"

"That's what *I* reckon."

"He'll break her 'art 'bout the third step," continued he, with a dismal relish, and speaking, doubtless, out of his extensive knowledge of the gaff and its drama.

"I hope he won't; it'll be a gallus shame if he does," I answered heartily.

"P'r'aps he'll welt her like the old man does, soon as he gets big enough," pursued Ripston; "like *your* old man used to welt *your* old woman—your fust old woman I mean, Smiff, eh!"

And this reflection of Ripston's calling up others, he sat a few moments, occasionally looking at me, and muttering incoherently such words as "jest ezackly!" "how rum!" "well, I'm blowed!" Somehow I seemed to know what he was thinking of, and it gave me no surprise when he presently whispered—

"I say, Smiff, it was jolly lucky that *you* changed, wasn't it?"

I could do no more than nod my head in reply to so cruel a question.

"You must have felt queer not to have no old woman to go home to—no reg'ler mother, I mean, when you changed," continued Rip; "it couldn't ha' been half such a settler with you as wot it was with me. Oh! when it come to that, don't yer know, and that 'orspidle cove what I was tellin' you on, ses he, 'Don't think on him as the wicked boy wot run away, mum,' ses he; 'but take him to yer arms,' ses he, 'like as if he was a kid what was jest born—like *he* was (that was me, don't yer know) when he was first born, and begin afresh;' blest if I didn' think my old woman would have busted herself; I thought she would ha' busted *me* too, a squeedging so jolly hard. Ah! that *was* a settler, I can tell yer, Smiff."

I felt the tears in my eyes, and Ripston's hand resting on my knee, I laid mine on it; and, only for shame's sake, would have there and then unburdened my guilty mind to him. There was a man came round with ginger-beer and biscuits between the acts, and he happening to approach our box at this moment, I called for and stood two two-penny bottles, and the change of the sixpence in biscuits, for the satisfaction of my secret self, and to convince that extremely private individual how lightly I held the money supplied me by the thief-training George Hopkins. It was shockingly rubbishy ginger-beer, and the biscuits were insipid as dry oatmeal, which seemed so like further spiting of George Hopkins, that while Ripston made wry faces at his, I consumed mine to the last dreg and crumb with infinite relish.

There appeared to be a long stride between the first and second steps, a stride of several years' length, for the curtain rising showed poor Mrs. Wildeye (the drunkard's wife) in widow's weeds, sitting in a wretched garret stitching shirts; while Frank Wildeye, (the Stepper, and late the infant,) a tallish boy, pale and emaciated as chalk and burnt cork could make him, reclined at the widow's feet, and did his humble best to assist her by threading the needles as fast as she exhausted them, which was at the rate of five or six per minute. Despite her misfortunes, the widow had contrived to preserve her furniture, as seen in the opening act, even to the bread-tray, which now, however, was not quite empty, inasmuch as it contained a solitary crust about the size of two fingers.

After working away at a rate that certainly would have secured her, had she been able to maintain it, several shillings a day, even at the fixed slop price of seven farthings a shirt, the widow suddenly paused, seeming for the first time to have observed the pale and famished appearance of her offspring. Frantically catching up the crust with one hand and her offspring with the other, she pressed him to eat. With tears and gesticulations he refuses; soliciting her with all manner of dumb entreaty to eat the crust herself; and then ensued a poking to and fro of the *crust from the offspring's* mouth to the mother's,

making a scene that might have melted the heart of a blackamoor. At last, with a wild cry of delight, the mother succeeded in forcing the crust between the offspring's lips, and while he tearfully munched it to the slow music of the harp and violin, the mother carolled the pathetic ballad of "Poor Dog Tray," with a strength of voice happily significant of the fact that seven years' poverty and privation had not affected her already disordered lungs.

This scene was a triumphant success. Compassion moved the audience as though it were but a single body with a great melting heart in it, and instantly there ensued a clinking and a chinking, and copper money flung from pit, boxes, and gallery, pattered on to the stage and rolled this way and that. This, as I knew, was the ordinary way in which the patrons of the gaff expressed their approval of a favourite actor, but in this case it was evident that at least a portion of them were actuated by feelings superior to mere admiration. Wholes and halves of penny loaves, apples, oranges, and a bit of seed cake, large enough to make considerable noise as it struck the boards, were generously contributed to the relief of the starving family. Nor was the family slow to garner the gifts so liberally showered. Without pausing in her song, Mrs. Wildeye bowed her acknowledgments left and right, (which, together with the action necessary to dodging the most bulky of the contributions, kept her pretty constantly on the move,) and scraped the halfpence together with her feet, while Frank, eking out his crust so that it might last as long as his mother's song lasted, arose from his recumbent posture and went about the stage with a business air, picking up the money, and having counted and pocketed it, he went and reclined by the bottomless chair again, to which Mrs. Wildeye, "Poor Dog Tray" concluded, presently staggered and sank down on it. The cause of her staggering was presently made painfully apparent.

In cases of consumption, as is well known, and as was vividly illustrated on the present occasion, appearances are treacherous; she had finished the ballad with the quaver of a hearty and robust woman, but now she rapidly sank and hurriedly blessing her offspring, expired.

The widow's demise was the signal for Frank Wildeye to enter seriously into the business of the drama. For a while he was overwhelmed by the suddenness of his bereavement, and wept and pulled his hair as though he held a grudge against it; but after about two minutes he recovered, and began to think about how his mother was to be buried. In dumb show he dug a grave, and lowered her into it, and filled it in, and planted flowers all over it; and then he wrung his hands and shook his head, signifying that, much as he desired it, he did not see how anything of the kind could possibly be done. At last a sudden idea seemed to strike him—an idea of so brilliant a nature as to quite dazzle him and induce him to turn his head from it, and put up both his hands as though the idea was coming it altogether too strong for him. By degrees, however, he seemed to grow used to it, and to be able to stare it boldly in the face. The idea in question seemed to have settled on the shirts his mother had been making, for, hurrying to where they lay, he pounced on them, gathered them in a bundle, and waving his cap, darted out, and disappeared.

In about three-quarters of a minute he returned empty-handed, and accompanied by an undertaker with a coffin on his back. What the bright idea was, and what he had done with the slop shirts, was now equally apparent—he had sold them to buy his mother a coffin! Indeed, any lingering doubts as to this being the state of the case, were speedily dissipated; for, scarcely had the undertaker set down his burden, when in walked two policemen and a gentleman, unmistakably a Jew slop-seller, from his countenance and the tape measure about his neck. In vain Frank Wildeye seized the bottomless chair and dared the owner of the misappropriated property, or the minions of the law, to approach so much as another inch; they rushed at him in a body, and doing no more damage than flooring the Jew by a blow of the chair-back, the heroic boy was secured and led away heavily handcuffed; being allowed, through the kind permission of the police, to pause at every third step and take a lingering and affectionate look at his dead parent. This was the second step.

"Werry good, but disapintin'," remarked Ripston; "he won't break his mother's 'art arter all, which he oughter, I think. Certinly, it makes him a horphin, and that tells up in a piece. I dessay it'll be werry good; but I shan't like one part on it, I'll lay a wager."

"Which part, Rip?"

"Why, the love part. Now his old woman's dead, and he's got no father, there's sure to be love in't, don't yer know? there alwis is. It spiles the actin', I think. If they'd leave it out, and make it up with fencin' or a duel, or a jolly good murder, that's wot I should like; summit wot stirs yer up; love don't stir yer up; leastaways, it don't stir me up, more'n dancin' do; jolly rubbish is wot I call all that sort of stuff in a piece, and werry much better left out on it."

Up went the curtain for the third step, showing a cellar in St. Giles's, and five thieves carousing round a tub, smoking short pipes, drinking pots of beer, and playing dominoes. That they were supposed to be thieves I learnt from the two young women in front, who had bought a playbill, and were reading from it. They were lanky, low-looking ruffians, with oily turned-under side locks, and shabby clothes buttoned up tight to the chin, giving rise to the suspicion that trade was not so flourishing as to admit of the luxury of a shirt. It gave me considerable satisfaction to see them such blackguardly-looking fellows; they were only thieves, but they were fifty times worse than I was; that was evident at a glance. Frank Wildeye was one of the five. The term of imprisonment adjudged him for stealing the Jew's shirts must have been a longish one; and, reasoning from his exceedingly corrupt manners, he must have derived the fullest advantage it was possible for evil communication to confer during the whole period. His pipe was the shortest, his side locks the oiliest, and the most determined in their under-hookedness, and, swelling the chorus to "Nix my dolly, Pals," as rendered by the oldest thief in the company, his voice was heard loudest and heartiest over all others, and he drank most beer. Presently a thief rapped the tub, and the landlord of the tavern appearing, more beer was ordered and promptly brought.

Cash on delivery, however, appeared to be the straight-forward system on which mine host conducted his business, and while he clapped down the pots with one hand he held out his other for payment. At this every thief slapped all his pockets, and looking at his neighbour, shook his head and laughed. Frank Wildeye did so, and followed the movement by facetiously offering the landlord a bit of chalk. The landlord, however, did not seem to see the joke, and furiously flinging the chalk from him, made as if he were about to take up the beer he had brought, when instantly four strong left hands seized his arm, and four vengeful right hands dived simultaneous into as many pockets in search of clasp-knives. Matters having arrived at this serious pitch, Frank Wildeye, who had stood aloof from this last-mentioned demonstration, laughingly interfered, and made certain signs to the landlord that so far satisfied him that he laughed, and they all laughed, and clapped Frank Wildeye on the back, and then the game of dominoes was resumed; the landlord joining, and Frank Wildeye quitting the stage.

In about as short a time as it would have taken him to have walked a hundred yards in a straight direction, Frank returned, bursting in at the door breathless, and with a face flushed with pride and excitement, and approaching the tub flung down upon it a fat-looking purse, that made a jingle like the dropping of a locksmith's tool-basket, whereat his brother thieves laughed loud and long; and the eldest one, by way of expressing his intense admiration for Frank's behaviour, immediately rose, and, approaching the footlight performed a hornpipe much in vogue in certain circles at that period, and known as the "cellar flap." Meanwhile, Frank and the rest had returned to their beer and dominoes, and were quietly enjoying themselves; all excepting the landlord, who, though he affected to laugh on the production of the purse when the thieves were looking at him, no sooner found himself unobserved than darting a look of implacable hatred at Frank and shaking his fist at him, he hurriedly retired from the apartment.

Scarcely, however, had the hornpipe and the applause consequent thereon subsided, when once more the cellar-door was heard to fly open with a crash, and looking in that direction the beholder was astonished to see two policemen with drawn staves, (singularly enough the same two who had previously arrested him on the shirt charge,) accompanied by the traitorous landlord, who, smarting possibly under the sneer conveyed to him by Frank Wildeye in that bit of chalk, had conceived the foul design of denouncing him for the recent robbery of the purse. Then came a fight, in which knives were drawn, and Frank, producing a pistol, fired it point-blank at the treacherous landlord's head; and, doubtless, it would have blown his perfidious brains out had not one of the officers opportunely struck up the weapon with his staff, on which the courageous young thief, resolved not to be entirely baffled, hurled the pistol with all his might at the landlord's head, from which the audience had the gratification of seeing a copious stream of what was very like blood instantly issue as the landlord lay extended along the ground. The audience was clearly of opinion that it served the landlord right, and so expressed itself in the most rapturous terms. Frank, however, though fiery and resolute, was of a soft and gentle nature; and, eyeing the prostrate and apparently murdered man for some seconds with an appalled look and hands upraised, he presently sank on his knees, and, withdrawing from his bosom a long ringlet of hair, which was instantly recognised as his mother's, he pressed it to his eyes, to his lips, to his heart, and appeared to be making some fervent vow. After which he replaced the hair, and passively and in meek resignation held out his hands for the handcuffs, and was led away to slow music.

The curtain rising on the fourth step, disclosed either that the landlord was not dead or that the law had taken a merciful view of the case, and for the joint crimes of robbery and murder condemned Frank to no more serious punishment than transportation. There he was, a convict at work at the stone quarries. He had fetters and chains on his legs; his oily locks were shorn, and his skeleton suit of serge was one half orange and the other half vermilion; seated on a wisp of straw, he was engaged in smashing a rock with a smallish brad-hammer. Several other convicts, attired as Frank, were squatted here and there similarly occupied; but for no apparent reason they presently rose from their labour and walked off, leaving Frank alone. Finding this to be the case, the young man laid down the brad-hammer, and, advancing wearily to the footlights, (pausing, however, on the way to re-adjust the bits of rags bound about his ankles to keep the iron from further galling him,) and withdrawing from his vermilion bosom the tress of hair he had exhibited at the close of his third step, he once more went through the ceremony of pressing it to the various parts of his body; and, kneeling down and shaking his head and turning up his eyes over it, and then dashing away a tear, he put the hair back, and, staggering to the wisp of straw, sat down on it, and went to sleep immediately.

Then ensued a scene of thrilling interest. No sooner had he composed himself for a comfortable nap than there arose from the shadow of the rock it was his business to smash, a ghostly figure—the spirit of his mother! Laying a hand on the young man's shoulder, he awoke; and, making a gesture of amazement, was for rushing to and embracing her, thinking that she was in the flesh—a pardonable error, seeing that she presented precisely the same appearance, even to her clean cotton gown and her side-combs, as when last seen stitching slop-shirts. She, however, at once undeceived him, by raising her finger, as only a ghost *can* raise a finger, and then pointing it graveward, as only a ghost *can* point a finger graveward. A correct understanding having thus been arrived at, the harp and violin played their solemnest, while Frank, with mouth ajar and staring eyes, concentrated his attention towards the ghost, who proceeded to execute certain mysterious dumb motions. It pointed in .the direction the convicts had taken when they struck work and strolled off the stage, and then it pointed in a contrary direction, which a convenient direction-post declared to lead " to the Governor's house." Then the ghost once more pointed after the convicts, and made motion with its hands of sharpening a knife on a steel, and *then she pointed the way the signboard pointed,*

and made the motion of plunging a knife into a heart. Then the ghost placed its finger on its lips, as though enjoining prudence, or secrecy, or silence, or something else; and, sinking into the earth, vanished.

A young man possessed of no more than ordinary intelligence would have been at a loss to make out what the ghost meant; not so Frank. He saw through the whole business instantly—it was a plot against the life of the Governor his mother's spirit had given him notice of! The convicts meditated revolt and murder, and his mother, watchful over his interest still, had disclosed the fact to him as a means by which he might regain his liberty! There could be no mistake that this was the state of the case, for at that very moment—and Frank held up his finger that the audience might listen and satisfy itself—there was to be heard in the distance such a sharpening of knives against steels as though a great public dinner was taking place in the neighbourhood. Hearing the approach of footsteps, Frank betook himself to smashing his rock as though nothing at all was the matter; and presently, sauntering up from " the way to the Governor's house," came the Governor himself, in a Newmarket coat and a cocked hat, smoking a cigar and carrying a large dog-whip in his hand. He made straight up to Frank Wildeye, and being of opinion that he had not smashed rock enough, (although there was considerably more than a saltcellar full lying pounded round the base of the bulk,) laid into him with the dog-whip without mercy. Frank, however, had a purpose to achieve, and as a preliminary step towards conciliating the Governor, went on with his work all the while the Governor was laying on to him without so much as winking. This seemed somewhat to astonish the Governor, who paused and regarded him as though he would be glad of an explanation.

In a few signs Frank Wildeye gave it. He motioned the Governor to listen, and as the process of knife-sharpening was still continuing, he heard it, and gave such a violent start of apprehension that his cocked hat fell off. When Frank gave him to understand that the knives were being sharpened for him, he began to shake at the knees, and his teeth to chatter, so that the cigar shared the fate of the cocked hat, and the Governor became a very abject picture indeed.

Frank Wildeye did his best to cheer him, and gesticulated his willingness to shed his last drop of blood in his behalf. The Governor was comforted. He seized Frank's hand, and on it pledged his eternal gratitude, and then ran to his residence, signifying that he would be back in a twinkling. If anything, he was back in less than a twinkling, bearing in his hands three guns, two pistols, and a sabre; and barely had he time to divide them with Frank, and to spring behind the rock Frank was engaged in smashing, than a wild hooraying and a rush of feet was heard, and on poured the five convicts, freed from their manacles, and each brandishing a gleaming carving-knife. Arrived at the fingerpost that pointed to the Governor's house, they paused, and gathering in a ring, crossed their blades, and dumbly took oath to do the job before them without flinching, and with another wild hooray were rushing onward again, when flash, bang! flash, bang! bang! from the rocks, and four convicts out of the five were stretched upon the ground, and the fifth brought to a state of complete bewilderment, rushing to the left and to the right, carving-knife in hand. Sabre in hand, Frank sprang out on this one, and then ensued a furious combat, which ended in the bloody-minded convict biting the dust. The Governor was not ungrateful. He took from his trousers-pocket a heavy purse, and from his waistcoat a free pardon, and handed them to the young man, who, affected to tears, turned away, and withdrawing once more his mother's ringlet from his bosom, pressed himself all over with it as before. He could not, however, content himself without performing an act of generosity, which was nothing less than soliciting the Governor to spare the life of the fifth convict, who still lay biting the dust, and scowling about him as though not at all liking it. The Governor refused. Frank persuaded. The Governor wavered. Frank implored. The Governor yielded, and taking from his waistcoat-pocket another free pardon, threw it to the ruffian, who snatched it up with a howl of triumph, which act finished the fourth step, and down went the curtain.

There was somewhat of a disturbance at this stage of the drama. The audience was very partial to sword combats, fierce, long-contested combats. That between Frank and the fifth convict was neither long-contested nor, on account of the inequality of the weapons, particularly spirited. The audience was dissatisfied. It whistled and kicked at the panelling and cried, "Combat! combat!" till the noise was deafening, and the manager in his shirt-sleeves and with an angry countenance came on the stage and demanded what the row was about. "Combat! combat!" was the reply that greeted him from all parts of the house. He waved them to silence. He was a broad-shouldered man with thick heavy arms. "Look here," said he, "you knows me pretty well by this time, don't you? Very well, then. Look here, you've had all the combat your goin' to have, and them as don't like it can hook it as soon as they like. There won't be no more performance till you hold your thunderin' row, so them that wants to see the rest of it had better keep the others quiet or else turn 'em out, whichever they like. It won't be good for 'em if I have to come and turn 'em out." This settled the difficulty. The cry of "Combat!" ceased, and in a few minutes the curtain rose once more.

Step five opened with Frank in London, once more a clean and respectable young man, in search of a job of work. With a bright and hopeful countenance, he makes known his intent to the audience, tucking up his sleeves, and going through the motions of sawing, hammering, and digging — ay, and of crossing-sweeping, rather than again be dishonest, a sentiment which the audience very heartily applaud. By good luck, by comes a master-carpenter, with his basket of tools on his shoulder, and to him Frank applies for a job. The carpenter makes several inquiries, but finally engages him, giving him his card, that he may know where to come to. Frank Wildeye is delighted—so much so that he cannot refrain from singing, in allusion, perhaps, to the burly master-carpenter, the song of "The Fine Old English Gentleman" right through at the footlights.

But, alas! poor Frank's promising nest of eggs are destined to be addled. Adverse influences are at work against him. While he is still blithely carolling his song, the carpenter once more crosses at the back of the stage, and is stopped and spoken to by—the very scoundrel whose life and liberty Frank Wildeye begged of the Governor of New South Wales. The scoundrel is well dressed, and wears a curly-brimmed hat and an eye-glass, and dandles an elaborate walking cane. He whispers the carpenter a little while, and points to Frank with a shrug of the shoulders, and the master-carpenter touches his cap, expressive of his thanks for the information the swell has given him. Swell walks off, and carpenter, approaching Frank Wildeye, by a snap of his finger and thumb, and a scornful curl of his lip, repudiates the engagement entered into so shortly before, and, with an impatient gesture, demands back his card of address. Poor Frank is thunderstruck, and, with clasped hands, beseeches the carpenter to make known his reasons for this sudden change; and the carpenter replies by laughing mockingly, and holding his head askew, raising his hand above it, giving the hand a jerk, as though tightening something about his throat, and making a choking sound, such as might be made by a man in the early stages of strangulation.

Frank Wildeye at once sees the true state of the case—the carpenter has discovered that he is a felon, who narrowly escaped the gallows, and on that account spurns him. In vain Frank begs and implores, and goes down on his knees to the carpenter; he is relentless, and, spurning the pleader with the toe of his boot, walks off. For a while Frank is overwhelmed by despair, but presently plucks up resolution, and drying his eyes on the ends of the clean cotton-handkerchief his bundle is tied in, departs with hope renewed in search of work.

While he is going, in comes the well-dressed scoundrel with the curly-brimmed hat and the eye-glass from the other side, and regarding the retreating form with the deadliest malice, shakes his fist at it, and laughs a bitter and diabolical laugh, which indicates as plain as spoken language his glee at the success of his fiendish plans, and his determination, from some mysterious and unexplained circumstance, to pursue and persecute Frank Wildeye to the death.

In something less than two minutes Frank returned, footsore and haggard, and with his bundle considerably diminished in size, which signs make it manifest to the audience that he has tramped in search of work through every county in England, until his scanty purse is exhausted, and he has been brought to selling things out of the bundle to keep life and soul together. All in vain, however—he is still an out-o'-work and an outcast, shunned by the world. He sits down on a bank, and covering his eyes with his hands, weeps. Suddenly a hollow and mocking laugh smites his ears, and looking up, there is Blue Lias, the well-dressed scoundrel, standing before him. With an instinctive cry of horror, Frank shrinks from the tempter, and catches up his little bundle. Blue Lias is not at all offended at this insinuation against his probity, and, good-humoredly slapping Frank on the shoulder, takes a seat beside him; then he withdraws from his pocket a capacious brandy-flask, and after some persuasion Frank is induced to take a swig out of it, the result of which is that his spirits are raised very considerably, and he laughs too, and accepts a cigar from Blue Lias's elegant case, and takes some more brandy, and makes himself comfortable.

Then, when he is well primed, Blue Lias whispers in his ear. Frank Wildeye starts as though some insect had bitten him, and holds up his hands deprecatingly. The tempter shows him a handful of loose gold and silver, and whispers again. With a reckless laugh Frank Wildeye springs to his feet, and, clasping hands with Blue Lias, the two go off together.

"It's a gettin' on, ain't it?" observed Ripston, taking a long breath.

"'Tain't so disappintin' as yer thought it would be; is it, Rip?"

"Not a half. There won't be no love in it arter all, I begins to think. There would ha' been though if it hadn't a been for the mother's ghost, you may depend upon it. It must make a cove feel orkard to see his mother's ghost, musn't it, Smiff? Hallo! my eyes, it *is* a stunnin' piece!"

The opening scene of the sixth step prompted this last remark of Ripston. It was a night scene, and masked with crape, Frank Wildeye and Blue Lias are seen breaking into a dwelling-house, or rather into a bed-room in a dwelling-house, for when, with their united exertions, and the free use of centre-bits and "jemmies," the door yields with a loud crash, the opening reveals an old gentleman calmly asleep on a sofa-bedstead. To make quite sure that he is asleep, Blue Lias flashes the fierce light of a bull's eye lantern several times across the old gentleman's eyes, and then the two proceed to ransack the strong box they drag from beneath the bedstead. Bags of silver and gold, candlesticks, and great rolls of bank-notes and parchment deeds, reward their search, when suddenly the old gentleman rouses, and proceeds to jerk the bell-rope at his bed-head, the result of which is a loud clanging sound at some other part of the premises. With a ferocious gesture, Blue Lias springs at the old gentleman's throat, and raises a life preserver to knock his brains out, but Frank Wildeye, who, though a thief, is no murderer, rushes to the rescue, and catches Blue Lias's hand just in time. With a howl of rage Blue Lias turns on Frank and knocks *him* down insensible with the life-preserver, and then, snatching from Frank's pocket his clasp-knife, (presumably with his name and address upon it,) plunges it into the old man's heart, and leaving it sticking there, escapes out of the window, thus bringing the sixth step to a close in a highly satisfactory manner.

Step seventh and last, and we have the wretched young man chained hand and foot, and securely padlocked to the wall of the condemned cell in Newgate. It is clear what has happened; he has been convicted on the false evidence furnished by his knife in the heart of the victim, and he is cast for death and awaiting execution. Evidently he is deeply penitent, so much so that the two-pound loaf and the gallon pitcher of water supplied him by the prison authorities remain untouched by his side, and he sits with his face on his drawn-up knees audibly sobbing. Suddenly he hears a well-remembered mocking laugh, and *hastily raising* his head there sees at his dungeon *grate the hated face of Blue Lias*, who, in the extremity of his hate and deadly spite, has come to taunt his wretched victim.

Owing, however, to the prohibition of the use of speech, his means of doing so are limited, and all he can do is to make faces—winking, thrusting out his tongue, and laying his forefinger along the side of his nose in the most exasperating manner. This last act goads Frank Wildeye to madness, and he rattles his chains and grinds his teeth at a tremendous rate. Blue Lias, however, is not destined to lord it to the end of the chapter. Suddenly, from amongst the straw in the dungeon, arises a white and ghostly form— the ghost of Frank's mother. She eyes the monster at the grate menacingly, and instantly he gives vent to a shriek, his forefinger drops from the side of his nose, his guilty jaw falls ajar, and his knees tremble so that you may hear them bumping against the dungeon door. The ghostly figure raises its hand, and first pointing up and then pointing down, with a louder shriek than the first, down fell the taunter with a crash that bespoke him dead beyond the shadow of a doubt.

Then the ghostly form came over to where its unlucky son was sitting, and regarded him pityingly, and took his hand in its and stroked his hair. With the violence of his emotion, Frank Wildeye's chains rattled, at which sound the tender ghost shuddered and wept, and taking the chains in its hand raised them that the captive might for a time be eased of their weight. All this time the harp and the fiddle were playing music sad and soft, and the motherly ghost leaned over Frank caressing him, while Frank's bosom heaved with a force that might be easily perceived by the people in the back row of the gallery. Then, taking from its bosom a similar scroll to that she exhibited when in the flesh in the first step, she unrolled it, and there was plain to all who could read, (I couldn't, but the two young women in front read it aloud and I heard them)—"A Mother's Love is Everlasting." Then, hearing a noise at the lock of the dungeon door, she hastily rolled up and replaced the scroll, and kissing her son on both cheeks and on the forehead, vanished the way she came; and Jack Ketch, (with the fatal noose in his hand,) and the Chaplain, and Sheriffs, coming in next moment to take the culprit off to the gallows, the play was brought to an end.

———◆———

CHAPTER XXXV.

IN WHICH MY DETERMINATION TO "CHANGE" IS SUDDENLY AND UNEXPECTEDLY BALKED, AND I APPEAR TO BE "GOING TO THE DOGS" AT A GALLOP.

AT the falling of the curtain the shouts of approbation were deafening, and there was a universal and tempestuous demand for Mr. Roshus Fitzherbert, the representative of Frank Wildeye, who, hand-in-hand with his ghostly mother, and still wearing his chains, came forward, expressed his everlasting gratitude for the handsome manner in which the audience had received the new piece. The ghost (whom I was given to understand was the wife of the manager) then spoke in similar terms, and announced that "The Seven Steps to Tyburn" would be repeated every evening till further notice. She then, in the most generous manner, made a pathetic appeal on behalf of the gifted author of the piece, whom she described as a struggling man with a large family, to which there had very lately, and on those premises, been an addition—a very heavy addition, in the shape of twins—a boy and a girl.

This last item of intelligence was received with renewed applause by the audience, especially the female portion of it, and there ensued a unanimous call for the author, or, as they expressed it, "the chap as made it up." With a promptitude that bespoke his vigilance as a public servant, "the chap as made up" "The Seven Steps to Tyburn" made his appearance; and when quiet was in some degree restored, he made a neat little speech concerning the piece, which, he said, he was afraid was weakish towards the end, excusing himself, however, on the ground that, circumstances kindly alluded to by the worthy manageress — coming sudden and unexpected, and just as he was in the middle of the fifth act—had naturally flurried him, to say nothing of the expense, which, however, as a husband and an Englishman, he was proud and happy to incur, and with their kind patronage hoped to be able to defray to the utmost farthing.

Again the gaff resounded with applause, seconded by a more substantial mark of the esteem in which the audience held the talented gentleman, as well on account of his literary worth as his domestic virtue and heroism, by a liberal shower of pence and half-pence. For my part I was too young to recognize his claims on public sympathy on part of the grounds urged. I only saw in him "the chap as had made up" the touching and deeply-affecting drama I had just witnessed, and in the fulness of my gratitude I threw him a fourpenny-piece out of my remaining one-and-tenpence. I was so completely subdued that I was ashamed to look Ripston in the face for fear he might see the tears in my eyes. As we were making our way out of the gaff, he observed:

"What a stunnin' piece, eh, Smiff? Just shows yer how a cove gets on to be wusser and wusser, till he ain't able to stop hisself! 'Mother's love is everlastin',' didn't that there bill say? I 'spose that means that arter mothers is dead they looks down on yer, and sees yer ways of goin' on, eh, Smiff?"

"I 'spose that's wot it does mean."

"The bills didn't say step-mothers, Smiff; that one of your'n 'ud have to look up 'stead of down, if she wanted to look arter you, arter she turned her toes up; what do you say, Smiff?" said Ripston, laughing.

I made something like a laugh by way of answer, but felt at the moment further from laughing than anything I can think of.

"Well, that makes no odds; you've got a regler mother to look down on yer, if she wants to; ain't yer, Smiff? Why, what's the matter? What are yer cryin' about, Smiff?"

We had got as far as the lobby leading to the street by this time.

"Oh, Rip!"

"Come on, yer young fool; you shouldn't come to see cuttin' pieces if yer can't stand 'em better than this. Hain't you got a hankcher? Here, ketch hold of mine." And Ripston kindly handed me from his jacket something that looked like a fragment of a dirty duster. We

had halted in a recess in the lobby, and the people hurrying out took no notice of us.

"Oh, Ripston!"

"Come outside and have some gingerbeer. You ain't well; that's wot's the matter with you; I can't abear to be seen walkin' with a cove wot's snivellin'; come on, and let's get out. It's gettin' late, don't yer know—past ten by this, I reckon; and ten's my time for gettin' in, and there's a tidy step for me to go. How far have you got to go, Smiff? What's your time of gettin' in?"

He asked this last question quite suddenly, and as though a shadow of the suspicion that once before in the course of the evening had flashed across his mind, had again occurred to him.

"Whereabouts is the draper's where you've got a place?" he repeated, laying a hand on my shoulder.

"I hain't got a place at a draper's at all, Rip," I whispered into his ear; making up my mind to the desperate resolve to tell him all about it, and take his advice on the matter.

"You don't live at a draper's at all?"

"No."

"Where do you live, then? at what shop, I mean?"

"At no shop at all."

"Well, if it ain't a shop, what bisness is it? It must be a bisness of some kind, don't yer know?"

"Bob yer head down lower, Rip. It ain't no bisness at all; leastways, unless the old trade was a bisness."

"The old trade!" repeated Rip, with amazement in his eyes as he scanned my respectable suit from top to bottom. "Why, you don't mean to say, Smiff, that you ain't bin and changed arter all? Oh, swelp me, Smiff, don't tell a cove that."

"Oh, yes, I've changed right enough," I replied in bitterness; "I've changed from wuss to wusser—jest like you was a sayin' jest now, Rip, that's how I've changed."

Ripston made no reply to this confession, but stood for fully half-a-minute scratching his head and staring at me as though considerably bewildered as to what, under such very peculiar circumstances, had best be done. He scratched his head at first, softly and meditatively, but the movement grew momentarily fiercer, which, from old experience, I knew to be an infallible sign that he was making up his mind as to the mode of treatment of the knotty point under discussion; presently, with a prodigious and sweeping scratch that nearly swept his cap off, he said,

"Was that wot you was a cryin' for, Smiff?"

"It was," I replied in all honesty.

"And you wishes it was different?"

"I'd make it different this minnit, Rip, if I only had the chance; you couldn't put a feller up to the chance, could you, Rip?"

"How could I?" asked Ripston, eagerly.

"Well, course I didn't know," I replied, still whispering; "but I was a thinkin' that p'r'aps your guv'ner "——

"That's jest exactly what I was a thinkin' on," interrupted Ripston, emphatically; "and since you was a thinkin' on it too, why I'm blowed if we don't try it at all events. Come on; don't let us stay here any longer, else the guv'ner'll be out of temper 'cos I'm so late; you can tell us all about it goin' along."

And fully resolved to dare all consequences and adopt Ripston's suggestion, I hurried with him along the now nearly deserted lobby towards the street.

Barely, however, had we reached the pavement, when an obstacle of an unexpected nature presented itself. The said obstacle took the shape of Mr. George Hopkins. He was very deliberately leaning against a neighbouring lamp-post, half hidden in the shadow of it, smoking a cigar, and, as soon as we emerged from the gaff, he came up and laid what may have appeared to an observer a kind hand on my jacket collar. I was, however, conscious that it was a tight hold, and one that I should have experienced considerable difficulty in escaping from, had I found the courage to try.

"So, here you are!" he exclaimed, in tones of mild reproach. "You unkind, disobedient boy you, how can you visit such low places when you know that your dear aunt is so averse to it? Will you never grow tired of such low-lived acquaintance? As for you, you young scamp," (this to Ripston,) "if I ever catch you leading this lad astray again I'll put you into the hands of the police. Be off with you."

I was taken so suddenly and completely by surprise that for a few moments I could not say a word, while Ripston, altogether taken in by long George Hopkins's gentlemanly exterior and authoritative language, could only stare at us with wide open eyes and his mouth ajar. At last, however, he mustered courage to say,

"Oh, well, if you ain't a comin' my way, Smiff, I'll bid you good night."

"Good night, Rip, p'raps I shall see you again soon."

And away he went at a trot towards Spitalfields, looking back again and again as though not at all knowing what to make of it.

"Who's that whelp I caught you with?" demanded long George, as still with his hand on my jacket collar he turned me about and we walked in the direction of Keate Street.

"He ain't a whelp, he's an honest boy," I replied, sulkily.

"Then he'd better keep away from a confounded young thief like you are, that's my advice to him," observed long George, with that peculiar laugh of his. "What the d——l have you got to do with honest boys? You mind your own business, which is my business, that's quite enough for you to do."

I felt too full of shame and confusion to make him any reply; he had taken his long fingers from my jacket and left me free to walk by his side; there was nothing to hinder my slipping away and running back after Ripston, and I believe that if I had a distinct and leading thought in my bewildered mind it was to do this; but, somehow or other, I durst not: there was something about Mr. Hopkins's way of speaking and looking that rendered me powerless, and with this lame and insufficient reason the reader must be content, for I can give him no other. Presently he spoke again :

"What was you talking to that honest boy about up in the corner—just before you came out of the gaff?"

"'Bout old times," I answered shortly.

"Old times, hey! Times when you was an honest boy?"

"No; times when he wasn't."

"Oh. He wasn't always an honest boy, eh, Jim? What was his line?"

I was conscious at the time that it was acting mean towards my old friend, Rip, to answer such questions respecting his past career; but, as before observed, I had no such thing as a will of my own with the thief-trainer.

"He used to pick up a livin' at Common Garden," I replied; "so used I; we used to lodge together under the 'Delphi."

"Ah. Where's he lodging now? What's he up to? How does he get a livin', Jim?"

"Works for it."

"I should say he did; hard, too, poor, dirty, little wretch," observed Mr. Hopkins, with his ugly laugh; "what does he earn, Jim?"

"Eighteenpence a-week and his grub."

Mr. Hopkins laughed outright.

"Your friend must have drove a lively trade in Covent Garden to turn it up for eighteenpence a-week, Jim! What does he work at?"

"Carries out coals and taters and that."

"Carries out coals—makes a horse of himself; goes about dirtier than a costermonger from Monday morning till Saturday night for eighteenpence! Do you know how much that is in a whole year, Jim?—all through the winter and all through the summer?"

"It comes to a good bit, don't it?"

"It comes to three pounds eighteen shillings."

"Well, that's a good bit."

"What! for a year's work? Do you know how much there was in that book you made this evening?"

"I didn't have time to count it afore you"——

"Just so. Well, there were seven-and-twenty pounds in that book, Jim. As much as he'd earn in seven years. I wonder what he'd ha' thought, Jim, if you had told him that, without making your hands dirty, you could earn as much in two minutes as he could earn in seven years hulking about at a dirty coal shop! It would have been a shame to tell him; it would have made him so precious miserable, wouldn't it?"

"Perhaps he'd ha' said, if I had told him about it, that he'd rather have the eighteenpence safe than "——

"Than what, Jim?" observed long George, encouragingly, seeing that I hesitated.

"Than—than run any risk," I mustered courage to remark.

"I daresay that's the answer he would have made," returned Mr. Hopkins, "being a canting little sneak that's turned ' good;' I think you've just hit it when you make that guess at his answer. Fox and the grapes, eh, Jim?"

"What grapes, sir?"

"The grapes that the fox said were sour and not fit to eat, because, after six hours' sweating and jumping, he found that he couldn't get at 'em," replied long George, affably. "As I remarked before, Jim, all boys are conceited; and it ain't for me to say anything to make you think more of yourself than you do at present; but, of course, you must understand, that it isn't every muff that could have done even the little that you've done; it wants spirit, pluck—talent, in fact, and that's what you've got in you, and what that poor coal-shop donkey hasn't. Oh yes, he'd preach, I'll be bound, if you was fool enough to listen to him. He has been preaching, or I'm very much mistaken."

"Pr'aps you might call it preaching, sir," I answered; "he told me about his changin' and that."

"And about how much better he felt, eh?"

"Yes."

"And how sorry he'd be to return to his old ways?"

"He said that, too, I recollecks."

"Of course he did. I know all about it, you see; and what did *you* say?"

"Say about what?"

"About me?"

"Nothing at all."

"What?"

We had got into a quiet and secluded quarter of the town by this time, and as Mr. Hopkins uttered this last ejaculation, he suddenly stopped and wheeled round on me, as though my audacity in denying that I had been talking about him, exceeded anything he had ever heard in all his life. You would have thought, from his tone and manner, that he had been in the box with us all the evening—lurking under the seats probably—and that we *had* been talking about him, and he had heard every word. Had I been talking about him —had I mentioned his name even—I should have been brought to immediate confusion and confession, I am sure; but as the reader is aware, I was innocent.

"I never said a single word about you," I answered him, meeting his searching look without fear. He was convinced, but it suited him better to make still a little more profit out of the capital he had so adroitly invested; or rather, by cunningly doubling on my words, to get back capital, profit, and all.

"You never said a word about *me*! By ——, that's the richest thing I've heard for a month! Ha! ha! I should rather suppose you did not. To a strange boy, too—a boy you happen to meet at a gaff! Well, well! we shall understand each other better by and by, I'll be bound."

And he went along musing pleasantly on my preposterous answer, as could be told by his frequent under-breath explosions of mirth. I have my doubts that to the astute even-minded reader all this, as set down, appears absurd, and as showing what a very slow and stupid boy I must have been; but I must remind him that in recording this last conversation between myself and Mr. Hopkins, I have not done him justice! I am not equal to the task. He was too much for me then, and he is too much for me now. There was something about him altogether incomprehensible, and not to be weighed by mundane weights and scales. "Something about him" exactly expresses my meaning. About him, but one couldn't say where particularly; everywhere; something under his perfect control, and ready at hand to season and flavour his every move and utterance! something——

But, there, I shall make my meaning no clearer by weaving fog at this rate, so I will say no more about it.

"What I was going to say," continued Mr. Hopkins presently, "about the young prig turned Methodist we were speaking of, is this. He's a cur; that's the long and the short of it. I don't mean to say he can help it; who can? But he *is* a cur; he tried his hand at a gentleman's life— no work and plenty of money; and, finding it no go, he sneaks back to carrying coals at three-

pence a day. Best place for him. But s'pose he *hadn't* been born a cur? S'pose he'd been born a boy with talent in him, such as you have! How then? Why, he'd have seen all the coal-shops at Jericho before he'd have consented to throw himself away on them; don't it stand to sense that he would?"

"Well, so it does, sir, when you come to look at it in that there kind 'er way."

"What other way can you look at it? It's the only fair way. What good does that boy get by working like a nigger for eighteenpence a-week? Who thanks him? Who thinks of him at all? Nobody says to him, 'What a first-rate sort of chap you are to turn honest and work for threepence a day.' What they say is—'Think yourself jolly lucky we let you come amongst us at all, and mind you toe the mark to half-a-farthing, because we all know about you, and have got our eye on you; and the least slip you make we're down on you, and off you go to quod as an ungrateful scoundrel.' Why, no boy of pluck could buckle under to such a way of living! and, what's more, he'd be a jolly fool if he tried— that's my opinion. Here we are at home."

So saying, Mr. Hopkins opened the street-door of the house in Keate Street with a latch-key; and, going into the parlour, there he found a hot and delicious beefsteak pudding, with a dish of mealy potatoes, and two bright glasses and a jug of beer, all ready and waiting for us.

"Draw up, Jim," observed Mr. Hopkins, helping me to a great plateful of the pudding, with several spoonfuls of the rich brown gravy over my potatoes; "don't spare it; there's plenty more where this comes from. Help yourself to beer."

Such a magnificent repast ensuing so immediately on long George's ingenious arguments was altogether too much for my newly-sprouted resolution to "change," as Ripston had done. As Mr. Hopkins remarked, it *was* all very well for a boy like poor Rip, who had no talent, (I didn't quite know the meaning of the word, but I liked it very much,) for anything better than nailing carrots and gooseberries, to turn coal-boy at threepence a day and his victuals, and very kind in him to advise me to do something of the same kind. Of course, *he* didn't know anything about my having pluck, and spirit, and talent, how should he? I had never told him how that I had been working for two months on my own hands as a regular pickpocket, and how easy it was, and how that any day you might stumble on a bit of luck—such as was contained in that pocket-book—that would admit of your living like a gentleman for months together, and wearing fine clothes, and going to as many plays and gaffs as ever you liked, or he might have altered his tune. After all, where *was* the use of making a dirty drudge of yourself, such as Rip was, just for the sake of being able to say that you are honest— commonly honest, like everybody else is, and nobody saying thanky?

"Have a bit more steak, Jim?"

"Just a little bit more, sir."

"I say! I wonder what that dirty young beggar of a coal-boy has got for his supper, Jim? A lump of dry bread and a bit of mouldy cheese, or something in that line, I'll wager. Ha! ha! I fancy I see the poor devil sitting on a potatoe-bin in the dingy shop, eating his supper! eh, Jim?"

9

"Ha! ha! I fancy *I* sees him!" I replied, like the selfish little traitor that I was.

"When he's finished his supper he'll make himself up a bed under the counter with coal-sacks, and go to sleep along with the rats, like a good boy; eh, Jim?"

"That'll be about it, I reckon," I replied again, laughing as Mr. Hopkins laughed.

"You'll find your bedroom pretty comfortable," continued Mr. Hopkins, after a pause. "You'll find some shirts and that sort of thing in a chest of drawers there. There's a suit or so of clothes, too, just about your size, I should think; if they ain't, I must get you measured; I shouldn't like to see you go in and out of my house in that shabby rig. Did you ever have a watch, Jim?"

I have a watch! Why didn't he ask me if ever I had a saddle-horse, or rode in a carriage with my own flunkies behind?

"No, sir, I never had a watch; I often thought I should like to have one, though."

"Of course, you shall have one; my boys always carry a watch; there's one up-stairs, I think, that will be just the ticket for you. I'll go and fetch it."

And up-stairs he went, and presently came down again with a beautiful silver watch, with a gold face, in his hand, and a long silver chain attached to it.

"I'll set it right by mine, and then you won't have to do anything else but wind it up when it wants it. You know how to wind up a watch, I suppose, Jim?"

Of course I did not, and I told him so; so in the kindest way he showed me how, and gave me the key, and, throwing the chain over my head, told me to put my watch in my pocket, which I did: the feel of it there, and the sight of the magnificent silver chain drooping from my waistcoat pocket, so widened the gulf between me and poor old Rip the threepenny coal-boy, that I could not think of him without a feeling of pity.

After supper, Mr. Hopkins took a glass of grog and a cigar, reclining at his ease on the sofa, and leaving me sitting by the fire, feeling very much more at *my* ease than I should have thought possible an hour ago.

"What did you see at the gaff, Jim? Anything very cutting?" he inquired.

"It was rather that way, sir," I answered.

He laughed a sneering bit of a laugh. "Tell us about it, Jim," said he.

Very readily I began. My description of the first step he allowed to pass with no further commentary than was expressed in a grunt of disgust.

The particulars of the second step he listened to with more attention, and when I told him all about it, said he:

"That's it. That's just the old play-acting rubbish over again; enough to make a cat sick. He stayed sprawling at home, the lazy hound, taking the last bit of bread from the old woman, too good to do anything naughty until she starves and dies, and when it's too late he takes to prigging! It would have been a —— sight more to his credit if he had stirred himself a bit earlier. So he would if it was real instead of play-acting: any fool must see that. Go on."

I related step the third.

"That's a rich touch," laughed he; "he puts himself to the trouble to make a purse, and he brings it in and throws it down for anybody to pick up to pay for a pot of beer! His next 'step' ought to have been to St. Luke's in a strait waistcoat. Go on, Jim."

So I went on, and at every "step" he had some derisive comment to make. He laughed and made a good joke about the "ringlet;" he pointed out clearly enough the impossibility of his getting a pardon in the manner described; he sneered at the ghost and made fun of her placard; in fact, after his peculiar manner, he turned the entire drama inside out as it were, and tore it into such ridiculous shreds that I became altogether astonished that I could ever have seen anything the least affecting in it, and I would no more have confessed to Mr. Hopkins that it had made me cry, than I would have explained to him my fancied discovery of similitude in some of the features of the drama with my own private and domestic experience. Indeed, for fear that he should have suspected how much the representation of "The Seven Steps to Tyburn" had worked on my disturbed conscience, I affected a keener appreciation and relish for his humorous criticism than I felt, and laughed longer and louder even than he did. We were capital friends. Presently, however, Long George referred to his watch.

"Hallo! we've sat it out prettily! Why, it's twelve o'clock! There's one thing, we don't rise very early in this establishment. Toddle off to bed, Jim, never mind about leaving me in the dark. Take the candle and call out when you're in bed, and I'll come and fetch it. Your room is the back one a'top of the stairs.

So, bidding him good-night in tones that must have convinced him how much my opinion of him had improved since we came home to supper, and how entirely I was now disposed to devote myself to his service, I took the candle as directed and made my way to the bedroom he had directed me to. He had informed me that I should find it pretty comfortable; but in my eyes it was many, many degrees beyond that. It was beautiful. I had never in my life seen such a bedroom. The bedstead in it was of the tent pattern, and hung about with chintz curtains that half-shut in the snowy bed, making it snug and downy-looking as a bird's nest. There were dimity hangings to the window, a warm carpet on the floor, a washstand and a lovely white towel hanging close by, a chest of drawers, and a looking-glass a'top of it. I put my head in at the door bold enough; but when I saw the interior I drew back in amazement, and looked out to make quite sure that this really *was* the only back room a'top of the stairs. There was no mistake about it, however; so, afraid almost to breathe too hard in such a paradise, I ventured in, pulling my boots off instantly, out of respect for the spotless red and green carpet. Only that I was aware that Mr. Hopkins was left in the dark in the parlour, there was so much to investigate in that wonderful room that I should have possibly spent a quarter of an hour very agreeably before getting into bed; as it was, however, I made haste to undress, and when the process was completed I went to the door to call out to that effect.

"Will you come and fetch the candle, please?"

Nobody answered; so I put my head out to

call a little louder. I could make out two voices raised to a high pitch, so high, indeed, that, although the parlour door was shut, the subject of the conversation in progress between Long George and the young woman who had opened the door for us in the early part of the evening, and who had treated me so unceremoniously, could be made out with tolerable distinctness.

"—— I'm to ask you, then, I suppose, when I'm to go out and when I'm to come home! it's likely, ain't it ? I'm the right sort."

"You're a —— bad sort, George! By G—d, I'll find out how bad. I'll follow you, if you kill me."

"Don't I tell you it's business ?"

"It's always business; the night before last, and again to-night, business! It's a lie, George; you know it's a lie."

"It's good enough for a —— like you, if it is a lie, if it comes to that; I'm going, that's enough."

There was a pause in the quarrel now.

"Will you fetch the light, please ?" I called once more, loud enough for them to hear, and almost before I could hop into bed up came Long George; and, without a word, carried the candle away. Almost immediately afterwards I heard the street-door bang.

There was nothing much to trouble me in the fag-end of the altercation I had heard between Mr. and Mrs. Hopkins. He wanted to go out, and she wanted him to stay at home, and he had gone out; that seemed to be all about it, and it was probably the novelty of my situation, rather than thinking about the squabble, that kept me from going to sleep as quickly as probably I otherwise should; at all events, I *did* lie awake for a quarter of an hour, I daresay, and was then comfortably dropping off to sleep when a rap at the bedroom door disturbed me.

"Who's there ?" I asked.

"Get up and dress yourself, and come down-stairs, my boy; I want to speak to you."

It was the young woman that spoke, and opened the door just wide enough to set a lighted candle within the room. Without another word she went down-stairs.

CHAPTER XXXVI.

IN WHICH, MOVED BY SPITE, MRS. LONG GEORGE MAKES CERTAIN DAMAGING REVELATIONS TO ME CONCERNING MY MASTER.

It was not for me to dispute Mrs. Hopkins's authority in her own house, or to question her right to order me out of bed if she chose to do so; since Mr. Hopkins was my master his wife must be my mistress, so although much puzzled and not a little alarmed as to what this singular proceeding on the part of Mrs. H. might portend, I simply replied, " Yes 'm " to her command, and prepared immediately to obey it. I was for dressing myself fully, boots and all, as she must have heard, for she called out from the foot of the stairs—

"Never mind your boots, leave them up there."

It raised quite a load from my mind to hear her say this; as the reader is aware she had not shown herself at all pleased to receive me as a lodger, and while I was dressing it occurred to me that she might possibly intend to turn me out to spite Long George. She couldn't very well turn me out without my boots.

When I got down stairs, I found her sitting in the parlour all alone, looking very pale, and with her eyes puffy and red as though she had not long ago been crying. She was standing with her face towards the fire-place (the fire had gone out) as I entered the doorway, but I could see her in the glass over the mantel-shelf.

"Come in, can't you ?" said she sharply, as I hesitated at the threshold; " come inside and shut the door."

Feeling each moment more perplexed and frightened, I did as she told me.

"Come here," said she, " I've barely seen you yet: set the candle on the table and let me have a look at you."

I don't know what she thought of me, but as she stood looking me in the face so earnestly with her red and swollen eyes my decided opinion was that she was intoxicated. I was altogether mistaken, however, as the reader will presently see.

"Sit down," said she, proceeding to question me—her scrutiny proving satisfactory I suppose —" Now what sort of boy are you ?"

"How d' yer mean what sort of boy, mum ?"

"Are you a downright bad 'un, born to bad, bad to the bone like all the other young scoundrels he has brought here ?"

She looked at me very hard as she asked me, and I could feel the colour mounting to my forehead. How did she want me to answer? The sort of boy I was had induced Mr. Hopkins to take me in hand and make me his lodger; still, it was not because I was a *good* boy I was very well aware.

"I don't know about a downright bad 'un, mum," I answered, " I hope I ain't quite that: I'm good at some things and bad at other things I s'pose. You ask Mr. Hopkins, he'll tell you what I'm good at."

"How long have you been a thief ?"

"Oh, a good many weeks."

"Only weeks! How often have you been in prison ?"

"Never."

"Never! Have you got a mother ?"

"No. Used to have one, but she died when I was ever so little."

"A father ?"

"I'd 'n know; he's dead, too, for all I knows. It don't make much odds to me whether he is or no."

"He's a thief I suppose. Always in prison almost, eh ?"

"What, my father! who se's so ? It wouldn't be good for 'em if he heard 'em sayin' it. Why, he's a reg'ler honest cove my father is." And her unjust insinuations against my father's character for a moment lent me courage to look her in the face in a way that made her smile.

"Then, how came you to turn thief ?" she asked. " How came you to take up with George ? Do you like him ?"

"Yes, very much," I promptly replied; " I think he's a nice sort of a genelman."

"Yes! he *is* a nice sort of a gentleman," observed Mrs. Hopkins, with a bitter little laugh.

"Shall I tell you what he is ? He's the devil in man's shape, if one ever lived; he's a spider, curse him, who gets you into his web before you know it, and sucks your blood to the last drop: then you're flung off."

"Sucks *my* blood, ma'am ?" Mrs. Hopkins spoke with a vehemence that alarmed and astonished me, even more than her expressions of hatred and contempt for Long George.

"Anybody's blood, he lives on it, the vampire," she replied, her swollen eyes flashing vindictively; "of course, he'll suck your blood: what do you think you are brought here for ?"

If she didn't know what I was brought there for perhaps it wouldn't please Long George if I told her; if she did know she didn't want telling. Most likely after all she was acting in this manner to set me against Long George, with whom, as I knew, she had had a row; and if I took her part, come to-morrow she'd most likely tell him all that I had said against him ! My experience of this phase of human weakness as developed in Mrs. Burke, was a sufficient safeguard to defend me from such a trap. Partly on these grounds, and partly that Mrs. Hopkins's demeanour (especially as each moment I grew more and more convinced that she was *not* tipsy) began to frighten me, I edged towards the door and laid my hand on the latch so as to be in a position to bolt upstairs at a moment's warning, and lock myself in my bedroom if necessary.

"Oh, it's all right, mum," I observed, in as conciliatory a tone as I could assume, "if it ain't, we'll see about it in the mornin'.".

She looked at me for a few seconds with a pitying look that was scarcely less embarrassing than her fury. "Please God you say that because you don't know, and not because you don't care," said she. "All right, is it ? Is it all right to be shut up in prison for months—years, perhaps; to be branded with a name that will never wear off, and will be a curse and disgrace to you and all who know you as long as you live ? Is *that* all right ? Supposing that you have no mother or father that cares for you, is there no one who was ever kind to you, and whom you would think of when you were shut up in prison —a felon ?"

Was there anyone ? Ay, there was indeed; there was one especially, and to that one she seemed particularly to point, (which, after all, I suppose was not extraordinary, considering that with the exception of Ripston there was none other)—to Mrs. Winkship ! Decidedly, I should *not* like that dear, kind old soul to know that I was a felon shut up in prison. I had only to reflect for an instant on that memorable night when she and Martha brought me in out of the streets and fed me, and clothed me, and did her best to set me in the right way, to feel that I should have some one to think a great deal about if ever so terrible a calamity as that which Mrs. Hopkins hinted at befell me. Still, there was Long George's promise that, if he could avoid it, it never should befall me.

"I shouldn't be *sure* to shut up in prison," I answered, ; t'an't likely I'd—I'd go on if I was sure."

"But you *are* sure—*certain*, as you stand there alive."

"I don't see why, mum; I've kept out on it

more'n eight weeks, and that wirrout anbody to help me."

I was conscious of fluttering for a moment c t of the dumps into which her strange conver tion had cast me, as I made this last observatic It was the boy of "talent" who spoke.

"You've got some one to help you now, God help you," replied she, shaking her head; "he'll help you as he has helped seven boys before you, since I've known him, the coward; he'll help you to the hulks. It's part of his plan to do it, I tell you. He's got that in view from the very first hour you start working for him. What have I heard him say a hundred times ? 'Never take up with a fresh hand till you've shopped your scarecrow.' The scarecrow is the boy who has served him until he is well-known to the police, and is so closely watched that he may as well stay at home as go out. Now, perhaps, you understand."

It was impossible to misunderstand.

"He told me different to that," said I, with a sensation of quaking at the ugly picture of Mr. George Hopkins as the woman drew it; "he told me that he could get people to swear to anything if he paid 'em for it, and that he'd get me out of a mess when I got into one."

"He told you true about the paying and swearing, curse him; there's no doubt of that," replied she bitterly. "Well I know it; well my poor Ted, ten thousand miles away, knows it. I wish I was dead. If I could kill him by wishing, he'd die this minute wherever he is, if they hung me for it to-morrow. Lord send I *could* kill him where he is now ! I'd give ten lives if I had 'em to be able to do it."

The pitying look her face had worn during the last few minutes faded as she gave utterance to these wicked wishes, and her swollen eyes flashed as before, and I could hear her teeth grate as she ground one foot against the floor as though in imagination crushing and killing some crawling thing hateful and abominable.

"Was Ted one of the seven boys, mum ?"

"No: my husband," she answered abruptly; "but there, it ain't for me to speak of him now; least of all to a child such as you are. Never mind why I hate the other one, the traitor, so that you get good out of it. I durst not have said a quarter as much to the last boy, nor any other that has lived here since he set me hating him, but I think I may trust you. May I ? You may tell him to-morrow all I have told you to-night, and you will have the pleasure of hearing him beat me—punch me with his fists and kick me, the coward, until I can neither stand nor speak—as he has done fifty times before. You may tell him if you like: I don't much care if you do, I'm so sick of it all; so heartily sick."

And she sank down on to a chair, and laying her face flat on her hands on the table, began to cry and sob in a way that brought tears to my eyes, little ruffian though I was.

"Don't you fear, mum; *I* won't tell him. I ain't the sort of boy to get anybody into a row what spoke up for my good."

"I do speak for your good," answered she, raising her tearful face from the table; "I don't speak it out of goodness, for there is none left in me, Lord help me; but may I never live to see daylight if all I have told you is not true, every word, every letter of it."

"So I b'lieve, mum; I can tell that from your ways of sayin' on it; but, look here, mum, what's a cove to do?"

"Go back to bed and think what you had better do," replied she, "I know nothing more about you than what you have told me; and, indeed, I don't want to know. You're awfully young to be a thief; go to bed and think a bit about it, think about where you may go and what you may do if you run away from this."

"But if I was to run away, don't you think he'd run arter me, mum? He said as much."

"Then you must think of a place to run to where he *dare* not follow you. Don't say any more. Go back to bed and think about it; you'll do better there than talking with me. Good night."

And so I was dismissed, and retired once more to bed in as pretty a state of bewilderment as can be imagined. It was very well for Mrs. Hopkins (or whatever else her name might be; it was clearly *not* Mrs. Hopkins, however) to say "Go to bed and think." How could I think with anything like a purpose? How could my thoughts be other than cross-grained, and at variance, after such an evening of blowing hot and then cold, and then hot again? From what point could I start for a good steady "think?" From the time of my meeting with Long George—from the time of my falling in with Rip—from my reconciliation with the thief-trainer? Should I go no farther back than my extraordinary conversation with his housekeeper, from which I had just returned with my heart nearly melted? It was all of no use; all was jumble and confusion.

Through all, however, stood out the plain conviction that the woman down-stairs had told me the truth to the best of her knowledge. I had not the least doubt that Long George Hopkins was just as black as his housekeeper had painted him; and that, if I stayed in his service, my fate would be just what she said it would be. What served to convince me of this more than anything else, more than her extravagant denunciations of him as a spider, and a vampire, and a bloodsucker, was her betrayal of his favourite and oft-repeated maxim—" Never take up with a fresh hand till you've shopped your scarecrow." They were the words of his own mouth, without doubt. I knew the meaning of the slang term "shopped" well enough. I had heard it under the dark arches any number of times in the course of the conversations that took place among the thieves lodging there, while relating the misfortunes of their brethren. What a "scarecrow" was the woman had sufficiently explained. I could think enough of all this, and could arrive at the conclusion that, after being warned, I should be nothing but a fool to remain at Keate Street. I would run away—but where? To somewhere where he *dare* not follow me. Where was that? Here I stuck; and, in order to shirk the difficulty, at least for the present, I encouraged a growing inclination to go to sleep. "I will have some more talk with her about it to-morrow, and I've no doubt that she will put me in the way of managing how to get away all right," thought I; and that was the last of anything I thought of that night.

It was eight o'clock by the splendid watch Mr.

Hopkins had presented me with, before I woke next morning, having slept through the night perfectly tranquil and undisturbed by dreams. I had not heard Mr. Hopkins come home, but it was the creaking of his boots going downstairs that woke me, so that it was clear that he *had* come home. He came out of the front room that adjoined mine, which, it seemed, was their bedroom. He went down in a hurry, without calling me as I expected he would, and walked quickly along the passage, and went out, shutting the door after him; and while I lay, still wondering whether I should get up just yet, I heard the street-door open again, and the sound of another pair of boots besides Long George's. Both men came up the stairs and went into the front room, and shortly afterwards Long George came into my room.

"Now, Jim, get up," said he; "you'll have to be housemaid and cook and the devil knows what to-day, I reckon; the missus is ill."

"Not very ill, sir, is she?" I asked, with a sudden and forcible remembrance of her strangely excited face last night.

"Ill enough to make me fetch the doctor in a hurry; she's got a fever, or going to have one, or something or the other, so he says; there's always some infernal bother or other."

CHAPTER XXXVII.

THE LAST CHAPTER, AND NOT A PARTICULARLY PLEASANT CHAPTER TO WRITE, INASMUCH AS IT INVOLVES THE STORY OF MY TREACHERY TOWARDS LONG GEORGE HOPKINS. THE FALL OF THE CURTAIN.

THE "fever or something," that attacked Long George Hopkins's housekeeper turned out to be no slight matter; it kept her a prisoner in her room for full three weeks.

During all this time I never once set eyes on her. An old woman of the neighbourhood came to wait on her, and do the housework and the cooking, at both of which domestic employments I assisted to the best of my ability. It was all I had to do. As for the trade my master had engaged to teach me, I was no wiser concerning it at the expiration of the three weeks, than when I first crossed his threshold; on the contrary, being an occupation at which one's hand very speedily gets out for want of practice, it is likely that I was a more indifferent sort of thief than on the evening when I picked my last pocket. The fact was, my master was never at home, the fever drove him away almost entirely. He took his meals with me in the parlour—with the window open, and the place smelling of vinegar like a pickling warehouse—and then he walked off and was seen no more all day, and, in general, through part of the night, it being my duty to sit up until he came home. He had a bed made up on the sofa in the parlour, and there he slept, and so on day after day.

I had nothing to complain of. My meals were regular and first-rate. I could always have a shilling by asking for it, and was allowed to go out of evenings from six or seven till ten. So far from encouraging me in dishonest courses, Long George never went out in the morning with out warning me against them. "Don't you go making yourself busy, you know," he would say, and I knew perfectly well what he meant; "and don't go to low and blackguardly places to amuse yourself; go to the theatre,—to the pit, mind, not to the gallery, or to some respectable concert-room; if you ain't got enough money, say so; I'd rather give you a pound than you should go helping yourself." So that, although there was never a day passed that I did not think over the advice Mr. Hopkins's housekeeper had given me, to have have run away under such circumstances appeared to me to be in the last degree foolish.

Besides, although I never saw the sick housekeeper, I frequently heard from her through the old woman that nursed her, and was of service to her in the way of going errands, and many other ways, and it would have been nothing short of ungrateful to have run away from *her*.

At the expiration of three weeks (a fortnight out of which Long George had never once seen his sick housekeeper; nor even, as far as my knowledge went, asked after her) she came downstairs, looking woefully thin and pale, and scarcely to be recognized on account of all her long hair having been shorn off, and wearing a cap. I was quite astonished to see how plain she had grown; as was Mr. Hopkins, to judge from the remark he made when, for the first time, he came in and found her sitting in the easy-chair, with a pillow behind her, by the fire.

"Well! you *do* look a sight! I'd ha' lived and died upstairs if I'd a been you, rather than show with such a figure-head as *that!*"

"I know you'd rather I'd died, but I'm going to live, my dear," she replied. "I wish my face was five times as ugly, for the sake of you and your handsome friends."

"I'd like to see a face five times as ugly as yours," laughed Mr. Hopkins; "it 'ud be worth something by way of a curiosity. The sooner you take it out of my house the better, that's all I know about it."

"You will have to turn it out to get rid of it, my dear," answered she, with a laugh as ugly as his own.

It was quite plain that the sick housekeeper's feelings towards Mr. Hopkins had not improved since the night when she had let me into the secret concerning them, and it was equally plain that there was not an atom of love lost on the gentleman's part.

Under such circumstances I was not a little surprised on coming home early the very next evening to find her sitting with Mr. Hopkins and two male friends of his in the parlour, chatting and laughing in the most cheerful way, and seemingly op the best of terms with him. The meeting, however, was rather of a business than a convivial character; for, after I had been in the room a few moments, and Mr. Hopkins had called the attention of his friends to me by a significant wink, and they had "taken my measure," as the saying is, by a few rapid glances, I was told that I might either go out again for an hour, or go to bed at once. Feeling tired, I adopted the latter suggestion.

How long I had been asleep I don't know; but I was awoke by a hand on my shoulder and a voice calling my name.

"Are you awake, Jim?"

It was the housekeeper.

"Yes'm."

"Have you thought over what we talked about the night before I was taken ill?"

"I've thought about it plenty of times, mum."

"And have you made up your mind to take my advice?"

"Yes'm; but I don't know where to run away to; that's the worst on it."

"You must settle that quick, then. If you don't go away to-morrow, you'll be sorry as long as you live. You saw the two men, Twiner and Johnny Armitage, down-stairs talking with him when you came in?"

"Yes, mum; I saw 'em. I saw 'em both look hard at me when master winked at 'm."

"Did you? I'm glad that you did. There's a job planned; a biggish job, and there's a part for you cut out in it."

"What sort of a job is it, mum?"

"A burglary. Hush; don't ask any more questions; it comes off to-morrow night or the night after; he'll tell you about it in the morning, I daresay. At Fulham the job is—Prescot House—Prescot House, Fulham. But he'll tell you, no doubt. You take my advice, and be off as soon as you can to-morrow—to somewhere, you know, as I told you before, where he daren't follow you, *and tell them all about it*—all, except that I had even so much as a single word in sending you away. It's for your good I interfere; you know *that*, don't you? And you won't even breathe my name at—at the safe quarters, you'll find your way to, will you?"

She laid her hand very earnestly (it was in the dark) on my face as she asked this last question.

"There's no 'casion for you to be afraid of that, ma'am," I answered.

"I am not afraid of it; you are too good a boy to bring hurt to any one who runs a risk for your good, I'm sure. Good-night. I must go down again; they have only gone as far as the public-house."

And, patting my cheek with her hot hand, she stole out of the room. It had come at last, then, it seemed. It was very odd that I should be required to engage in a job of so much importance as a burglary without any of that useful training Mr. Hopkins had promised me; but, no doubt, he had his reasons for the step. Mrs. Hopkins, too, had *her* reasons—reasons that, while they perplexed me very much, I couldn't, bother my head how I might, get anything like a satisfactory clue to. Why did she want to inform me of as many of the details of the projected burglary as she had? If it was her simple intention to give me warning that I might by going away avoid plunging deeper into crime, why had she so carefully enunciated the names of Mr. Hopkins's pals? Why was she so particular in impressing on me the place at which the burglary was to be perpetrated? It was a queer business altogether; and, lying awake through half the night reviewing it thoroughly, it most undoubtedly appeared to be my best plan to give such dangerous company the slip at the very earliest opportunity. This resolution I arrived at before I closed my eyes, as well as at another—that when I ran away next day I would go straight to Spitalfields, find out Ripston, and take his advice as to what I had best do next. There were only two persons to whom I could apply for advice in my extremity —to Mrs. Winkship and Ripston—and for some time I was undecided which it should be; but when I came to reflect on the danger of encountering my father—especially if the authorities had been troubling him respecting the resurrectionist business—and again on the view Mrs. Winkship might possibly have been led to take respecting my behaviour towards Mr. Belcher, her son-in-law, I at once made up my mind.

The housekeeper was wrong in her surmise that Long George would tell me "all about it" in the morning. All he said was, as he dressed himself to go out after breakfast,

"Don't you go driving about to-day, and making yourself as tired as a dog before night, because I shall want you."

"What for, sir?" I asked, with affected innocence.

"What the —— is that to do with you? You 'll see when the time comes," was Mr. Hopkins's answer.

A little time after he called me from the little wash-house at the end of the passage. There was a small window in the wash-house—just a single square of glass framed and hinged opening into the kitchen; he was standing by this little window.

"Show me how neatly you can get through a hole of this size," was his strange request.

There was bare room for my shoulders; but I contrived to squeeze through with tolerable ease, and jumped down on the other side.

"Don't you think you could make a little more noise in doing it?" asked he, sarcastically.

I got through it again; this time as quietly as possible.

"That 's better," said he; "try again—come down on your toes."

I tried again, and still again; twenty times at least.

"That 'll do better," he remarked; "let 's see, what sort of boots do you wear, Jim?"

"Lace-ups, sir."

"Then *they* won't do. You must have a pair of shoes—something that you can kick off and put on easy. You may as well go and buy yourself a pair at once. Go out into Bishopsgate Street for 'em."

He gave me half-a-sovereign, and away I went. He was still in the wash-house, and I had to pass the parlour door on my way out. The housekeeper was there, and as I passed and glanced in she nodded her head and made "now be off" with her lips too plainly to be misunderstood, and I nodded back again.

It was plain that she had told me the truth. Mr. Hopkins had told me nothing of the nature of the job he wanted me to assist him in by and by, nor was there any necessity that he should; setting his behaviour by the side of what she had told me last night made it all clear enough. My share in the burglary was to get through a window, and I wanted the shoes so that I might slip them off without waste of time, and in order to go about the job the quieter! I was a little incredulous when the housekeeper had applied the harsh word "felony" to simple pocket-picking; but there could be no mistake about burglary being felony—felony for which the certain punishment was transportation. The housekeeper was right. I *should* be lost for life unless I got out of the mess as quickly as possible; and

quite determined to do so, I made all haste in the direction of Spitalfields.

Of course, I had not seen Ripston since that remarkable night at the gaff, and all that I knew of his address was that it was "somewhere nigh the church." Without doubt, he meant the old parish church; and, though there were a good many streets thereabout, there could not be a great number of coal and potato shops. When I found the one where Ripston worked, I would go boldly in, ask for him, and tell him all about it.

So I comforted myself; but I found the task much more difficult than I had anticipated. There were, after all, a very great number of little and big coal and potato shops in the vicinity of the church, and I asked at least half-a-dozen of these —asking if "Ripston" worked there—without any success. I began to despair. Perhaps he didn't go by the name of Ripston now. Perhaps he had left his situation and gone quite out of the neighbourhood. When just as I had applied at my seventh greengrocery store, and been snapped up very short indeed by the person that kept it, and who evidently had a suspicion that I was making game of her, just as I turned out of the shop once more disappointed, and was looking up and down wondering which way I should go, there I spied Ripston with half-a-hundred of coal on his shoulder, and a bunch of greens in a basket on his other arm, lumbering along on the other side of the path, but not so bowed down by the great weight but that he could whistle "Jim Crow." When I, skipping across the road, clapped him on the back and called on him by name, so much was he startled that there would have been coals to pick up had I not assisted him in saving the toppling sack.

Scarcely giving him time to recover his breath, there and then, with the coal-sack still on his shoulder, I poured into his amazed ears the story of my connexion with Long George Hopkins, and how I had run away and why.

"Here, ketch hold!" exclaimed he, excitedly, and before I had quite finished my narrative, at the same time thrusting into my arms the basket of greens, "carry that, and we shall get along all the quicker. It's on'y round the corner. I told my guv'ner all about what you told me at the gaff, and about the cove wot said he was your uncle as met me comin' out, and he ses, ses he, the werry next time you sees him, if he ain't too far gone, ses he, you bring him along to me; come on."

And, despite his half-hundred weight of ballast, Ripston, in his eagerness to introduce me to his master, stepped out at such a rate that I, much lighter, freighted with the greens, could hardly keep pace with him.

"Here he is, sir!" exclaimed Rip, turning into a thriving-looking green-grocer's shop and addressing a little bald-headed man busy at the potato-bin, "this is the one I was a speakin' on, sir; this is Smiff; he ain't gone a bit furder, sir, than when I last seed him, if you wouldn't mind talkin' to him."

The little bald-headed man adjusted his spectacles, and deliberately surveyed me. "So this is the lad, is it?" said he. Then he went to the door of the shop-parlour and called "Sarah!" who came up from somewhere below. She was very little younger than he was, and she had white hair in tidy little plaits, just showing under the frill of her round cap. He spoke a few words to her; and then, turning to me, said, "Go in there, my boy; I'll speak to you when I've finished my job."

But I didn't have to wait to be talked to till that time. The green-grocer's wife began to question me in such a soft, motherly way that I was speedily in deep conversation with her. In the midst of it, she went to the door and called her husband.

"Come in here, Tibbit," said she; "of all the strange stories I ever heard, this bangs everything."

So old Mr. Tibbit came in, and I told *him* the story. Its effect on him was no less astonishing than on his wife. As I approached the end of it, he got up from his chair; and, taking a coat from a peg behind the door, put it on, and pulled off his blue apron, and all the while I narrated the particulars of Long George Hopkins's singular behaviour that, morning—showing him the half-sovereign I was to buy the light shoes with—he was fidgeting from one leg to the other and brushing his beaver hat with the cuff of his coat.

"What's to be done, father?" asked Mrs. Tibbit; "where are you going? what are you going to do?"

"There's only one thing to do that I see, my dear," replied the old greengrocer in a decided tone; "I shall take the lad round to the police-station at once; it's much more their business than mine. You'll come, boy, won't you?"

"What for, sir?" I inquired, tremendously alarmed at the unexpected turn affairs had taken. My last business with the Ilford constabulary had not ended so satisfactorily as to make me anxious for a fresh introduction to the police.

"To prevent this burglary. That's the first thing to be seen to, whatever we do afterwards. Don't *you* be alarmed, my lad; the police will put Mr. Long Hopkins where he can't hurt you, never fear. Come along."

I would much rather not have gone; but there was no help for it, and in five minutes afterwards I was face to face with a police-inspector. Once more I told the story; but the effect of it on my two previous listeners was flat and dull compared with this one. He wasn't still an instant when once his interest warmed, which it did as soon as I mentioned the names of Twiner and Johnny Armitage. He made frequent signs by holding up his forefinger for me to stop for a moment while he dashed down a hurried note with his quill-pen; he brushed up his stubbly hair fiercely on each side with both his hands; he took tremendous pinches of snuff with startling rapidity, and nodded and winked, and clicked his finger and thumb as pleasantly excited as a man who has had a swinging and unexpected legacy left to him. When I ceased talking he looked towards me with startling abruptness.

"That's all? There's nothing behind? Out with it, if there is; you know, we're sure to find it out."

"That's all, sir."

"Now, don't say that, or I shan't believe a word of it," observed the inspector, glaring at me savagely; "what about the woman? You hav'n't told us half of what you know about her—not a quarter; out with it. She told you not to mention her name in the business, I know, but you mustn't mind that, *she'll* be all right. Now, then, what made her split on George?"

With all sincerity I assured Mr. Inspector that I couldn't tell, but proceeding to cross-examine me in his peculiar manner, he found out in a very few minutes, and to his perfect satisfaction.

"The old story you see, Mr. Tibbit," said he, rubbing his hands gleefully. "Bless the women! I don't know how *we* should get on without 'em. Not that he's to be pitied; he's earned his leg irons years ago. How he's kept out of 'em is one of *the* wonders. We'll have another cast for him now, at all events, and land him, too, if bait and tackle will do it."

The inspector took one or two hurried turns up and down the room, and then suddenly turning to me, inquired what time it was when I came away from Keate Street.

It was ten minutes to ten, for when I looked into the parlour where Mrs. Hopkins was making signs I noticed the time by the clock that stood on the mantel-shelf.

"Now it's five minutes to eleven," remarked the inspector, consulting his watch. The watch was of the sort known as a "hunter," and with his chin in one hand, and the timekeeper in the other, he regarded five minutes to eleven with a profound air, until it must have abated at least forty seconds of that time. Then he suddenly closed the case of the hunter with an emphatic click and replaced it in his fob, while his face wore the expression of a man who has quite made his mind up.

"He told you to go into Bishopsgate for the shoes, didn't you say?" asked he. "Did he mention any shop in particular?"

"No, sir."

He went to the door and called in a private-clothes man.

"Take off one of your boots, my lad," said he. "Jones," (this to the constable,) "take this boot and this half-sovereign and buy a pair of light shoes the same size—light thin-sole shoes, with a single tie in front. Go to the first shop, and be quick about it. As you go past Martingale's livery yard, tell them to send some light fast-going trap round here in half an hour."

I couldn't make it all out. What was the light-going trap for? Why had the inspector sent for the shoes? If I was not going back to Keate Street any more I didn't want the shoes; it seemed like throwing a good half-sovereign into the gutter.

"You've no 'casion to send for the shoes, sir," I ventured to remark, "I don't want 'em; my boots are werry good as yet."

The inspector whispered to Mr. Tibbit, who left the room; and then he beckoned me towards him in a very kind and confidential manner.

"You are a sensible lad," said he; "another little step the other way and it would have been all over with you. Thank your lucky stars you stepped *this* way. It will be the making of you. If you'll only help us to finish this little bit of business neatly I give you my word that you shall be set up respectably for life. You want to get out of your present life and be made respectable, don't you?"

"That's what made me run away, sir," I replied; "but I don't see how I can do more'n I've done."

"But I do," observed the inspector, affably;

"I see how you can help us exactly how we want helping. You can do so by making as much haste back to Keate Street, when the man comes back with your shoes as you possibly can."

"Back to Keate Street! back to Long George!"

"Back to Long George, just as though nothing had happened; it is impossible for him to know that anything *has* happened, you know."

"But what for, sir? What must I go back for?" I inquired, growing more and more alarmed at the depth to which the foot I had put into it, as the saying is, was sinking.

"Because we want this burglary to come off just as it would if you hadn't found the pluck and sense to blow on it," answered the inspector, positively winking at me in his excess of professional enthusiasm. "You ain't a fool. You are wide awake enough to see what I want, and how I should like to have it brought about, I'm sure."

"There's no danger in it, you know; not the least in the world," continued Mr. Inspector, seeing that I *did* understand what he wanted, but dreaded to entertain it. "Why, my dear fellow, where can the danger be? If you had gone with the burglars in the regular way, there might have been danger; no doubt, there *would* have been a pretty good amount of it; but now you don't go to break the law, but to assist it, and don't you be afraid but that the law will protect *you*. Take my word that from this time until the job's over you won't be lost sight of by the police for so long as a single minute."

The inspector made this latter remark with peculiar emphasis, so as I suppose that I might quite understand that if I meditated playing the law a trick I should pretty soon find myself in the wrong box.

"But," said I, "if I go back, what will Mrs. Hopkins say?"

"What odds what she says? All you've got to answer is that you have altered your mind, and don't mean to run away; say that and no more, and stick to it. *She'll* understand. She's got her teeth into him, and she'll hold on like a badger, no fear of that."

The latter part of this observation was spoken rather to himself than me by the inspector, as he once more dashed down a note in his memorandum-book. Just at that moment in came the policeman with the new shoes.

"Just try 'em on; ah! they'll do: now be off, or he'll begin to wonder what keeps you. Stop a moment, though," and he laid his hand on my shoulder, "just one word with you,—may I trust you?"

He fixed his twinkling gray eyes on mine as he asked.

"Yes, sir; if you think it's all right and it'll be the better for me, and you'll look arter me, you *may* trust me. I'll do just what you've tell-ed me."

"Then that's enough. All you've got to do is to go back, and if the woman asks you, tell her you've altered your mind. One word· more. Unless I'm much mistaken you'll find yourself being put through a small window-hole by and by. Don't be afraid—when they put you through, you'll find me there inside and waiting for you. It'll be in the dark, no doubt, but you'll know it's me by my pulling your hair so—now be off."

It would be quite useless my attempting to describe my sensations as I left the police-station and hurried back to Keate Street. I could think on nothing distinctly; through all, however, I preserved a dogged resolution to keep my word with the inspector, who had given me his promise—and the promise of an inspector of police was no slight matter—that I should be set up respectably for life if I did so. I was not at that time aware of the extent of the tremendous risk I was running, or it is very likely that I should have treated the Whitechapel police with no more respect than I had treated those of Ilford.

When I got back to Keate Street, Long George was gone out, and his housekeeper opened the door to me. I had thought that she would have evinced considerable surprise at seeing me return; but, after looking at me very hard she exclaimed lightly, very lightly indeed as it occurred to me when I afterwards thought about it:

"Back again, then, Jim?"

"Yes'm; I've altered my mind."

"That's right," said she, quite cheerfully; "I was looking for you to come back again."

"Didn't you want me to go away then, mum? What made you say you wanted me to if you didn't?"

"Of course I wanted you to come back if you saw fit to alter your mind," replied she, laughing in an odd sort of way that made me feel extremely uncomfortable.

A few minutes afterwards she suddenly asked me:

"What was the name of that place at Fulham I told you of last night, Jim?"

"Prescot House," I answered, readily. I had repeated it too frequently that morning not to have it at the tip of my tongue when called for.

"Yes. And the names of the two men who join George in the job?"

"Twiner and Johnny Armitage."

"That's the ticket," she observed once more, laughing her odd laugh; "*you're* the chap to let into a secret, no fear of your forgetting it;—or losing it either, eh, Jim?"

I could make her no answer, but stooped down and hid my face by busying over my new shoes.

"Ha! ha! it's a nice world, isn't it, Jim?"

"Yes'm," I answered, and then sneaked up into my bedroom in a terrible state of mind.

Whatever she knew or suspected, I got no further hint of it throughout the remainder of the day; indeed, about four o'clock in the afternoon she dressed herself and went out, leaving me alone to mind the house until Long George came home, which happened somewhere about seven o'clock. For a moment he seemed annoyed to find that his housekeeper had gone out, but his good humour speedily returned, and he chatted as pleasantly with me over the tea as ever I had known him to. I would very much rather he had not done so; I should have liked him to snap and sneer at me as he most commonly did, it would have made me feel much more comfortable.

After tea said he:—

"Do you know Fulham Bridge, Jim?"

I told him that I did not.

"Well, it don't matter; you walk up as far as the Bank—put your shoes on—and take the Fulham omnibus. Then ask for the bridge, and in the third street on the left-hand side over the bridge you'll find a beer-shop; go in and ask if Mr. Mason is at home. Go at once."

Glad enough to be out of the house and in the open street, I at once set about doing as he requested. I put my shoes on and made my way towards the Bank. Just as I reached Threadneedle Street a butcher came up to me—

"Can you tell me the way to London Bridge, my boy?" he asked.

I told him.

"Thanky," said the butcher; and then, to my great astonishment, he continued in a low voice, "It's all right; I'm the man who bought the shoes this morning. Going to Fulham?"

A glance at the man's face convinced me that he really was the individual he represented himself to be, and heartily thankful that the inspector had not forgotten his promise to look after me, I told him in a few words where I was going, and all about it.

"Thanky," replied he; and off he walked towards London Bridge as innocent-looking a butcher as ever stepped.

At nine o'clock I reached the third street over Fulham Bridge and found the beer-shop. Mr. Mason, the man behind the bar told me, was waiting for me in the private parlour, and going there I discovered Long George, and Twiner, and Johnny Armitage, playing a quiet game of whist, single dummy. "My name's Mason," said Long George, winking; "come and sit down, my lad."

They played on, drinking very moderately, until half-past eleven o'clock, the landlord joining in the game part of the time, and conversing with the three as though they were something more than chance customers. At half-past eleven, the night being very dark, we came out of the beer-shop and walked—George and I together, and the other two arm-in-arm, a hundred yards or so behind—along the main road for nearly a mile, I should say. Going along, Long George confided to me the nature of the business in hand, and the part in it I was expected to perform. Nothing could be more simple as he explained it; it was merely to squeeze myself through just such a hole as the little window at home covered, to feel cautiously along the wall of the passage until I came to a door, and to shoot back the bolts thereof, top and bottom.

"You must see that there's no danger about it, or I wouldn't trust a green hand like you are with it. You'll be able to manage it easy enough, won't you?"

"Course I shall," I replied, my teeth chattering.

"It's as easy as cracking a filbert," said Long George; "nobody but the old gentleman, and the old butler, and a deaf old housekeeper on the premises, and no dog or anything."

We turned down a short lane and halted against some palings, and in a short time up came Twiner and Johnny Armitage. The first job was to scale the palings, which was accomplished by the whole party with little more noise than as many cats would have made. Then we made our way across a green and a gravel path, and halted again in the shadow of the house, which was as silent and pitchy dark as a house could be. Not a word was spoken; but I could dimly make out Johnny Armitage screwing two bright tools together, and presently Twiner "laid him a back," and he stood upright on it, and worked away with just a slight scratching noise against the wall, and in a minute or two there was a clinking sound, and he jumped down.

"Shoes off, Jim," whispered Long George.

Trembling with excitement, I slipped off my shoes, and then Long George mounted on Twiner's back, with me in his arms, and thrust my legs through a hole.

"You'll find it rather a tight fit, Jim," whispered he; "but you'll do it. Keep one arm straight to your side, and get that in first. That's the ticket! Hold on the ledge and drop—it ain't more than six feet! That's your sort; you know what I told you about the door and the bolts."

As he spoke, I hung my full length by the inner ledge of the little window, and dropped as requested; and, to my inexpressible relief, my hair was instantly pulled by an unseen hand. Another hand was clapped over my mouth, and I was led noiselessly to a side room, and gently pushed in.

What immediately followed I only know from hearing. Listening with all my might, all alone in the strange room, I heard the gentle creaking of the withdrawn bolts of the back-door, and then a sudden tramping of feet, and a terrible uproar of voices—Long George's loudest amongst them, and a gleaming and flashing of lights, as I could see through the chinks and crevices of the closed door. That was the end of it. The bait *had* taken as Mr. Inspector hoped it might, and the last-named worthy, besides the other two loose fish had hooked and landed that curiously slippery eel, Long George Hopkins.

And here closes the history, as promised at the beginning. Its narration has proved a long task —longer than at setting out I anticipated; therefore, with the reader's kind permission, I will not go beyond the strict letter of my contract. With the capture of Long George ended my career as a Little Ragamuffin. There is much more that I could tell of his interesting trial and tremendous sentence, of the suicide of his wretched housekeeper, of the kind friends I found through the intercession of good Mr. Inspector, of my life at the Reformatory, of my emigration to Australia, and my various fortunes there. Some day I may find opportunity to enter into these particulars at their fullest. Thank God, I have lived to be a grown man, and am prosperous and happy, but for my Ragamuffin recollections. Mister Ripston —my coal merchant—respectively intimates that, taking it altogether, he doesn't see that I've much to regret; but, you see, Ripston, even up to this time, doesn't know everything. If I could discover all the people who have been made the poorer by my larcenous propensities, I would willingly expend all my savings in making restitution. But this is impossible. The best I can do, and, please God, I will do it, is to assist the little Ragamuffin wherever I find him.

THE END.

Printed in the United States
86137LV00006B/19/A

9 781432 668662